Table of Cont

CW00736287

Introduction

Some of the best stories in the annals of American history often have nothing to do with the great decisions, climactic battles, and leaders. Sometimes the forgotten lives and experiences of ordinary and everyday individuals, including forgotten outliers barely existing on society's margins, often tell us far more about the American experience in unique narratives. Indeed, these outlier narratives are often more revealing than the traditional narratives in multiple ways. The unforgettable story of the remarkable life of a former Missouri slave named Cathy Williams has provided one such notable example of this phenomenon.

Today, the life of Cathy Williams has been largely forgotten. This situation is a striking paradox because her story is especially important and meaningful to American women, black and white, today when American society has been more focused on gender issues and identities than ever before.

Few chapters of American history have been more overlooked than the lives of those women who had been long relegated to lowly socioeconomic positions and subordinate roles far outside of the mainstream of America's patriarchal society. And this negligence has been especially the case in regard to African American women throughout the course of American history. These obscure individuals of African descent have truly been the most forgotten players in America's story.

For good reason, it was once thought that no individuals in American history have been more overlooked than those relatively few white women who early served in the United States military disguised as males. But such is not the case. In fact, this unique, but notable, distinction has applied to black women who disguised themselves as males to serve in the army, because they were far fewer in numbers. Of course, this situation has inevitably developed because of the lack of documentation and collaborating evidence about these little-known black women, when combined with their lower class and minority status, which had often guaranteed illiteracy to ensure a lost history.

However, there is one notable exception to this general rule. Fortunately, filling a host of significant voids in the historical record is the odyssey of an African American woman who served in the United States Army disguised as a male, Cathy Williams. Cathy's life has provided us with a fascinating look into the triumphs, heartbreaks, and tragedies of a young ex-slave woman struggling for survival on the western frontier. Indeed, the story of Cathy Williams has given us an unforgettable glimpse into the secret life of one of America's forgotten black female warriors. She served capably as a United States regular soldier during America's westward push toward the setting sun during the post-Civil War period.

Fortunately, in a rare occurrence, ample evidence and documentation (Cathy Williams' military service record is located in the National Archives, Washington, D.C, and a little-known oral interview that she gave to a St. Louis, Missouri, journalist of the *St. Louis Daily Times*) have revealed that she was the first black female ever to have served in the United States Army. Cathy Williams served in the ranks of the 38th United States Infantry for nearly two years. This regular United States Army regiment was one of a half dozen black (Buffalo Soldier) units organized in 1866 for arduous service on the Great Plains.

As the only documented African American woman to have marched in the ranks of the United States Army during the nineteenth century, Cathy Williams set a precedent for the tens of thousands of black women who later served in the modern United States military. Significantly, she compiled an unblemished military record for nearly two years, including service during a risky campaign against the elusive Apache in New Mexico's mountains. Entirely unknown to her at the time, Cathy Williams was in fact a ground-breaking pioneer for the thousands of dedicated and courageous African American women who serve their country today in combat zones around the world. Quite simply, she was the first to go where no other black female had previously gone: a unique distinction that was unprecedented in the annals of American military history.

But Cathy William's life is much more than simply a narrative about military service on the western frontier. After all, Cathy's service in the United States Army only lasted for a nearly two year period, from mid-November 1866 to mid-October 1868. Most of all, Cathy's remarkable story is especially unique and revealing because her life blended seldom explored aspects of military history with even more obscure chapters of black history and western history in entirely unprecedented ways. Far less known than her service in a Buffalo Soldier regiment was the fact that Cathy Williams was also a western pioneer, who accomplished what was rarely achieved by a free black woman at the time: creating a successful life for herself on the western frontier in the pioneering tradition. Significantly, she took full advantage of the ample opportunities that the untamed western frontier offered to an enterprising and hardworking single woman, after her Buffalo Soldier service ended in New Mexico in mid-October 1868 on her own terms.

Like generations of American males who took the sage advice of Horace Greeley, the influential editor of the *New York Tribune*, New York City, to "Go West Young Man," many women (black and white) likewise heeded that stirring call to migrate west. Consequently, large numbers of single women, unmarried and widows, pushed toward the setting sun after the Civil War. Cathy Williams was one of these single pioneering women, who created a new life for herself (first as a soldier and then as a pioneer) at a time, when the vast majority of women migrated west with their families and friends in no small part because of safety concerns during the long trek across an inhospitable land. Long unrecognized by mostly male historians, independent single women (black and white) played larger roles in the frontier's settlement than has been realized.

Cathy Williams first journeyed west as a Buffalo Soldier in April 1867, and then decided to remain on the western frontier as a settler. Here, she fulfilled her great dream of living an independent and self-sufficient life in a pristine land far from where she had been born. In a beautiful land that she loved, Cathy lived most of her life on Colorado's southeast frontier, creating a fulfilling life for herself in a picturesque region. Here, at the small frontier town of Trinidad, Colorado, among a people (mostly whites and Latinos, but also other ethnic groups—especially European immigrants —because of the coal mining industry), Cathy lived life on her own terms after overcoming seemingly insurmountable odds and severe adversity: the most common and enduring theme of her life.

Cathy's decision to join the United States Army was motivated by her desire to maintain her personal and financial independence in order not to burden family members, who were also former slaves. Clearly, Cathy Williams' amazing story is entirely unique for a host of reasons, representing a rare merger of African American, Women's, American military, and Western history to present a host of distinct perspectives seldom seen simultaneously together in a single historical narrative.

All in all, therefore, this is a remarkable personal odyssey of a single black woman, who succeeded against seemingly insurmountable odds. In addition, this is also very much of a redemption story about a former slave who lived life outside of traditional boundaries by her wits and resourcefulness. Most of all, Cathy Williams was the ultimate survivor. Cathy's life revealed how a highly-adaptive, resourceful, and opportunistic individual of considerable versatility and ingenuity was able to succeed in life even in the most disadvantageous situations. Significantly, Cathy Williams' life has transcended the stereotypical definitions of American, western, military, and black history to present an uplifting personal story. In many ways, Cathy's life was a true triumph of the human spirit.

Cathy Williams proved that a highly-adaptive African American woman of lower class status and without means, education, or financial resources could accomplish what was considered impossible for her to achieve. She demonstrated the uncanny ability to literally orchestrate the means to move forward in life by utilizing innovativeness and flexibility. Cathy Williams created an entirely new identity by successfully enlisting in a Buffalo Soldier regiment. Cathy's ultimate challenge required the ability to act, talk, and walk like a male (nearly four years of service as a cook and laundress in the camps of Union Armies on both sides of the Mississippi had provided invaluable experience) for nearly two years, which was quite a remarkable performance. From 1866 to 1868 while serving as a Buffalo Soldier, Cathy knew that one slip could reveal her true identity.

Like few women of her day, Cathy went far beyond traditional gender boundaries and society's expectations to create a decent and independent life on the western frontier. After the Civil War, meanwhile, the vast majority of ex-slaves continued to live traditional lives in the rural South, which remained an oppressive environment for newly-freed blacks. But Cathy Williams aspired higher, and she went farther in life than the vast majority of ex-slave women.

She became America's first documented female Buffalo Soldier on a cold Thursday, November 15, 1866. At that time, this young African American woman successfully enlisted in the 38th United States Infantry by stealthy means and great deal of ingenuity. Embarking upon her greatest challenge, she transformed herself into Private William Cathay (thereby preserving her name which was an act that demonstrated pride and a healthy self-esteem, despite risking the discovery of her true identity for nearly two years) at America's primary military installation west of the Mississippi, Jefferson Barracks, Missouri.

Born as a slave in the fertile Missouri River country in western Missouri near Kansas City, Cathy Williams was not destined to spend most of her life in Missouri. In eastern Missouri, she embarked upon a new life as a Buffalo Soldier in one of the recently-formed black regiments. These black soldiers of the postwar period were assigned to the nasty job of pacification of hostile Great Plains tribes. Buffalo Soldiers, including Cathy Williams, were needed partly because relatively few white males, who were weary of military service after four years of service in America's bloodiest war, were reluctant to embark upon difficult military service and thankless job of pacification on the western frontier.

Cathy Williams' enlistment in this regular regiment at Jefferson Barracks on November 15, 1866 represented a personal rebirth: quite literally a case of a phoenix rising. She had taken the bold step of accomplishing what was considered not only impossible for a woman, but also a gross transgression of the traditional norms and expectations in a strict patriarchal society. Indeed, this young woman relied upon a clever utilization of a far-sighted strategic plan to overcome the almost insurmountable obstacles that had been unfairly set in her path by American society because of her race and sex.

Consequently, enlisting in the United States Army was very much a story of personal liberation. Significantly, in serving for nearly two years of competent military service to her country in the 38th United States Infantry, Cathy Williams was not only a pioneer but also a trendsetter. Indeed, she was a ground-breaker for the large number of dedicated women who serve with distinction today in America's military around the world, including in the War against Terrorism. In charting upon a radically new course by going her own way in life and beyond all traditional expectations, America's first and only known female Buffalo Soldier served faithfully as "a good soldier," in her own words, for an extended period of time. All in all, this was no small accomplishment.

Therefore, this book will explore the unique life challenges and experiences of Cathy Williams as a Buffalo Soldier and then as a single black woman on the western frontier. This work will also emphasize her special place today in American history and memory, especially in terms of culture, gender, and race. As mentioned, what Cathy Williams accomplished outside of military service was equally, if not more, impressive than what she achieved while serving in the United States military on the western frontier.

Indeed, in a double distinction, she pushed west not once by twice in order to embrace a host of new challenges in creating a new life for herself: first, as a Buffalo Soldier, and then as a pioneer in search of greater opportunities in an unspoiled land of beauty on the western frontier. On the historic Santa Fe Trail at Trinidad, Las Animas County, in southeast Colorado, she supported herself by hard work and thrifty means (the secrets to her success as an independent single woman) in the Purgatoire River Valley. Here, along the river's clear waters that flowed through the frontier mining town surrounded by mountains near the border of New Mexico, Cathy Williams finally found her permanent home on the western frontier.

In this unruly "Wild West" town of Trinidad, she basked in her frontier surroundings and benefited from a friendly people who treated her fairly and as a person worthy of respect: the fulfillment of her lifelong personal aspirations and ambitions, especially to a former slave. This brighter future for her had only been possible by first developing a novel solution for getting out of the United States military, when she felt that she had no choice but to end her military career. To exit the military establishment, Cathy allowed the post surgeon at Fort Bayard, New Mexico, to discover her gender during a routine medical examination, after she had complained of physical ailments. By this means (the solution to a personal dilemma was obtained by her with an official discharge), Cathy won her freedom which allowed her to escape an unfavorable environment that included racial discrimination and hostility.

Ironically, this was still another day of personal liberation (October 14, 1868) for Cathy Williams, and not unlike her June 1861 release from slavery by Union troops seven and a half years before in her native Missouri. Living in the frontier town of Trinidad (both before and after Colorado became a state in August 1876), Cathy Williams was a pioneer both inside and outside of the military.

Repeatedly throughout the course of her remarkable life, Cathy Williams went where relatively few other women dared to go, or even thought about going. Throughout the annals of American history, only the most adventurous women embarked on the dangerous trek west to the frontier, but these were almost always civilians (wives, mothers, and daughters) rather than single women. But no other black woman in the annals of America's western expansion embraced the unique dual challenges as a United States soldier and a pioneer on the western frontier.

As a "good" soldier in a blue uniform, Cathy Williams marched all the way to the southwestern frontier and into New Mexico's depths. Here, while stationed at isolated frontier forts, she performed all of her assigned duties beside her male comrades (mostly other former slaves who served under white officers) of the 38th United States Infantry.

While most other women (black and white) cooked meals and took care of children on the western frontier in traditional domestic roles and familial settings, Cathy Williams embraced far more unconventional and challenging experiences both in and out of uniform. She marched for seemingly endless miles across the broad prairies, over the rugged mountains of Colorado and New Mexico, and forded creeks and rivers, including the Rio Grande River. Because the Buffalo Soldiers formed part of the spear tip of America's push west after the Civil War, she not only trekked hundreds of miles across the untamed west, but also campaigned against the southwest's fiercest Native American warriors, the Apache.

Symbolically, Private William Cathay risked her life in serving a nation that she owed a great personal debt because of her liberation by Union troops and President Abraham Lincoln's freeing of the slaves. Consequently, she faithfully fulfilled her obligations to her country, regiment, and male comrades of the post-Civil War military establishment that became her surrogate home for nearly two years. As a slave, a competent soldier, and pioneer on the western frontier, she faced a host of obstacles that were almost unimaginable to modern Americans today. These formidable challenges were overcome by her with an inordinate degree of flexibility and adaptability.

In the end, Cathy was most of all a cagy and resourceful survivor, thanks to a powerful will to succeed. Clearly, Cathy Williams had to employ a most novel means of defying convention and orthodoxy of a patriarchal society to overcome gender and race barriers during her quest to secure a more independent and rewarding life.

Most importantly, the narrative of Cathy Williams' life has provided us with a timeless example of what it takes to succeed in life(then and today), revealing invaluable life lessons that still apply: the winning formula of hard work, perseverance, willpower, and a determination to succeed against even the most formidable odds. Cathy's story has revealed how thoroughly a woman, regardless of color, must rely on flexibility, resourcefulness, and God-given smarts to overcome seemingly insurmountable obstacles to succeed in life.

Because the unorthodox course of Cathy's life was deemed improper by the arbitrary dictates of a patriarchal society and tradition, negative stigmas about the mere concept of a female Buffalo Soldier have lingered to this day. Cathy Williams and her service in the United States military have been often seen as a threatening example by males (black and white), because she so boldly defied society's traditional gender role. When she was older, on her own, and in great need of assistance, consequently, she had to pay a high personal price for her transgressions: the official denial of a well-deserved invalid pension by Washington, D.C. authorities primarily because of her color and sex at a time when she was in bad physical shape that stemmed from the arduous demands of military service.

A number of modern artists have depicted Cathy Williams' imagined appearance while wearing the full uniform of a Buffalo Soldier. Allowing their imaginations to soar to produce highly-marketable works of art for higher sales, these artists have created overly-romanticized images of a light-skinned woman of inordinate beauty. But, of course, these are hardly realistic portrayals of a tough and resilient woman who long maintained a false gender identity among large numbers of men in blue uniforms. In truth, she needed to look as plain, if not outright ugly, as possible, or no one (beginning with the army recruiters at Jefferson Barracks, where she enlisted on November 15, 1866) would be fooled by her clever ruse. Some evidence has indicated that she might have worn her short hair in a dred lock ("dreds") style, while serving her country. Military service records have revealed that Cathy Williams was dark in color, and without any mixture of white blood as portrayed by some modern artists to appeal to a wider audience.

Unfortunately and like her highly-romanticized image created by artists, too many voids in Cathy's life have been filled with fabricated romance and gross embellishment by fiction writers, obscuring the fundamental truths about her life. In consequence, the primary emphasis of this book has been to present the true story of Cathy Williams without the usual layers of romance and myths. Her struggles in life have provided enduring lessons today about the importance of perseverance and determination—sheer willpower—to achieve success (more in personally rewarding terms rather than in financial terms) in life. She managed to survive with uncommon ingenuity in a struggle against odds that were stacked high against her from the beginning: a situation that forced her to rely on her own intelligence, resourcefulness, and innovativeness to an inordinate degree for simple survival.

Contrary to the romantic myths about her life, the real Cathy Williams does not fit into the romantic imaginary and fiction that has been created by over-imaginative writers and artists. Therefore and as mentioned, the overall purpose of this book has been to provide a more realistic view of the triumphs, heartbreaks, and tragedies of her amazing life. Significantly, the real story of Cathy Williams has revealed the complexities and contradictions about the female western pioneer and Buffalo Soldier experiences that have been seldom previously explored in the historical record. Additionally, this book has emphasized the timeliness and relevance of the inspiring example of Cathy Williams for people in the twenty-first century.

Cathy Williams' life has also revealed how the western frontier consisted of more ethnic and cultural diversity than generally realized today. No doubt to her surprise, Cathy discovered that the Trinidad region was a melting pot of many races (white, Indian, black, Latino, recent European immigrants from the Emerald Isle to eastern Europe), languages, cultures, and religions. This multicultural environment was the antithesis of the stereotypical portrayal of the mythical "Old West" without ethnic and multi-cultural roots. Indeed, this mining town in southeastern Colorado was also the antithesis of the traditional antebellum planter world of Cathy's native Missouri, where she had been born in slavery. African Americans, European immigrants (especially Irish and Germans), Chinese, Latinos, and Native Americans worked together in the frontier community of Trinidad. Here, the arbitrary barriers of race, class, gender were far less oppressive for a single black woman than in the South. Cathy broke her restrictive gender and racial chains, which allowed her free spirit to soar in the more egalitarian environment of the "Old West," after her October 1868 discharge from the army.

Significantly, Cathy Williams' unforgettable life story is not unlike the struggle of many modern women today: overcoming the still existing discriminatory limitations and societal barriers because of gender and race. And for Cathy, the only solution to gain a better life had called for bold, imaginative action that required a thorough deviation from her female identity to take advantage of a rare existing opportunity. For Cathy, this novel and unorthodox solution was the only means of escaping from the lowly status that a racist society had ordained for her.

Against the odds, she excelled in serving as a Buffalo Soldier and then as an independent, self-sufficient business woman on the western frontier. Without a choice under crippling circumstances and in a seemingly impossible situation, she was forced out of necessity to directly challenge society's most entrenched values and restrictions in the most innovative manner. Cathy, therefore, became exceptionally flexible and imaginative in finding a most unique solution to an almost impossible situation, relying on ingenuity to survive.

Cathy Williams' life has revealed the extent of the enormous challenges of the female experience as a soldier and civilian on the western frontier: a rare composite glimpse into dual gender identities in two entirely different and distinct worlds. Significantly, Cathy Williams' story has filled a large void in the historical annals of the West by providing a host of fresh and new insights into the complexities of the Buffalo Soldier and female experiences (a unique combination of the two) on the western frontier.

Cathy Williams' life has highlighted the seemingly endless struggles of a common American black woman, who achieved uncommon things and soared higher than her peers because of her resourcefulness and determination to succeed against the odds. She was also the first and only woman to serve as a United States regular in America's Indian Wars, while performing her duty longer and more faithfully than hundreds of white male soldiers during this same period. After all, this was a time when desertion—including from Lieutenant Colonel George Armstrong's Custer's famed 7th Cavalry —and misbehavior in the frontier army were epidemic.

Most importantly, Cathy Williams was not the stereotypical so-called Amazon and perverse neurotic (the longtime traditional male-based explanations to deride the military service of women disguised as men) to explain the unconventional life that she led with such careful calculation and stealth. Presenting us with an universal and unforgettable story of courage and faith that is still relevant to this day, Cathy Williams was also just an ordinary woman, who was forced by circumstances beyond her control to adapt to a good many harsh realities in extraordinary times. Because American society has been steadily evolving and gaining greater awareness of gender and transgender issues, the story of the first documented female Buffalo Soldier actually has become more important to even more Americans in the twenty-first century: a classic case of history's lessons and examples coming full circle.

Each year with monotonous regularity, the same standard cast of African American heroes and heroines have been routinely celebrated across America —Harriet Tubman, Frederick Douglass, and only a handful of other distinguished black achievers. Although these relatively few black notables are certainly well deserving of national recognition, the excessive commercialization of these icons (deemed acceptable to the white public for marketing purposes and to ensure greater corporate profits) have guaranteed the overlooking of hundreds of other forgotten African Americans, who are equally, if not more, deserving of recognition and celebration. In this way, the American marketplace has still arbitrarily dictated who we recognize in history to this day, while so many other noteworthy black heroes and heroines (but less commercially acceptable) have fallen by the wayside to ensure their permanent historical obscurity in this sanitized version of black history.

Cathy Williams is one of these marginalized individuals whose remarkable life story certainly deserves greater recognition today, because she carved out a very special and unique place for herself in the annals of Western, United States Military, Women's, and black history.

Most of all, Cathy Williams embodied the essence of the American spirit and represented a triumph of the human spirit. Consequently, this is the unforgettable story of a single woman's seemingly endless struggles, and what extreme efforts it took to successfully overcome insurmountable odds that led to her personal redemption and rebirth as a new person on the western frontier. Consequently, the life of Cathy Williams has revealed a remarkable personal resurrection—literally the case of a phoenix rising—and the fulfillment of the American Dream for a determined young woman who had the misfortune of having been born in slavery.

Phillip Thomas Tucker, Ph.D.
Washington, D.C.
October 15, 2016

Part I

Chapter I: Phoenix Rising

A young former slave named Cathy Williams was entirely without prospects or hopes for a bright future at the Civil War's conclusion, after General Robert Edward Lee's Army of Northern Virginia surrendered at Appomattox Court House, Virginia, on Palm Sunday April 9, 1865. Having grown up in the ugly grip of slavery in the fertile Missouri River country of mid-Missouri, she had been denied an education by law, because educations were deemed by slave-owners as too dangerous for slaves.

Therefore, this young woman named Cathy Williams could not read or write. Of course, the combination of color and illiteracy all but ensured a permanent lowly place for her in postwar American society. As a former slave, she had no connections, savings, or clout when on her own after the end of America's bloodiest war.

Facing a serious quandary about having to learn to survive when handicapped by a most unpromising future, Cathy's bleak post-Civil War situation was especially ironic, because she had played an active support role with the Union Armies for most of the war. She had served as a laundress and cook for Union troops on both sides of the Mississippi River. Discriminated against because of her sex and color, Cathy realized that her future was especially bleak, if she remained passive and allowed the usual course of events to take their due course. But Cathy Williams was determined not to willingly permit an unkind fate to dictate the rest of her life.

Confronted with a host of disadvantageous circumstances, however, what was this young ex-slave woman to do in order to survive without an education, financial means, or a husband, when suddenly stranded on her own at the war's end? Where and how could she find permanent safety, shelter, and employment in order to survive in an unkind world after the Civil War? How could Cathy possibly make a decent life for herself when it was virtually impossible for a young and single former slave woman to do so?

This disadvantageous postwar situation that seemed to have no solution was even more daunting because Cathy Williams decided not to become a "fallen woman" or prostitute. Such a decision would have been a short-sighted and risky one, because it was full of personal peril for a young woman. Of course, such an unwise decision (especially for her in the long-term) would have all but guaranteed Cathy a permanent place in society's underclass and lowest order, while insidiously wrecking self-esteem and character.

Most of all, this resourceful young woman, who had grown up in Jackson and Cole Counties, Missouri, knew that she could not go back to her native Missouri River country, where slavery's bitter memories still lingered. Haunted by a tragic, if not traumatic, past, Cathy Williams still bore the emotional scars (deeper than physical scars), because she had been a slave for most of her life.

Therefore, without any future prospects after the Civil War's conclusion and with so many avenues for any kind of advancement closed to her, she now found it absolutely necessary to somehow develop an innovative solution to her dilemma to increase her chances for survival in a harsh world. In relative terms, this disadvantageous situation was far more challenging than for former male slaves (they could always perform manual labor to make a living) and even for the average lower class white women of her age. At this time, post-Civil War America offered very little, if anything, to an ex-slave woman on her own. Consequently, Cathy Williams had to shift for herself in attempting to navigate an entirely new course in life, and it was not easy.

To survive this unforgiving world, consequently, Cathy Williams was forced out of necessity to develop a novel means to overcome the seemingly endless barriers that had been so unfairly stacked-up against her, because of her gender and race. These obstacles were so great that Cathy was forced to formulate a very proactive and unique strategy that was entirely unprecedented in the history of black women in America.

Increasing her chances of developing an innovative solution to her personal dilemma, she possessed an inordinate degree of flexibility and an adaptive nature that God had given her. These were well-honed qualities (from her varied experiences in slavery and in the Civil War) necessary for survival that enhanced the possibility of developing a novel solution to overcome obstacles that seemed insurmountable. Despite the low, almost zero probability of finding a solution, Cathy was determined to cut the proverbial Gordian knot that had long placed such severe restrictions on her future possibilities of getting ahead in life.

Equally important in facing such formidable challenges that had been long ago set in place by society, Cathy also possessed a healthy sense of self as a resilient survivor of hard times. Her well-honed survivor instincts and skills were rooted in her background long before the Civil War: the nurturing Missouri's slave community, her family, and a vibrant maternal-based culture based on West African traditions. Combined with her service as a cook and laundress for Union Armies during the Civil War, these early formative experiences had provided her with a psychological buffer against some of the most dehumanizing effects of slavery. These were invaluable life experiences on multiple levels that bolstered Cathy's can-do attitude when facing a truly disadvantageous situation. But more than any previous time in her life, Cathy was now forced to rely on all of her cunning and innate abilities to survive as a single black woman on her own in the postwar world.

She possessed relatively few skills—all domestic —because of her slave past. However, Cathy at least possessed ample experience (from 1861 to 1865) about soldiery ways that she could still utilize to her advantage, if the right opportunity was presented. Because of her extensive experience from the Civil War years, she possessed considerable knowledge about how to act, move, and even talk (no doubt including cursing like a veteran trooper, or an angry teamster employed by the Federal Government) like a Union soldier of the Civil War.[1]

For a young black female just out of slavery, the extent of this challenge to create a decent new life seemed almost much too daunting for her to possibly overcome. Former slave Booker T. Washington explained the dilemma for ex-slaves after the Civil War: "The great responsibility of being free, of having charge of themselves, of having to think and plan for themselves [because] freedom was a more serious thing than they had expected to find it [and the most important question was how] to earn a living in a strange place and among strange people, even if they had been sure where to find a new place of abode."[2]

Out of urgent necessity, Cathy Williams most of all needed to devise a brilliant plan to literally beat a deeply-entrenched discriminatory system that had her trapped to a lowly place in life. Thanks to a creative and flexible mind, therefore, she began to devise her own novel strategic plan that promised to provide a new life, while also gaining a measure of dignity and respect that society had denied her only because of her sex and gender. Cathy was destined to develop a unique strategy that set her on an unprecedented course in life, allowing her to secure what she most of all desired: a chance of gaining a measure of dignity and honor while serving in the United States Army.

Although not recognized or appreciated by anyone at this time, Thursday, November 15, 1866, was a historic day not only for Cathy Williams, but also for the United States Army. Cathy Williams never forgot the autumn day along the Mississippi River in eastern Missouri, when the course of her life took a dramatic turn, thanks to her own bold initiative. Indeed, this Thursday in mid-November was the major turning point of Cathy's life, and destined to set her life on an entirely new course of her own choosing, after careful deliberation. A novel plan had been born of a fertile imagination to set the stage for a thorough transformation of this young woman, who was about to gain a surprising new identity.

On this Thursday on which she planned to no longer be known as Cathy Williams based on her own careful calculations, this young woman was now going for broke to literally begin life anew. At a time when the autumnal colors of the hardwood trees still dominated the high bluffs that overlooked the Mississippi River only around ten miles south of the major Mississippi River port of St. Louis, Cathy was about to gamble on her future as never before.

Thursday November 15, 1866 was an ordinary day at the busy military base located near the town of Carondelet, Missouri. This small town had been settled by French settlers before the first American settlers pushed that far west. Jefferson Barracks had been named in honor of the third United States president, who had long promoted westward expansion, Thomas Jefferson. This revered Founding Father hailed from his peaceful hilltop mansion known as Monticello, near Charlottesville, in the Virginia Piedmont. Jefferson had penned the Declaration of Independence at Philadelphia, Pennsylvania, during the exciting summer of 1776, when a new nation conceived in liberty was created.

The military outpost of Jefferson Barracks (established in 1836) now served as a training center for the fighting men of America's infantry regiments, before these new units were dispatched to their respective assignments on the Great Plains. Young soldiers in blue uniforms drilled on the wide parade ground, after countless hours of practice. A large United States flag fluttered in the river breeze that swept across the grassy parade ground, waving over America's largest military outpost west of the Mississippi River.

Since its establishment a decade before the Mexican-American War of 1846-1848, this important military base that overlooked the Illinois prairies to the east on the other side of the "Father of Waters" had long served as a launching point of past military expeditions against the Great Plains Indians. For decades, tons of supplies and troops (and shortly ebony recruits of African descent, who were mostly former slaves like Cathy Williams) had been dispatched from Jefferson Barracks to reinforce far-flung remote outposts across the Great Plains. Cathy Williams probably never realized that Jefferson Barracks had long served as the nerve center of America's western expansion. For her, this was an ideal time and place to attempt to embark upon a military career of her own, because America was once again on the verge of continuing to expand west with renewed vigor after the Civil War.

Less than sixty days remained in 1866 (the nation's first full year without conflict since April 1861), a proactive Cathy was determined to secure a brighter future for herself, and this goal required the most artful means possible. Cathy also fully understood that she could not now rely on anyone or anything else in the future—not even her country, family, or society. Therefore, she would have to depend upon her own resourcefulness and ingenuity for future survival.

Although having actively supported Union troops during the war years, Cathy Williams was not aware that Robert E. Lee, as a young engineer officer in United States service, had been stationed at Jefferson Barracks during the prewar years. At that time, the erudite Virginian of the Tidewater planter class had helped to save the threatened St. Louis harbor on the Mississippi. He had orchestrated the creation of a system of underwater dikes to keep the river's main channel from shifting from St. Louis east to the Illinois side (lower ground than on the St. Louis side of the river). General Lee had surrendered his Army of Northern Virginia at Appomattox Court House to Lieutenant General Ulysses S. Grant on a beautiful Palm Sunday, while Cathy had continued to serve as a cook and laundress with Union forces in the eastern theater.

Ironically, Generals Lee and Grant possessed personal and prewar connections to St. Louis. Before the Civil War, Grant had lived on a small farm, which he called "Hardscrabble," located near Jefferson Barracks in the quaint community of Carondelet. Living in the westernmost border slave state, Grant had even owned a slave (given to him by his in-laws, the Dent family) at his St. Louis County farm. Grant had given this lucky man his freedom in 1859, when Cathy Williams had been a slave in mid-Missouri around 150 miles to the west.

On November 15, 1866 and barely a year and a half after the Civil War's conclusion, the American nation was attempting to move forward much like young Cathy Williams. With an easy, self-assured manner, but more pronounced by deliberate design given this high stakes situation, and with a measured confidence calculated not to arouse suspicions, Cathy Williams walked toward the post gate at Jefferson Barracks. In the disguise (baggy and loose-fitting clothing, large hat, etc.) of a black male, she was about to enter Jefferson Barracks with a bold and well-conceived plan in mind on this cold Thursday. No doubt, this young woman was almost certainly nervous given the overall tense situation because she was taking a considerable risk. After all, she now had to completely fool every male who she encountered at this busy army post, especially at the post's recruiting office.

Cathy realized that she had to perform her well-rehearsed male act in a flawless manner to arouse no suspicions about her true identity. Indeed, her overall performance at Jefferson Barracks before white officers, soldiers, and recruiters needed to be flawless and convincing to one and all. Could she now fool all of these army veterans, including older and educated men (officers), in blue uniforms by pretending to be a male?

Meanwhile, the cold winds of mid-November that swept down the brownish-hued Mississippi made the high ground at Jefferson Barracks feel even colder to this young African American woman on this Thursday, when winter was on the horizon. With a typical male-like stride and the self-assured look (necessary facades for her ruse to be successful) that revealed how she knew exactly what she was doing, Cathy Williams continued to walk toward Jefferson Barracks' main gate on her nerve-wracking mission.

Cathy now realized that she would have to give the acting performance of her life at the recruiting office to fulfill her lofty dream of ensuring a brighter future for herself. She was determined to join the United States Army as a male soldier (it was officially illegal for a woman to serve) and then embark upon an entirely new course in life. However, a good many experienced officers, some of the smartest and most educated men at Jefferson Barracks, would present the greatest challenge to the fulfillment of Cathy's bold plan. If they even suspected that she was not exactly what she pretended to be for only a moment, then her entire plan would completely unravel.

Besides the immediate desire to secure a guarantee of regular food, clothing, and shelter on a long-term basis, Cathy also desired to join the military to defend the nation that had only recently delivered the death stroke to slavery. As Cathy Williams fully appreciated, this bitter conflict had been waged in part to end forever the greatest blight on America's republican experiment. Of course and from the beginning, no other institution had more thoroughly mocked the republic's founding principles than slavery.

Leading abolitionist Frederick Douglass, the son of a white Maryland master and black slave, lamented America's hypocrisy in 1846 at the beginning of the Mexican-American War, not long after Cathy Williams had been born in Jackson County, Missouri. He emphasized how: "three millions of people [including Cathy Williams] are held in the most abject bondage, deprived of all their God-given rights–denied by law and public opinion to learn to read the sacred Scriptures by a people professing the largest liberty and devotion to the religion of Jesus Christ."[3]

Douglass's vision finally began to take permanent shape when President Abraham Lincoln issued his preliminary Emancipation Proclamation in September 1862, and then his final Emancipation Proclamation on January 1, 1863. But, of course, the real blow to slavery's existence came with the Confederacy's defeat in 1865. Having long advocated such a bold decision by President Lincoln, abolitionists and free blacks (like Douglas) across the North had rejoiced at the long-awaited news (like Cathy Williams who had been then serving as a civilian in support of Union troops at the time) that had brought a new birth of freedom in America. Reverend William Henry Hurness rejoiced that President Lincoln had finally opened up the door to a "new world," which came "into existence arrayed in millennial splendor, wherein the distinctions of race, which have always been such active causes of contempt and hatred and war shall be obliterated, and men shall live together in the relations of a Christian brotherhood."[4]

The reverend's words in regard to a "new world" now applied to Cathy Williams. Consequently, to the best of her ability, Cathy Williams was now determined to take full advantage of new opportunities that had been presented to African Americans not long after the Civil War's conclusion: in this case, the Congressional authorization of America's first black regular regiments (only black volunteer regiments fought in the Civil War) in July 1866. Another northern man of God had rejoiced at the fulfillment of

President Lincoln's moral vision of eliminating the stain of slavery that had long tarnished America's national character and soul: "our shame, our misery, our deadly sickness will be taken away; no more that poison in our politics, no more that degradation in our commercial relations."[5]

As mentioned, because of Lincoln's Emancipation Proclamation and the triumphant march of Union armies across the South that had freed around three million African Americans, Cathy Williams now desired to serve that nation which had brought liberation, the golden day of Jubilee. What had been accomplished by this wartime moral crusade to forever change America now still inspired young Cathy, who remained idealistic. After all, she had embraced this great righteous cause like a holy shroud during the war years.

Slavery's death, therefore, continued to serve partly as a strong motivation for her to try what no other woman had ever attempted to do at Jefferson Barracks. Like other freed blacks, the joyous feeling gained from the great moral crusade to end slavery was still part of the heart and soul of Cathy Williams. Therefore, the flag of red, white, and blue that she saw waving high over the parade ground of Jefferson Barracks meant something very special to this young woman on the most important day of her life, November 15, 1866.

Learning about Military Life, The Civil War

Indeed, Cathy's determination to enlist in the United States military can be partly explained by what she had experienced during the war years. She now desired nothing more in life than to have the much dreamed about the opportunity to wear a blue uniform and serve in the United States Army, just like the brave northern men who fought to end slavery's existence. What was never forgotten by Cathy was that she had been liberated in June 1861 by this moral crusade that had destroyed slavery. She had been a lowly slave at the William Johnson place located at the Missouri state capital of Jefferson City in Cole County at the outbreak of the Civil War.

Ironically, like Jefferson Barracks situated on the high ground overlooking the Mississippi, the state capital that stood on the heights above the Missouri River had been named in honor of Thomas Jefferson. He had early promoted the exploration of the West, including by the famous Lewis and Clark Expedition, which had reached the Pacific Ocean on November 1805: exactly 61 years before Cathy Williams targeted Jefferson Barracks as the place where she hoped that she could forever alter the course of her life.

For many reasons, therefore, the United States flag and the blue uniform held great significance and special meaning, if not a certain symbolic beauty, to Cathy, because of what they represented to former slaves. Cathy Williams never forgot that glorious mid-June 1861 day of liberation when, in her own words, "the United States soldiers came to Jefferson City" and broke her lifelong bonds of slavery. Unlike the vast majority of America's slaves, Cathy was fortunate that Missouri had become a bone of contention early in the war to hasten the convergence of invading Union troops from neighboring states to ensure her own freedom, after their arrival in central Missouri.[6]

Unfortunately, Cathy Williams failed to elaborate upon the depth of her feelings on that glorious day of liberation, when she was later interviewed by a newspaper reporter of the *St. Louis Daily Times* in late 1875 or on the first day of 1876 (most likely the former).

The words of Booker Taliaferro Washington, who was the son of a white father and female slave in Franklin County which was located among the rolling foothills of the Blue Ridge Mountains in southwest Virginia, and was destined to become America's top black leader by the late nineteenth century, described the same exhilarating experience felt by Cathy Williams in Missouri in mid-June 1861, when "the day of freedom came [and] It was a momentous and eventful day to all upon our plantation."[7]

Consequently, Cathy never forgot that great day of her life when Jefferson City had been captured by Union forces on June 14, 1861, bestowing a long-awaited freedom. Quite suddenly, the teenage Cathy was no longer owned by the William Johnson family. While enduring years of bondage, she had only known Jefferson City and a relatively small area of Cole County during her early adulthood. Cathy's early memories were much like that of Booker T. Washington, who explained how: "The earliest impressions I can now recall are of the plantation and the slave quarters" of rustic log cabins, usually located in a neat row behind the so-called "big house" of the master.[8]

Compared to the much more difficult daily existence as a common field hand who labored outdoors from sunup to sundown, Cathy's life in slavery was better in overall terms because "I had always been a house girl." In this role, she had performed domestic chores (primarily washing, cleaning, taking care of children, etc.) at the mansion house.[9] Compared to the field workers who occupied the lowest spectrum of slave society, Cathy benefited from a relatively privileged position. She had also possessed an even more elevated status on the William Johnson place in part because "my father was a free man," while her mother had been a slave, evidently a field hand. Therefore, Cathy had known both the slave and free world, while living in bondage in Missouri. What she almost certainly learned from her father at some point was about the sweet taste of freedom and the benefits of a free life outside slavery.[10]

Cathy Williams' earliest memories were from slave life on a plantation in Jackson County in western Missouri, before William Johnson moved his family and slaves east to Jefferson City. But Cathy's fortunes had been dramatically reversed, when she first caught sight of the blue uniformed soldiers, who marched into Jefferson City with pride and flags flying in mid-June 1861.

Ironically, as mentioned and fortunately for her, Cathy's liberation in mid-Missouri had been hastened because of the strategic situation of Missouri and the state's overall importance at the war's beginning. President Lincoln had early realized that the North needed to win Missouri, because of its overall strategic importance: the westernmost border state that served as the Confederacy's left flank and the new Southern nation's northwest corner.

President Lincoln had early correctly realized that the Union needed to secure the all-important border states, especially Missouri and Kentucky. Therefore, liberating Union forces, under red-haired General Nathaniel Lyon, an irrepressible West Pointer from New England, and his troops had pushed west up the Missouri from St. Louis by steamboat to take possession of Jefferson City on June 14.He was determined to crush the rising revolt of Missouri rebels in the pro-Southern heartland of the Missouri River country.

Along with large numbers of St. Louis Germans under General Franz Sigel, Lyon's strike deep into the state's interior forced secessionist Governor Claiborne Claiborne Fox Jackson, the pro-Southern Missouri legislature, and his fledgling Missouri State Guard (militia) under General Sterling, "Old Pap," Price on the defensive. After capturing the state capital of Jefferson City, General Lyon then shortly delivered another blow after moving farther west up the Missouri River on June 17. He won the battle of Boonville while commanding around 1,700 troops, which forced Price's pro-Southern

Missourians to withdraw south toward Arkansas.

As a young woman who had been recently freed from slavery by the Union Army, Cathy Williams became attached to the forces that had liberated her, because many freed slaves gravitated to the invaders for safety, food, and shelter. Without a home after having been freed from the ownership of the William Johnson's family ("My master [earlier] died," in Cathy's words, before the war at Jefferson City, so that she was legally owned by his widow in June 1861), Cathy was on her own.

Therefore, she became a permanent fixture with the Union Army like many other liberated slaves. But this situation suddenly became more complicated for the black teenager when orders came for Union forces to advance out of Cole County to resume active campaigning against the Missouri Rebels. While receiving payment in the form of food, shelter, and protection provided by the Yankee soldiers, former slaves provided much-needed logistical support to Union troops during active campaigning by cooking, washing uniforms, collecting fire wood and performing other camp duties.

Consequently, when the Union Army marched out of Cole County and headed south to resume active campaigning, Cathy went with it. Like other liberated slaves, she became part of Union forces advancing toward northwest Arkansas. But never before having left her family and home region, she departed the Missouri River country only reluctantly. After all, as a young woman who was vulnerable especially around so many men who were strangers, Cathy possessed numerous reasons for concern at this time.

First and foremost, Cathy Williams did not know where the army was headed and how long it might take to get there, while on the march south. In addition, she was no doubt concerned being around so many strangers (almost all males) from far-away areas that she had never seen before. These men in blue uniforms talked differently (generally faster than residents from the rural Missouri drawl of the "Little Dixie region," including Jackson and Cole Counties), and acted differently from Missourians, who she had known all her life in the Missouri River Country.

Because she did not want to leave family members, including her mother if still alive at this time and the place that she had known for most of her life (despite slavery, Jefferson City was still home to her), Cathy had initially balked at the Union Army's utilization of her in an unofficial support role during active campaigning far from her home. In her words that betrayed the insecurity and anxiety of this young woman on her own: "I did not want to go."[11]

But in the end, Cathy overcame this initial reluctance. She might have decided to leave mid-Missouri because of growing fears about the possibility of re-enslavement, after the bluecoat soldiers departed this region situated along the Missouri River. Clearly, this was a good reason for her to remain in the presence of Union troops.

However, in overall terms, the Civil War experience bestowed a new self-assertiveness and activeness for women, including Cathy Williams, which had been unattainable to them before the Civil War. In this sense, therefore, Cathy Williams was very much in the mainstream of this overall process of greater self-actualization experience among women in the North and South, because of the new opportunities and roles created for females by the war's demands.

Like so many other women across America from 1861 to 1865, Cathy's energies were then directed toward supporting the war effort that had galvanized millions of her fellow Americans of all colors. She embarked upon an odyssey had not ended for nearly four years and only after journeying hundreds of miles to far-away places that she had never seen before. This young woman of African descent eventually acclimated so thoroughly to the once-mysterious ways and rigors of military life that she considered the army her personal refuge and surrogate home.

Even more, the military became a way-of-life that she grew accustomed to and even eventually enjoyed, after acclimating to a domestic role in the military machine to save the Union. Cathy Williams' support role with the Union Army also had legal justifications. To circumvent the 1850 Fugitive Slave Law that required the return of escaped slaves to owners, General Benjamin Butler, a brilliant Massachusetts lawyer and the conquer of New Orleans, Louisiana, in late April 1862, declared that escaped slaves were "contraband of war": a legal definition and effective means by which to retain and utilize this vast manpower resource of former slaves (male and female), while denying it to the manpower-short Confederacy.

Therefore, in legal terms, Cathy was officially considered "contraband of war" during the Civil War years, which in part allowed her to embark upon her longtime role in supporting the Union Army. Because of this wartime situation, she was legally utilized by Union forces in the war effort calculated to destroy not only the Confederacy, but also the institution of slavery: an overall policy, when combined with her own inclinations after an initial reluctance to depart Cole County, that motivated her to serve for an extended period in a support role to Federal troops. In fact, these combined factors ensured that she remained with Union Armies until the war's end.[12]

Especially in the beginning and as mentioned, there was nothing glamorous about Cathy's initial entry into military life, because the transition period was an overall difficult one for a young woman, who had never been far from home before. Like other former slaves who linked themselves to liberating northern armies to provide support to America's fighting men by cooking and washing uniforms, Cathy was eventually utilized in domestic services for non-Missouri Federals. Fortunately, she benefited from a kind benefactor in a compassionate and humanitarian Union officer, who was a model Christian warrior. A Mexican-American War veteran, Colonel William Plummer Benton, a former lawyer (admitted to the Indiana bar in 1851), commanded the 8th Indiana Volunteer Infantry, which had been organized in Indianapolis, Indiana. In early 1862, he utilized Cathy's services as a laundress for his officers. Most importantly, Colonel Benton became her supporter and protector.

Destined to gain a general's rank in April 1862, Benton was sympathetic toward Cathy and felt concern about her fate. Colonel Benton, born in New Market, Maryland, knew a good deal about personal suffering in his own life. These sad experiences in part allowed him to empathize with Cathy's plight. One source of Colonel Benton's empathy was rooted in personal tragedies. The colonel's wife, Sarah A. Wiggins, had recently died of disease at age twenty-seven, leaving his children, Walter, Jessie, and Mary, under their father's care. But despite his benevolence, the kind-hearted colonel's fate continued to be unkind in the years ahead. In fact, Cathy Williams outlived the unlucky Indiana colonel. He died of yellow fever during the postwar Union occupation of New Orleans, where General Benjamin Butler had ruled since 1862 like a feudal warlord, in mid-March 1867. Benton was only age thirty-eight when he died near the ten year anniversary of his marriage to the woman of his dreams.

Cathy's domestic work now supported the officers of Colonel Benton's Indiana regiment, when attached to General John C. Fremont's Army of the Southwest. She was provided food, shelter, and clothing, while Benton's officers benefited from her domestic services. Clearly, this was a reciprocal relationship that benefited both parties in an informal business arrangement of mutual support. Eventually, the Indiana colonel decided that Cathy would make an ideal cook for his officers evidently to allow her to remain with the Union Army. To Colonel Benton's reasoning and according to the pervasive northern stereotype, black female slaves were known to be good cooks.

But ironically this general assumption about black women (former slaves) did not apply to Cathy. She had been stereotyped by the boys in blue, and that assumption was entirely misplaced. In Cathy's own words that revealed the dilemma, Colonel Benton "wanted me to cook for the [8th Indiana] officers, but I had always been a house girl [at the William Johnson residence just outside of Jefferson City] and did not know how to cook."[13]

But this popular stereotype about female slaves was also rooted in some fact. Providing a good representative example, Booker T. Washington emphasized how the young white daughters of his master "were not taught to cook, sew, or to take care of the house."[14] While Cathy had not been taught to cook at the William Johnson place in Cole County, she had been assigned to taking care of domestic chores at the main house. As she had grown taller and stronger in her teenage years, so her responsibilities had increased and her work became more demanding.[15]

Later in the Civil War in 1863 when Cathy was cooking for Union troops, another young slave woman recently liberated from slavery's bonds became the cook of General George Armstrong Custer, Eliza Denison Brown. During the summer of 1863, Eliza was part of a group of Rappahannock County, Virginia, contrabands (runaway slaves), who entered the Army of the Potomac's cavalry encampment. Custer needed a cook for himself and the officers of his headquarters staff.

Therefore, Eliza began a six-year period of service as cook for him. This faithful service was extended by Eliza, at Custer's personal request, all the way to the Great Plains during the post-Civil War years. Well-deserving of recognition for her generally forgotten influential role at Custer's headquarters and in the lives of the famous Ohio-born general and his wife Elizabeth, who was the pampered daughter of a Monroe, Michigan, judge, Eliza was destined to "become a figure of no minor importance in the Custer story."[16]

Indeed, in time, Eliza evolved into far more than simply a cook and servant. This larger role represented a significant transition that Cathy Williams also might well have undergone at some point with the Union Army, but to a lesser degree. Eliza became an effective organizer and manager, who "began to rule [Custer's cavalry] headquarters as effectively and firmly as Custer commanded on the battlefield."[17]

However, like Cathy Williams in the beginning, so young Eliza (near the same age as Cathy during the Civil War's years) feared the prospect of life in a far-flung army engaged in campaigns to destroy the Army of Northern Virginia, which might well in turn to destroy the Yankee army. If so, then Eliza (like Cathy) might be caught amid a raging battle, and perhaps killed or even re-enslaved, if captured by Southern soldiers. As Eliza explained her initial fear in 1863 that she also eventually overcame like Cathy Williams during the summer of 1861: "Oh, how awful lonesome I was at first, and I was afraid of everything in the shape of war [and] I used to wish myself back on the plantation with my mother."[18]

Cathy Williams felt much like Eliza because nothing was more challenging for a young woman than a wartime environment, when serving in support of an army (even in a non-combat role) during active campaigning far from home. When Cathy Williams initially embarked upon a support role for the officers of the 8th Indiana Regiment in early 1862, she had unknowingly continued a longtime tradition. Black women, slaves and free black females, had long played comparable support roles for American soldiers. This forgotten role had existed since the beginning of the nation's founding, when General George Washington's Continental Army had contained large numbers of female camp followers, black and white, during the American Revolution.[19]

When Cathy began campaigning with the Union Army before the arrival of the 8th Indiana which joined the Army of the Southwest in January 1862, during the summer of 1861, she had no idea how far this duty in support of Union troops would take her from her native Missouri River country homeland. After General Sterling Price's defeat at Boonville, Missouri, on June 17, Cathy accompanied General Nathaniel Lyon's Army south and deeper into Missouri in its pursuit of the ragtag Missouri State Guard, under

"Old Pap" Price. Fortunately for Missouri slaves living south of the Missouri River, fortunes continued to decline for Price's undisciplined citizen-soldiers during the summer of 1861. The Missouri Rebels were forced to retire into Missouri's remote southwest corner located not far from the Indian Territory and the Boston Mountains of northwest Arkansas.

Leaving the Missouri River country behind, Cathy accompanied the Union Army south to Springfield, Missouri, which served as the logistical base for the operations of General Lyon's Army of the Southwest. Here, in Missouri's southwest corner, Springfield was located more than 130 miles southwest of Jefferson City. At this time, Cathy Williams had never been so far from home in a more remote region that was more heavily-wooded and less cultivated than her native Missouri River country, which was dominated by large hemp, cotton, and tobacco plantations.

Cathy then heard the roar of thousands of muskets on August 9, 1861 during the battle of Wilson's Creek, a tributary of the James River, just outside Springfield, Missouri. With the Southerners encamped along the picturesque creek that flowed through the rolling hills of Greene County, Missouri, General Lyon embarked upon bold but risky tactics. Gambling on the tactical premise that the best defense was an audacious offensive effort, he decided to strike his opponents' large encampment. Despite facing superior odds, Lyon divided his command to attack simultaneously from two different directions in true Napoleonic fashion. General Lyon delivered a frontal assault that caught the Southerners by surprise, while his top lieutenant, General Franz Sigel, delivered a flank attack: an effective one-two punch.

However, the bluecoat attackers only stirred up a hornet's nest of Rebels, who rallied and fought back with spirit. Shot off his horse in leading an attack, Lyon's death sapped the Union troops' morale and initiative to reverse the day's fortunes. The homespun Missouri Rebels and their Arkansas and Louisiana allies won a hard-earned victory at the battle of Wilson's Creek. [20]

Lyon's spunky army of Missouri, Kansas, and Iowa troops was defeated but not destroyed, which would have resulted in Cathy's re-enslavement, if she had been captured. After the slugfest at Wilson's Creek, the Union Army withdrew to Rolla, Missouri, some 110 miles to the northeast and about half-way to the state's largest and most strategic city, St. Louis. Cathy marched northeast and toward St. Louis during the army's withdrawal to Rolla, located northeast of Springfield. Rolla served as the new supply base after Springfield's loss to the resurgent Southerners. With so many wounded Federals from the battle of Wilson's Creek and medical staff short of helpers, Cathy might well have briefly served as a nurse to assist overburdened Union surgeons in makeshift field hospitals.[21]

Meanwhile, Price's victorious army pushed north from Springfield in an ambitious bid to reclaim the home state. The Missouri Rebels advanced north just inside the state's unmarked western border with Kansas and all the way to the Missouri River country, where Cathy Williams had been born. Here, in western Missouri, a surprising September 1861 victory was won by "Old Pap" Price's resurgent Missourians, perhaps including male members of the William Johnson family that had once owned Cathy, when the Union garrison at Lexington, Missouri, surrendered after a siege. But in the end, Price's bold invasion to reclaim Missouri was thwarted by the advance of sizeable Union reinforcements. Therefore, the Missouri Rebels were once again forced to withdraw south and back to Springfield, which was relatively close of Confederate Arkansas and sizeable reinforcements.

The fate of Missouri, the strategic border state west of the Mississippi, was permanently decided at the battle of Pea Ridge, Arkansas, in early March 1862. Like at the battle of Wilson's Creek in southeast Missouri, Cathy was with the Army of the Southwest when it won the decisive Union victory at the battle of Pea Ridge in northwest corner of Arkansas. After Confederate defeat at Pea Ridge, Price's Missouri State Guard was no longer a threat to the home state that was now lost forever to the Confederacy. Meanwhile, the Trans-Mississippi Theater became a secondary arena of operations in 1863 to General Ulysses S. Grant's Campaign to capture the strategic Mississippi River port of Vicksburg, Mississippi, on the east bank of the "Father of Waters." Vicksburg fell on the Fourth of July 1863 to the relentless and highly-capable Grant, who was never discouraged by initial setbacks during an extremely challenging campaign. Here, at Vicksburg, he won the victory that gained Union control of the strategic Mississippi River and Mississippi Valley, after the subsequent fall of Port Hudson, Louisiana.

Confederate fortunes continued to sag on the Mississippi's west side, after Vicksburg's fall. After the capture of Little Rock, Arkansas, by General Frederick Steele's forces on September 10, 1863, still another opportunity was presented to Cathy Williams. She continued to adjust to the sudden changes brought about by the unpredictable fortunes of war. Once again, it almost seemed as if a strange fate and destiny were pulling the young former slave not only ever-farther from home (farther south and to more remote and warmer regions compared to her frigid Missouri River country homeland in winter), but also to new roles to play in this war.

Cathy Williams now gained culinary skills in Little Rock, which had been liberated and its slaves freed. As Cathy described the personal situation that was still another unpredictable phase of her personal odyssey with the Union Army: "they took me and other colored folks [of Missouri] with them to Little Rock. Col. Benton [now promoted to a brigadier general] of the 13th army corps [Army of the Southwest] was the officer that carried us off [and] I learned to cook after going to Little Rock . . ."[22]

When Cathy had been liberated from slavery in mid-Missouri during June 1861, President Abraham Lincoln had not issued the Emancipation Proclamation in part because the time was still not right because of a delicate political situation stemming from pro-slavery sympathies in the border states, including Missouri. Because of having been raised in slavery that had ensured no educational instruction for Cathy during her formative years, she was not able to read the words of the Emancipation Proclamation when finally issued, even if a copy had been placed before her.[23]

As a cook for Union troops west of the Mississippi, Cathy gained a more elevated status of a skilled position rather than an ordinary laundress in washing soldiers' clothing. She continued this longtime black tradition of black women cooking for American fighting men, evidently officers, and even top civilian leaders. Prized female black cooks had even long prepared meals, including their favorite Southern dishes, for Southern-born presidents at the White House from George Washington to Lyndon B. Johnson, both Southerners, Virginia and Texas, respectively.

Hercules had been George Washington's slave and favorite chef, who had been brought by the president to the nation's first capital of Philadelphia, before it was established in Washington, D.C., along the Potomac. Likewise Thomas Jefferson, the third president, had long utilized his black "chef for life" at Monticello and including in Philadelphia, when the red-haired Virginian had served as secretary of state. James Hemings had been trained in the art of French cuisine in Paris, France. He was the brother of Sally Hemings, whose father was white (the father of Jefferson's wife and Sally Hemings) and mother black.[24]

On February 22, 1797 when Washington had celebrated his sixty-fifth birthday, Hercules escaped the nation's capital of Philadelphia and the republic's first president. Clearly, despite his elevated status in slave society, Hercules' love of liberty had never diminished, burning deep inside him despite the passing of years–something that his aristocratic Virginia slave-owner could never fully understand, despite his lofty intellectualism and love of liberty.

Nevertheless, Washington, a much sterner slave-owner than the more cerebral Jefferson, had made determined efforts to track down the escaped Hercules and return him to slavery. Like in regard to Cathy Williams and her own free black father, the little daughter of Hercules fully appreciated her father's love of freedom. When a white foreign visitor asked if she was saddened that her own father had left her and his family mired in slavery under Washington's ownership, she declared with spunk, "Oh! Sir, I am very glad, because he is free now."[25]

Compared to her service as a laundress to Yankee troops, the relatively elevated status of a cook enjoyed by Cathy was echoed in the words of Booker T. Washington. He described how, "The [family's] cabin was not only our living-place [in Franklin County, Virginia], but was also used as the kitchen for the plantation. My mother was the plantation cook [and] One of my earliest recollections is that of my mother cooking a chicken late at night . . ."[26]

Like many newly-liberated blacks, Cathy continued to faithfully perform her assigned duties for Union fighting men month after month. Although the overall transitional period since departing mid-Missouri had been personally uncomfortable for her in the beginning, Cathy shortly realized that she had found a secure home in the army. Indeed, the Federal Army served as her surrogate family, with individuals, black and white, bonded together by the common goal of saving the Union and destroying slavery.

Of course, other black cooks and laundresses (former slaves and no doubt fellow Missourians) were Cathy's friends, because of their shared background and experiences in not only slavery, but also the Civil War. As a cook, Cathy Williams served in Union armies on both sides of the Mississippi until the war's end. All the while, she continued to learn intimately about the ways of military life, including army protocol and martial customs. Cathy also learned a good deal more about the fighting men and boys (including teenagers who had never shaved) in blue, who were so unlike the pro-Southern Missourians.[27]

Although the Yankees were liberators of slaves, Cathy also encountered her fair share of anti-black sentiment in the army (especially from soldiers born in the border slave states). After all, these young men often represented slices of a prejudiced society, most often rural and provincial. Quite literally, these young Union soldiers were the products of their mostly backwater and less progressive environments. In a letter, one Federal soldier declared that he would rather fight against blacks than for them. Clearly, the Union Army consisted of a wide spectrum of American society, including men of every class, social structure, and ethnic group, especially the Irish (who were often known for their hostility toward blacks primarily because of stiff economic competition in civilian life) and the Germans (but generally more liberal than the Irish), who also served their adopted country in large numbers.

But overall the treatment of contraband men and women in the Union Army was often so relatively good that it sometimes caused resentment among some members of the rank and file. One Maine soldier complained in a letter how: "Contrabands [now] have better places to sleep in and better grub than we do . . . "[28] As mentioned, this relatively favorable situation partly explained how and why Cathy Williams found a secure refuge—even a surrogate home —in the military during active campaigning.

In this war to save the Union, the overall role of ex-slaves was a factor in the final victory in 1865, because large numbers of former slaves provided all manner of support to Federal soldiers in the field. Historian Nell Irvin Painter described how, "Hundreds of thousands of black men, women, and children advanced the Union cause inside and around the organized armed forces [and] Without their support, the Union cause would not have won this war on Southern territory. The enslaved were not given their freedom; they earned it."[29]

When Cathy was first taken into the Union army and given assignments in supporting the North's fighting men, she was in essence paying the country back for her newly-won freedom by her service. This fact was a realization that brought a sense of satisfaction to her, fueling her motivations while serving the liberators of her people.[30]

As mentioned, Cathy Williams was still serving in a support role with a Union Army in the western theater, when President Lincoln's finally issued his two Emancipation Proclamations, with the first, or preliminary, coming in September 1862 to exploit the Union success at the battle of Antietam at Sharpsburg, Maryland, on September 17, 1862. This hard-earned victory amid the rich farmlands of western Maryland on the war's bloodiest single day forced the Army of Northern Virginia to withdraw back south into Virginia, ending Lee's first invasion of the North.

Ironically, however, this first proclamation issued from the White House failed to apply to Cathy's home state of Missouri, where her mother, if still alive at this time, and other relatives remained in bondage. Slavery in Missouri was not officially abolished until January 1865. Most importantly for the overall war effort, former slaves officially enlisted in large numbers in the Union army from 1863-1865: ironically, nearly two years after Cathy Williams began her support role for the Union Army.

As a native Missourian, it was also symbolic that Cathy served the Union cause because her home state provided more men to Union Armies in proportion to its total population than any state. The conflict in Missouri was an example of total war, including a vicious guerrilla conflict waged by wide-ranging Missouri partisans, such as William Clarke Quantrill's band of hard-riding guerrillas. These Southern partisans sought to win their home state from Union occupation troops. In this sense, Cathy Williams was actually fortunate to have departed the state with the Union Army by moving farther south into Arkansas, instead of remaining in a war-torn Missouri, where the most brutal brand of guerrilla warfare seen anywhere in America raged for years.

As mentioned, President Lincoln's final Emancipation Proclamation was issued on January 1, 1863 to bring a new birth of freedom to many African Americans. Because Cathy had been freed in June 1861, she more intimately understood how this war for America's heart and soul was most of all about freeing the slaves, even before many Union soldiers (who initially fought more to save the Union rather than destroying slavery) came to this realization. Northern abolitionists proclaimed that America was now truly living up to its idealistic egalitarian promise of 1776 that all men were created equal as proclaimed in the Declaration of Independence, Cathy no doubt wondered at some point about the unfairness of the blatant inequality of women and blacks in American society. After all, the two groups had been denied—one for gender and the other for race —what had been promised in the Declaration of Independence and the Constitution.[31]

After President Lincoln's first proclamation, newly-freed blacks, including from Cathy's home state, began to flood into the ranks of new regiments of the United States Colored Troops (USCT). Had she known this fact that played a large role in Union victory because of pervasive war weariness among the northern population during the most murderous war in American history, Cathy would have taken pride in the fact that a total of 8,344 black soldiers from Missouri served in USCT regiments. This figure was more than the number of blacks who served from the northern states except Pennsylvania.[32]

Large numbers of these African American males were playing their parts to destroy slavery, just like Cathy, who had embarked upon this lofty goal earlier than the highly-motivated USCT soldiers. Cathy first saw these black soldiers either in camp or marching in column in 1864 or 1865. Cathy Williams' own cousin (a future member of her own Buffalo Soldier regiment after the Civil War) was one soldier who very likely served in a USCT regiment from Missouri. If so, then he would have been one of the nearly 40 percent of black males from Missouri who wore the blue uniform that now represented a symbol of liberty to former slaves.[33]

Cathy Williams' most significant role during the Civil War years came after the 8th Indiana was transferred east to the Army of the Shenandoah and participated in the 1864 struggle for possession of the vital Shenandoah Valley. This fertile valley, the breadbasket of the Confederacy, had long funneled resources and supplies to Lee's Army of Northern Virginia, whose primary mission was to protect the Confederacy's capital of Richmond. Therefore, Union strategists determined that this lush valley of plenty had to be razed to deprive the enemy of resources in this modern war of attrition.

Here, Cathy's skill and experience as a cook landed her a coveted position (compared to working solely for the 8th Indiana's officers) at General Philip Henry Sheridan's headquarters. "Little Phil" Sheridan was one of the North's chief architects of decisive victory in the eastern theater. Cathy often saw the dynamic general, a diminutive and feisty West Pointer of Irish heritage, up close. She also became familiar with the sight of the general's prized black war horse named "Rienzi." As Cathy explained in her own words: "at the time Gen. Sheridan made his raids in the Shenandoah valley [in 1864] I was cook and washerman [woman] for his staff."[34]

Ironically, as the strange fate of her life would have it, Cathy was destined to serve as a Buffalo Soldier during the Indian Wars when General Sheridan commanded the Department of the Missouri (that included the Great Plains) and sought to subdue the hostile Native Americans. Angry warriors of the Great Plains tribes hampered settlers and railroads from moving west, and a vibrant national destiny called for them to be pushed aside.

Since the 1863 Gettysburg Campaign and as mentioned, General Sheridan's top cavalry lieutenant, Brigadier General George Armstrong Custer (the "Boy General"), likewise employed his former slave female cook, Eliza, who managed the internal functioning of Custer's cavalry headquarters. Like Cathy when liberated in mid-June 1861, the legal designation of contraband had played a role in shaping the course of Eliza's life. After "having learned of the new dispensation by which people of her race were no longer to be regarded as chattels, left their plantation on which she had been reared" and as mentioned, Eliza had then "'jined up with the Ginnil'," as she called the flamboyant Custer.[35]

Like Cathy, Eliza also found a secure refuge and safe home at the headquarters of one of the Union's most dynamic cavalry officers. Hard-driving, young cavalry officers on the rise, Generals Custer and Sheridan were kindred spirits. These two West Pointers formed one of the most effective leadership teams of the United States cavalry during the Civil War. Of course, a stationary position of working at a general's headquarters was well-protected behind the lines during active campaigning, which gave Cathy Williams and Eliza additional security that enhanced their personal safety compared to being assigned to a single regiment like the 8th Indiana (Cathy's old regiment that she had supported), if a Confederate attack was launched.

At Custer's headquarters, Eliza faithfully supported one of the North's youngest and best cavalry generals, who inflicted havoc upon the enemy at seemingly every opportunity. Therefore, this former Virginia slave felt satisfaction and a sense of pride in assisting this bold cavalry commander, who played a key role in ridding the republic of slavery's curse: a situation that equally applied to Cathy Williams' support to "Little Phil" in the Shenandoah Valley. Such factors explained in part why Cathy remained with Union armies on both sides of the Appalachians and faithfully performed her duties year after year.[36]

Eliza described the same kind of transformational experience that Cathy herself underwent in the Union Army, "There's many folks says that a woman can't follow the army without throwing themselves away [by succumbing to vice and easy money from exploitative Federal soldiers who were overpaid—in relative terms —and often ill-spent their money] but I know better. I went in, and I cum out with the respect of the men and of the officers."[37]

In an army filled with young, healthy men of differing characters distinguished by virtues and vices, it is not known if Cathy might have been tempted by offers of easy money from lustful soldiers, who had not come into close contact with young females for extended periods. But acting in a support role for the Union Army provided far more positive aspects that benefited former slaves. Like Eliza who served General Custer for six years during the Civil War and the Indian Wars, so Cathy Williams also gained a greater sense of self-identity and accomplishment in serving in a support role in the Union Armies for nearly four years.[38]

Chapter II: Overcoming the Bleakest of Beginnings

The determination of Cathy Williams to embark upon her life as a United States soldier could not have been greater on perhaps the most memorable day of her life, November 15, 1866. Clearly, the Civil War years had resulted in a life-changing personal experience for Cathy. Indeed, Cathy Williams would never be the same thereafter. While planning to enter the United States Army compound known as Jefferson Barracks in her ambitious bid to enlist in a Buffalo Soldier regiment on his mid-November day, perhaps Cathy briefly reflected upon the strange course of her life and how fate itself seemed to have ordained the special destiny of a soldier's life for her.

As mentioned, she had been born in Jackson County, Missouri, which was located at the eastern edge of the Great Plains, in September 1844. Therefore, she knew about life on a western frontier environment from having grown up first in western Missouri, and then mid-Missouri where her last owner lived. In her words about the most inauspicious start in life, that could not have begun less promising: "I was born near Independence, Jackson County, Missouri."[39]

However, despite the adversity, this young black woman was now able to draw strength and inspiration from the positive aspects of her past life and religious faith. Significantly, Cathy William's free black father had left her a lasting personal legacy that was even more important than a moneyed inheritance in terms of bestowing an independent nature and a desire for freedom like he had enjoyed as a free man. While Cathy had been enslaved, he had lived outside the horrors of slavery, minimizing its psychological and emotional damage that destroyed so many black lives.

As Cathy explained her earliest and fondest memories about her father, who had provided her with an inspirational example for her to continue to look for a better day in the future. Many slaves, like Cathy Williams and Booker T. Washington possessed relatively little knowledge about their free black fathers, because slave-owners kept the dangerous example of free blacks as far away from their own slaves as possible. After all, free blacks represented the fulfillment of the dream of freedom. In Cathy's own words:

"My Father was a free man, but my mother a slave, belonging to William Johnson, a wealthy farmer [and] While I was a small girl my mater and family moved to Jefferson City . . . My master died there" before the war.[40]

Cathy's father, with the last name of Williams, was one of the few free blacks who had resided in Jackson County during the antebellum period. Located in the Missouri River country, Jackson County was part of a high-productive agricultural region known as "Little Dixie." This fertile region had been heavily populated with slaves. Cathy's father almost certainly had been born a slave, before gaining his freedom. It is not known, but he might have been freed by an enlightened Missouri master by a court ruling in the 1850s. Indeed, because Missouri was a slave state, Cathy's father most likely gained manumission legally. If so, then he would have been very careful to carry the legal paperwork with him to prove his freedom, just in case his free status was ever contested by authorities or any unscrupulous white Missourians. After all, opportunistic whites could make easy money by kidnapping and then selling a free black man as a slave.

A young Cathy might have seen her father's free man papers at some point in her life while growing up in Jackson County. Or if Cathy's father had been a free man before the 1840s, then his early absence from Cathy's life might have been legally mandated by an 1847 state law, which had forced free blacks to depart Jackson County, because they were viewed as disruptive influences (possibly inciting slave revolts) to slavery's stability.

However, the more enlightened environment of bustling St. Louis, the state's largest city on the Mississippi, had been much different from rural areas like in the Missouri River countryside to the west. In this cosmopolitan urban environment, slavery had long been a dying institution compared to the fertile Missouri River country, where cash crops (primarily hemp, cotton, and tobacco) had been grown on large plantations during the antebellum period. Therefore, most free blacks of Missouri had lived in St. Louis. Here, 1,398 free blacks were counted in the "Gateway to the West" city, as revealed in the 1850 Census.

Only a decade later, free blacks outnumbered slaves in St. Louis, where many free blacks worked in skilled positions, especially as artisans. By comparison, Cathy's native Jackson County was primarily a rural region long dominated by staple crops, plantations, and large numbers of slaves (21 percentage of the county's total population). As the sectional crisis over slavery intensified in the 1850s, especially on the Missouri Kansas border, the free status of Cathy's father had grown more precarious.

Therefore, if he had been freed in the 1850s, Cathy's father very likely took the wise precaution of departing Missouri, and then moved west to escape across the nearby border to the safety of Kansas. Here, in the decade before the Civil War, anti-slavery Kansas settlers, mostly northern immigrants, protected African Americans, including slaves who had trekked west and crossed the lengthy north-south state border of open prairies to escape from Missouri. During the antebellum period, Missouri was a state where slavery thrived almost as much as in Georgia or Mississippi.

If this was indeed the case in regard to Cathy's father, then her father's relentless spirit to move west was not lost to his adventuresome daughter. Indeed, she eventually followed in her father's footsteps in pushing toward the setting sun in search of a better life after the Civil War, leaving Missouri far behind. Life in nearby abolitionist Kansas towns, like Lawrence, was good for free blacks. Before the Civil War and like escaped slavers, many free blacks had migrated from Missouri and other pro-slavery states to live in the free havens of Kansas. Here, they merged into the frontier communities of Kansas with a relative smoothness that was impossible in Missouri.[41]

A Name's Importance

When she had been trapped in the tight grip of slavery, Cathy had early witnessed a number of upheavals in her life. But fortunately for her, these setbacks had only made Cathy stronger and more determined to succeed. She had proved resilient, adapting to unexpected changes that often came her way, when least expected and at no fault of her own. Most significant and as revealed when she finally enlisted as a Buffalo Soldier, Cathy had refused to take the last name of her master (Johnson) unlike most other slaves.

Instead, Cathy had kept her father's last name, because it was a reminder of home, family, and heritage that obviously meant a great deal to her. This preservation of her father's last name revealed a healthy respect for her past. Cathy's decision to cast off her master's name and then resurrect her father's name revealed a sense of pride in not only herself, but also in her father and his elevated free status that had set him apart from the vast majority of other blacks in Missouri before the Civil War.[42]

Booker T. Washington described this subtle, but important psychological and symbolic change of a personal name that clearly represented something very significant to Cathy Williams: "After the coming of freedom there were two points upon which practically all the people on our place [in Franklin County, Virginia] were agreed, and I find that this was generally true throughout the South: that they must change their names, . . . In some way a feeling got around among the coloured people that it was far from proper for them to bear the surname of their former owners, and a great many took other surnames. This was one of the first signs of freedom. When they were slaves, a coloured person was simply called 'John' or 'Susan.' [and] If 'John' or 'Susan' belonged to a white man by the name of 'Hatcher,' sometimes he was called 'John Hatcher,' or as often 'Hatcher's John.' But there was a feeling that 'John Hatcher' or 'Hatcher's John' was not the proper title by which to denote a freeman" or freewoman.[43]

In much the same way on this cold November 15, 1866, Cathy Williams now planned to have her real name written by the recruiting officer on the enlistment form at Jefferson Barracks. But this name would be written down in a totally unique way that revealed a great deal more about this young woman, who had been hardened by her years of service with Union Armies on both sides of the Mississippi. Obviously when she had first developed her risky plan to enlist in the United States Army at Jefferson Barracks, Cathy knew that she could not use her first name as Cathy. Interestingly, the name of Cathy might not have been short for the English name of Catherine as generally assumed. The possibility existed that Cathy was in fact an African name with West African antecedents, and that this name might have possessed special meaning to her in consequence. The name "Kessie," which might have been corrupted into the name of Cathy, was a Fante and Ashanti, of Ghana, West Africa, female name that meant "born fat."[44]

While Cathy Williams continued to walk toward the front gate of Jefferson Barracks on that Thursday November 15, 1866 with the determination to enlist as a Buffalo Soldier in her boldest undertaking to date, she still possessed a distinct sense of pride in the name Cathy. And, most importantly, she was determined not to lose her birth name, even when that singular ambition placed her at greater risk by doing so in the upcoming enlistment process. After all and as mentioned, this name meant something very significant to her, representing a distinctive identity that bolstered her sense of self and self-esteem.

Therefore, she developed a premeditated plan to merely use Cathy as her last name by having an additional letter of "a" included near the end for a new spelling of Cathay. To embark on his new career as a United States soldier, the name of William Cathay was her final choice for her new identity. And, most importantly, she could also still carry forth and preserve her father's name of Williams by simply removing the last letter of the last name.

To maintain her sense of self and a healthy self-image based on pride in her own personal legacy in regard to name and family, Cathy's decision to have a single letter added, the "a" into her first name was decided upon by her (although illiterate she at least knew how to spell her name) revealed that her past was atypical for a female slave. Having served as a house slave, the distinct possibility existed that the master's wife or children (who might have been of Cathy's own age) might have taught Cathy Williams at least to write her name. Or perhaps her free father had taught her how to write the name of Cathy. Unfortunately, we will probably never know for sure because of the lack of documentation about Cathy's life.

But more likely, Cathy had evidently gained some rudimentary informal schooling during the Civil War years, when she had been attached to the Union Army. Significantly, what was clear was that she did not want to completely lose her true identity and sense of self in regard to her first and last name, while simultaneously creating a new identity for herself as a male soldier of a new Buffalo Soldier regiment eventually bound for service on the western frontier.[45]

To increase the odds for the fulfillment of her novel concept of disguising herself as a male as envisioned when her new manufactured name would be signed to the enlistment papers by the army recruiter at Jefferson Barracks, Cathay benefited from the fact that this was a legitimate last name unlike Cathy. It is not known but perhaps Cathy also might have known a person by the last name of Cathay. However, the existing evidence has indicated that Cathy most likely developed the spelling of the last name of Cathay on her own to maintain her separate and distinctive identity in her bid to begin her life anew in the United States military.

United States Colored Troops, USCT

Besides pride in name and self, Cathy also almost certainly wanted to continue the distinguished tradition of the more than 200,000 blacks, who played key roles in winning the war for the Union. As mentioned, she had seen some of these ebony fighting men during the Civil War. Nearly 3,000 soldiers of African descent died in the Civil War. In fact, the battlefield successes of African American soldiers from 1863 to 1865 had paved the way for the official establishment of the Buffalo Soldier regiments in 1866. Therefore, in this sense, the roles of the Buffalo Soldier regiments were actually a continuation of the impressive combat performances of the USCT regiments during the Civil War.[46]

At the Civil War's beginning, the general assumption in the North and South was that blacks would not make good soldiers like white men: one of the oldest and most timeworn racial stereotypes in American history. This most outrageous of stereotypes was one of America's most enduring myths, entirely lacking in any solid foundation or substantial evidence. However, overcoming his own initial prejudices, one erudite journalist of the *New York Times* had early known the undeniable truth. With clarity, he saw well beyond the pervasive racism that proclaimed that blacks would not fight as well as white soldiers, because of nothing more than differences in skin color: a longtime racial assumption and pervasive stereotype so laughable, as fully recognized by Founding Father Alexander Hamilton during the American Revolution, that people with good sense and intelligence knew better.

Born in the Caribbean, the gifted Hamilton was open-minded about matters of race when he had served with distinction as General George Washington's chief of staff during the American Revolution. At risk to his own career, the young lieutenant colonel boldly advocated for the use of black soldiers at a time (1779) when white manpower shortages were dooming America's resistance effort, especially in the Southern theater. Firm in his convictions, Hamilton ignored the fact that the wealthy Washington was a large Virginia slave-owner. Seeing through the society-induced fog of racial stereotypes and prejudices, one knowledgeable journalist informed his readers on May 12, 1861 and barely a month after the Civil War's beginning: "The most efficient troops in the French Service at the present day are the Turcos, who are Africans, while England, also, has kept black troops in the West Indies, and at other places" in the British Empire.[47]

In a May 30 letter, 1864, Adjutant General of the United States Army, Lorenzo Thomas, understood one reason why the black troops (mostly former slaves) made ideal soldiers, echoing Hamilton's unconventional late 1770s views that he had masterfully emphasized to the president, John Jay, of the Continental Congress during the American Revolution. As Thomas explained with insight to a senator how, "The negro in the state of Slavery is brought up by the master from early childhood to strict obedience, and to obey implicitly the dictates of the white man, and they are this led to believe that they are an inferior race. Now, when organized into troops, they carry this habit of obedience with them, and their officers being entirely white men, the negro promptly obeys his orders. A regiment is thus rapidly brought into a state of discipline. They are a religious people, another high quality for making good soldiers. They are musical people and thus readily learn to march, and accurately perform their manoeuvres. They take pride in being devoted as soldiers, and keep themselves as well as their camp-grounds, neat and clean. This I know from personal inspection, and from reports of my special inspectors . . ."[48]

But, of course, these views from a high-ranking white Union officer failed to provide a fully adequate explanation in regard to what other key factors made African Americans such good soldiers, in camp and on the battlefield: the simple fact that these ebony fighting men were so highly-motivated because they fought to destroy slavery and liberate millions of slaves in bondage across the South.

During her service in supporting Union troops in Virginia in 1864-1865, Cathy might have learned of the dozen USCT highly-decorated soldiers of the Army of the James. They had been the first blacks to receive the Medal of Honor on April 6, 1865 for demonstrating heroics in attacking strong Confederate defenses at the battle of New Market Heights near Richmond on September 29, 1864.

Cathy had been in the Virginia Theater at that time, and a grapevine of free-flowing information existed among the black cooks and laundresses about the distinguished battlefield accomplishments of African American soldiers, who were greatly admired by them. Symbolically, William E. Barnes was one of these black Medal of Honor winners, and a proud member the 38th USCT regiment (a volunteer regiment). In contrast to this fine USCT regiment of the Civil War, Cathy Williams was destined to serve in the 38th

United States Infantry Regiment (a regular regiment instead of a volunteer regiment) from 1866 to 1868.[49]

Sergeant William Carney became the best known winner of the nation's highest award for valor. He won the Medal of Honor for heroics in the bloody attack (celebrated in the popular 1989 movie *Glory*) of his 54th Massachusetts Volunteer Infantry Regiment upon the defensive bastion of Fort Wagner, located just outside Charleston, South Carolina. Besides the sixteen African Americans who won the Medal of Honor while serving in USCT infantry regiments, another sixteen blacks of the United States Navy won the Medal of Honor for exhibiting gallantry.[50]

As mentioned, because of bonds of race and shared experiences, Cathy also felt that she had a debt to pay to the legacy of the more than 200,000 troops (mostly former slaves), who served during the Civil War. They had marched forth to ensure the extinction of slavery, and to prove their worth as equal men. One northerner described why the black troops were so effective during the Civil War years: "Their loyalty, their devotion to the cause they espoused, their fighting qualities, are all established, beyond dispute; while their thousands of dead upon various bloody battlefields tell of the sacrifices they have made that the Government might be sustained" by the Confederacy's defeat.[51]

Therefore, while Cathy Williams continued to walk toward the main gate of Jefferson Barracks on this cold Thursday (November 15, 1866), after which her life would never be the same, she carried with her the inspiring memories of when she had been liberated in mid-Missouri and the enduring memory of black troops of the Civil War. That mid-June 1861 day of liberation in Cole County had been the happiest day of Cathy's life. Other than that special day, this November 15, 1866 was destined to be the most important day of Cathy's life: literally a time of renewal and rejuvenation for her, but only if all went well for fulfilling her well-thought-out plan to enlist in the United States Army. If Cathy's ruse succeeded, then November 15 would be as memorable as that unforgettable day of liberation back in Missouri, when her life was so suddenly changed forever by the ever-unpredictable winds of war.[52]

From 1861 to 1865 and like the fighting men (black and white) who had reaped the final decisive victory for the Union, Cathy Williams had been hardened by her Civil War experiences for nearly four years, even more than her life in slavery. As a youth and later during her teenage years, she had been a "house girl," in Cathy's own words. Now about to pay dividends to her at Jefferson Barracks, Cathy had learned to rely upon an arsenal of interpersonal skills and survival mechanisms, including the art of deception, derived from a diverse range of past experiences that well prepared her for undertaking her greatest challenge of enlisting and serving in the United States Army.

Contrary to the popular "Sambo" stereotype–the myth of the docile, submissive slave —as long perpetuated by Southern whites, including in popular novels and plays, to demonstrate an alleged black inferiority, Booker Taliferro Washington understood the kind of personal transformation that had been undergone by Cathy Williams in slavery: changes that had created a savvy and resourceful individual, who was the very antithesis of the mindless "Sambo" stereotype. Washington fully realized how the difficult experiences of slavery (and also the Civil War years in Cathy's case) had created a highly-resilient and versatile person. Like Cathy, Washington had been forged by the searing experiences in the school of hard knocks of a kind not experienced by whites: "notwithstanding the cruelty and moral wrong of slavery, the [blacks who] went through the school of American slavery, are in a stronger and more hopeful condition, materially, intellectually, morally, and religiously, than is true of an equal number of black people in any other portion of the globe."[53]

As mentioned, Cathy had developed a clever enlistment plan in the hope of securing a better life for herself, a guaranteed income of $13.00 per month as a Buffalo Soldier private, and a decent supply of clothing and rations. Cathy William was just the sort of resourceful person who Washington described with admiration and respect. He fully understood about how such resourceful individuals—true survivors--had been thoroughly transformed by the dual experiences of slavery and the Civil War.[54]

At Jefferson Barracks on November 15, 1866, Cathy also wanted to validate her claim to a newly-bestowed citizenship of a morally reborn United States, thanks to the North's great moral crusade that had destroyed slavery. Like the Buffalo Soldiers in general, she had embarked upon her own personal fight "for recognition as citizens in a racist country." And this struggle was one that had existed long before the Buffalo Soldiers took the fight to Native Americans on the Great Plains.[55]

Rather than being an alleged neurotic or psychologically-disturbed individual that her distracters have employed to explain her unorthodox decision to dress as a man and then enlist in the United States Army as emphasized by her male (generally more white than black to basically reflect fundamental cultural differences) distracters of today, Cathy Williams desired to become a Buffalo Soldier for primarily the same reasons that so many of today's men and women, black or white, have decided to enlist in the United States military: love of country, a sense of adventure, greater social and economic opportunities, and the promise of a better life in the future. Clearly, these universal and timeless desires—from Cathy Williams to the large number of women (black and white) in today's United States military—were fundamentally the same ones in 1866 as today.

But of course, Cathy Williams faced far greater challenges than women in today's military, because a host of more complex factors in regard to her unique situation primarily because of slavery's dark legacies. Quite simply, Cathy was going against not only society's most entrenched gender values of a patriarchal culture but also history in attempting to become a United States soldier. First and foremost of course, warfare had always been the longtime province of males in western culture. And this dominance of a male warrior ethos in the western military tradition had long deemed that such female transgressions into this exclusive masculine realm only resulted from some kind of psychological, sexual, or emotional deviance: an enduring gender stereotype and misconception that was part of the cultural, societal, and gender inheritance of western societies from time immemorial.

However, like Cathy's world during the Civil War years, women had been always shaped by war and its stern demands on the home front, suffering hardships and traumas like men, but of an entirely different variety. Although far from the front lines, these women (who served as the soldiers' support network) were the forgotten heroines of conflict. They have long been unrecognized largely because of this traditional male-focus of war. If necessary, Cathy was fully prepared to go to the front lines to fight for her country, which was unprecedented for an African American woman in the ranks of the United States Army, if she successfully enlisted at Jefferson Barracks on November 15.

Therefore, for such cultural and societal reasons, this unique side of war (women's roles) has become a forgotten wartime sacrifice in the western world, including in the United States. Of course, this was especially the case in regard to women who disguised themselves as males and then went to war. But in truth and as mentioned, these latter women were fundamentally no different from men in regard to a strong attraction of the virtues of military service, a deep-seated desire to serve their nation, and even in fighting for one's country: a fundamental part of the overall human condition and experience from time immemorial.

Almost certainly because this was a universal psychological and emotional priority of individuals who served their country, Cathy Williams might have been personally concerned, if not intrigued, by a perpetual question in regard to military service. This was the central thesis famously explored in the Stephen Crane's novel *The Red Badge of Courage*: could Cathy master her natural fears (like any young and inexperienced male soldier about to experience combat for the first time) and face the formidable challenges posed by the stern demands of combat situations? Like any rookie male soldier, Cathy's moral resolve and strength of character would be severely tested when under fire for the first time. Buffalo Soldier service was dangerous, resulting in the stiff demands of arduous campaigning against the Great Plains warriors in some of the most remote and inhospitable regions of the western frontier. Perhaps not even realized by Cathy at the time, her chances of eventually going to war against Native Americans were all but inevitable at this time.

After the four years of fratricidal war, America was now on the move toward the setting sun. Thousands of settlers, including many European immigrants, and the railroads steadily pushed west and into remote western regions that supported the wide-ranging existence of nomadic native tribes. Indeed, open warfare was now inevitable and only a matter of time between the Indians and the newly-formed Buffalo Soldiers, after the nation's push west was resumed. This clash of two very different cultures (red and white) with two completely different world views and societies ensured years of future warfare on the Great Plains.

Consequently, Civil War veterans, including Lieutenant Colonel George Armstrong Custer and General "Little Phil" Sheridan, who Cathy knew from her days in the 1864 Shenandoah Valley Campaign, were about to resume their respective distinguished military careers against resisting Indian tribes. These Great Plains tribes stood in the way of the American nation's push west and the fulfillment of national ambitions. Therefore, the native people had to be pushed aside by military might.[56]

Cathy Williams' First Great Challenge, Joining the United States Army

Fortunately for Cathy Williams, on this Thursday November 15, 1866, the temperatures were low, which was the seasonal norm at this time of year. The cold weather allowed Cathy the opportunity to utilize her well-disguised plan of wearing men's thick winter clothing, including a baggy pair of pants. Such apparel hid her feminine shape to sharp-eyed army recruiters, who she knew would closely look her up and down during the enlistment process. After the mild weather of Indian summer had passed in Missouri, she almost certainly had deliberately waited for an especially cold day to embark upon the daring attempt to change her life forever. And now this opportunity finally came at this large military installation (Jefferson Barracks) that now served as headquarters of the newly-created 38th United States Infantry. In regard to fulfilling her clever ruse, Cathy Williams was equally fortunate in benefiting from a slim, athletic build and a height above that of the average woman.

As she had carefully devised for a proper demeanor to deceive, Cathy appeared masculine to the casual eye, especially because of her height combined with suitable male attire to hide her physical form. In truth, this accomplishment was not as hard as it would seem in a day when sexual differences were most clearly marked by only the most simplistic of distinctions between the sexes: individuals who wore pants were all males. Cathy also might have heard stores of female slaves who had escaped by masquerading as men, which was a strategy that extended to before the American Revolution.

Most importantly, Cathy had succeeded in cultivating a male appearance as much as possible on November 15, exaggerating an overt maleness for the upcoming act that she knew would have to be performed flawlessly before the sharp eyes of army recruiters. Cathy had to convince the white soldiers, including officers, that she was exactly what she now appeared to be at first glance: an ordinary African American male eager to join the United States military and serve his country.

For young Cathy, however, just the formulation of such an audacious plan was no small undertaking. She was now relying on considerable cleverness and guile to ensure a successful enlistment effort at the recruiter's office. Clearly, this was a bold design based upon a confident self-assured conviction that she could fool every white soldier, especially officers, not only on November 15, but also far into the future. Hence, Cathy's masterful disguise, well-honed mannerisms, and even rougher manner of talk had to be precisely that of a young black male in entirety.

If she was caught in so audaciously attempting to pass off her ruse at a major United States military installation, however, Cathy might be punished for trying to fool the white soldiers, including officers. Very likely, they would feel insulted, if not angered, that a former slave woman's ruse had almost made fools of them. If her true sex was discovered, then the distinct possibility existed that officers would even hand Cathy Williams over to civilian authorities, a local sheriff, to be placed in jail in Carondelet or St. Louis. After all, a woman enlisting in the United States Army was an illegal act. Or she might even receive a minor beating or whipping from white soldiers for having attempted to mock the integrity of the military establishment that she desired to join by such audacious guile.

If Cathy was lucky if caught, she only would be escorted out of Jefferson Barracks. But to her way of thinking, this daring attempt to become a United States soldier was well worth the high risk. After all, this was a rare chance for her to serve her country, a future guarantee of food, shelter, and safety from a hostile world, and secure monthly pay for an extended period.

Formidable social, economic, and financial inequalities (only because of her race and gender) were obstacles that Cathy had to overcome, and now she hoped to negate these significant barriers on November 15. Of course, such stiff obstacles had long kept women of all colors and races in lowly places in this patriarchal society. Cathy was determined not to spend the rest of her life as a domestic worker. She now wanted something more significant in life, after having long served as a lowly domestic and menial worker: first in slavery for her Missouri owners and then for white soldiers during the Civil War. She was determined to maintain her financial independence, and this required an entirely new identity and life. Clearly, a successful enlistment in the United States Army represented a quick rise to higher social status that Cathy had never previously enjoyed.

Other factors enhanced Cathy's chances for a successful enlistment on this cold Thursday. She also possessed the advantage of having taken the initiative, which enhanced the possibility of a successful ruse: a rare example of a young black recruit coming on their own to Jefferson Barracks, especially during the fall and winter of 1866.Now that the army was expanding to fill-up the ranks of the new black regiments, the vast majority of white recruiters (officers) were now away from Jefferson Barracks in search for young black men to sign up in towns and cities. However, recruits were hard to find, including even in the cities.

The 10th Cavalry, a mounted Buffalo Soldier regiment authorized at the same time as Cathy's future infantry regiment, counted only one volunteer who stepped forward to enlist at Fort Leavenworth, Kansas, by September 1866. And even this prospective volunteer was stricken with malaria. Meanwhile, white regimental recruiters went to great lengths and distances, including to New York, Boston, and Philadelphia, in attempting to fill up the ranks of the six newly created half dozen Buffalo Soldier regiments (all officially established on July 28, 1866) with new recruits. Therefore, Cathy now possessed the advantages of the element of surprise by attempting to enlist at Jefferson Barracks on her own initiative on November 15.

Indeed, Cathy's overall chances for a successful enlistment were actually quite good at this time for other reasons as well. Female slave children had grown up in an environment in which males and females were treated more equally to obscure the boundaries of gender differences compared to their white counterparts, where gender roles were more sharply defined along traditional lines. But for Cathy, the Civil War years had provided the real training ground about how to behave like a male and a soldier, and she had learned her lessons well.

Long before ever putting on a blue uniform as a Buffalo Soldier, therefore, Cathy Williams already knew how to look, act, and talk like a young male soldier, after having been around fighting men, mostly middle-class farm boys, from 1861-1865. As mentioned, this was an invaluable learning experience that had led to the acquisition of considerable knowledge about soldiery ways that was now about to benefit her at the recruiting office at Jefferson Barracks.

Although she had only served as a cook, laundress, and perhaps nurse during the Civil War years, these diverse experiences over an extended period of nearly four years had been sufficient to give Cathy not only a decided edge for a successful enlistment on November 15, 1866, but also a distinct advantage. After all, she would shortly face experienced white recruiters who were soldiers. In regard to background knowledge and common experiences, especially during the Civil War years, Cathy was also closer to males than females, and closer to these bluecoat soldiers at Jefferson Barracks than the average civilian.

Other factors boded well for Cathy's successful enlistment. Former black cooks, painters, bakers, waiters, and even cigar makers became troopers of the 9th Cavalry, which also drew recruits (former slaves and free blacks) from St. Louis like the 38th United States Infantry. This competition made it much more difficult for the 38th United States Infantry to gain recruits for less glamorous and more difficult infantry service compared to the more popular cavalry service. In the prevalent thinking of the day, the average man (black or white) naturally preferred to ride rather than walk, and cavalry service also possessed an irresistible romantic lure to American males, black and white.

However, this was not the case with Cathy Williams who thought differently about cavalry service for obvious physical reasons. She needed to become a soldier in the infantry, rather than cavalry, service for the best chance of continuing a successful ruse for an extended period of time. In addition, she had little, if any, prior experience with horses, because she had been a domestic house servant in Missouri, and she had only accompanied infantry units during her Civil War career.

Bestowing Cathy with added confidence for a successful enlistment was the fact that this military environment was a familiar one to her. Cathy knew Jefferson Barracks and its daily routines, after having lived in Union encampments from 1861 to 1865. These past experiences now fueled a mixture of confidence and boldness in her audacious bid to fulfill her ambitious goal of smoothly fitting into the military establishment.

Most encouraging was the fact that she had previously lived for a period of time at Jefferson Barracks only last year. This advanced knowledge about Jefferson Barracks almost certainly provided a measure of comfort to Cathy at this time. In fact, she might even have been familiar with the recruiting office before November 15.Not long after the Civil War's conclusion, she had been sent to "Jefferson Barracks, where I remained for some time," in Cathy Williams' words that revealed her intimate knowledge about this military installation on the Mississippi.[57]

Most importantly, Cathy had developed a well-conceived strategic plan for not only entering Jefferson Barracks without a hitch, but also for then going straight to the recruiter's office in a sudden and unannounced visit. All of this was set in place in order to circumvent the initial obstacle to her enlistment: an overly-prepared recruiter who expected her arrival. After having carefully formulated her plan to fool the recruiters by every trick that she could possibly imagine to maximize her chances for success, Cathy now relied upon the element of surprise to avoid closer scrutiny by the recruiter.

Quite likely, the recruiters at Jefferson Barracks were relatively inexperienced compared to those recruiters (officers), who were now engaged in searching for men from the large urban areas, where blacks were primarily concentrated in separate ethnic communities, because of segregation. Custer's wife, Elizabeth "Libbie" Bacon-Custer, the privileged daughter of a Monroe, Michigan, judge and the antithesis of Cathy's lowly slave background, described the chief obstacle (a knowledgeable and experienced eye) that this young black woman might not have been able to fool, if she had attempted to sign up with a world-wise recruiter in St. Louis or another city: "The recruiting officer in the city . . . casts his critical eye over the anatomical outlines [of a new recruit], as he would over the good points of a horse destined for the same service."[58]

Because of Cathy's varied background and Civil War experiences, the mere act of confidently approaching the main gate of Jefferson Barracks, informing the guard of her purpose, and then entering the sprawling military compound would be a relatively easy for one who knew exactly how to look and act like a soldier. As mentioned, she knew how to mimic the talk and manner of a young black man, such as those men who she had been around for most of her life. In this sense, Cathy was very much of an actress (or an actor in this case because of her male disguise), who knew how to play this part extremely well and with consummate skill: very much a revival at Jefferson Barracks of what she had learned from her Civil War experiences.

Even her years of living as a slave in western and central Missouri now paid dividends on November 15. Out of necessity, slaves had evolved into clever masters of artful deception: a key to receiving better treatment, and even guaranteeing survival in some cases. A slave, especially a female, had to long cater to the whims and vanity of the master, and conceal their intelligence, especially if one possessed a greater amount of brainpower than the master. Working in the "big house" in Jefferson City had conditioned

Cathy to be extremely careful and smart around whites out of necessity.

Therefore, she had evolved into a young woman who was very skilled in the art of hiding her true self by acting the way that she knew the master wanted her to behave. Quite simply, surviving slavery meant becoming an astute actress, sharpening interpersonal skills to an inordinate degree. This well-honed talent based on many years of experience was about to serve her well on November 15.

Upon nearing the main gate at Jefferson Barracks on November 15, nevertheless, Cathy no doubt now wondered if she could possibly keep her sex a secret, and not arouse the slightest suspicion. Could she actually trick these experienced and older military men—all white men like her own Missouri master William Johnson? She, however, had almost certainly fooled Union soldiers, perhaps officers, during her Civil War service, so she was now probably confident that she could accomplish the same at Jefferson Barracks.

But Cathy almost certainly possessed some nagging doubts about the possibilities for success on November 15. What if her ruse of wearing heavy, loose-fitting, and baggy clothing on this cold November day was not sufficient to fool the guards and recruiters? As mentioned, standing five feet and nine inches was another invaluable asset that certainly assisted her at this time, but this might not be sufficient for Cathy to succeed in her mission.

However, Cathy might have thought that she needed something more in perfecting her disguise. Therefore and although it is not known, she might have taken the precaution of having bound her breasts to create the impression of a flatter chest. To achieve her great goal, Cathy had accomplished almost everything possible so that no one would even suspect that she was a female, when she finally appeared before the armed guards at the main gate and then attempted to enlist.

Entering the Main Gate

For all of these reasons, Cathy was easily able to enter the main gate of Jefferson Barracks. She simply informed the sentry that she wanted to sign up to join the United States Army. Here, at this entry post, she might well have been just casually waved on by the guards to proceed to the recruiter's office on her own: the first test for Cathy Williams, and it was one that she had passed. No one suspected that this tall, young person in typical civilian winter clothing was a woman. For all practical purposes, she was just another black male not long out of slavery, and eager to enlist in the United States military.

It is not known, but perhaps Cathy was freely allowed to go by herself to the recruiting office without an escort, especially if she expressed (almost certainly the case since a friend and cousin were now training in the 38th United States Infantry at Jefferson Barracks) prior knowledge of its exact location. She evidently knew where the recruiting office was located because she had already spent "some time," in her own words, at Jefferson Barracks. Therefore, Cathy no doubt told the sentry that she knew exactly where to sign up, which would have helped to diminish any initial suspicions about her sex, if any had risen to the fore.

Masked by her easy manner and nonchalant demeanor in a calculated bid to fool the recruiters, Cathy's ruse entirely escaped detection by the first soldiers who saw her at Jefferson Barracks. This was a comforting realization that fueled her confidence to go for broke. She played her part in a well-rehearsed performance that she had often gone over in her mind in minimize the chances for error.

Even after she entered the recruiting office in a confident manner which was a calculated move not to betray anything out of the ordinary or reveal any telltale nervousness, the recruiting officer was not suspicious by the sight the young, athletic African American standing before him. Her height—taller than the average soldier of both Company A and the 38th United States Infantry—erased any initial suspicions that might have otherwise developed.

Evidently, the recruiter was just happy to see a new recruit in the office on this mid-November day. Perhaps no other recruit had walked into Jefferson Barracks and straight to the recruiting office without escort if that was the case. Like so many times in the past, the recruiter pulled out the enlistment papers for what appeared to be nothing more than a routine enlistment of another former slave man, who was eager to begin a new life as a United States soldier, as if only wanting to escape a dark past.

Despite her calm outward appearance, Cathy was naturally nervous inside while maintaining her ruse with considerable nerve. Most importantly, whatever level of uneasiness felt by Cathy did not show at the recruiting office. Nevertheless, this young woman, age twenty-two, must have now wondered if her true gender was about to be discovered at any moment. Consequently and although it is not known, perhaps beads of sweat began to form on Cathy's forehead under her hat. If any first hint of perspiration—a sign of excessive nervousness—was ascertained by the recruiting officer, then he naturally would become suspicious.

After all, this was a cold November day and seemingly only a routine enlistment in which a recruit should display no such telltale signs that indicated something might well be amiss. Consequently, there should be no obvious signs of nervousness in this new recruit. With so much at stake (her entire future), Cathy Williams was naturally anxious, while standing before the white soldiers inside the recruiting office. But, performing like a true actress, she gave no outward sign or appearance of any nervousness. Cathy realized that her lofty goal of successfully enlisting in a Buffalo Soldier regiment would have to be a flawless acting performance.

When she was asked the first routine question, Cathy gave the recruiting officer her new name. The recruiter then signed her name on the enlistment papers. Her new name "William Cathay" was dutifully written down on the enlistment form. Because of an 1847 Missouri law had made it illegal for anyone to teach a slave to read or write, Cathy had been legally banned from receiving an education. If she had received some basic education when having been with the Union Army and, therefore, could write her name, Cathy had a good reason not to sign her name to the enlistment form. It was wise not to sign her name, which of course meant that she would have to get close to the recruiting officer to sign the paper and hand it to him. Obviously, Cathy knew that keeping more than a respectful distance from the recruiting officer was smart.

All the while, her clever ruse at the recruiting office continued to succeed without rousing any suspicions among the white soldiers, who saw nothing more than a black male recruit before them. However, one slip of the tongue and her audacious plan would immediately unravel. Under additional questioning, she stated to the recruiter that her occupation was "cook," which reflected but one of her roles during the Civil War. This occupation was then written down by the recruiter on the enlistment form. Without much fanfare or even a thorough medical examination, Cathy Williams became the newest private of Company A, 38th United States Infantry Regiment: the new black unit of regular infantry that had been first authorized by Congress on July 28, 1866.

Against the odds, she had succeeded in becoming the first and only documented black woman to serve in the United States Army in the nineteenth century, before women were officially allowed to enter the United

States military in the twentieth century. Indeed, in Cathy's own words, "on the 15th day of November 1866, I enlisted in the United States army at St. Louis, in the Thirty-eighth United States Infantry, company A, Capt[ain] Charles E. Clarke." Clarke was a veteran white officer who commanded Company A.[59]

Clearly, Cathy's stealthy plan of entering the recruiting office unexpectedly in a surprise visit paid dividends: a very good tactic because no medical man (a surgeon or attendant) was in the recruiting office at this time to give her a routine medical examination. If a long period of time would have been required in awaiting the surgeon's arrival to the recruiting office to give Private William Cathay a medical exam, then the new recruit might have had a change of heart and simply walked away. It is not known, but Cathy might have even possessed some prior knowledge that the post surgeon was absent at this time when she entered the recruiting office on this particular Thursday for the express purpose of avoiding a more rigorous physical examination.

After all, her cousin and friend were already regimental members, and might have known about the surgeon's non-availability on this particular Thursday. Official enlistment papers indicated that Cathy had undergone a thorough physical exam, but this was not the case. The enlistment form might have been falsified by white recruiters in order to ensure the quick signing up of the new recruit in a physician's absence, because manpower was in short supply and their job depended upon signing up as many volunteers as possible until their quota was met.

Assignment to Company A, 38th United States Infantry, indicated that Cathy was one of the first volunteers to join this infantry regiment, filling the initial, or first, company of this new regular regiment that began to be organized at Jefferson Barracks on October 1, 1866. Cathy enlisted exactly a month and a half after the 38th United States Infantry Regiment had been officially established by Congress. As in other Buffalo Soldier regiments, like the 10th United States Cavalry (established on the same day in July 1866 as the 38th United States Infantry), recruitment had been slow in the fall of 1866. In fact, recruitment of black soldiers was not to increase until the spring of 1867 with the arrival of warmer weather. This was an additional reason to get this new recruit named Cathay signed up and entered into service as quickly as possible.

Most importantly, the sight of Cathy Williams suddenly arriving at the recruiting office at Jefferson Barracks on this autumn day had been not only unexpected, but also had been a most welcomed appearance to the manpower-hungry recruiters, as she had calculated. After all, the job of these men and their good standing with superiors was dependent upon securing additional new bodies to fill the new regiment's ranks. For a host of such reasons, Cathy Williams had been quickly signed-up without hesitation or close inspection: an advantageous situation that she had in part helped to set in place by her foresight. Of course other than her sex, Cathy was typical of the other male recruits, former slaves who were illiterate and from rural backgrounds. In a testament to her interpersonal skills, nothing about Cathy or her behavior at the recruiting office had aroused any suspicions whatsoever.[60]

To the recruiting officer during the enlistment process, she gave her age as twenty-two, and he wrote it down on the enlistment form. But in fact, Cathy very likely had no exact idea of the actual date of her birthday or age, which was usually the case with most individuals, male or female, born in slavery. In this regard, she might have been much like Booker T. Washington. He described how, "I was born a slave on a plantation in Franklin County, Virginia [but] I am not quite sure of the exact place or exact date of my birth . . . I do not know the month or the day [and] Of my ancestry I know almost nothing [because] In the days of slavery not very much attention was given to family history and family records–that is, black family records."[61]

Or if actually younger than her stated age at Jefferson Barracks, Cathy might have chosen the age of twenty-two to make sure that this number was well above the minimum enlistment age of eighteen. In fact, the distinct possibility existed that she was still a teenager, age nineteen. By succeeding in her ruse at the recruiting office when her ambitions and future hung in the balance, Cathy had accomplished more than simply joining a new Buffalo Soldier regiment. She had become the first female member of a United States military unit, while keeping a measure of her personal pride and dignity intact by emphasizing her new name of Private William Cathay: a clever inversion of her name that allowed Cathy to retain her first name that had now become her last name.

Although now only a lowly private of Company A, 38th United States Infantry, Cathy was eager to learn and become a good soldier to the best of her abilities. She already knew enough about the military's stern requirements from her Civil War experiences to make a conscious decision to try to perform at her best in order to avoid future problems with white officers. Cathy realized that a common soldier's life was much easier if one caused no problems, just kept quiet, and followed the seemingly endless rules and regulations, while making as few mistakes as possible and obeying orders. Cathy knew that she had to remain on the good side of the white officers, just like when she had attempted to remain on the good side of her master William Johnson and his wife back in Cole County, Missouri.

Cathy's personal motivations could not have been higher at this time. Now suddenly deserving of more respect in society in general than had she remained a single black woman in the civilian world, Cathy Williams now embarked upon an entirely new life with a new identity. The embracing of the new challenges of a soldier in a United States regular regiment represented a thorough personal transformation that had been unimaginable, when Cathy had been a house slave vulnerable to a master's whims and punishment in Jefferson City, Missouri, barely five years before.[62]

Unfortunately, Cathy's exact thoughts of how she felt upon succeeding in her clever ruse of successfully enlisting in a regular United States regiment, and then the long-awaited moment when she put on a blue uniform for the first time have not been recorded. However, she almost certainly felt pride, if not exhilaration, in accomplishment in becoming a United States soldier, after having fulfilled her initial goal that was masterfully achieved with stealthy ingenuity. Almost certainly, Cathy also experienced some apprehension in regard to the many stiff challenges (some known, but far more that were entirely unknown to her at this time), which lay ahead for her in her new role as a private in the United States Army.

In addition, Cathy already felt satisfaction in having made her own decision about her future, dictating her life's future course in her own special way and by her own bold actions: a rarity for an African American female not long out of slavery. Clearly, this determined young woman was not willing to allow herself to become another victim like so many other females, black and white, mired in a patriarchal society's restrictions and limitations. But of course, this situation was especially the case for African American females who still experienced the lingering effects of slavery's trauma and emotional pain.

Cathy had already overcome the odds by successfully joining a Buffalo Soldier regiment in an audacious bid to gain a brighter future by staking all while serving in the disguise of a man. Cathy almost certainly realized that she had succeeded in becoming the first female Buffalo Soldier in United States history. Indeed, November 15, 1866 was a most historic day, which was literally a life-changing one for Cathy Williams. In becoming America's first female Buffalo Soldier, she basked in this self-satisfying realization, after achieving her lofty goal.

On this cold Thursday at this military installation located just south of St. Louis, Cathy had charted a new course in life. Becoming a United States soldier represented a remarkable evolution brought about by her own skill in orchestrating a well-calculated plan. For the first time in her life, she was now officially no longer a young woman named Cathy Williams. By determining her own destiny and making her own major life choices for a brighter future, this young black female was now officially Private William Cathay. She was a proud member of an army that she had long admired and respected.

At this time, Cathy Williams was more than ready to embark upon a new life, because the golden promise of a better day was something that she had long held close to her heart. She became another person altogether, with an entirely new identity to everyone at Jefferson Barracks except her cousin and a friend, who were members of the same regiment. They no doubt marveled how Cathy had set her own course in life to ensure a fresh start in life, thanks to her guile: an unprecedented accomplishment for a black woman at this time. She now only wanted to serve her country to the best of her abilities, because she dreamed of making a career out of soldiering.

However and as mentioned, Cathy had not completely left the past behind, because she was reunited with a family member (cousin). She now became part of a small kinship group—almost certainly of Company A—that provided support and assistance for her transition to an entirely new existence. Therefore, this young female private was not entirely on her own at this time, because of the presence of these two individuals. This situation provided a distinct advantage to her that helped to ensure a smoother acclimation into the military's unique martial culture based on strict discipline and a warrior's ethos.

Most of all to fuel her determination, Cathy's decision was all about the future and what it promised. In explaining her motivations in becoming a United States soldier, Cathy Williams emphasized that she wanted to be independent as much as possible in regard to her personal choices in life. This was the antithesis of her dependent life as a slave, and even during her years of service as a cook and laundress during the Civil War, but to a lesser degree. In Cathy's own words that revealed the extent of her sheer determination to succeed, "I wanted to make my own living and not be dependent on relations or friends."[63]

Even in the context of being reunited with her cousin and friend, Cathy was still very much of an independent entity even while serving in the United States Army. She had made her first career choice, despite the inherent risks and against all expectations. This personal choice was a good one for a young black woman and former slave, who had been long denied a decent opportunity in life only because of her gender and race.

To overcome the widespread discrimination, she had finally discovered a most novel and innovative way to embark upon a meaningful career, which was a rare achievement for an ex-slave. Despite a rough beginning in life, Cathy had found a most unique way to gain a distinctive measure of pride and dignity, when entrapped by the severe limitations of an oppressive society. She had refused to become a victim in life by continuing to make her own choices about the direction of her life and future. Clearly, this was a bold example of self-assertion by a young black woman, who was determined to succeed in life at almost any cost.

As mentioned, Cathy's transition into the insular world of the 38th United States Infantry, where the strictest discipline was required, was made easier by the presence of a male cousin and friend (faithful supporters and protectors of her true identity) in the regiment's ranks. They almost certainly also served in Captain Clarke's Company A. But even so, these two individuals were less important than would have been the case under normal circumstances, because of Cathy's overall familiarity with military life from her Civil War days.

As Cathy Williams explained in her own words: "The regiment I joined [were] only two persons, a cousin and a particular friend, members of the regiment, knew that I was a woman [and] They were partly the cause of my joining the army."[64] It is not known but quite likely at least one or both of these supportive individuals (the friend and cousin) had served in a USCT regiment (if so, then most likely that command had been recruited in Missouri, because they were native Missourians like Cathy) during the Civil War. Such past experience would have partly explained the enlistment of the two men in the 38th United States Infantry. Missouri had contributed more than 8,000 of her black sons, almost all former slaves, to defeat the Confederacy.[65]

Like Cathy, her cousin and friend had also felt the need to serve their country, after Union victory and official legislation (both national and state) had ensured slavery's permanent end. On January 11, 1865 at the state convention held at the Mercantile Library Hall in the heart of St. Louis, Missouri Governor Thomas C. Fletcher had officially abolished slavery across Missouri: "henceforth and forever, no person within the jurisdiction of this state shall [now] now any master but God."[66] Officially, all of Cathy's relatives in Missouri, including her mother if still living in Jackson or Cole County, had been set free by this state law. Even her cousin and friend had been officially freed by this 1865 law.

Cathy's explanation of exactly why she had decided to join the 38th United States Infantry sheds considerable insight into the character and psychological make-up of this young woman. In addition, some degree of maternal consideration was also involved in her unorthodox decision that changed her life forever, perhaps because she had no children of her own. Cathy's years of wandering service with Union Armies on both sides of the Mississippi had precluded the possibility of acquiring a husband and family. At this time in emotional and psychological terms, consequently the new black regular regiment served as a familial organization, especially for Cathy because of her cousin's and friend's presence. But the majority of the regiment's former slaves also provided a sort of extended familial network, forging a common bond between Cathy and other regimental members.

In addition, her cousin might have been younger, and perhaps in need of assistance from another family member, especially a nurturing female. Therefore, Cathy's decision to enlist also perhaps can be seen as a deliberate effort to reunite family members (Cathy and her cousin) who had been torn apart by the dual ravages of slavery and America's most destructive war. For a variety of reasons, Cathy's motivations to enlist in the United States Army were not fundamentally ego-based and masculine-driven as portrayed by a patriarchal society's stereotypical negative view of her most unorthodox decision: the brazen Amazon (a traditionally negative, almost insulting, connotation) that has long applied to women, who embraced non-traditional roles in society that were considered reserved only for males, especially as a female warrior in the military. After all, the military realm had long been believed to be the exclusive reserve for the demonstration of male courage.

The possibility of Cathy's choice of joining the regiment to watch over a younger cousin has considerable merit under the circumstances. This strong maternal influence and bond of black females had long served as a central foundation of the slave community. In general, these qualities were less evident among American Caucasian women, because they hailed from a patriarchal society and culture in which such maternalism was generally less strong. Out of necessity, slave women played a larger role as the head of the family than black males, because slavery had eliminated the traditional protective male role. Cathy's true culture and society, in regard to that of her African ancestors and even during slavery, were decidedly maternal.

Interestingly, this same kind of prevalent maternalism among American blacks was also seen in the Latino culture. In consequence, this strong maternal Latino tradition (not unlike the black family tradition which was a cultural legacy from west and central Africa's maternal societies) also led to a greater support role by women for Mexican soldiers in the field than historically had been the case in United States Armies—except during the colonial and Revolutionary War periods.

Continuing the fabled martial tradition of Aztec women fighters of Mesoamerican warrior societies of Mexico since the pre-Columbian period, the soldaderas served in the Mexican military during its revolutions, civil wars, rebellions, and military expeditions, including north of the Rio Grande River. Hundreds of the faithful women had served in support roles during General Antonio Lopez de Santa Anna's 1836 invasion of Texas that resulted in the battle of the Alamo at San Antonio de Bexar and then the final clash at San Jacinto near the gulf coast barely a month later. Throughout the course of Mexican history, large numbers of Mexican women provided vital support roles to the army primarily because of familial loyalties and maternal priories rather than from a sense of nationalism.

During active campaigning, these Latino women looked out for the welfare of male relatives, including brothers, sons, and husbands. Besides often fighting as women warriors for their mixed-raced people (primarily from intermixing between Spanish and Indian to produce mestizos) and republic (established in 1821), the soldaderas also made contributions to Mexican military forces as foragers, nurses, cooks, supply-carriers, laundresses, comforters, spies, and gun-runners. Still another contribution came from iconic female fighters, known as the "La Adelita," of Mexican revolutionary armies.[67]

Cathy Williams identified with the black military tradition, especially from the Civil War years. While growing up in the Missouri River country whose commercial ties based on trade along the "Father of Waters," were closely connected to St. Louis and New Orleans, Louisiana, Cathy also might have heard stories from former seamen (especially when she had served near the east coast in Virginia during the Civil War) about the black warrior women of the French Caribbean colony of St. Domingue (today's Haiti). These women, mostly Africa-born and of African descent (Creoles), were determined revolutionaries against white domination (French colonialists and imperialists) and slavery. After the largest and most successful slave revolt in history that consumed the sugar plantations on St. Domingue's northern plain during the early 1790s, black women often served as front-line fighters during the next decade of bitter conflict.

These black rebel women wore the same apparel–civilian pants or uniform pants–as the male revolutionaries, who were former slaves, the Black Jacobians. General Charles Victoire Emmanuel Leclerc, Napoleon Bonaparte's brother-in-law, had been dispatched in command of a mighty expeditionary force to conquer St. Domingue in 1802-1803 and restore slavery. But the young general died of yellow fever like so many of his ill-fated troops. A former member of Napoleon's staff, a stunned Leclerc wrote with a growing respect and admiration for the courage of the black rebels in late August 1802: "The men die with an incredible fanaticism; they laugh at death. It's the same with the women," (black and mulatto), who fought and died for liberty like America's male revolutionaries, including black soldiers, from 1775-1783.[68]

In later describing her uniform to the St. Louis newspaperman whose story of Cathy's life was presented to the American public for the first time on January 2, 1876, Cathy utilized a popular French term (Zouave) that was well-known throughout America, because of its popularity in the Civil War.

Among illiterate former slaves, they might have used this term to describe their uniform, although it was an improper designation. Young Colonel Elmer Ellsworth had made the name of Zouave popular across America during the years immediately before the Civil War. He was the commander of his famed Zouave company that had toured America's major cities. Ellsworth and his men had performed drill exhibitions across the country to great fanfare and acclaim. The handsome colonel became a special friend of Abraham Lincoln and his family, especially the president's sons Tad and Willie, until his May 24, 1861 death. Ellsworth was killed by a shot-gun blast at close range from a pro-Southern innkeeper named James Jackson for having torn down a Rebel flag that flew from a hotel rooftop in Alexandria, Virginia, and within sight of the capitol on the river's east side.

Consequently, in later speaking to the St. Louis reporter, Cathy was certainly mistaken in having used the term of Zouave, because she—except perhaps when newly enlisted at Jefferson Barracks—wore regulation Civil War surplus uniforms of an infantryman. She wore a uniform that consisted of the dark blue 1851-pattern frock coat and light blue pants. This was the standard uniform of the Union soldier from 1861-1865. Her use of the word Zouave was the most obvious error in Cathy's Williams' story of her life, as she presented it to the *St. Louis Daily Times* reporter more than a decade after the Civil War's conclusion.[69]

Colonel Ellsworth had continued the martial legacy of the original Zouaves. These were French troops, who had served in North Africa's northern deserts, while battling local tribes on France's colonial version of the "Old West" frontier. In the name of French imperialism, these French fighting men waged war against indigenous people of the Muslim faith, including the fierce Bedouin tribes that roamed the desert and showed no mercy to white interlopers. This aggressive "pacification" had been the most pronounced in Algeria, where the French Zouaves battled Bedouin and Islamic warriors to expand France's colonial empire in North Africa.[70]

The vivid colors and flashy style of this exotic Zouave uniform appealed greatly to young soldiers of the Civil War generation. The standard Zouave apparel–baggy red pants, red fez skull cap with decorative tassel, red sash, and short red and blue coat —was distinctive, including "the flashy, Algerian colors in the uniform."[71] These fancy uniforms, especially those imported from France, had enjoyed considerable popularity among troops on both sides at the Civil War's beginning. In fact, larger numbers of fighting men from New York volunteer regiments had marched off to war wearing Zouave uniforms than any other state. Most Zouave regiments of the North were eastern units. New York contributed the highest number of these colorful regiments that earned distinction on battlefields across the eastern theater.[72]

In addition, the possibly—although remote —existed that Cathy was perhaps initially outfitted in an old surplus Zouave uniform from the Civil War at Jefferson Barracks. After all, she was one of the earliest recruits assigned to Company A, 38th United States Infantry, only a month and a half after the regular regiment's official formation. Of course, such wholly impractical uniforms, especially for western frontier service, would have served as only temporary wear for a new recruit for only a brief period, before the issuing of standard blue uniforms. As mentioned, Cathy enlisted less than four months after the regiment's official authorization during the summer of 1866 and organization at Jefferson Barracks on October 1. If this had been a temporary uniform, then Cathy was not mistaken in stating how she "wore the Zouave uniform" temporarily before the issuing of regular infantry uniforms.[73]

During the Civil War, Union regiments had guarded the nation's capital and maneuvered on parade grounds in performing the well-known "Zouave drill," Cathy might have seen Zouaves or heard of the term Zouave in the eastern theater most likely before the onset of the 1864 Shenandoah Campaign. Therefore, this term was a common word that Cathy Williams was familiar with during the war years, as later revealed in her newspaper interview with the St. Louis reporter.[74]

It is not known, but because the name Zouave was so common throughout the Civil War, she might have even mistakenly believed that the United States regulation uniform of blue was called a Zouave uniform. Again as a house slave, Cathy had possessed no prior military knowledge before her liberation by Union forces in mid-June 1861. Or the white reporter (a male probably unfamiliar with black dialect of a former slave) of the *St. Louis Daily Times* who conducted the future interview of her in Trinidad, Colorado, perhaps might have added this word himself in error, or perhaps in hastily writing down Cathy's story in haste. Or perhaps the reporter misunderstood what she said, because Cathy still spoke in a slave dialect with a rural Missouri drawl of the Missouri River country: a regional way of speaking that might have been entirely new to this reporter if he was a native easterner or New Englander.[75]

As mentioned, Cathy's use of the word Zouave, if that was indeed the case, was her most glaring contradiction of her oral account about her life that she gave to the St. Louis newspaperman in either late 1875 or perhaps even as late as January 1, 1876, if the reporter telegraphed her story to the office of the *St. Louis Daily Times* in St. Louis on New Year's Day.

However, another possibility existed. A recently discovered photo of an 8th Indiana soldier can perhaps shed some new light on this obvious contradiction in Cathy's use of the term Zouave. An antique dealer recently offered a tintype of Jacob Mullin, 8th Indiana. The old script identification was written behind the photo inside the wooden case that housed the tintype. Mullin hailed from Hancock County, Indiana, like the rest of the men of Company B, 8th Indiana. What was significant about this photo was that Mullin was shown wearing a non-regulation blue uniform (although looking much like a Union musician's uniform), which had an elaborate design comparable to a Hussar light cavalryman. Hussars had long served in Europe's Armies, including Napoleon's Grande Armee, during the nineteenth century.

The design of Mullin's uniform was distinguished by braid extending across the uniform's front on either side of a roll of brass military buttons: a popular herringbone trim design. Significantly, this 8th Indiana soldier's uniform was only worn by these Midwestern troops early in the war, when Cathy was connected to the Hoosier regiment.

Then, nearly fifteen years later, perhaps the word Hussar might have become Zouave to the thinking of some civilians, because the reporter would have been more familiar with the term Zouave rather than Hussar, if Cathy had actually used this word during the interview. It is not known but this might be still another possibility that explained why the word Zouave appeared in the January 2, 1876 article about Cathy Williams' life.[76]

Not long after her enlistment on November 15, the new recruit, now officially known as Private William Cathay, was issued a United States musket. The principal Union firearm of the Civil War, this reliable weapon (the standard Springfield Model 1861 musket) was a surplus item from 1861-1865. Weighing 9.75 pounds, the Model 1861 Springfield rifle (caliber .58) was 56 inches in length. Cathy had often seen this percussion rifled musket that had been manufactured in Springfield, Massachusetts, during the Civil War.[77]

One Buffalo Soldier described the procedure practiced by Cathy during her intense training at Jefferson Barracks that began in the last two weeks of November: "We got de ole fashion muzzle loaders [and] You puts one ball in de muzzle and shove de powder down wid de ramrod."[78]

The Buffalo Soldiers

Unknown to her at the time, Cathy Williams was actually part of a military experiment it was believed, because many officials still doubted the martial qualities and courage of ex-slaves. Therefore, for a host of reasons, she was determined to demonstrate her worth as a proud member of the 38th United States Infantry.[79] The 38th United States Infantry had been authorized only by Congress during this so-called Buffalo Soldier experiment. After the vast demobilization of the North's more than one-million man war machine that reaped decisive victory in the Civil War, America's peacetime military requirements diminished dramatically thereafter.

The American military now focused on protecting settlers moving west and the resulting Indian problem on the Great Plains. As could be expected, indigenous people west of the Mississippi were determined to preserve their distinctive way-of-life and hunting grounds from white encroachment. Thanks to the significant contributions of USCT troops during the Civil War, including the 33,000 black soldiers who died in helping to save the Union, Congress had taken note of the distinguished performances and sacrifices of these ebony fighting men. Therefore, politicians had seen the wisdom of utilizing former slaves for service in the post-Civil War army (but only if commanded by white officers), but only after much heated debate in both houses of Congress.

Initially, only black infantry regiments of the regular army had been contemplated, until Senator Benjamin Wade, Ohio, advocated for the formation of two black cavalry regiments, the 9th and 10th United States Cavalry, for the peacetime regular army. After the final details were worked-out by Congress, President Andrew Johnson had then signed the law that created the six new Buffalo Soldier regiments (4 infantry and 2 cavalry) on July 28, 1866: the 38th, 39th, 40th, and 41st United States Infantry Regiments, and the 9th and 10th United States Cavalry. With one stroke of the pen by the Southern-born president, the peacetime regular army was radically transformed by the inclusion of black regular troops for the first time, because the USCT of the Civil War years had consisted of volunteer regiments.[80]

Despite the USCT's success in the Civil War in continuing a noble "tradition of courage under fire" that extended back to when at least 5,000 black soldiers had fought as patriots during the American Revolution, the Buffalo Soldiers were still seen negatively by many whites. When offered command of a black regiment, George Armstrong Custer had refused a lieutenant colonel's rank in the 9th Cavalry. Instead, he later took command of the all-white 7th Cavalry with the same rank. Ironically, Custer perhaps would have been wiser to have made a post-Civil War career in leading the 9th Cavalry: a decision that would have spared him a tragic fate (along with five 7th Cavalry companies) the high ground above the Little Big Horn River, Montana Territory, on June 25, 1876.

Other respected Civil War leaders should have known better than to doubt the already well-proven martial abilities and combat prowess of black soldiers, but they were blinded by color prejudice. Nevertheless, in clinging to old racial stereotypes about race, they now still refused to believe that blacks were capable of becoming good soldiers, despite the overwhelming amount of evidence (going back centuries in various parts of the world) that clearly indicated otherwise. As appreciated by Cathy Williams, the formation of the Buffalo Soldier regiments represented the first time that African Americans had ever served in the premier regular regiments in the history of the United States military. Therefore, this fact alone caused some uneasiness among many elitist and conservative white officers, who deplored the crossing of this color line as the ultimate taboo.

After all, what if blacks truly proved equal to whites in regard to the most admirable manly qualities, especially courage and strength of character? Such obvious truths threatened to overturn longtime racial stereotypes that had existed for centuries, while mocking the established social and racial order based of myths. As mentioned, this was the first time in history that African Americans were allowed to serve as members of regular army regiments (the Army's elite combat units), and they, including Cathy Williams, took full advantage of this unprecedented opportunity. The American military now led the way in the so-called experiment of black regulars that eventually helped to change American society for the better, including Cathy's life, while overturning a host of racial stereotypes.[81]

After having survived slavery's horrors and her nearly four years of varied Civil War experiences with Union armies on both sides of the "Father of Waters," what Cathy Williams had accomplished by joining the Buffalo Soldiers was quite literally the embracing of the American dream: rising higher in life by way of her own initiative and actions. But in a racist and patriarchal society that kept blacks and women in the lowest positions, especially black females, Cathy had been able to outsmart and circumvent the deeply entrenched paternal system that had been long structured to keep her in a lowly place in society.

In the end, the gaining of this unprecedented opportunity (enlistment in a regular United States regiment) for her was only possible because of Cathy's own innovativeness and adaptability. Quite simply and in the most creative way, she had disguised herself as a male to force America to live-up to its still unfulfilled promise to her and other former slaves: in essence, America's "promissory note" (Dr. Martin Luther King's emphasis during the Civil Rights struggle) that Cathy had cashed-in on the promise of gaining a better life for herself.

What she received in return for her personal commitment to serve in the United States Army was something in her day not unlike today's winning the lottery for a young lower class female, who had spent most of her life as a slave: regular pay, shelter, and clothing combined with a healthy dose of self-respect and pride in serving as a United States soldier, while marching under the flowing colors of "Old Glory."

Cathy Williams could not wait for the arrival of full equality for blacks and women that would not come in her lifetime, because the righteous rhetoric of freedom only existed on the surface to hide America's ugly racial realities for former slaves: a no-win situation that required not only bold, but also extremely thoughtful action to essentially speed-up this belated process of obtaining greater equality for herself by outmaneuvering the entrenched discriminatory system that kept her in such a lowly place.

Therefore, with social and economic advancement virtually impossible for a young, former slave woman, Cathy had forged ahead on her own by innovatively creating a novel opportunity for herself in the most unorthodox manner. Against the odds and all expectations, she had accomplished her lofty goal with considerable innovativeness and resourcefulness on November 15, 1866.[82]

But the hard part was still to come for this resourceful young woman, who only desired to aspire ever-higher in life. Cathy now possessed new confidence in her abilities, because she had literally reached out to grab an ever-elusive and rare measure of greater equality for herself. Clearly, this was Cathy's unique way of taking charge of her life by manipulating her own personal destiny and molding it to fit existing opportunities to her maximum advantage.

First and foremost, she was now determined to become the best possible United States soldier by not only learning, but also obeying all army rules and instructions to the fullest. And this secretiveness of hiding her sex had to be accomplished on a daily basis, while under the sharp eyes of experienced white officers and ever-observant black drill instructors, who watched her every move. Indeed, this would be a non-ending and most demanding challenge for her. From beginning to end, this was an overall situation that excessively taxed all of Cathy's ingenuity and intelligence to maintain her masterful ruse over an extended period, while coping with the related stress and anxiety that was inevitable under the circumstances.

Clearly, in the months ahead while wearing the blue uniform, Cathy needed to maintain her elevated level of poise and nerve in the most challenging circumstances and unexpected situations. A seemingly endless of number of mentally taxing and nerve-racking situations required considerable composure and thinking fast on her feet over a lengthy period. Of course, Cathy's early life as a slave in the "big house" of William Johnson had provided good practice in challenging situations for the many upcoming trials that lay ahead. After all, fooling the master and other whites was simply part of basic survival for a female slave. And now the complex art of deception in regard to interaction with white officers now became the central feature of

Cathy's life as a new Buffalo Soldier.

Making Cathy's challenges even more daunting, some white officers, especially the more conservative and racially-intolerant types, were still unhappy about African Americans having been allowed to serve in the postwar regular army, where they had been previously excluded, by Congress. These white traditional and elitist types were determined to make soldiering as hard as possible on young black recruits like Private Cathay. At Jefferson Barracks and like other ebony recruits at Jefferson Barracks, she faced a regular pattern of harassment from officers in the name of proper training and instruction.[83]

A racist white commander had the potential to become the ultimate nightmare for Cathy Williams, who still had much to learn about becoming a soldier. A respected Union division commander who won distinction at the two-day battle of Pea Ridge, which had been witnessed by Cathy Williams, where Confederate forces were defeated on March 7-8, 1862, Brevet Major General Eugene A. Carr proclaimed that blacks simply "would not make good soldiers." He clearly should have known better.[84] Ironically, Cathy might have seen General Carr, when he had commanded the Army of the Southwest in early 1862. In Cathy's words: "I . . . was with the army at the battle of Pea Ridge."[85]

Of course, General Carr could not have been farther from the truth because his racial prejudice was directly contrary to the facts relating to black soldiers found throughout history. Commanding the 10th Cavalry and a celebrated Union cavalry hero of the western theater, Colonel Benjamin Grierson, who was highly valued by Generals Ulysses S. Grant and William T. Sherman, fought against this pervasive racial prejudice.

He stood up in behalf of his black soldiers when discrimination was hurled upon his new black recruits by white officers, including the intolerant commander at Fort Leavenworth, Kansas. Here, Grierson not only defied the orders of Fort Leavenworth's commanding officer that forbid black cavalrymen to stand beside white troops on the fort's parade ground, but also took official action. The fair-minded native Pennsylvanian lodged an official protest to department headquarters, complaining of discrimination against his men from high levels.

Enlightened white officers, including Colonel Grierson, were not safe from the inevitable backlash from unified members of the conservative army power structure, whenever they were sufficiently bold to demand fair treatment for black soldiers. Famous for leading one of the Civil War's boldest mounted raids deep into the Confederacy —in Vicksburg's rear (Grierson's Raid) in 1863—, Colonel Grierson was also a talented composer. On his own at great risk to his military career, he battled against the racial discrimination imposed by his less open-minded superiors. High-ranking white leaders had also relegated his Buffalo Soldiers to the worst places to encamp, including on low ground that often flooded, which then led to the spread of sickness.[86]

An angry Grierson, therefore, wrote how senior officers found easy targets in the Buffalo Soldiers: these "powers that be [were determined] to wreak their spite and wrath upon" on the 10th Cavalry troopers, who were mostly former slaves like Cathy Williams.[87] In a letter to his wife, Colonel Grierson complained about prejudiced "Old Forgies" at Fort Leavenworth who caused a long list of difficulties in the hope of forcing the disbandment of the black regiments, so that only white troops remained in the pre-Civil War army.[88]

Clearly, unknown to Cathy, the 10th Cavalry's unfortunate situation at Fort Leavenworth was comparable to the racial trouble that lay ahead for her and her male comrades of the 38th United States Infantry, when stationed in far-away New Mexico. Of course, Cathy had long experienced such harsh racial attitudes as a Missouri slave.

Almost philosophically, she knew that these deeply-entrenched racial views among whites (part of an Anglo-Saxon cultural and racial inheritance extending back to western Europe, especially England) could seldom be changed. In Trinidad, Colorado, she eventually settled down partly because these good people of this western frontier town were the antithesis of less intolerant conservative types in the military establishment, especially in the higher ranks.

Remaining optimistic because she knew that harboring resentments and anger toward others because of their racial insensitivities and prejudice did her no good in the long term, Cathy refused to be consumed by the same kind of racial animosities that defined the narrow mentality of others. She was sufficiently wise to know that this exercise of misplaced anger was a waste of time and energy. Cathy Williams, therefore, continued to look forward for a better day and a brighter future. And this most of all meant keeping a positive outlook about life in general, despite adversity and setbacks.

Training as a New Recruit at Jefferson Barracks

First and foremost, Cathy's main focus as a new recruit at Jefferson Barracks was now mastering the difficult challenge of becoming a disciplined and well-trained United States regular. And this stiff requirement meant a seemingly endless regime of instruction and drill on a daily basis, while black sergeants barked out orders in her face on the drill field. Cathy's own words revealed that she was determined to become the best soldier possible, because this was the most effective way to keep her greatest secret concealed. Consequently, Private William Cathay realized that she had to be even more competent and harder working than the male soldiers in order to avoid suspicion about her true identity.

Under no illusions and better mentally prepared for the daunting challenges than the typical recruit without prior experience and knowledge about military life, Cathy already knew enough about soldiering from the Civil War years to realize what was expected of her at Jefferson Barracks. Consequently, she was psychologically prepared for life in the United States military and its demands. Indeed, in relative terms, there were probably few severe shocks left for this young woman, who had long marched with Federal armies from 1861-1865. Cathy had already learned a great deal about military life, and this knowledge about soldiering was now employed to her advantage.

Enduring the verbal abuse of drill sergeants and harsh treatment with a stoic patience was a necessary requirement for fulfilling her larger ambitions. Cathy learned the basic drills and maneuvers of conventional warfare, almost as if the Buffalo Soldiers would never face Great Plains warriors who fought a traditional guerrilla-style of warfare. Therefore, throughout November and December of 1866 while the weather grew colder and reminded her of winters back in her native western Missouri several hundred miles to the west, Cathy rigorously trained on a daily basis with a singular intensity on the wide parade ground of Jefferson Barracks.

Unlike other young soldiers who had known only civilian life, she easily picked up the finer details of soldiering, including aspects of military protocol and courtesy. After all, she had long observed interaction between officers and enlisted men during the Civil War years. In addition, she had even grown accustomed to being around high-ranking officers from her days of cooking and washing for General Philip Henry Sheridan and his staff officers at headquarters during the 1864 Shenandoah Campaign in Virginia. All of these past experiences now paid dividends to her, helping to obscure the secret that she was now the first and only black female soldier in the history of the United States military.

No doubt with a typical survivor's sense of humor that had long served as the antidote for helping to endure the horror of her former life in slavery, Cathy might well have enjoyed what she perhaps viewed (especially if her sense of humor was finely-honed as often the case among members of the African American community) as a joke played on so many white soldiers, especially officers. From the first day, she had completely fooled "the man" about her true identity week day after day. Therefore, what she was now doing—becoming an excellent soldier who obeyed orders and faithfully performed her duty as required by regulations and officers—might have been a source of some amusement to this spunky young woman, who continued to do her best under challenging circumstances.

As colder winds and the snow descended upon Jefferson Barracks on the high ground overlooking the Mississippi after November had passed, Cathy stood in ranks at attention for extended periods. She also marched in Company A's and the regiment's formations in unison beside her fellow Buffalo Soldiers, performing precision drill on the parade ground. All the while, noncommissioned officers, especially the hardened sergeants, shouted directives that rang across Jefferson Barracks to remind Cathy that she was far from home and family. She knew that to become a true United States regular, who were more disciplined than the volunteer soldiers of the Civil War, the thorough mastering of all aspects of training was required by her.

Indeed, the military standards were exceptionally high and exacting in this regular regiment that was now preparing for the western frontier duty. Therefore, Cathy realized that she must successfully meet each order and new requirement to the letter. If not, then she might be dismissed from service for not making the grade, especially if any suspicions about her sex were aroused. In consequence, Cathy was forced to work twice as hard as the average male recruit, because she could not allow anyone to become suspicious or question her abilities that even vaguely might hint of the so-called weaker sex.

Week after week, she needed to perform exceptionally well so that nothing might cause a sergeant or white officer to question why Private Cathay's soldierly performance was noticeably inferior in comparison to her comrades. Such questions about her strength or endurance might lead to the much-dreaded exposure of her true gender. This situation, of course, was Cathy's greatest fear day after day. If her sex was discovered, Cathy would be then instantly returned to a bleak existence without a decent future in civilian society, where prospects were especially slim for a young black woman on her own.

Like her fellow soldiers, she also learned the new skill of marksmanship at Jefferson Barracks. She loaded and fired her musket properly during target practice that required sharp eyes and steady aim to ensure accuracy: a skill that Cathy Williams had not gained during the Civil War years.[89]

All the while, Cathy had to live-up to the high reputation that the elite white regulars had earned not only in the Civil War, but also during the Mexican-American War of 1846-1847. Some officers and noncommissioned officers at Jefferson Barracks had seen service during that conflict in Mexico. In early 1847, General Winfield Scott had led a relatively small army of mostly regular regiments more than 250 miles inland, after an amphibious landing at Vera Cruz, Mexico. Scott's little army had then pushed west and all the way through the Central Valley to Mexico City. General Scott won a series of victories over larger Mexican forces, defying the odds and experts on both sides of the Atlantic. By relying upon the tactical mix of frontal assaults and flank maneuvers, this little American army of less than 10,000 men captured Mexico City in September 1847.

General Scott's capture of Mexico City had brought an end of America's first foreign war, resulting in Mexico losing nearly half of its territory to a young republic that had flexed its Manifest Destiny muscles. This success would not have been possible without Scott having utilized so many well-trained regulars, especially those of an elite officer corps. These young regular officers vindicated the importance of the nation's reliance on its promising sons educated at America's military academy at West Point, New York. West Point had educated an entire generation of highly-capable leaders, who had then risen to the fore during the Civil War. Some of these talented regular army officers (like "Little Phil" Sheridan, Custer, and Grant who had lived in Missouri when Cathy had been a slave) had played key roles in saving the Union.[90]

Clearly, against the odds, Cathy had now carved out a unique and special place in the history of women who served in the United States military. As she realized, Cathy Williams was the first black woman to wear the uniform of a United States regular. Most of all, she was a determined and committed soldier, and her service for her country was destined to extend for nearly two years.

However, Cathy Williams was not the first American woman to have served in America's military. The most widespread participation of white women disguised as men serving in the American military occurred during the Civil War. Disguised as men, young women from North and South served in the ranks of their respective armies with equal enthusiasm, fighting and dying beside male comrades. Historian Garrison Webb emphasized this long-overlooked female contribution during the Civil War in his book *Amazing Women of the Civil War, Fascinating True Stories of Women Who Made A Difference*: "The Civil War was fought largely–but not exclusively–by men. Long ago, someone came up with a ballpark figure of about three hundred women who actually fought in either blue or gray. Although that figure cannot be documented or confirmed, it is widely cited. The truth of the matter is that no one knows precisely how many females went Rebel and Federal fighting forces because many of them disguised as males and were extremely clever. What makes this number even less accurate is that the most clever of them were probably never discovered."[91]

Of course, Garrison might well have been describing Cathy Williams' service as a Buffalo Soldier from 1866 to1868, because the word "clever" certainly applied to her case. In her own words, Cathy performed well as a young soldier was fully verified by the details of her military service record at the National Archives, Washington, D.C.: "I was never put in the guard house, no bayonet was ever put to my back [because] I carried my musket and did guard duty and together duties" as ordered by officers and noncommissioned officers.[92]

Because male traditionalists and conservatives, including historians, have continued to dismiss the possibility of female soldiers serving in male disguise partly because postwar accounts about their roles have been often embellished by excessive romantic fiction, the following examples from primary sources (Northern and Southern newspapers) have provided additional solid evidence of women who served as soldiers during the Civil War.

In October 1861, the *New York Times*, New York, New York, reported the arrest of a nineteen-year-old women dressed as a soldier in Baltimore, Maryland. The young woman's personal story was featured in her own words: "My name is Hatty Robinson, of Auburn, New York . . . I have no father, mother, brother or sister [and] It has been about seven months since I put on boys' clothes [and] I went by the name of Charles D. Knipe," and served in the 46th Pennsylvania Volunteer Infantry.[93]

Providing evidence how Cathy Williams' own clever ruse could have been successfully continued for nearly two years and a reminder that she could not afford to become pregnant just like during the Civil War years, if she had developed a love interest when serving in Union armies as a cook and laundress, the same newspaper reported to its readers on May 2, 1863 how: "A corporal in a New-York City regiment gave birth to a fine boy . . . For two years, this female soldier has served in the ranks without any suspicion of her sex, even by her messmates."[94]

Like those in the North, readers across the Confederacy were astounded to read about another young woman's personal story under the heading of "A Female Soldier" in the December 12, 1863 edition of the *Richmond Examiner*. This article was reprinted in the *New York Times* for northern readers on December 19, 1863. This revealing article told about a young Yankee prisoner in Richmond, who was a woman, "about 19 years of age," after having been captured with her comrades: "Yesterday, a rather prepossessing looking lass was discovered on Belle Isle [at the Confederate prison camp on this island located in the James River within the city limits] She gave her name as Mary Jane Johnson, belonged to the Sixteenth Maine [Volunteer] Regiment, [and] she gave an excuse . . .that she was following her lover, to shield and protect him when in danger. He had been killed in battle . . . The heroine of a novel yet to be written in Yankeedom was considerably sunburned and roughened by the hardships she had encountered, but still retained marks of some womanly comeliness, which would be heightened by a calico frock and crinoline."[95]

Clearly, this Southern editor from a leading newspaper in the

Confederacy's capital on the James River certainly knew a good story when he saw one, just like the opportunistic newspaperman, who eventually interviewed Cathy Williams to publicize her remarkable life story in the January 2, 1876 edition of the *St. Louis Daily Times.*[96]

However, Confederate prison authorities at Richmond still considered this particular female Yankee dangerous, and refused to set her free from captivity. Instead, this female Union soldier was transferred to Castle Thunder, the Federal officers' prison in Richmond, because more privacy existed at this place of confinement than at rocky Belle Island in the James River.[97]

In addition, women in Cathy's home state likewise disguised themselves as men to serve in Missouri Union regiments during the Civil War. The possibility existed at some point that Cathy might have even heard about these soldier women from her own home state of Missouri, including females who served in the western theater like herself, in the war's beginning. A story in the *Memphis Argus*, Memphis, Tennessee, reprinted in the *New York Times* on August 26, 1864, told of two women, who served with the 26th Missouri Volunteer Infantry, which had been organized in St. Louis.

One of these Missouri females served as a drummer "boy," while the other woman performed duty as a regimental wagon driver. The drummer had enlisted "under the name of Charley Davis and William Morris [the teamster, but] The drummer's real name is Jane Short." Jane had been wounded at the battle of Iuka, northeast Mississippi, on September 19, 1862, when Cathy Williams had been serving in domestic roles west of the Mississippi. This incredulous reporter described how, "In uniform, one would never suspect her [much like Cathy Williams] to be a woman [as] She looks like an unsophisticated country lad of twenty years, and assuming modesty!"[98]

And "Lou Morris, alias Bill Morris [had] resided in St. Louis, from which placed she had enlisted in the 'Red Rovers' of the Tenth Missouri Cavalry [and] served nine months, passing unhurt through several engagements. She then deserted, and coming to Memphis, lived as a woman until meeting with Jane Short, with whom she started for the wars again, as teamster for the Twenty-first Missouri Infantry. They claim that they have not revealed their sex, nor was it discovered by any of their comrades since they entered the service, and that their enlistment was prompted by patriotic motives only; they wanted to do a small share towards 'licking the rebs,' as Lou said. Lou, when dressed in uniform looks as little like a woman as her companion [Charley Davis, or Jane Short], and presents the appearance of a hardy boy of eighteen. They are much tanned by exposure."[99]

Of course by this time, Cathy Williams also could have readily identified with the personal struggles and challenges of a young African woman from England (evidently descended from slaves in the British West Indies, and most likely from the largest island of Jamaica) who had served in the British Navy. She went by the name of "'William Brown' (a negress so rated on the books of Queen Charlotte), who was proved to have served eleven years when the ship was paid off in 1815, and was conspicuous for her agility as a captain of the main top no less than for her partiality for prize money and grog."[100]

Cathy Williams was now facing comparable challenges that had been experienced by this ebony female sailor, who had boldly taken the identity of William Brown to sail the seas and enjoy a measure of equality.

Chapter III: A New Year, 1867, and New Challenges

The new year of 1867 presented unprecedented and formidable challenges to young Private William Cathay. All the while, she continued to train and drill at Jefferson Barracks, becoming more of a model soldier in keeping with her main objective. Cathy steadily improved her steadily-evolving soldierly skills of a United States regular, which included deploying in skirmish lines and refining her marksmanship, which were necessary to confront some of the most lethal Native American warriors of the Great Plains.

Meanwhile, the warm weather of the spring of 1867 brought an increase in the same daily routine to Cathy that seemingly had no end: drill, drill, and even more drill. Simply living a daily existence of a Buffalo Soldier at Jefferson Barracks was not without risk for Cathy Williams, although the conflict with hostile native tribes was still far away on the Great Plains.

The Most Lethal Enemy, Disease

The greatest danger of serving as a United States soldier always came from disease, and not Indian bullets or arrows as generally assumed. Any concentration of soldiers living in close quarters for an extended period was in itself a considerable risk., when sanitation was poor. Cathy, therefore, endured the omnipresent risk of succumbing to the ravages of disease, while stationed at Jefferson Barracks, where a large number of men were concentrated within the installation's relatively narrow confines. In such an unsanitary setting, sickness could spread like wildfire. Not surprisingly, Cathy became sick. She was hospitalized in St. Louis by the time that a sufficient number of recruits (75) were mustered for duty and stood in the ranks, when Company A was officially organized on February 13, 1867.

The exact cause and nature of Cathy's illness is not known. However, the ravages of Asiatic cholera had often swept through the ports of St. Louis and Carondelet, including Jefferson Barracks, because of their locations on the Mississippi River and heavy water traffic that brought many people together from different regions. This dreaded disease had first made its lethal appearance in St. Louis in 1832, after spreading north from Jefferson Barracks. Immigration, heavy riverboat traffic, and urban congestion led to the spread of disease in this area.

Of course, Cathy had no idea that she performed drill maneuvers with her comrades across deadly ground long ravished by disease epidemics. Even more, this young former slave was also not aware that slaves often had been not only the first to die, but also had suffered more heavily from the spread of Asiatic cholera than whites. Cholera had most recently struck the St. Louis area during the summer of 1866 only several months before Cathy enlisted. This epidemic was more severe than the one that had ravished St. Louis in 1849.[101]

After recovering from her illness and returning to Jefferson Barracks in better overall physical shape, Cathy felt invigorated by spring's arrival. The fact that Cathy was able to maintain her true identity revealed the overall poor quality of medical service that had been provided for lowly enlisted soldiers. Of course, white officers received the best medical care.

Because the training and high standards of the 38th United States Infantry were so demanding, the daily activities of learning to be a regular soldier continued to leave William Cathay exhausted at night and ready for sleep at her assigned barracks, especially after having been weakened by the recent unknown illness.

All the while, Cathy's cousin and friend provided not only good companionship, but also protected her if any situation developed that might lead to her discovery as a woman. This additional layer of security had been another reason why she had first decided to join the regiment in which they served together and stayed close together in Company A's ranks. Most importantly, Cathy's cousin and a friend helped to ensure that Cathy kept the secret of her sex safe from prying eyes, or perhaps even parried questions from curious soldiers about the tall, quiet soldier, who was their close friend. After all and as mentioned, any discovery of her sex would ensure an automatic dismissal from Buffalo Soldier service and a quick exit from Jefferson Barracks, leaving Cathy on her own and even more vulnerable.

In a strange way, the twisting course of Cathy's up-and-down life seemed to have been somehow tied to the two greatest rivers of the Mississippi Valley, the Missouri and the Mississippi. These two mighty rivers had been connected to Cathy throughout her life like an invisible umbilical cord, uniting her life and fate to America's heartland. Having grown up in slavery in the Missouri River country, she was still part of the soil like other former slaves, who had once worked this land of plenty. She was part of the Missouri and Mississippi River Valleys that she had known intimately all her life, and they were now part of her core being.

Even her Civil War experiences with the Union Army, when sometimes serving more than 1,000 miles away from her place of birth, had not severed her personal connection to her native homeland deep in America's heartland. Even the Federal Army that she had first joined had been focused on winning control of the strategic Missouri and Mississippi Valleys.

Additionally, despite having journeyed through large sections of the South on both sides of the Mississippi during the Civil War years, Cathy had still always thought of this fertile agricultural region as her home. Therefore, this Missouri homeland west of the Mississippi had drawn her back like a magnet after the war ended, explaining in part why she had enlisted at Jefferson Barracks.

As mentioned, Cathy had been born not far from the Missouri River in Jackson County in western Missouri, and grew to adulthood in Jefferson City that overlooked the Missouri River which flowed into the Mississippi. And now Cathy had learned to become a United States regular within sight of the Mississippi River and just south from where the two mightiest rivers of mid-America intersected just north of St. Louis. For all of these reasons, the great "Father of Waters" had a special place in this young woman's life, and helped to define her. For Cathy Williams, the memories of these two wide rivers (the Mississippi and Missouri) that symbolized the American heartland were almost like long-lost family members, providing a degree of familiarity.

In contrast to the life of a former slave that had been marked by instability, these two legendary watercourses were constant and reliable entities (something personal and almost familial-like because slavery and service with Union armies for nearly four years had made her largely a rootless person) in an ever-changing world, where the course of one's life could so suddenly change. Therefore, like people of color in general, so Cathy almost certainly felt a sense of solace that she could at least count on these dual entities which were as timeless as their dark currents. Consequently, these two great rivers of destiny that had long defined America's fertile heartland and drained most of the North American continent were still part of the heart and soul of Cathy Williams.

On the lonely nights in the wooden barracks located atop the hills above and just west of the Mississippi while the winds howled outside her sleeping quarters at Jefferson Barracks, Cathy often heard the mournful whistle of the train of the Iron Mountain Railroad. This train rumbled down the tracks that ran along the bluff's base near the river bank. The iron tracks led north toward the gas lights on the streets of the vibrant city of St. Louis that illuminated the northern horizon just upriver. However, this haunting sound of the train that echoed in the night brought little comfort to this young woman, while perhaps she thought back upon her life's unpredictable course.

Cathy might have wished that the up-and-down course of her life had been as straight as the churning locomotive making its way north to St. Louis, or the Mississippi's relentless currents flowing south to New Orleans and then the Gulf of Mexico since time immemorial. However, at least in one context, the distant whistling from the train moving at a brisk pace in the night might have reminded Cathy that her life was not unlike this locomotive, because she was now headed in an entirely new direction and uncharted course.

But, of course, Cathy Williams did not know what lay ahead around the next bend in a most unconventional life. As she had learned throughout the past, seemingly impossible turns of fate that always had something unexpected in store for this young woman, who nevertheless always kept her faith and hope for a brighter future. It is not known if Cathy was religious or not. But very likely the Protestant faith (either Methodist or Baptist) that she had first learned about as a child also provided spiritual comfort to her in her darkest days of uncertainty and adversity.

As the twisting course of her life had long verified, Cathy Williams knew not what to expect next, including whenever the 38th United States Infantry was finally ordered to move west for new assignment far away from her native homeland.[102] Nevertheless and despite any possible lingering doubts, Cathy had firmly set herself on an entirely new course in life which revealed what she believed was most important to her: "I wanted to make my own living and not be dependent on relations or friends."[103]

Private William Cathay Heads West as a Buffalo Soldier

After months of the seemingly endless drilling on the parade ground of Jefferson Barracks, the long-awaited moment that Cathy and her comrades had long dreamed about finally arrived during the spring of 1867. New orders came from headquarters, bringing a new challenge with the warmer weather of spring: the traditional time to begin military campaigning. The 38th United

States Infantry received directives to depart Jefferson Barracks and embark upon its first mission beyond Missouri's western borders. Just the thought of active duty brought a sense of exhilaration to the young Buffalo Soldiers, and no doubt Cathy Williams as well. Now fully recovered from her wintertime illness and with spring in the air to reinvigorate spirits, Cathy Williams was now ready for duty on the western frontier.

This new assignment on the Great Plains might well provide an opportunity for non-veterans, like Private Cathay, to prove themselves in active campaigning and combat situations: ultimate tests of endurance and courage that had special meaning to a young woman now carrying a musket for the first time. Consequently, the more philosophical regimental members pondered a fundamental question. What newly-minted soldiers, like Cathy, of the newly-formed 38th United States Infantry would demonstrate courage on the field of strife, or would be overcome with fear in a crisis situation? Of course, no one knew the answers to these nagging questions at this time.

However, such personal concerns had been contemplated by some 38th United States Infantry members during the intensive training at Jefferson Barracks. Often the soldier who talked the loudest about his fearlessness in combat and how he would vanquish opponents proved to be the first to run in a dangerous combat situation. Meanwhile, the meekest soldier, even a quiet bookworm-type of diminutive stature, sometimes demonstrated more courage in the face of danger than the loudest braggarts. Only the great trial of combat would tell the truth, separating coward from hero before the eyes of regimental members. For one, Cathy would have to find out for herself exactly what she would do when the much-anticipated moment of crisis came in the heat of battle. She would either rise to the occasion or prove not to be a good soldier, as she had tried so hard to become during her training at Jefferson Barracks during the winter of 1866-1867.

But in broader terms, Cathy Williams was about to play a role in America's great drama of westward expansion, which had long propelled the most adventuresome young men and women of a vigorous nation toward the setting sun for generations. She was about to become part of a national epic movement of the American people to the western frontier. To an ex-slave or even an average American settler, the West represented a romantic ideal and a bountiful land of promise. Here, Cathy was to eventually learn that a hard-working person could be reborn by taking advantage of new opportunities. In the West, a person could be literally transformed and made anew in a pristine land unspoiled by man's corruptive influences compared to farther east.

By this time, Cathy needed a dramatic change after the long months of routine training and a mundane existence at Jefferson Barracks. She looked forward to a fresh challenge, which was now provided by duty on the western frontier. For the first time in her life, Cathy was about to enter a fabled land located west of her native western Missouri. She had never before seen Indian and buffalo country, but Cathy had often heard about this remote frontier region. For young Cathy Williams and like so many others, there was something invigorating about the prospect of moving toward the setting sun and experiencing the West.

Indeed, like no other personal experience in Cathy's life to date, the challenges of the West were destined to provide almost like a healing effect of sorts, because she was finally getting the opportunity to leave a dark past farther behind to enter a land of beauty that had never known slavery's horrors. Indeed, Cathy Williams sought to escape the ghosts and demons of her past. This comforting realization alone must have been exciting to the young female Buffalo Soldier, who had never been farther west than Jackson County, where she had been born when her prospects in life had been at their lowest ebb.[104]

Forgotten Western Women

One of the myths of American history was that the course of westward expansion was devoid of African American pioneers and settlers, especially single black women. However, nothing could have been farther from the truth. The true life stories of Clara Brown and many other black pioneers have revealed how African American women were an integral part of America's westward expansion. Like white women who pushed toward the setting sun, they were in the forefront of the West's settlement. In fact, they helped to shape the western experience in unique ways long overlooked by generations of historians. From beginning to end, these so-called forgotten "Madonnas of the prairies" played vital roles in the overall saga of the taming of the West.

Brown had been born a slave around 1803 in Tennessee and around four decades before Cathy Williams' birth in western Missouri. Brown and her mother were sold to tobacco farmer Ambrose Smith, who then moved to

Kentucky. Clara not only worked in the fields, but also cleaned as a domestic (like Cathy at the William Johnson house) and cooked in the master's house. She early found comfort from slavery in a reliance on a powerful spiritual faith stemming in part from the emotional religious revivals in the open air, which immeasurably helped Clara to endure her darkest days. She married another slave, Richard, and they had four children together. However, one child, Paulina, died from drowning. Luckily for Clara, Smith was a God-fearing slave owner. He refused to split up the little family by selling family members on the auction block to gain a hefty profit.

Then, an unkind fate intervened. Unfortunately, her life and the family were shattered forever when Smith died, and his assets, including the slaves, were sold to pay off mounting debts. Therefore, Clara was not able to avoid the horror of having been sold at the busy town square of Russellville, Kentucky, in the summer of 1835. Fortunately, Cathy Williams never endured this searing experience, although owner William Johnson died before she had been liberated by Union troops from slavery in June 1861. Because Johnson owed no significant debts, Johnson's widow had kept Cathy as her own.

Consequently, Cathy never carried Brown's deep psychological scars from this ultimate family tragedy, because she was never placed on the auction block to live a nightmare-come-true for a young black woman, who was fated to be severed permanently from family and friends. Clara had even endured the horror of having seen her youngest daughter, Eliza Jane, and two older children (Richard, Jr., and Margaret), and her husband, Richard, sold to different owners.[105]

Clara was then sold to George Brown. She took her new owner's last name, which was the custom of the day among enslaved blacks. For the rest of her life, Clara never gave up the hope of finding her husband and children. But it was destined to be a heartbreaking quest, because she met with endless frustration. However, displaying strength of character, she refused to allow herself to become consumed by bitterness or anger. Clara placed her faith in God, while forsaking resentment and hatred. As she emphasized, "My little sufferings was nothing [because] the Lord He give me strength to bear up under them."[106]

When new master George Brown died in 1857, his will set Clara free. As if to escape the haunting memories and because of a law that gave a freed slave a year to depart the state (Kentucky) or be sold as a slave, Clara then headed west. She hoped that Richard or her children were now located somewhere in the West. She prayed long and hard to have a long-awaited reunion with them, despite the great odds against any such possibility.

She then journeyed west across Missouri and through Jackson County town of Independence, near where Cathy had been born. All the while, Clara was also motivated to continue trekking west because she had heard "that blacks enjoyed more freedom on the western frontier." Clara Brown then settled down in Leavenworth, Kansas. Here, Clara found domestic work in a friendly land without the curse of slavery. However, blacks in eastern Kansas risked periodic kidnapping by unethical Missourians, including ruthless men from Cathy's native Jackson County that bordered Kansas. These opportunists often launched slave-catching raids across the border. Therefore, after joining a wagon train bound for Colorado in April 1859, Clara then continued to push west to further distance herself from slavery and heartless slave-owners: much like Cathy Williams in exorcising her slave past and any lingering personal demons by shortly departing her home state of Missouri as a Buffalo Soldier.[107]

Earlier than Cathy Williams' own personal odyssey in trekking west, Clara then settled in the rustic frontier mining town of Auraria, Colorado. Here, in a makeshift community of miners and prospectors located just south of the confluence of the South Platte River and Cherry Creek, Clara found steady work at a bakery that sold bread to hungry laborers. In the frontier community established by Georgians in late 1858 and later like Cathy Williams when she eventually settled down in Trinidad, Colorado, Clara discovered that working class whites (as opposed to those of a more elevated class, especially slave-owners) were much friendlier toward her.

What she discovered to her great relief was that the West was far less socially restricted and class conscious than the South. Clara not only gained wide acceptance in the new western community, but also became popular among the miners and common people, who recognized her value to their community as a devout Christian. This more tolerant environment in the West was still another significant development that Cathy Williams was destined to enjoy one day in Trinidad.

Clara earned the affectionate nickname of "Aunt Clara" and "Aunty" among the local whites, who respected her because of her Christian kindness.

What food was left over at the bakery was given to a Methodist church, and she fed the homeless and destitute, regardless of race. The irrepressible "Aunt Clara" secured a one-room cabin to conduct regular prayer meetings. She fixed up the place, transforming the log cabin into a makeshift church. Here, Clara began to spread the gospel with her own fiery brand of religious faith like which had long served as a central foundation of black (slave and free) communities. All the while, her personal example served as a model of true Christianity to others, black and white.

Like Cathy Williams in later moving throughout the West in search of greater opportunities after her Buffalo Soldier service finally ended in the fall of 1868, Clara eventually moved to Central City, in north central Colorado. Here, she opened the state's first laundry. Because of the May 1859 gold strike (part of the Pike's Pike Gold Rush), a new boom reinvigorated the town, along with small businesses. In this shallow valley surrounded by the picturesque mountains, Clara made her financial dreams come true. Taking full advantage of the opportunities offered by the gold rush miners (almost all single men) who paid in gold for having their clothing washed, she saved her profits to amass sizeable funds. Demonstrating a savvy business sense, she then smartly invested her money in property, mining claims, and grub stakes. In property alone, including more than a dozen town lots in Denver and properties in Boulder and other Colorado frontier towns in the area, Clara's worth grew to around $10,000 by the Civil War's conclusion, when Cathy Williams had been still attached to Union forces in the eastern theater.[108]

As the first black female settler and first successful African American entrepreneur in Colorado, Clara Brown left an enduring legacy. Even more, she also was Colorado's first black humanitarian who garnered a widespread reputation. She donated her sizeable profits to helping others, especially the needy and poor. She assisted destitute miners and their families, and working men who had been injured in the mines. Clara's charity work and her remarkable life story were described in the pages of the *Denver Republican* in 1890, like Cathy Williams' own life story that appeared in January 2, 1876 issue of the *St. Louis Daily Times*. As if to replace the great emotional and psychological void left by the loss of her family members, who had been sold on the auction block, Clara devoted her life to helping less fortunate others. She earned the renown as the "angel of the Rockies." Clara was not only widely known for her compassion, but also for the depth of her spiritual strength that inspired many others to live decent lives on the lawless frontiers.

But as a sad fate would have it, ironically, Clara could not help herself, after assisting so many unfortunates. Driven by her ever-lasting dream of reuniting with her last remaining loved ones, Clara journeyed back to Kentucky in search for her family. She never relinquished her greatest hopes and desires. These beloved family members were not found despite Clara's tireless efforts, however. Instead, she found a good many destitute former slaves, including her own nephew, in Kentucky, and bestowed assistance to them, as if to ease the depth of her personal pain. Spending her own resources, Clara even brought some of these unfortunate African Americans back to Colorado, where they thereafter led better lives, unlike if they had remained in Kentucky (a former slave border state like Missouri).

After securing donations in Colorado because she was so well known for her humanitarian work as the irrepressible "Aunt Clara Brown," she also assisted around 5,000 black settlers who were known as the Exodusters. These hopeful people had fled the South to start life anew in Kansas during the late 1870s. But, as if a final reward for her tireless humanitarian work for having assisted so many others in need, there was fortunately a happy ending for Clara. After many years of searching and when nearly age eighty, Clara finally found her daughter, Eliza Jane, married and living in Council Bluffs, Iowa, in 1882.[109]

A fellow Missourian like Cathy Williams, Sylvia Estes-Stark was another black female pioneer of the West. She had been born in 1839 in "a shed" behind the master's house, where he mother–Hannah Estes—had been a domestic servant, in western Missouri (perhaps Cathy's own Jackson County) only a few years before Cathy's birth. She lived with her Bible-reading mother in an urban setting, while her father, Howard Estes, a mulatto whose father was white, lived outside of town. Howard visited his family on the weekends. With the 1849 Gold Rush in California, Howard obtained permission from his master to work as a miner in the gold fields. Here, he earned enough money to eventually buy freedom for himself and his family. Howard then returned to western Missouri with high hopes for a better life. Hannah and Howard were then united in marriage. The family of free blacks purchased land in western Missouri, and began to farm the land. Hannah's former master then hired Howard Estes, Sylvia's brother Jackson, and others to drive a herd of cattle to California and sell the beef to miners.

On April 1, 1851, the cattle drive began from western Missouri, and the Estes family, accompanied black and white cowboys, trekked west in a covered wagon. After an arduous six month journey, the family's migration west finally ended at Sacramento, California. Then, the Estes family settled down in an old miner's cabin just outside Placerville, California, in late 1851.Here, Howard worked in a gold mine, and family members planted crops in an environment that was far more promising than in Missouri. After much hard work, they created a better life and brighter future for themselves in the West, where the dreams of black pioneers came true.[110]

First Assignment out West

Meanwhile, like these pioneer black women, so the West now beckoned to young Private William Cathay in much the same way. She was destined to engage in some of the most demanding military service on the western frontier. All the while, Cathy still worried that her true identity would be discovered, if she made a single mistake or a careless slip of the tongue. If so, then everything would completely unravel around her, and the new life that Cathy had created for herself by her own ingenuity would be no more.

Now on her way to the regiment's new assignment at Fort Riley in the Kansas Territory in April 1867, Cathy traveled west with Company A in a lengthy journey. As fate would have it, the young private's trek west passed through the Missouri River country where she had been born near the town of Independence, Jackson County, Missouri. Cathy might have reflected on how much she had grown in overall maturity to become a more self-actualizing person since when she had been a vulnerable house slave and catered to her owners' whims.[111]

If she had relatives still living in western Missouri, Private William Cathay had no time to stop and visit. Orders were orders, and the legendary discipline of the regulars had to be maintained at all costs. Therefore, all personal desires and priorities were set aside by Cathy, because she had no choice in the matter. For all that she knew, Cathy might never see her Missouri relatives and homeland again.

Meanwhile, she and her fellow black troops, and their white officers, of Company A, 38th United States Infantry, traveled west on the rails of the Kansas Pacific Railroad (a branch—the Eastern Division —of the Union

Pacific Railroad). All the while, Cathy moved farther away from her native Jackson County. For the first time in her life, she entered the rolling plains of eastern Kansas. Here, this landscape began to gradually change with different topography and vegetation, bestowing a new look. During the trek west, Cathy Williams saw the terrain gradually become more arid and hence less wooded compared to her native Missouri. All the while, the number, size, and varieties of timber continued to get smaller as she journeyed west, except in the more fertile river and creek valleys.

For the first time in her life, Cathy had entered the prairies of the eastern edge of the Great Plains, leaving the United States for the first time in her life, after entering Kansas. The farther that Cathy rode the iron rails west across Kansas and ever-closer to Fort Riley, Kansas, which the railroad had reached in the fall of 1866, the grasslands of Kansas became more extensive. She must have marveled how the prairies flowed to the horizon in every direction. This was a novel sight to Cathy and quite unlike any other area that she had seen during her Civil War sojourns. The farther west that she traveled west from Kansas City, the prairies became gradually larger to a size unseen in her native western Missouri. Consisting of a vast expanse of bluestem prairies of so-called buffalo grass that had long supported the immense herds of the "monarch of the plains" (the American Bison), the grasslands rolled ever-onward and closer to where Cathy Williams' destiny now called and awaited her.[112]

About to be assigned to Fort Riley (like Cathy Williams and her Buffalo Soldier command), where his 7th Cavalry had been ordered by headquarters in Chicago to be organized, Lieutenant Colonel George Armstrong Custer, born in an Ohio long removed from the western frontier experience, was impressed by this pristine region. He marveled at the Great Plains that touched the romantic side of his soul and fascinated him to no end. An enchanted Custer described how: "this immense tract of country . . . is now known as the Plains [and] Comparing the surface of the country to that of the ocean, a comparison often indulged in by those who have seen both, it does not require a very great stretch of the imagination, when viewing the boundless ocean of beautiful living verdure, to picture these undulations as gigantic waves . . . ."[113]

At some point west of Jackson County and across the Missouri border in

Kansas while riding the rails of the Kansas Pacific Railroad, Cathy saw her first herd of buffalo, after entering the bluestem grasslands of traditional buffalo country. She had almost certainly heard about the great herds of buffalo before, but had never seen these majestic animals in her native Jackson County. The last buffalo of this county had been killed by the first pioneers who migrated to western Missouri decades before Cathy's birth. Along with the extensive grasslands which sustained the vast herds that migrated in search of fresh grass and water during the spring and summer, Cathy's first sight of the buffalo in eastern Kansas reminded her that she was entering a western frontier region that was still untamed compared to her native homeland.

After eating the rich grasses all summer and gaining fat to store energy and gain strength for endurance during the lean winter months, these durable animals survived the harshest Great Plains winters, including the bitter cold of howling Arctic winds and blizzards. This natural hardiness of the buffalo not shared even by modern domestic cattle. Such sights during her journey to Fort Riley perhaps brought the realization to Cathy Williams that the Buffalo Soldiers (a respectful name eventually bestowed by the Indians because the black soldiers' hair resembled wooly buffalo hair to native people of the Great Plains) had been assigned to duty in this frontier land to safeguard the railroads and the wagon trains of migrants pushing toward the setting sun. [114]

Marveling at the sight of herds not unlike Cathy Williams on her first journey beyond Missouri's borders, Custer described how, "Nearly all graminivorous animals in habiting the Plains except the elk and some species of the deer prefer the buffalo grass to that of the lowland [and] Both are often found in large herds grazing upon the uplands . . . the buffalo grass [is] beyond question that it is the most nutritious of all varieties of wild grass [while] The favorite range of the buffalo is contained in a belt of country running north and south, about two hundred miles wide . . . The habits of the buffalo incline him to graze and migrate from one stream to another, moving northward and crossing each in succession as he follows the young grass in the spring, and moving southward seeking the milder climate and open grazing in the fall and winter [and] Throughout the buffalo country are to be seen what are termed buffalo wallows." [115]

Providing a sense of wonderment to her, Cathy viewed this unique natural environment of the eastern edge of the Great Plains, which she was about to intimately know. This wild region was about to become her new home during her first assignment. But the farther that she journeyed deeper into the sunbaked grasslands of eastern Kansas, the closer Cathy came to Indian country.

Indeed, this was the ancient homeland of Great Plains warriors, who were enraged over the ever-escalating white encroachment into their hunting grounds. To defend their land, families, and ancestral way-of-life and enhance their reputations in their tribe, these seasoned warriors would have enjoyed nothing more than killing and taking the scalp of a young Buffalo Soldier inexperienced in the cunning ways of Indian warfare. For these veteran warriors, it made no difference if one of these Buffalo Soldiers, who had been ordered to protect (western migration and national expansion) what was gradually destroying the Indians' sacred world, was actually a woman disguised as a man. In this case and above all else, a blue uniform all but ensured a death sentence and an ugly one, if Cathy Williams was ever captured by Great Plains warriors. Ritualistic torture and even dismemberment were part of the warriors' cultural traditions and ethos, including the belief that they would not have to face a whole enemy in the afterlife.

Fort Riley Becomes a New Home

Situated on the muddy Kansas River (known to locals as the Kaw River) that sliced through the rolling grasslands of north central Kansas that were located one hundred and sixteen miles west of Fort Leavenworth, Fort Riley was a remote outpost located in the Department of the Missouri. This expansive military department on the western frontier was commanded by General Winfield Scott Hancock, a hero of the battle of Gettysburg, and then later by General Philip Henry Sheridan, Custer's old commander from Civil War days, who replaced him.

But this "important center of service school instruction and military administration" located at Fort Riley was not distinguished by a traditional wooden frontier palisade of upright logs to protect the garrison from Indian attack. Although it is not known, perhaps this realization came as a shock of Private Cathy Williams. One of the oldest military outposts on the Great Plains, Fort Riley had been established in 1852 in preparation for the eventual pacification of the hostile tribes that roamed the Great Plains at will. This so-called fort only consisted of one and a half story stone buildings, quarried from local sandstone, which surrounded the parade ground. Situated amid the wide prairie that seemed to stretch endlessly to the horizon, this group of buildings consisted of six barracks for soldiers and half a dozen double houses for officers and their families.

Lieutenant Colonel Custer and his 7th Cavalry had been garrisoned at Fort Riley to protect the workers who were spearheading the relentless advance west of the Union Pacific Railroad. The expansion of the iron rails ever-farther west through buffalo country had infuriated the Indians, whose nomadic culture depended on the vast buffalo herds (that were disturbed by the wagon trains and railroad to interfere with their migratory routes) for survival. Fort Riley provided troops to protect the seemingly endless miles of iron track that stretched across the broad prairies and the westward expansion of thousands of migrants.

At this time, Fort Riley contained five lengthy horse stables, Sutler's stores, mess buildings, "laundress houses,' quartermaster employee houses, a small chapel and his reverend's house, post office, a 'Billiard House,'" in the words of Elizabeth "Libbie" Bacon-Custer. Other small structures were located behind the larger stone buildings. Presenting "the appearance of a little city," in the opinion of Libbie who was a small town product from Monroe, Michigan, Fort Riley was nestled on the north bank of the Kansas (Kaw) River. This river flowed west below Fort Leavenworth, which was located just east of the mouth of the Republican River.[116]

Elizabeth (Libbie) Bacon-Custer and Eliza Denison Brown (the former Virginia slave who had escaped slavery to join Custer's command to cook for the young general's staff in 1863) arrived at Fort Riley on the Union Pacific Railroad from St. Louis on October 16, 1866 (just a month before Cathy Williams enlisted). By this time, Custer's dreary Reconstruction duty in the South had ended, and the 7th Cavalry had been ordered to organize at Fort Riley. Libbie described the parade ground, after her arrival from her hometown of Monroe, Michigan: "This square is a large lawn for parade, a flag and two cannon in the centre [and] A Carriage drive runs all around the parade ground."[117]

Of course, Libbie and other 7th Cavalry officers' wives rode in nice carriages and were treated like royalty by Custer's men. Cathy Williams, therefore, no doubt marveled about the comfortable lives of these women, who were privileged members of the upper echelons of the military hierarchy. This situation was not unlike the existence of slave-owners' wives, including when Cathy served as a domestic who worked at the "big house" of William Johnson in Cole County. While Cathy existed on bare essentials of basic rations of hardtack and beef at Fort Riley, Libbie described the good life that she now enjoyed in her letter to her cousin in Michigan: "We are so much more comfortably situated here than we were at Winchester [Virginia and] we are living almost in luxury. It does not seem [like] life in the army for you know I have had mostly a rough time [and] The [officer's] houses all have wide verandas . . . Our house has a large parlor, my bedroom back of it . . . So, you see, we are comfortable. I have a carpet on my bedroom also and expect to have one on the dress-ing room."[118]

By comparison, Fort Riley's stone barracks in which Cathy slept was drafty and unsanitary, especially in winter. The barracks provided no cozy existence for the young Missouri-born female private at Fort Riley. Therefore, like more than a dozen other privates of her Buffalo Soldier command dispatched from Jefferson Barracks, Cathy came down with an illness not long after arriving at this post in April 1867. It was very likely that Cathy was still paying a price (like her first illness at Jefferson Barracks) for her arduous service and rough living—mostly outdoors —in support of Union armies for nearly four years.

The fort was named for Mexican War hero General Bennett Riley. He had established this western frontier fort to protect the nation's push west. Of Irish descent, Riley had been the first regular army officer to lead United States soldiers down the Santa Fe Trail that stretched from Cathy's native western Missouri and southwest to Santa Fe, New Mexico, and then into northern Mexico. Located near the confluence of the Republican and Smoky Hill Rivers just to the southeast, Fort Riley's construction had begun in the summer of 1855.

Hoping to revitalize a spectacular Civil War career, after having accepted the rank of lieutenant colonel, Custer had been ordered to Fort Riley (before his wife's arrival with Eliza Denison Brown in tow) in October 1866. In mid-October, Custer had taken command of four companies of his newly-organized 7th cavalry during General William S. Hancock's punitive expedition against the Cheyenne and Sioux—"Hancock's War." In a poorly-executed campaign that only caused greater difficulties with the Indians than solutions, Hancock's expedition, in which Custer led the 7th Cavalry, pushed west from Fort Riley at the end of March 1867. This expedition had been launched not long before the arrival of Private William Cathay and her Company A, 38th United States Infantry to Fort Riley. Unfortunately, for the Buffalo Soldiers, General Hancock's over-aggressive actions caused greater hostility from the Great Plains tribes, while operating unsuccessfully during the summer, which was Cathy's first on the Great Plains.[119]

At some point relatively early during her 1867 duty at Fort Riley, Cathy Williams saw Lieutenant Colonel Custer leading his troopers with his usual dramatic flair and colorful military attire that caught everyone's eye, especially the females. As mentioned, Custer had earlier refused a lieutenant colonel's rank in the black 9th Cavalry largely because of an omnipresent factor that was only too well-known to Private William Cathay. By declining to accept command of the black cavalry regiment, he had bided his time that allowed him to obtain the coveted command of the newly-created 7th Cavalry, an all-white regiment, which had been authorized by Congress at the same time that Cathy's infantry regiment had been organized: Custer (who proved to be a contradiction in matters of race) had made his final decision based largely on color and, of course, a good deal of pride and vanity.

Like many white officers, Custer considered commanding a black regiment a smear on his name and reputation, because of the old myth—something that never completely died despite the Civil War heroics of tens of thousands of black troops —that these fighting men of African descent somehow lacked the same combat prowess and the same sterling qualities of character, especially courage, as white soldiers. Of course, this was a central myth of the American experience that somehow continued to endure generation after generation.[120]

To the thinking of Custer and so many other officers (infantry and cavalry) at this time which only reflected society's pervasive racial views, blacks were best suited for serving whites because of their alleged inferiority. However, Custer's opinions about blacks and race were as complicated as they were hypocritical, while mirroring the common beliefs of white society that extended back generations. As the Union's popular Civil War cavalry hero, he had embraced the North's holy war against slavery and demonstrated a highly creditable degree of enlightenment in racial matters. He believed that the slaves should be freed and repeatedly risked his life on major battlefields of the eastern theater in part because of these moral convictions. Custer had fought with great distinction against "this evil," (slavery) in his own words in a letter to his father-in-law Judge Daniel S. Bacon (Libbie's snobby and class conscious father who had been initially against Custer's marriage to his pampered daughter because of his middle-class background), in Monroe, Michigan.

However, Custer also simultaneously believed in the inferiority of blacks, especially former slaves. Therefore, while he had long fought against slavery, including with great distinction on July 3, 1863 at Gettysburg, and like the majority of whites of his day, Custer was still racist to a degree to reveal a central paradox of his character. But as mentioned and to be fair to Custer, this racial prejudice was a pervasive sentiment in American society, North and South, at this time. Haunted by unfounded racial stereotypes, Libbie was terrified of the black soldiers of the 38th Infantry. Unfamiliar with blacks, she was obsessed with the traditional unwarranted white fear of the possibility of rape by black men because of the persistent stereotype of their sexual aggressiveness rather than by their actual behavior. Although a northerner, Libbie was a victim of the longtime racial obsessions and fears of white Southerners, especially women.

While serving on Reconstruction duty in the South before his reassignment to Fort Riley, Custer had closely identified with the elite of the Southern planter class. He admired their elevated social status and entrenched positions. The native Ohioan was only a middle-class product of the West and the son of a lowly blacksmith. Consequently, he was easily impressed by the superficial façade of the aristocracy, and had been easily seduced by it. The ambitious Custer aspired to move up the social ladder and join the upper class, which he had closely associated with in cosmopolitan places like New York City.

Nevertheless, out of a sense of compassion, he had also personally long related to individual former slaves in need, like Eliza Denison Brown. She faithfully served Custer for six years during the Civil War and the Indian Wars. Despite his lofty general's rank during the war and later with a lieutenant colonel's rank in leading the 7th Cavalry on the Great Plains, he had always treated Eliza with a distinct measure of respect and dignity that would have appalled upper class Southerners. In this sense, Custer was truly egalitarian in regard to race.

Clearly, Custer's personality was far more complex and nuanced than has been generally portrayed by historians, who had simplified him according to long-existing popular stereotypes. After the war during Reconstruction duty, he and his wife Elizabeth had once sat together in quiet reverence at a black prayer meeting in Texas. They had enjoyed the free-spirited religious service and the well-harmonized gospels of former slaves, whose distinctive manner of worship was so different from what Libbie had seen for her entire life in Monroe, Michigan.[121]

Despite his pro-Southern leanings that made him a staunch Democratic supporter of President Andrew Johnson, a Southerner (Tennessean) who had taken office after President Lincoln had been assassinated at Ford's Theater, Washington, D.C., in a heady April 1865 when the North had been basking in decisive victory, Custer revealed his more enlightened side when he wrote: "I am in favor of elevating the negro to the extent of his capacity and intelligence, and of our doing everything in our power to advance the race morally and mentally as well as physically, also socially."[122]

In performing her daily duties at Fort Riley, Private Cathay often saw Libbie who could not have imagined that one of the 38th soldiers who she feared was actually a young woman also from the Midwest. At this time and as mentioned, Custer household still included former slaves Eliza Denison Brown, Custer's favorite cook who he treated as part of the family, and Henry. The little household of the Custer family had been together at Fort Riley since October 16, 1866, which was less than a month before Cathy Williams enlisted to begin her Buffalo Soldier odyssey.[123]

During the Civil War years, Eliza's life had been much like of Cathy Williams, sharing a host of common experiences. The Virginia-born Eliza had been with Custer and the boys in blue since the 1863 Gettysburg Campaign, which was the Civil War's turning point. At that time, young Custer had been promoted to brigadier general, and his star was on the rise. He formed his staff of capable officers of promise. Dark-skinned without a hint of white blood much like Cathy and as mentioned, Eliza had been Custer's first choice in the summer of 1863 to attend him and his staff as a cook. He had picked her out among a group of escaped Virginia slaves, who flocked to their bluecoat liberators who they viewed as saviors. Custer had asked Eliza if she would cook for his newly-created staff, and the young black woman readily consented.

Like Cathy Williams, she had then embarked upon a new challenge and entirely new life-style with the Army of the Potomac and Custer's cavalry. Also like Cathy Williams because of orders, Eliza's own strange destiny had now brought her to Fort Riley situated on the wide Kansas prairie. As during the Civil War while serving in the eastern theater, she continued to faithfully follow Custer's fortunes on the western frontier.[124]

As mentioned, anti-black soldier sentiment was prevalent among many white Civil War officers. A stroke of luck and of course unknown to them at the time, the black troopers of the 9th Cavalry benefited from Custer's racial prejudice and ambition in the end: a situation that perhaps ensured that these black cavalrymen would not be wiped out with the former Civil War hero on the high ground above the Little Big Horn in the Montana Territory on the bloody afternoon of June 25, 1876.[125]

Now assigned to her first frontier fort, Cathy Williams almost certainly felt a sense of vulnerability at Fort Riley, which was situated amid the vast expanse of open prairies. The young private from Missouri was now even more vulnerable while lying in a sickbed at the post hospital for most of April and half of May 1867, when unable to defend herself, if the Indians suddenly attacked. Cathy had heard about Fort Riley in the past, but nothing about this remote installation on the western frontier looked like the kind of fort that she had imaged when training back at Jefferson Barracks. In a December 6, 1866 letter to her first cousin, Rebecca Richmond, Grand Rapids, Michigan, Libbie Custer described how Fort Riley "was not a fort, tho' called so, it is a garrison. For there are no walls enclosing it!"[126]

The initial shock that Libbie had experienced at Fort Riley because of obvious safety concerns was no doubt also felt by Cathy Williams, her cousin and friend of the 38th United States Infantry. Cathy was now situated in the eastern Great Plains and Indian country: an alien environment to her. Perhaps now feeling that enlisting as a Buffalo Soldier might not have been a wise choice after all, young Private William Cathay almost certainly had initially expected to have seen protective walls, or vertical wooden palisades, around

Fort Riley and its small garrison of soldiers.[127]

Most significantly, Cathy Williams' legacy lived-on at the black community in and around Fort Riley for generations, because of the existence of a vibrant oral tradition of the local black community: a hallmark of the richness of the African American experience (oral history) and due partly to the legacy of illiteracy stemming from slavery. Of course, little did Cathy realize in 1867 that an enduring legacy was destined to be left behind by this young woman during her first assignment at a western outpost: the enduring memory of her Buffalo Soldier days at Fort Riley.

An African American United States Army officer of the Vietnam War period never forgot what he had first learned about the legacy of this young Buffalo Soldier named Cathy Williams. In a December 2, 2002 letter to the author, Bernard C. Duse, Jr., described how "Some 38 years ago, in 1964, I was stationed at Ft. Riley, Kansas as a 2nd Lieutenant in the Second Brigade of the U.S. Army First Infantry Division. (The Big Red One).I recall very distinctly having to break-up a barracks fight between two young enlisted soldiers. One of them had stated that he had been very convincingly informed by some African-American residents of the town of Junction City, Kansas, which is just outside of Fort Riley, that there had been a female soldier in the Buffalo Soldiers. The other young soldier, who apparently viewed himself as a Buffalo Soldiers historian, took great offense at the statement and the fight ensued. At the time of the fight, I was only concerned with re-storing order in the barracks. I took no sides on who was correct or incorrect [but ample evidence and documentation] confirms the oral history maintained by those Junction City residents."[128]

Ironically, this barracks' fight between two latter-day Buffalo Soldiers at Fort Riley took place near the location of the stone barracks where Cathy Williams had been quartered on her first assignment on the western frontier, while serving her country more than three-quarters of a century before. Symbolically, the legacy of the first and only female Buffalo Soldier was something that never died in the black civilian and military community around Fort Riley, because of a deep appreciation of history and the vibrancy of the black oral tradition that had kept the memory of Cathy Williams alive for generations. Meanwhile, the rest of the world was destined to forget about Private William Cathay for generations, when her memory was kept alive by black men and women who appreciated their history.

Chapter IV: Forgotten Apache Campaign

The warriors of the Great Plains had never seen black soldiers before, and the sight of Buffalo Soldiers came as a shock to these nomadic people. At this time, many Native Americans, especially the most hostile types, lived by the astute wisdom of simply staying "away from all white people" in order to avoid armed conflict. Because the native people possessed darker skins (more generally bronze-colored) than light-skinned mulattoes, who were the offspring of black and white, this difference skin color justified subjugation in the minds of many white westerners. The Great Plains warriors now realized that they would have to fight both white and black men to retain their ancestral homeland and nomadic way-of-life.

Initially to overconfident Native American warriors who had never seen Buffalo Soldiers before, the black troops "were something to wonder about and to laugh about . . . they were nothing to be afraid of."[129] However, this was a premature conclusion based on lack of familiarity. At the first sight of the African Americans in bluecoats, including soldiers of Cathy's own 38th United States Infantry, some warriors called out to the Buffalo Soldiers in derision, "The black whitemen . . . The Buffalo Soldiers!"[130]

In time, this distinctive name became a distinguished badge of honor to these African American soldiers, including Private William Cathay. Then, back in their remote villages on the Great Plains, the warriors gathered to sing war songs around campfires that mocked the usual color of the African Americans, "Soldiers with black faces . . . you can't take off your black faces."[131]

But as mentioned, this initial ridicule (ironically, from both Native Americans and white Americans) shortly turned into deep respect, after the warriors faced these black fighting men in combat situations. Therefore, the sobriquet of Buffalo Soldier evolved into a complimentary one among the Great Plains tribes. After all in the world of these nomadic people who loved this pristine land of their ancestors, the majestic "Monarch of the Plains" was the most highly revered animal of the Great Plains. As mentioned, the buffalo had long served as the central foundation of the indigenous people's religion, philosophy, and culture of the Great Plains. To sustain them and their rich native culture that had been perfectly adapted to a nomadic life on the rolling prairies, the Great Plains tribes' entire existence was based on following the buffalo herds during the bison's relentless search for fresh grasslands that were lush and green in springtime.

The first Spanish explorers and subsequent white interlopers of the western plains had marveled at the sight of the immense buffalo herds that seemed to have no end. And as realized by the nation's highest ranking military officers who had learned how to wage total war in subduing the Confederacy during a war of attrition, the power of the Great Plains tribes would not end as long as these great herds of buffalo moved freely over the open prairies in a life-sustaining dark mass: the invaluable logistical support system of the warriors and their people for generations.

Therefore, in what was a logistical war, the vast herds had to be destroyed, because this was the key since the Indians' dependence on the animals was total. The powerful bulls demonstrated a well-known aggressiveness against threats posed by attackers, man (white and red hunters) and packs of hungry wolves. With a hardy resilience and legendary toughness, the buffalo survived the terrible blizzards that poured south from the Arctic each winter and swept down the Great Plains.[132]

Meanwhile, Private William Cathay continued to face a set of unique challenges as a soldier, who was still learning the business of frontier service at Fort Riley. After duty at Fort Riley and then Fort Harker, also located in Kansas southwest of Fort Riley, by the summer of 1867, Cathy Williams and her Company A, 38th United States Infantry comrades, along with other regimental companies of the Buffalo Soldier battalion, marched southwest to Fort Union, the Territory of New Mexico.

High heat and humidity made the trek miserable for Private Cathay during the longest march of her life. Fort Union was reached by Cathy and her comrades on July 20, 1867. The fort then provided a welcoming respite from the long march south. Protecting travelers and settlers moving along the Santa Fe Trail, Fort Union was the largest United States military establishment in the Southwest.

Private Cathay had survived a harrowing ordeal. Trekking more than 500 miles from the Kansas plains and over the Santa Fe Trail was a most demanding experience for Private Cathay. After trudging over northeast New Mexico's mountains in the ranks of her battalion of four companies, she learned about the harsh realities of military life in the Southwest. This was a wild and remote land that Cathy had never seen before, and it presented new challenges.

Like other Buffalo Soldiers, what Private William Cathay saw around her in the Southwest left her with a sense of wonder, because of the sheer beauty of this unspoiled land. What Cathy had experienced during the long march south from Fort Riley to New Mexico never left her in the years ahead. During the southwestward trek to Fort Union that had included her swimming across the Rio Grande River and marching in full gear up the rugged mountain (a two-day climb) that led to Raton Pass, Cathy Williams recalled a little frontier town situated along a small river and surrounded by towering mountains to frame the picturesque river valley, Trinidad. Southeast Colorado was the kind of attractive place that she might want to settle down in one day in the future, if Buffalo Soldier service suddenly ended with the discovery of her true identity, and if she decided not to return to her native Missouri.[133]

Another new assignment called for the first female Buffalo Soldier and her comrades when the battalion of the 38th United States Infantry, including Cathy's Company A, was ordered to Fort Cummings in early September 1867. Fort Cummings was situated in the southwest corner of New Mexico and about 375 miles slightly southwest of Fort Union, about halfway between Raton Pass and Albuquerque, nestled in the Rio Grande River Valley. This new assignment called for still another demanding march over rough and unspoiled terrain for Cathy Williams. In the column of black soldiers who marched steadily onward with muskets on right shoulders, she struggled in full gear over a sprawling landscape of mountains, strewn with boulders and little vegetation in an arid region.

But as during the long march from Fort Riley to Fort Union, Cathy withstood the hardships and inclement weather. Exhibiting a stubborn endurance in her determination to prove that she was a good soldier, she kept up with the pace of her comrades. She and her fellow soldiers ignored wet uniforms and sore feet in stoic silence during the long trek. Of course, one challenge that Cathy faced in hiding her true identity in the midst of so many soldiers, especially the white officers, was from the complications that developed because of her menstrual cycle. The sheer stress of ceaselessly struggling to keep her greatest secret and the tough physical demands of soldiering, especially the lengthy march to Fort Union, might have resulted in the ceasing of her normal menstrual cycle. Whenever the opportunity allowed, Cathy might have bathed in a creek or river, like the Rio Grande during the trek to Fort Union, in the fading light near sunset to safeguard her secret from prying eyes.

With flags (national and regimental) flying at the column's head on October 1, 1867, the command of weary black troops finally reached their destination. Cathy and her comrades marched into Fort Cummings, located in the southwest corner of New Mexico, after the exhausting ordeal of pushing farther south.

Here, near Cooke's Springs, Luna County, New Mexico, and located not far from Arizona's southeast corner, Cathy had never been so far south in her life, or so close to another independent nation beyond the United States' borders. The Republic of Mexico, a largely mixed-race nation that had won its independence from Spain in 1821, lay just to the south. Situated around 350 miles of southeast of Phoenix, Arizona, and west of the Rio Grande River that flowed southeast to Texas and eventually into the Gulf of Mexico, Fort Cummings was one of the most forlorn military outposts on the North American continent.

As fate would have it, this isolated fort in an untamed land was the new home of Private William Cathay and her 38th United States Infantry comrades for the next eight months, from October 1, 1867 to June 1868. The reputations of the black troops for combat prowess had preceded them, because warriors had learned that the Buffalo Soldiers were "heap bad medicine"—the ultimate compliment.[134]

New Challenges in Dangerous Apache Country

Cathy Williams was now situated deep in Apache country, which was a wild, arid region far from population centers. This was the homeland of the most feared warriors in the West, the Apache. By this time, the war chief named Cochise was the most aggressive and resourceful leader of the Chiricahua Apache. He had become so adept at battling white interlopers that one conflict became known as "Cochise's War." Highly adaptive products of one of America's harshest regions, these unsurpassed fighting men roamed the rugged mountains and deserts of southern Arizona and northern Mexico with impunity.

However, Cochise drew his devoted followers far and wide, including farther east from western and central New Mexico and all the way to the Rio Grande (the eastern Chiricahua was one of the tribe's four major bands). By this time, he had emerged as the most powerful Native American war chiefs in the Southwest. The White Mountain Apache were centered in the forlorn mountains located west of Fort Cummings just across the Arizona border, while the Mescalero (meaning mescal makers who created a popular intoxicating drink among Apaches and Mexicans) Apache ranged over the wild lands located just east of the Rio Grande in central and south central New Mexico. This remote Apache home region that was so dangerous to white settlers and soldiers was known as Apacheria.

Besides waging war on American settlers and miners who were vulnerable while working at remote locations across the southwestern frontier, the Apache also often raided across the border into northern Mexico. These hard-hitting raids were so destructive that the farms, or haciendas, located in the north Mexican states of Sonora and Chihuahua became largely depopulated. A product of a harsh land where survival of the fittest was the cruel philosophy that dominated life in the unforgiving deserts, the Chiricahua warriors were the most feared Apache fighters and their toughness was legendary.

No Apache leader fought the whites, especially United States soldiers, with more tenacity than the ever-elusive Cochise. One United States officer, John G. Bourke, was impressed by the Apache's disciplined warrior ways. In regard to the tribe's total dedication to warrior ethos and with the ancient Spartans in mind, Bourke concluded how "the Apache resembled some of the nations of antiquity . . ."[135]

In regard to Cochise and his slashing raids that had brought destruction for so long on both sides of the border, Cathy Williams was relatively fortunate now that she was stationed in this easternmost part of Apache country. After having stirred up a hornet's nest, Cochise had made the wise strategic decision to avoid Americans, especially the pesky soldiers in blue jackets. Therefore, he now restricted his raids to striking at more lucrative targets in northern Mexico, hitting isolated Mexican settlements and rancheros, while battling Mexican soldiers (soldados) who attempted in vain to protect small, far-flung Latino settlements in a most inhospitable region.[136]

But while the Buffalo Soldiers were stationed at Fort Cummings, the

Apache threat continued unabated. Cathy Williams and her 38th United States Infantry comrades still faced the threat of the easternmost Chiricahua west of the Rio Grande. The small garrison and Fort Cummings, located on level ground of a broad valley and surrounded by mountains, were vulnerable in this remote setting. With her ample Civil War experience in supporting Union troops, Cathy almost certainly realized the extent of the existing dangers of this lonely outpost, because so much open ground lay around the military installation. Here, at one of the most isolated forts in the Southwest, Private William Cathay performed her required daily duties and fulfilled her assigned responsibilities, before her health again faltered, after the exhausting marches so far south.

In early 1868 and in still another attempt to eliminate an omnipresent threat, a new campaign was about to be opened against the ever-elusive Apache. At this time, the Buffalo Soldiers of Fort Cummings occupied a strategic location on the east flank of the most warlike Apache in neighboring Arizona to the west, where Cochise had returned after raiding into northern Mexico. As usual, trouble developed when least expected. As ordained by headquarters at Santa Fe, the target of this new offensive campaign was a Chiricahua village from which raids had originated, or so it was believed at headquarters. One of these Apache raids included a bold attack on Fort Bayard, which was located about fifty miles northwest of Fort Cummings and closer to the Arizona border.[137]

The antithesis of the traditional military campaigns of the Civil War that Cathy had witnessed on both sides of the Mississippi, warfare against the Apache was the most demanding service for United States soldiers who trained for conventional warfare. Generals Ulysses S. Grant and William T. Sherman, the primary military architects of destroying the Southern people's will to resist and the Confederacy's war-waging capabilities during a war of attrition, now sought to repeat these earlier successes that had saved the Union. At their comfortable headquarters located far away from isolated military installations like Fort Cummings, they developed aggressive plans to subjugate a free people, who fought to defend their homeland and way-of-life as it had existed for centuries, before the coming of the white interlopers.

Developed into an art form by General Philip Henry Sheridan (Grant's top lieutenant during the Civil War by 1864), the strategy of striking Indian village in the depths of wintertime provided the means of catching these elusive warriors by surprise. At this time of year, the Indians were stationary and their legendary mobility—swift horses that allowed them to conduct effective hit-and-run tactics—was dramatically reduced, because of harsh winter conditions. Indian horses were thin and weak without grass to eat during the coldest mouths of the year. In surprise cavalry attacks that struck sleeping villages at dawn, Indian women and children were inevitably killed during the confusing swirl of close-range combat that caused panic and flight. [138]

Here, at Fort Cummings, Cathy Williams made her preparations to participate in General Sheridan's winter war strategy that called for striking a vulnerable Indian village as part of his concept of "total war."[139]

Three columns of troops were ordered to converge on the Chiricahua village that they believed to have been the source of the recent raids. As fate would have it, the troops of the 38th United States Infantry, including Cathy's Company A, were about to join this ambitious offensive effort in the hope of catching the Apache village by surprise. But the stiff challenges of accomplishing this mission were more formidable than imaged by top United States officers, whose strategic and tactical decisions were too often based on analyzing inaccurate maps at a far-away headquarters. The nation's foremost military leaders had never seen the remote area that they had targeted.

Indeed, the targeted Apache village was located in the vast mountain recesses far from Fort Cummings and headquarters. This remote target required long and hard marching by the Buffalo Soldiers just to reach their assigned advanced position from which to strike the hidden Apache sanctuary. Cathy Williams now prepared for this special mission that was as dangerous as it was historic: she was about to become the first and only female soldiers of the United States Army (regular or volunteer) to play an active part in an offensive operation against an enemy during a far-flung expedition deep into Apache country.

All the while, the weather had grown colder, with winter's depths having descended over dreary Fort Cummings that seemed to be located in the middle of nowhere to Cathy. Preparations for the offensive operations were finally completed at the fort by the arrival of New Year's Eve. However, Cathy Williams was not celebrating the nearness of New Year, because discipline remained tight among the black regulars.

During bitter winter weather, Cathy now prepared to embark on her first large-scale offensive operation in her military career, cleaning her gear and musket that she had yet to fire in anger at an enemy. Therefore, Cathy no doubt felt a sense of heightened anxiety in regard to facing the upcoming stern challenge of campaigning deep in dangerous Apache country. It is not known if Cathy's cousin and friend were still members of the regiment at this time. If not, then Private William Cathay would have very likely felt a greater sense of loneness and isolation on the eve of her first military expedition against the legendary Apache warriors, when close friends would be needed, especially in a crisis or combat situation.

Splitting the cold air, trumpeters blew sharp notes that echoed from their brass bugles and swept across Fort Cummings on the cold morning of January 1, 1868. On the double, the Buffalo Soldiers, including Private William Cathay, poured out of the wooden barracks to align on the broad parade ground. Meanwhile, the red glow of the sun peaked over the treeless mountains to the east in a typical desert sunrise on the New Mexican frontier. Cathy aligned in Company A's ranks and stood in a neat line of bluecoats who were ready for the challenge. Lieutenant Henry F. Leggett, a veteran Civil War leader, now commanded Company A. Private William Cathay was fortunate to have a capable company officer in charge.

Such an experienced officer would certainly keep a cool head in a close combat situation and make the right decisions, thankfully for Cathy and her comrades. However, Cathy might have been concerned by the alarming fact that Company A (below its peak strength of 75 soldiers) was low on manpower at such a critical time, when every Buffalo Soldier was needed in the ranks for the daunting mission of striking deep into Apache country during wintertime. When the black soldiers marched out of Fort Cummings on the cold of January 1, they represented the smallest of the three columns that had been ordered to converge on the hostile village of the Southern Apache.

With her musket on her right shoulder and while the United States colors flew at the column's head, Cathy and her fellow Buffalo Soldiers left the frontier fort farther behind at the beginning of a lengthy march. They trudged north over mountainous country and parallel to the Rio Grande River that flowed to the east. Hour after hour and like her comrades, Cathy pushed onward in the column of blue-clad fighting men of African descent. The full gear and musket that she carried seemed heavier with each passing mile.

While steadily marching north toward Colorado's southern border, the Buffalo Soldiers crossed numerous creeks that flowed east toward the Rio Grande River.

With no bridges spanning across these uncharted watercourses, Cathy and her comrades got their feet wet in icy waters, when crossing numerous streams and creeks. However, there was no time to build fires to warm and dry feet. Because of the need to keep moving at a good pace in order to meet the other two columns in accordance with the campaign's timetable of multiple columns simultaneously striking the Apache village, the Buffalo Soldiers of the 38th United States Infantry continued onward into the unknown. Despite falling snow, sleet, and rain, the column of black fighting men (and a solitary woman in this case) steadily surged north to keep pace with the ambitious schedule to fulfill the planned three-column convergence on the Apache village.

Meanwhile, Cathy must have marveled at the unspoiled natural beauty of the surrounding landscape. Jokes and laughter or even singing—perhaps even old slave spirituals once heard in the cotton fields of the South —might have occasionally erupted from the ranks to lift spirits during the lengthy ordeal. With legs and feet sore from the exhaustive marching over long distances, Cathy might have now wished that she had instead enlisted in the 9th or 10th Cavalry of a regular infantry regiment. Rocky canyons and high mountains appeared strange and eerie to Private William Cathay and her comrades in daylight hours. However, they also appeared hauntingly beautiful in the red glow of sundown and sunrise, when the sun's rays bestowed vivid colors that shined over the mountains. No doubt, Cathy and her comrades sensed that they were being watched by a savvy and highly-skilled opponent, who was rarely, if ever, seen.

This untamed Apache country was quiet and still, betraying the eerie sense that this was an especially dangerous country for any unwary Buffalo Soldier bold enough to enter it. They realized that a band of Apache warriors could suddenly strike or spring an ambush in the most rugged countryside that they had never seen before. This nagging feeling of vulnerability steadily grew among the black soldiers during the relentless trek north, especially since the Fort Cummings column was relatively small. This was an unsettling reality that became more apparent to Company A's soldiers the farther that they distanced themselves from Fort Cummings. The Buffalo Soldiers seemed almost to have been swallowed up by the immense size of the vast landscape around them, while they continued marching mile after mile in a northerly direction. Clearly, in this land of great natural beauty, a small column of blue-uniformed soldiers could become lost and never seen again.

Like her 38th Infantry comrades, Cathy Williams might have wondered if she would ever see Fort Cummings again, while the column pushed deeper into unfamiliar terrain of Apache country. When the Buffalo Soldiers marched near an elevation or in crossing a creek, Cathy no doubt worried if her life might be suddenly cut short by a hail of bullets or arrows from an unseen Apache ambush. While marching toward an uncertain future and perhaps a grisly end for all she knew, young Private William Cathay might have now contemplated her fate, and the strange course of her life that had brought her to this isolated place so deep in Apache country and so close to danger.

Therefore, under the stress and hardships of active campaigning in Apacheria, this young soldier from Missouri might have thought more about her life's course and the past decisions of her life. Had she survived slavery's horrors and campaigning with Union Armies on both sides of the Mississippi only to get killed in an Apache ambush when so far from family, friends, and home? If so, then she would be buried in some unknown location in New Mexico's wilds that family members would never know about. Cathy Williams probably had not expected the possibility of encountering such an unkind fate in the remote reaches of New Mexico, when she had signed up as a Buffalo Soldier at Jefferson Barracks more than 1,000 miles to the northeast.[140]

But in fact, Cathy had no need to worry if she would survive the upcoming strike on the Apache village and at a time when a band of infantrymen were much more vulnerable than cavalry in such a disadvantageous tactical situation. As developed at General Sheridan's headquarters far from the harsh realities of campaigning in inhospitable and unfamiliar terrain, the overly-ambitious plan of three separate columns converging simultaneously on a hidden village situated in the mountains was simply too complex and impractical.

Lieutenant Leggett wisely avoided a potential ambush by refusing to march his thin column of weary and nervous infantrymen through a deep canyon near the village. This savvy Civil War veteran now made another smart decision. He prudently awaited reinforcements before venturing forth into the rugged mountainous terrain that was ideal for an ambush: the specialty of the cunning Apache, who were the consummate warriors. The lieutenant realized that the column dispatched all the way from Fort Cummings was entirely too small for the dangerous mission that it had been assigned. And, of course, the top leaders at headquarters knew nothing about the rough terrain or the dangers of a small column of black soldiers passing slowly through this rocky canyon that they had never seen before.

As Lieutenant Leggett now fully realized, the fort's commander had basically only sent out a token force of Buffalo Soldiers to comply with the unrealistic orders from headquarters, because he was seemingly more concerned about Fort Cummings's (and his own) safety. Consequently, far too many soldiers still remained at Fort Cummings. In this sense, Lieutenant Leggett, Cathy Williams, and the remainder of Company A had become little more than pawns, and ones that might never return to Fort Cummings in consequence.

Therefore, Leggett early realized that he could not afford to take any unnecessary risks with so small a force, because they might prove fatal to the entire command. Besides possessing the advantages of familiarity with this region, especially in the clever art of setting up ambushes, Apache warriors also possessed the tactical advantage of being mounted that allowed them to suddenly strike out of thin air. Clearly, this small infantry command of black infantry and their white officers were vulnerable to a mounted attack as Lieutenant Leggett fully realized, while so far from Fort Cummings and reinforcements.

Cathy and her comrades, consequently, remained under cover after the sun set over the mountains to bestow a red and yellow glow, maintaining defensive positions in the cold blackness. For good reason, Cathy and the other Buffalo Soldiers were ordered not to light fires so as to not betray their exact positions, because they were now close to the targeted village. Private Cathay endured the cold nights without the warmth of fires or hot coffee: a situation that later caused her to suffer from an illness before the end of January, after the command's return to Fort Cummings. All the while when positioned near the Indian village, Cathy and her comrades maintained a strict vigilance and gripped their muskets tightly in case the Apache warriors ascertained the small command's vulnerability and suddenly struck.

And if Company A's soldiers lacked proper clothing (which was very likely the case because they had been assigned to such a remote frontier fort at the end of a lengthy supply line) to stay warm during winter nights in this mountainous region, then the Buffalo Soldiers endured even more frigid misery. However, in this regard, Cathy Williams may well have been relatively more fortunate than her comrades, because extra layers of baggy clothing had long been part of her disguise in wintertime to conceal her sex. But almost certainly, what she could not disguise was a fear about her fate if captured by the Apache, who would then discover that Private William Cathay was a young woman.

Lieutenant Leggett fully realized that the Fort Cummings column, already too small for succeeding in its mission, was not supported as planned. The Fort Cummings troops were to have united with a column from Fort Bayard, but these soldiers never arrived for the anticipated united effort to descend upon the hostile Apache village, while the other column was to strike from the opposite direction. Fortunately for Cathy Williams and her comrades, Leggett demonstrated tactical flexibility and strategic insight. He wisely made his own decision depending on the then existing tactical situation on the ground, because the expected Fort Bayard column continued to be nowhere in sight. Knowing that his task force was much too small and too far advanced in an overly exposed position, Leggett ordered the Buffalo Soldiers to turn around and march back to Fort Cummings. Making a smart decision, he cancelled his part in the offensive operation, because it had become just too risky for this small column to continue forward on its own.

With muskets on right shoulders, Cathy Williams and her fellow Buffalo Soldiers formed in column. They then began to march south toward Fort Cummings, moving by the same route that they had recently come. These mostly former slaves, especially Cathy, were thankful that their small force had not been ambushed and destroyed as Lieutenant Leggett had feared.

Meanwhile, the two other columns failed to deliver the anticipated blow to surprise the village in its remote mountain sanctuary, because the Apaches had caught wind of the converging movement of slow-moving bluecoat soldiers. As so often in the past, the wily Apache had abandoned their village by the time that the two converging columns arrived to strike. Therefore, this was just another wasted effort of the United States troops deep in Apache country, which was an all too familiar experience for America's soldiers, black and white.

Like Lieutenant Leggett and his 38th United States regulars, the two columns of frustrated soldiers likewise turned around and marched back to their respective forts, after failing to achieve their tactical objective. But the Buffalo Soldier infantrymen, including Private William Cathay, had proved hardy and durable during this demanding Apache campaign deep into the most inhospitable of environments during wintertime.

Indeed, Cathy Williams had performed well during this most demanding of campaigns, doing her duties as required and successfully meeting each new challenge. She had fulfilled her obligations to her comrades and commander during this Apache Campaign so far removed from Fort Cummings' safety.

Had Cathy fought the Apache as had been fully anticipated during this risky campaign, then she would have continued an ancient legacy of warrior women, including the courageous Argive (a citizen of the ancient Greek land known as Argos located in the fertile plain—known as Argolis--in the southern Peloponnese and a rival of Sparta) women. These women warriors had defended their beloved city with an "impulsive courage, divinely inspired" against legendary Spartan invaders, who were the elite Greek fighting men of the ancient world.

Because these ancient Greek women had saved the day, the Argives thereafter celebrated these brave heroines at an annual festival on the battle's anniversary by "putting the women into men's [warrior] tunics and cloaks and the men in women's dresses and head-coverings."[141]

Cathy Williams would have almost certainly identified with the resolve and courage of these ancient female Greek warriors, who had astounded the fighting men on both sides with their valor in a crisis situation to create an ancient legend.

Another Liberating Moment

When Cathy Williams had been freed by Union troops at Jefferson City in mid-June 1861, she had felt that this exhilarating moment of liberation could not be possibly equaled by any other experience. As mentioned, freed slaves called this joyous time of release from slavery's bonds, the day of jubilee. [142]

She was mistaken in the assumption that everything would be relatively easy in her life once freed, which was perfectly logical to have assumed under the circumstances partly because she was young (only a teenager) and had known only in slavery. Of course, Cathy had viewed her decision to join the Buffalo Soldier regiment barely a year and a half after the Civil War's end as still another liberating moment because it was also all about escaping a lowly existence in life.

But after what she had experienced as a humble private while serving in the 38th United States Infantry over an extended period, Cathy was very much of a changed person in attitude and spirit by this time. She was no longer the same young woman in her early twenties, who had enlisted at Jefferson Barracks with high hopes. Nearly two years of hard duty in the United States Army, a difficult and thankless undertaking, had lost much of its appeal to her by this time. Even worse, the long marches, cold nights, and unsanitary remote forts on the western frontier proved damaging to Cathy's health that had become more fragile by this time.

Wearing a blue uniform no longer represented something special, as it had when she had first enlisted. Significantly, as a person, Cathy Williams had evolved considerably by this time. Cathy had grown a great deal as a person in the last nearly two years of faithful service in the United States military. Consequently, this female Buffalo Soldier now looked at things quite differently than before. If nothing else, Cathy was resilient and flexible. She had always proved highly-adaptive in regard to facing new situations (almost chameleon–like in this regard), and this time was no different. After nearly two years of excellent service in the ranks of Company A, 38th United States Infantry, Cathy Williams had become a person who now little resembled that more naïve young woman, who had entered the recruiter's office with the burning desire to fulfill a lofty dream on Thursday November 15, 1866.[143]

Indeed, after her Buffalo Soldier experiences, Cathy Williams had matured during the last nearly two years in ways that she had not originally expected, when she had first enlisted at Jefferson Barracks that now seemed like ages ago. Most of all, military life—its endless rules, personality clashes, and backdoor politics that caused deep internal divisions and endless infighting, including ugly racial animosities —had lost its appeal to her by this time. Quite simply, she had grown far beyond that more innocent stage of her life when she had first enlisted, acquiring new insights about life in general. Cathy had become aware of the Faustian Bargain that she had made for service in the United States military and its increasingly high personal costs: mental, emotional, and physical. As mentioned, the demanding duty on the western frontier had seriously affected Cathy's health, which continued to suffer from exhaustive duty and excessive demands, especially during the recent Apache campaign.

Other factors explained the depth of Cathy's disillusionment with military service by this time, because she was not a quitter by nature. In general because of her natural maternal instincts and sense of compassion derived partly from her experiences as a slave and a person living on the margins of society, Cathy was naturally more sensitive than her more roughhewn male peers in regard to the plight of more vulnerable women and children regardless of race. She more readily felt a sense of uneasiness, if not repulsion, at America's growing aggression against indigenous people, who only wanted to be left alone to live free lives like generations of their ancestors. Cathy now realized that these were a beleaguered darker-skinned people who were not unlike African Americans, who had suffered for so long because of color. At some point during her service as a Buffalo Soldier, therefore, she began to identify more closely with the Indians' dismal plight and desperate fight for survival as a distinct people.

Cathy now understood that this national and race-based conquest—the so-called "winning of the West"—was in many ways comparable to slavery: the classic case of the exploitation of the land, its people, and resources for the profit of a relatively few whites of power, wealth, and privilege. Therefore, Cathy Williams suddenly found herself burdened by two dark historical legacies (slavery and conquest) that nagged at her moral conscience and inner soul. Whereas the Civil War had been the North's moral crusade to liberate slaves, the conquest of the West was about subjugating indigenous people, who were relatively weak in regard to overall manpower, especially when divided by ancient tribal rivalries. Consequently, this was now an entirely different situation in strictly moral terms as when Cathy had marched with the boys in blue in a support role during the Civil War years.

For such reasons that Cathy Williams now understood more intimately than when she had first enlisted, a certain affinity had long existed between Indian and black people throughout the course of American history. Both were people of color who faced a common antagonist who sought to dominate them for their own benefit. Cathy now understood how the United States fighting men, including the Buffalo Soldiers, were merely used as the head of the spear for imperialistic and expansionist designs against Indian people in a "total war" as developed by ruthless leaders, Generals Grant,

Sherman, and Sheridan. After all and as mentioned, these were experienced leaders who had destroyed the South's manpower-short armies in a brutal war of attrition. This same destructive formula for achieving decisive success was now turned upon the Indian people.

Therefore, the Great Plains people were about to suffer the same tragic fate as the Southern people: complete subjugation by superior military might and an even more merciless war of extermination against their primary resource that formed the basis of a nomadic culture, the buffalo. In this sense, Cathy could no longer view the men in blue as liberators, as when they had freed her from slavery. Clearly, everything in her world had dramatically changed for Cathy Williams, including the meaning of right and wrong, because the times and the overall situation had changed dramatically since the Civil War. At that time when she had first seen soldiers in blue uniforms, there had been no questions or doubts about which side was right and wrong.

Significantly, this young woman had become more politically conscious and keenly aware that this war against native people was unjust from a strictly moral lens. She now realized that America's war was now waged to destroy the warriors' support system that sustained the existence of women and children that explained why the warriors fought so fiercely in defending all that they loved.[144]

Quite simply, the boys in blue had now become more oppressors rather than liberators, because their primary mission was to subjugate a free native people, who owned ancestral lands now coveted by whites and their Machiavellian government in Washington, D.C. Private William Cathay had seen first-hand exactly what kind of ugly war was transpiring in the remote section of New Mexico. What could not be denied was that this transformation of moral purpose had made the Buffalo Soldiers into essentially the unwitting pawns of imperialistic designs of pushing native people aside and then forcing them to remote western reservations, where they could be controlled by the military and the government.

As if their skins were not black, the Buffalo Soldiers were fighting in behalf of the national conquest and domination of still another people of color. This was an unsettling realization to a more politically astute (especially which combined with her already-existing social consciousness rooted primarily in having experienced slavery's horrors) and racially-sensitive Cathy Williams. Cathy's eyes had been opened wider by her

Buffalo Soldier service, and she saw the harsh realities that could not be denied.

With an even greater awareness in which she saw blacks and Indians (and all dark-skinned people) as victims of imperialistic aggression of a powerful Anglo-Saxon people on the relentless march west under the nationalist banner of Manifest Destiny, Cathy could now identify with the sentiments of one Sioux woman. A member of the largest tribe on the Northern Great Plains, the woman saw blacks and whites in blue uniforms as essentially the same because, "Buffalo Soldiers and the white man killed my people."[145]

One of the myths fostered by even leading Buffalo Soldier historians and writers was that the affinity and identification between blacks and Indians were nonexistent, as if the bonds of color played no influential role. But such was not the case, because these shared bonds had long existed and even before the American Revolution.[146]

As she had learned from her western frontier experiences, Cathy Williams now realized the truth of the words of one historian, who concluded how the United States Army during the post-Civil War period was "not so much a little army as a big police force."[147] Indeed, like other Buffalo Soldiers, Cathy now saw that the blue uniformed soldiers, black and white, were no longer engaged in a holy crusade to save the Union, destroy slavery, and bring significant social change in America. Instead, the Buffalo Soldiers were now the enforcers of arbitrary and cynical dictates from the White House and military headquarters, where war-hardened men made decisions that dictated the fate of native people.

To Cathy's consternation, United States soldiers were attempting to deny freedom to the ever-independent Indian people, who were fighting to defend an ancestral homeland and nomadic way-of-life under severe threat. Because of Lieutenant Colonel George Armstrong Custer's attack (ordered by headquarters) on the peaceful Southern Cheyenne village of Black Kettle on the Washita River, located in today's Oklahoma, in late November 1868 that resulted in the deaths of an estimated 40 women and children, one disgusted white Indian agent turned in his resignation to end his career because: "I must emphatically pronounce [Custer's attack was] wrong and disgraceful."[148]

At this time, therefore, Cathy Williams now understood a host of ugly truths about military service on the western frontier, fueling greater disillusionment in wearing the uniform of blue. Other soldiers, including high-ranking officers, had also derived these same conclusions. A disillusioned General George Crook, a Civil War veteran experienced in battling the Apache in Arizona by 1876, concluded that fighting Indians, especially the most fierce warriors of the southwest, was "the most dangerous, the most thankless, and most trying" of all America's wars.[149]

Slavery in the Southwest

The fact that black soldiers (the head of the spear of America's military on the western frontier along with white troops) were themselves used merely as tools of America's race-based Manifest Destiny and expansion was viewed by African Americans with increasing disgust. Having been victims of slavery for most of their lives, blacks in general were increasingly sensitive to the unfortunate plight of the Great Plains Indians, who faced not only losing their homes, lives, and lands (the initial fate of their enslaved African ancestors, including Cathy Williams' own relatives), but also the grim prospect of slavery in regard to the Apache.

What Cathy Williams had no doubt also discovered in the Southwest was that slavery was still alive and well: not black, but Indian slavery. The Spanish had long continued an especially horrific tradition of launching slave-catching raids to supply the lucrative slave markets of Mexico City with Indian captives. Beginning in the 1620s, Spanish governors of New Spain had ordered the seizure of Apaches in northern Mexico's mountains to work as slaves in the silver mines to the south. In fact, slavery was the most forgotten source of the Apache's legendary hatred of the Spanish that fueled generations of bitter conflict.

Spanish governors had even sold peaceful Christianized Indians as slaves to work in the hellish mines, because of their greed to reap greater riches from this supply of cheap labor. Spanish slave-raids were also launched to gain slaves for the domestic market in Mexico City throughout the seventeenth century, because the Spanish wealthy class desired permanent housekeepers and gardeners. However, including in the mid-nineteenth century when Cathy Williams served in the West, the "enslavement of Apache captives [by the Spanish and then private Mexican citizens became just another ugly fact] of life on the northern frontier."[150]

During the Civil War when Cathy Williams had provided support to Union Armies, one Confederate general advocated an ambitious plan for selling captured Navajos and Apache into slavery. Actually, lifelong servitude was actually perhaps a more humane fate compared to the often more popular (among top military leaders and much of the American public —especially in the West —who desired the Indians' elimination) policy of outright extermination. A cruel economic factor was part of the ruthless equation of subjugation. One Confederate officer, who fought in part for the goal of enslaving blacks and Native Americans, wanted "to kill all adult Indians and sell the children to pay for the cost of killing their parents."[151]

Cathy Williams almost certainly learned that the Spanish, Mexicans, and Americans had been initially much alike in regard to their harsh treatment of Apache and blacks for centuries. Indian slavery was so common in New Mexico by the Civil War's conclusion that President Andrew Johnson had been forced to take action. He had ordered his military commanders to attempt to put an end to the brutal Indian slavery trade at a time when the prices for slaves reached new heights. Latinos and whites had long bought Indian slaves, including children, mostly for domestic services in private homes.

In March 1867 and months after Cathy Williams had enlisted at Jefferson Barracks, Congress passed a new act, "An Act to Abolish and Forever Prohibit the System of Peonage in the Territory of New Mexico and Elsewhere." But slavery continued to thrive unabated because it was a well-established tradition that had long thrived across the Southwest, including when Cathy Williams served as a Buffalo Soldier in New Mexico.

Quite likely, she herself had seen Apache and Navajo slaves, including children, serving in white and Mexican households at isolated rancheros in New Mexico and elsewhere in the Southwest–a disturbing sight that must have brought back the dark memories of her own searing experiences in slavery, when she had been "a house girl" in Missouri.[152]

Fighting against a dark-skinned people defending their own sacred homeland and the sickening presence of Indian slavery were undoubtedly twin factors that played a part in Cathy's final decision to end her career as a United States soldier. While slavery no longer existed in the South or her native Missouri, she had also certainly discovered that the most hated institution and greatest evil of her lifetime was still thriving in the New Mexico Territory. During this period, an estimated 2,000 Apache and Navajo, including children, were held in lifetime bondage in this southwestern land, where she served in a blue uniform.[153]

Private William Cathay also had learned that President Lincoln's promise of equality in the Emancipation Proclamation had proved to be a hollow promise in regard to slavery in the Southwest, and that the vast majority of former black slaves remained little more than "slaves" of an institutionalized economic, social, and political structure firmly set in a lowly place in the Deep South.

Rather than a proclamation based purely on moral and humanitarian motivations, that historic document issued from Lincoln's White House had stemmed more from war-related priorities of 1862 and 1863, when the life of the Union was at stake. These foremost priorities included reinvigorating the northern war effort by bestowing a righteous moral motivation to fuel patriotism and fortify the flagging resolve of the northern people to prosecute the war to the end, while negating the possibility of foreign (England and France) intervention in support of the Confederacy and tapping into tens of thousands of black troops to serve. Lincoln's extensive utilization of former slaves, therefore, helped to open the doors to decisive Union victory in 1865, but not to full racial equality.

Therefore, not only losing faith in the United States military, Cathy Williams had also lost some of her once boundless faith in America 's lofty utopian visions (often more rhetorical than practical or realistic) of full social and political equality that were still out of reach for blacks and women. For a host of reasons, including the increased racial tensions and even open hostility that had risen to the fore between Buffalo Soldiers and racist white officers on the southwest frontier, she had finally made up her mind in regard to another important decision that transformed her life: it was now time to cut her ties and permanently leave the military service and the blue uniform that she had once loved.

But this decision called for developing still another novel plan by Cathy, after she and her Company A had been transferred from Fort Cummings to Fort Bayard in early June 1868. As mentioned, health factors were still another consideration for her to leave the military, because Cathy continued to suffer from numerous physical ailments. Her physical conditions worsened, and there were days when Cathy was unable to perform her required duties. Consequently, for a host of reasons, she planned to get out of the military by the quickest and easy way possible. Such a sudden departure from the military called for a surefire short-cut solution to end this once meaningful chapter of her life (a true personal odyssey), which was entirely unique in the history of the United States military.

Now eager to depart military service on the southwestern frontier, Private William Cathay had to resort to drastic action. Feigning an illness for the first time in her Buffalo Soldier service to go against her own value system that had long made her a "good soldier"(in her own words), the now healthy Cathy allowed her sex to be discovered by the post surgeon at Fort Bayard. This, of course, was the certain guarantee for a quick release from military service. Her much coveted release from the United States military was still another form of Cathy's winning her personal freedom on a day that she never forgot on another important day of her life, October 14, 1868.[154]

As Cathy explained the problematic situation at Fort Bayard that resulted in a long-awaited day of personal liberation to start all over again in a life full so many twists and turns: I "finally got tired and wanted to get off. I played sick [for the first time], complaining of pains in my side, and rheumatism in my knees. The post surgeon found out I was a woman [evidently in examining her side when required pants removal] and I got my discharge."[155]

Finally, Cathy's masterful ruse that had worked magnificently for nearly two years was finally over on this Sunday, October 14, 1868. However, a personal dream had died for Cathy, when she had decided that it was finally time for it to all finally come to an end. But there were other dreams for her to embrace in the future. Once this young woman made up her mind, there was no going back. For Cathy Williams, her successful ruse of nearly two years of service was certainly a most bittersweet experience in the end.

For the only female Buffalo Soldier in the annals of American history, there would be no fond farewells, affectionate good-byes, or best wishes for Cathy Williams. There would be no thanks for her faithful service as a "good soldier" for an extended period: her words that revealed a sense of pride in what she had accomplished against the odds and all expectations. Cathy, however, felt that she had little choice but to leave and acted accordingly. As mentioned, her failing health also had been a key factor in Cathy's final decision to leave the military. Even her captain had become frustrated that Cathy had been often sick and unable to perform her required duties as a Company A member.

As could be expected, the discovery of her true identity sent shock waves through Fort Bayard and the small garrison. Cathy's male comrades of the 38th United States Infantry even became angry at her. They believed that they had been fooled for nearly two years by her clever ruse, which indeed was the case. Therefore, to Cathy's shock, the sharp backlash, even from her old friends in blue uniforms, was severe.

In fact, it was beyond anything that she had expected. She was hurt by the extent of this hostile reaction, because the "men all wanted to [now] get rid of me." This reaction hastened her early exit from the fort, where she evidently, at least initially, expected to stay as a civilian for a brief period. Of course, some men, the common Buffalo Soldiers as opposed to white officers, were angered because they realized that they had missed countless sexual opportunities with Cathy on many lonely nights.

Final Departure

Therefore, it was once again time for Cathy Williams to simply go away as seemingly everyone, including old friends, now desired at Fort Bayard. After she received her final orders and back pay from the United States military, it was time for her to depart Fort Bayard and never to return. That "good soldier" named Private William Cathay was no more, only a fading memory and an obscure name of a young soldier that had gained a permanent place in a military service record located at the National Archives, Washington, D.C.

At long last, the service of the first and only documented black woman to have ever served in the United States Army during the nineteenth century was suddenly over: quite possibly, this was perhaps the most masterful ruse ever played on the United States military establishment during the post-civil war period. But despite the unexpected backlash for old friends at Fort Bayard that had cut her soul like a knife, Cathy Williams simply walked away from her military service with a certain sense of pride in what she had achieved, after having succeeded in doing what no one thought was possible for a young woman to achieve.

Clearly, it was now time for the next chapter of Cathy's life to unfold, and she was now more than eager for a new and significant change in her life. Cathy had already achieved all that she had sought to accomplish during her service as a Buffalo Soldier. In this sense, Cathy's military career had been a satisfying one in terms of achieving her personal goals and proving to herself that she could live-up to the highest standards of the United States regular army: no small accomplishment.

At this point after nearly two years of service, there existed no other obtainable goals for this young Buffalo Soldier, who had already achieved far beyond what anyone had imagined possible for a young African American female. She now looked forward to a truly independent life far from unbending rules and regulations of the United States military: a life that was too confining and restrictive for a free-spirited and independent-minded young woman over an extended period.

Consequently, true individual freedom now beckoned to Cathy almost as much as when she had been a slave back in Missouri. Therefore, Cathy Williams now embraced a set of new goals and ambitions by focusing on her new life outside of the military establishment for the first time since she had been liberated by Union troops in June 1861. In her own words: "I wanted to make my own living and not be dependent on relations or friends."[156]

Finally escaping the military establishment's strict restrictions was not a dead end for this former slave woman, as it would seem at first glance. However, a good many stiff challenges lay ahead because she had willingly forfeited all regular pay (monthly), clothing, shelter, and daily rations that had been long forthcoming to her as a soldier. Even more of a disadvantage, Cathy was now located far from family and friends in a remote part of the southwestern frontier, and she was not in overall good health. Therefore, the future was not as bright as it had initially seemed to her.

However, new hopes shortly replaced any existing self-doubts and the boring monotony of military life, which had long stifled Cathy's individual spirit and creativity. In fact, her decision to finally have her sex discovered by the post surgeon at Fort Bayard only signaled a bright new beginning for Cathy Williams, who now resumed her true identity with renewed enthusiasm.

Almost certainly for Cathy, this change back to her old identity provided a great sense of personal relief that resulted in the lifting of a heavy psychological burden and considerable stress that had a cumulative effect. In fact, the task of maintaining her ruse to a high degree of perfection for such a lengthy period might have also played a part in negatively affecting her health in the past. After all, she had been living a lie for nearly two years.

For a young woman like Cathy who had all of the normal personal feminine needs beyond the strict requirements of a military life, service in a Buffalo Soldier regiment had become not only a dead end, but also an oppressive one. She could no longer tolerate the toxic brew of seemingly endless politics, racism, and pettiness that had made her military existence miserable. Clearly, Cathy badly needed a fresh start in life far from the military establishment's restrictions that had long smothered her spirit and individualism. Most of all, she could once again live her life as Cathy Williams and not Private William Cathay of Company A, 38th United States Infantry.

All in all, departing the United States Army was also an escape from a racially-charged situation—abusive white officers and institutionalized discrimination —that had become unbearable for Cathy, and perhaps even a life-saving one (certainly a spirit-saving and psychologically-significant release) for her. Even some high-ranking white officers on the western frontier often failed to escape the most negative efforts of their chosen profession—especially arduous and thankless duty on the Great Plains—by simply taking off the blue uniform and walking away with their remaining health and sanity, before it was too late. Western frontier service could be fatal to heart and soul of a once idealistic young soldier, as realized by Cathy in the end. Cathy Williams accomplished this new personal goal of simply surviving by stepping away with a measure of dignity and the pressing desire to preserve her health, when she realized that the military life on the southwestern frontier had become too toxic for her.

Some distressed officers committed suicide because of their total disillusionment with army politics and unrewarding service on the bleak Great Plains. This tragic last resort was preferable to quite a few troubled enlisted men and officers, who served on the western frontier, including members of Custer's 7th Cavalry.[157] Captain Frederick William Benteen, a Civil War veteran who was one of Custer's top 7th Cavalry officers (senior captain) at the Little Big Horn disaster of June 25, 1876, penned in a letter how a "Capt. Thompson . . . had blown his brains out in camp,–cause, sickness, whisky, etc."[158]

By departing the military establishment in mid-October 1868 and leaving Fort Bayard never to return, Cathy Williams at least avoided this possible tragic fate. Indeed, a high level of suicide existed among service members (then and today in the United States military, especially serving far from home and family). This was one of the forgotten means of death for American fighting men on the western frontier.

However, in the end, Cathy Williams was destined to pay a high price for her nearly two years of military service and her final decision to leave the military and accept the equally stiff challenges of a free life as an ordinary civilian. She now decided to remain on her own while living on the western frontier, going her own way once again. This was a risky decision because of her limited resources, lack of personal connections in the civilian realm, and when far from family, while a single woman on her own: the antithesis of the secure military environment that Cathy had known for years and since her June 1861 liberation from slavery.

But something significant in Cathy Williams' life would not change, despite the radical alteration of her status, after having put aside her blue uniform to begin her life anew on her own. In the future, she continued to boldly defy the deeply-entrenched restrictions of her male-dominated world and prevailing conventions of a patriarchal society that had seemingly been expressly designed long ago (patriarchal legacies that stemmed from western Europe, especially England) to keep her in a lowly place for the rest of her life.[159]

Nevertheless, Cathy had willingly taken the risk of leaving the military establishment and a guaranteed stable existence and security behind forever. However, and most importantly, Cathy Williams continued to be highly-adaptive and flexible, boding well for the future. These invaluable personal qualities, especially surviving on the western frontier, enhanced her chances for succeeding in civilian life.

Cathy certainly agreed with the words of teenage Emma Edmonds, a Civil War soldier while disguised as a male. She explained her decision to live a life in male clothing (wearing pants in this case that primarily defined the visual differences between the sexes), because it presented an unprecedented opportunity for her to "step into the glorious independence" of a male identity. Ironically, Cathy's personal freedom now called for exactly the opposite: leaving a male identity behind by once again become Cathy Williams, which was now even more liberating. Assuming her old female identity had finally once again made Cathy a whole person, after nearly two years of playing a difficult part like an accomplished actress in keeping her greatest and most intimate secret.[160]

Just as Cathy Williams had first embarked upon a new life as a Buffalo Soldier on November 15, 1866 at Jefferson Barracks, so she now prepared to enter an entirely new life on her own on the western frontier. Quite simply, complete personal freedom (not obtainable while campaigning with Civil War Armies or during her service as a Buffalo Soldier) had beckoned to Cathy more than ever before. As she desired and on her own terms which was no small accomplishment in itself, Cathy had fulfilled her latest ambition by leaving the military life behind forever and having no regrets in her abrupt departure from the 38th United States Infantry. A fresh start and a new day once again now called to Cathy Williams as never before, and her life would never be the same.[161]

Chapter V: Gambling in Once Again Going Her Own Way in Life

Cathy Williams felt secure in her decision to stay in the West that she had grown to love by this time. But she would have to now carve a new life out for herself on the western frontier well outside of the military world in which everything (shelter, clothing, regular pay, food, etc.,) that was necessary for survival had been provided to her for nearly the last two years. Therefore, Cathy Williams would now have to survive on her own, while saddled with a host of disadvantages.

For true equality and any chance for a decent independent life, she could no longer depend on the United States, its much-celebrated Constitution, high-minded proclamations, or self-serving military and civilian leaders. A hard-earned lesson, Cathy Williams had discovered that true equality was still out-of-reach and only a vague dream for a young African American woman who had once been a slave.

In regard to ex-slaves across America, the republic had failed to live-up to its most enlightened and cherished principles in regard to having bestowed full equality to former slaves. When it came to black people in general, an entire different reality existed far beyond the republic's lofty egalitarian rhetoric about freedom for all that had long drawn so many hopeful immigrants to America's shores. After October 14, 1868, the soldier once known as Private William Cathay was no more except a name in outdated regimental muster rolls of Company A, 38th United States Infantry. Most of all, Cathy now fully realized that she could depend only upon one person in the future of succeed in life, herself.[162]

As with others who had boldly defied societal values and convention in a strict patriarchal society, so Cathy Williams had to pay an inevitable high price for what were widely viewed as her transgressions and open defiance against white societal expectations about race and gender. No doubt Cathy thanked her lucky star for having gained her military discharge to escape the dysfunctional environment dominated by an ultra-conservative power structure and petty politics that she had grown to detest with all her heart. Clearly, Cathy was not one to conform permanently to group thought or a hierarchical organization based upon like-minded individuals with comparable agendas and goals. As Cathy had learned as a lowly private, this sterile military environment was barren of individuality and freedom of thought, because a non-thinking conformity had been required above all else.

For Cathy Williams in the long run, consequently, it was best for her physical and psychological health, self-esteem, and personal dignity to move far away from remote military installations like Forts Cummings and Bayard. As mentioned, Cathy almost certainly avoided a dismal personal fate by departing military service just before the second year anniversary of her enlistment. Even the fates of some Buffalo Soldier Medal of Honor winners ended sadly on the remote western frontier. After having served for decades because they were career soldiers, these black fighting men simply could not overcome deep-seated prejudice, army politics, and the institutionalized racism in the United States Army.

Therefore, because of reasons that Cathy Williams had grown to hate which helped to ensure her permanent exit from military life without ever looking back, not one of the black Medal of Honor "recipients achieved any post-military successes [because] Most were essentially used up by their service, and all were affected by the lack of opportunity in the pervasively racist climate of their time."[163]

And this overall intolerable situation was even worse for a lowly private without having won comparable distinction. However, such grim realities about race relations in the military were not to doom Cathy Williams to a less rewarding life, because of her own far-sighted decision-making. She had been wise enough to make her own decision to get out of the military once she ascertained the extent of the ugly realities of army life, especially racism, instead of wasting away year after year in an unfulfilling life of seething in frustration, if not bitterness.

Most importantly, Cathy departed the military establishment, when still young (just before her mid-twenties), and at a time when duty on the western frontier was exceptionally harsh, especially for Buffalo Soldiers stationed at lonely western outposts. Significantly, because Cathy Williams' service to her country had been relatively short, she still possessed a sense of bright optimism about life in general that allowed her to embark upon a fresh start and the next chapter of her life with considerable enthusiasm.

But as mentioned, Cathy's decision (literally a Rubicon crossing moment in her life because there was now no turning back) to leave the familiar security of a predictable military life came at considerable risk for an unmarried women on her own in an untamed land. Indeed, the overall western frontier experience was the most difficult for single women who lived on their own without husbands and families. Married women, widows, and young single women were part of the migration west, and they came on foot, aboard wagons, by steamboat, or by railroad. But none of these pioneering women came from the ranks of the United States military like Cathy Williams.

Compared to other women, especially Caucasian females, it was far more challenging to attempt to survive on the western frontier for a young, single woman of African descent, without resources or personal connections. To escape troubled pasts and looking for adventure, many women across America headed west.

But the vast majority of female pioneers pushed west in the hope of finding a better means of supporting themselves and their families. And now as a civilian for the first time in years, Cathy Williams was part of this self-sufficient group of relatively few African American women, who were pioneers in a frontier land with relatively few blacks. The cousin and friend (Cathy's early personal support system in Company A, 38th United States Infantry), who had been regimental members when Cathy had enlisted, were no longer with her during her sojourn to find a better life for herself.

For Cathy by this time, there was much less heady romance in regard to the western experience not only because of its harsh realities for a single woman, but also because she still faced greater odds to overcome because of gender and color. However, Cathy's life in slavery and during the Civil War had bestowed a savvy realism and common sense practicality that had laid a sturdy foundation for a high level of resiliency that boded well for her chances to succeed in the future. Cathy's highly-developed qualities and interpersonal were well-suited for the many future challenges that existed for a single black female without a familial support system. For naïve women with less experience than a world-wise Cathy Williams and by way of comparison, the harsh realities of life on the western frontier often came as a severe blow, resulting in a devastating personal experience.

Therefore, tragedy was often in store for naïve and romantic-minded women, when the bright dream of a better life in a promised land of milk and honey was quickly crushed by the randomness of chance or a cruel fate, including the worst case scenario for a single woman: a sad, tragic life of wandering as a vagrant or a begging women without an adequate means of support. Of course, such a tragic fate ensured greater vulnerability and a descent into the dark outer fringes of western frontier society well-known for its debauchery and cruelty. There was no romance about life in the "Old West" for such unfortunate women, who saw luck and fate turn against them.

Cathy Williams now faced a daunting challenge now that she was on her own living on the western frontier. Relatively few jobs or opportunities of any kind were open to women, especially African Americans. As so often in the past, therefore, she now had to rely upon her own intelligence and instincts to survive, because so many potential pitfalls lay in her path for not only success, but also for simple survival.

Young and single women (black or white) on the western frontier, where males made-up the vast majority of the population, often survived by prostitution. But there was no glamour for a young woman who found herself trapped in this dark profession that was nearly as old as mankind, proving to be a cruel Faustian Bargain in the end. Prostitutes in the West seldom prospered beyond a basic subsistence level, with ill-gotten income barely covering the high costs of food, clothing, housing, and bribes to law enforcement officials. Chances for getting ahead in life by prostitution led to misery, moral corruption, alcoholism, and even suicide.[164]

The ultimate survivor, Cathy Williams possessed higher ambitions for herself, and never lost sight of her lofty goals, however. She was not one to give in to temptation or to take the easy way out of her personal dilemma, even in the toughest times. A central hallmark of her character that had been forged in adversity, Cathy was determined to never give up. Cathy most of all wanted to follow her dreams wherever they led her.

But she was not about to take any shortcuts in attempting to create a new and better life for herself. Consequently, Cathy refused to take the easier route of making quick money by prostitution in a busy mining town that was mostly all-male. Savings that she had accumulated from her monthly salary of $13.00 per month as a Buffalo Soldier now served as an initial financial cushion against any sudden turn of bad luck now that Cathy was on her own. Faithful service for nearly two years in the United States Army had proved conducive to saving money. She had enjoyed a steady income for the first time in her life and for nearly two years, and her savings now bestowed mobility, flexibility, and opportunity.[165]

Cathy had learned to be thrifty from her past experiences as a laundress and cook for the Union Army (meager monetary rewards had been forthcoming from individual soldiers, most likely officers). And now after nearly two years in service as a Buffalo Soldier, she might well have saved more than $200.00. Most significantly, this amount of money would at least buy an extended period of time for her to find steady work and settle in the West.[166]

The fresh opportunity of embarking upon a new life energized Cathy, who knew that she could not afford to fail. She readily accepted new challenges, and this time was no different, because it was now necessary for achieving any future success (personal and economic) that she had long dreamed about obtaining. As mentioned, she had already decided not to return to Missouri partly because of slavery's dark memories stemming from the trauma that she had endured. In addition, Cathy's home state was now more than 1,000 miles away. No longer was the government providing her with transportation as when serving as a Buffalo Soldier. Therefore, she probably had departed Fort Bayard in an empty supply wagon, since she evidently did not know how to ride a horse.

All in all, Cathy found ample good reason to remain in the free spaces of the West. For one, this pristine environment of the western frontier was healthier and more invigorating than back east. Cathy's feelings no doubt can be partly seen in the words of one western migrant, who boasted how the "climate is dry, clear, and invigorating"–the setting and environment that Cathy Williams desired to make a fresh start in life.[167]

Like other women who migrated toward the setting sun at considerable risk, Cathy Williams was now "follow[ing] a dream that hung like a bright star just out of their reach in the purpling skies of the great" west.[168]

Without any connections to family and now truly on her own, Cathy's first priority was to find steady employment at a decent place to live. Cathy, therefore, decided to journey to a place that was already well known to her, Fort Union, in northeast New Mexico. Here, at the largest military installation in the Southwest, she gained steady employment. Cathy now made a living by cooking and washing for a colonel and his family from 1869 and 1870. But Fort Union failed to provide a permanent home for Cathy, because greater opportunity beckoned elsewhere.

She then heard of work to the north in Colorado's mineral-filled mountains, where gold, silver, and coal mining enterprises provided jobs for large numbers of miners. Therefore, she traveled north—probably by wagon rather than on horseback—from Fort Union and across the state line to enter Colorado, leaving New Mexico and a good many memories (good and bad) behind her. As she explained: "I went to Pueblo, Colorado, where I made money by cooking and washing" for two years and into the new decade of the 1870s.[169]

Ill-Fated Marriage

As in facing severe limitations and insurmountable obstacles of a patriarchal society and the stern demands of survival on her own, so Cathy Williams faced another vexing situation (not unlike what military service had become for her to hasten her departure from the service) with a dramatic change that was about to take place in her personal life. By a chance encounter and perhaps when least expected by her, this young black woman was about to meet a man and fall in love in either 1871 or early 1872.

However, quality pickings for a young woman (white or black) among the motley collection of men were especially thin on the remote western frontier. Consequently, finding the right man and a good one was almost impossible in vice-filled "Wild West" towns like Pueblo, Colorado. This frontier town's pre-Civil War antecedents extended back to Fort Pueblo. Pueblo was located on the Arkansas River amid the high desert region at the front range of the Rocky Mountains. Here, a good many drunks, wife-beaters, criminals, cowboys, pimps, killers, psychopaths, misfits, frontiersmen, and simple plow boys from the farm literally ran wild in this lawless environment in which social standards and morals had collapsed, when so far from eastern society. Of course, these seedy types were anything but suitable life partners for Cathy Williams, who was still relatively inexperienced in regard to love relationships, because of the years (more than half a decade) in supporting Union armies and her service as a Buffalo Soldier.[170]

And for a young black woman like Cathy Williams, the chances of finding a decent man on the western frontier were far higher because of the scarcity of other African Americans, until the odds were stacked astronomically high against her. As mentioned, Cathy's friend and cousin were no longer with her like when she had first enlisted at Jefferson Barracks. For a number of such reasons, therefore, Cathy was now personally more vulnerable—psychologically, emotionally and perhaps even spiritually—because she had just served as a Buffalo Soldier for nearly two years in a regiment (a mini-black community that had provided a stable environment like the military establishment). This regiment had served as a surrogate home and family of sort: a highly-disciplined environment that had naturally precluded love or marriage for Private William Cathay.

Of course in personal terms, the sacrifice of a healthy and satisfying personal life was a high price that had been paid by a young woman to emotionally and psychologically pay, but Cathy had no choice under the circumstances. For any chance of getting ahead in life, she simply had to make such necessary personal sacrifices, revealing an ambitious and far-sighted view of life.

Quite likely although it can only be speculated upon because of the relative lack of documentation about her life, one of Cathy's motivations to get out of the military might also have been to open up the possibility of finally pursuing a loving relationship or a husband, if she could find one among the ragtag group of males on the western frontier.[171]

Here, in Pueblo, Colorado, where she cooked and washed clothes for miners and diligently saved her hard-gained earnings that continued to grow because of her thrifty nature and hard work, Cathy Williams finally met a man to her liking. Very little is known about this mysterious man. But because a mixed relationship between black and white would have been highly incendiary in this small town frontier environment that was decidedly provincial and included native Southerners, Cathy almost certainly found an African American male. If so, then he was among a relatively few black men in this remote part of the Colorado frontier. In her own words: "I got married and while there, but my husband was no account. He stole my watch and chain, a hundred dollars in money and my team of horses and wagon. I had him arrested [by Pueblo's sheriff] and put in jail . . . "[172]

What was significant about this unhappy chapter in her life was that it demonstrated not only Cathy's strong will and strength of character, but also revealed that she was smart about money management: unfortunately for her, quite unlike in her choice of a husband, who was wiser in devious ways of the world than Cathy. In contrast to her new-found husband of unknown background, she had accumulated considerable savings (mostly from washing and cooking rather than the remaining financial reserves leftover from her accumulated soldier's monthly pay) that were coveted by her opportunistic husband.

He clearly had an eye for easy money, especially the funds of a trusting new wife, who was a hard-worker and saver unlike himself. As mentioned, Cathy was somewhat personally vulnerable during this period when she was in the difficult process of adjusting to life as a civilian, because she was relatively inexperienced in love relationships, and this man took full advantage of the situation. It is not known, but perhaps what had most attracted the new husband to her was that Cathy operated her own business with skill: a relatively easy target for an unethical husband eager to take advantage of a trusting young woman, who had created a decent life for herself with hard work and business savvy.

Utilizing interpersonal and management skills, she had long negotiated her own work arrangements, laboring responsibly to ensure a steady income flow. This income was not wasted as in the case of so many other men and women who lived only for the moment on the free-wheeling western frontier. Therefore, Cathy had accumulated so much money that the temptation was evidently too great for her husband to resist.[173]

As could be expected for a young woman who had never had an opportunity to embark upon a long-term relationship of a serious nature, a suddenly shattered marriage with what was very likely her first love came as an emotional blow. This sharp setback in her personal life would have been especially the case, if Cathy ascertained that he had married her expressly for the purpose of thief.

Most importantly, she quickly recovered from this harsh emotional blow that would have completely shattered many other women. Throughout her life, Cathy had learned how to put personal missteps and unhappiness behind her, while keeping focused and always looking ahead to a brighter day in the future: well-learned life lessons about to be utilized by her after having made the wrong choice in a husband. Cathy learned the hard way about the pitfalls of a one-sided relationship, a bad marriage (her first), and the high risks of becoming emotionally attached to the wrong man. Cathy would not make the mistake twice in her life.

As throughout her life, Cathy Williams now refused to become a victim in an emotionally-charged and negative situation that was personally devastating. She would not allow herself to be defeated by an inequitable system, including the military, or by any man, even the one who she had loved. Most revealing, Cathy had refused to allow her once strong love felt for her husband to stand in the way of having him arrested to regain her possessions, and then to rid herself of him entirely. Even more and most importantly, Cathy wisely realized that she could not permit herself to fall back into a bad relationship with this unscrupulous man, who could do worse to her in the future, if she ever made the mistake of reconciling with him. [174]

Despite the Pueblo setback of a failed marriage, she continued to look ahead with a cheery optimism that could not be shattered by misfortune or a person of low character. She always tried to make the best of this painful situation, and this meant sacrificing immediate emotional and physical gratifications for the obtaining of a larger goal and more important objective: a rewarding life of dignity and self-respect.

Fueled by a never-say-die attitude, this steely determination that burned deep inside this former slave was additional proof that Cathy would allow no one—not a husband, family member, or officer—to drag her down in life, especially after she had worked so long and hard to rise higher by her own efforts and sacrifices. As in the past, nothing had been given to Cathy Williams, or had come easily to this determined young woman, who knew that she could only rely upon herself to have any chance of succeeding in life.

Cathy Williams had now learned the hard way that her primary life goals could be best achieved, if she remained unmarried and single. Most of all, she was a hardy survivor of a series of unfortunate situations and misfortunes that were no fault of her own. Nevertheless, Cathy never lost her faith for a better day and a brighter future. After having given her all in Cathy's first and only marriage, she now realized that this kind of an emotional and psychological bond was simply too risky, and even dangerous, for an independent-minded and decent woman, who was honest and wore her heart on her sleeve.

Therefore, Cathy never again placed herself in another such personally vulnerable and compromising position by way of marriage, when her emotional and physical health and psychological well-being (not to mention her financial state and future welfare) were at stake.

As so often in her life, Cathy most of all now needed still another fresh start in life after the unraveling of her personal life at Pueblo. Fortunately, for her, the West provided many places where one, especially a former slave and a single woman, could go to make a fresh start: America, the fabled land of endless opportunities and possibilities, was now best represented by the western frontier. Cathy was now in the right part of the country and at the right time.

Now the picturesque country of southeast Colorado situated south of Pueblo beckoned to Cathy Williams, after her failed marriage that haunted and nagged her at her conscience. She must have asked herself how she could have made such a mistake? It was time to move on and leave Pueblo and bad luck behind her. Cathy Williams' quest for a better life was destined to continue to take her on a solitary sojourn and toward a future that was still unknown to her.[175]

A Decent Life in Trinidad, Colorado

The repeated setbacks in her life, especially slavery but including the failed marriage, came as personal blows that would have been sufficient to crush the spirit of many other young women. However, such reversals were nothing new to Cathy Williams, who literally rolled with the punches. She became even stronger as a person and even more resilient by these character-forging experiences and reversals. As in the past, she knew how to recover from severe setbacks and then look forward to a brighter future.

Cathy realized that what was most important was not how many times one fell down in life in suffering personal reversals that were inevitable in life, but how quickly one got back up, while continuing to move forward in life. She knew how to live for the future without dwelling on past failures and mistakes that might totally consume her in a negative way, if she proved mentally weak and allowed a dark past to drag her down. As demonstrated repeatedly throughout the past, Cathy possessed an uncanny ability to bounce back with spirit, demonstrating a great deal of flexibility and adaptive qualities that immensely benefited her, despite all manner of adversity.

Therefore, each new setback in Cathy's life had then led to a better situation than what she had just left behind with no regrets: a cause-and-effect relationship that played a large part in shaping Cathy's strong will and determination to succeed in life. After the sheriff of Pueblo, Colorado, had jailed her husband for stealing her hard-earned savings, Cathy regained her stolen property, including her horses and wagon, which had been originally bought from funds that she had earned and saved. Cathy decision to go straight to the law resulted in a turning point in her life that allowed her to continue her quest for a more rewarding life. Significantly, after having her thief husband arrested and placed in jail, Cathy's regained her stolen possessions which allowed her the means to leave Pueblo forever and a no-good husband behind forever.[176]

Driving a team of horses, she departed the mining town of Pueblo in a wagon, heading south. Once again, she embarked upon a fresh start like so often in the past. Traveling along the Santa Fe Trail which she had already marched down with the 38th United States Infantry in the same direction toward New Mexico, she continued south from the high desert region and toward the New Mexico border. Once again, Cathy was heading toward a fresh beginning at a little frontier town that now provided a new opportunity to her. This town in southeast Colorado was named Trinidad.[177]

After journeying on her own south around 75 miles south of Pueblo, Cathy reached her destination in 1872. In many ways, this was a place—around 900 miles from where she had enlisted as a Buffalo Soldier—which she had been searching for all her life. At long last, Cathy Williams reached her new destination that offered a fresh start in life. Located barely a dozen miles north of the New Mexico border, Trinidad was a special place that Cathy had previously seen before, and never forgot.

Nestled in the foothills of the Rocky Mountains about halfway between Denver and Santa Fe, Trinidad now became Cathy's permanent home in the unspoiled region of southeast Colorado, because so many opportunities abounded in this frontier boom town: a new environment that had drawn her south to Trinidad like a magnet. Although small and isolated, this frontier community was an ideal town for an enterprising young woman like Cathy Williams. Indeed, Trinidad offered her the possibility of making a decent living, thanks to the rise of profitable coal mining and the large number of miners who lived in town.

Because relatively few women resided in Trinidad and most miners were single men, domestic work was in high demand. These miners needed their clothing repaired and washed after each day's labor in the dirty mines. This was an advantageous situation that allowed Cathy to acquire sufficient money to allow for the quick accumulation of funds. Here, in this little town nestled in a valley of the Purgatoire River (known as the River of Souls) with mountain peaks, towering at more than 6,000 feet, overlooking the frontier community, she finally found a good place that entirely suited her. Cathy grew to love the hard-working citizens of this multi-cultural town in the Purgatoire River Valley. The frontier community of Trinidad, situated between the mountain peaks known respectively as Simpson's Rest and Fisher's Peak, provided Cathy Williams exactly with what she was looking for on multiple levels.

To Cathy's liking, the residents represented a broad mix of people from across the West and Europe. They had migrated to Trinidad to labor in the coal mines. Cathy's timing was excellent beyond the fact that good opportunities abounded in Trinidad. In overall terms in regard to the possibilities of a brighter future for the entire community, this period was an exciting time for Trinidad's hard-working citizens. This frontier community was destined to be incorporated as a town on February 1, 1876. The Colorado Territory was about to gain statehood, which finally became a reality in August 1, 1876, and Cathy was destined to witness the birth of a new state.

In late 1875, Cathy Williams' words about her life in Trinidad, located barely 20 miles north of Raton (along the Santa Fe Trail), New Mexico, were illuminating, especially with Colorado's statehood drawing near and the town's official incorporation. An optimistic Cathy revealed not only a sense of jubilation, but also her ambitious nature and strong will to succeed: "I like this town [Trinidad].I know all the good people here, and I expect to get rich [by continuing to work hard and save money] yet. I have not got my land warrant. I thought I would wait till the railroad [Topeka and Santa Fe Railroad, whose terminus was only five miles away from Trinidad by the beginning of 1877 and finally arrived in 1878] came and then take my land near the [railroad] depot. [Land or President Ulysses S. Grant, or Federal Government] Grant owns all this land around here, and it won't cost me anything," because of her military service from 1866 to 1868.[178]

With a steady flow of work and in demand among the locals because of the quality of her labor, Cathy acquired sufficient funds to become financially secure in Trinidad, and more so than at any other time of her life. In addition, some evidence has indicated that she also worked as a nurse at Trinidad.

Year after year, Cathy had continued to closely embrace the core tenets of the American Dream that she refused to let fade away from her grasp: working hard, saving money, and gaining financial stability by increasing the size of her business (washing, sewing, cooking, and nursing), especially when combined with the rising land values in this frontier boom town. Revealing the extent of her happiness, peace of mind, and sense of self-reliance, Cathy emphasized how: "I shall never live in the states again . . . I've got a good sewing machine [probably a Singer Sewing Machine with a patent in 1851] and I get washing to do and clothes to make [and] I want to get along and not be a burden to my friends or relatives."[179]

To explain why she had migrated to Trinidad to make this place her permanent home after an adventurous life of wandering over so much of America beginning in the summer of 1861, Cathy Williams steadily made money, while continuing to dream big. The dream of creating a brighter future was a lifelong pursuit that had long sustained Cathy during slavery's darkest days, the challenges of the Civil War years, and during her Buffalo Soldier service. For all of these reasons, consequently, the year 1876 was the best yet for Cathy.

At this time and as mentioned, the future prospects for Trinidad and Colorado were most promising, especially in regard to official incorporation and statehood, respectively. After what she had already endured in life, Cathy Williams had earned every bit of her personal happiness, success, and contentment that she found at Trinidad. This frontier community suited her easy-going style personality and zest for life, because the western frontier embodied the independent and irrepressible spirit of Cathy Williams, which now soared.

Indeed, far from the restrictive and ultra-conservative world of the United States Army, Cathy's personality and sense of self-esteem blossomed in Trinidad partly because of the "good people," in her own words, of this frontier community that she fully appreciated. At Trinidad, she became more social in part because her business enterprises resulted in a good deal of personal contact and interactions with customers, who then became friends rather than clients. Of course, this refreshing, if not comforting, situation offered a psychological release and the lifting of a heavy burden compared to her tense Buffalo Soldier days of constantly maintaining her secrecy (almost as personally restrictive and confining as life as a Missouri slave) and the omnipresent fear of her gender suddenly being detected.

Here, at Trinidad under the shadow of Raton Mountain, Cathy most likely lived in a small adobe house, one of around 75 such dwellings on "Mexican Hill," among a warm Latino people. Because a new settler (or squatter) could take possession of any abandoned "adobe hut" within the friendly Latino section of town that was a true Christian (Catholic) community, Cathy most likely found a secure and safe place to reside on "Mexican Hill."

This elevation of arid ground was safely located a good distance from the river's flooding in the valley's depths below. Other key advantages of living in the Mexican community appealed to Cathy. Greater personal safety lay in a good number of people who had gathered on "Mexican Hill," as Cathy Williams realized in part from her military experiences. After all, Trinidad, surrounded by mountains, was vulnerable to Indian attack. During an emergency, the sturdy adobe homes of "Mexican Hill" could serve as defensive structures if the Indians suddenly struck.

Because of her training as a Buffalo Soldier and familiarity with firearms, Cathy almost certainly owned a rifle (perhaps even an old Springfield musket like the one she had carried in her old Buffalo Soldier days), or a six-shot revolver—perhaps an Army Colt--that could be turned against Indians, thieves, intruders, and even an angry ex-husband, who might desire revenge for having been imprisoned by Pueblo's sheriff. For safety, the Latinos of Trinidad stayed closely together on their hill community in a separate and insular Hispanic society at a safe distance from the often less tolerant Anglos.

Several hundred Hispanics lived in the "Mexican settlement" on the hill that overlooked the river. Because these Latinos were a people of color of mixed Indian and Spanish heritage and open-minded in regard to race, Cathy fit easily into this distinctive ethnic community of a graceful, kind-hearted people, who sympathized with Cathy's trials in life and her dark past in the miserable depths of slavery. A devout people with large families, they worshipped the Catholic faith with supreme devotion, unlike Cathy who was either a Baptist or Methodist.

Sister Blandina Segale, a zealous Catholic missionary who had migrated to Trinidad in the same year (1872) as Cathy Williams, also loved the kind-hearted and close-knit Latino people of Trinidad in part because of the redeeming qualities of a God-fearing people. She described how everyone "I've met has an innate refinement." Cathy certainly appreciated such admirable characteristics among these Latinos, who she had never lived around before. This was still another new experience in learning about different people and cultures and a most rewarding one for her. This little Colorado mining town, not yet located on any map and still a haven for outlaws who had fled north to escape New Mexico's law enforcers, was segregated. The Anglos lived primarily in the heart of the little frontier community closer to the river unlike the Hispanics, who lived in their separate community located on their own hill.[180]

Trinidad remained turbulent and wild like other western frontier towns during this period. Bat Masterson later served as the town sheriff who sought to clean-up the town's lawless section along the river, especially among the troublesome saloons and brothels, which were breeding grounds for all matter of trouble. Therefore, the Latino community known as "Mexican Hill" was certainly safer for Cathy, who was still single, than the town proper: a situation based on race and class that also explained why she would have preferred to reside in the Hispanic part of town. Wyatt Earp and his brother (while living on both sides of the law, depending on the situation and existing opportunities to exploit), and their cronies eventually rode into town to visit Bat Masterson in late April 1882, when Cathy lived nearby and around age thirty-six.

Now enjoying life more than 550 miles slightly southwest from where she had been born a lowly slave in western Missouri when she had no future prospects at all, Cathy Williams discovered in Trinidad what she had always been looking for in life. In Trinidad situated along the little river, which the Latinos called "Purgatorio," that flowed through the frontier town, she basked in what meant most to her in life at this time: a permanent home, peace of mind, a quiet dignity, and a personally rewarding life among a friendly people, especially the Latinos, who she loved because of their easy-going manner and decent Christian lives based on their devotion to Catholicism and close-knit families.[181]

Chapter VI: America's Centennial 1876 and Cathy Williams' Interview to a St. Louis Reporter

New Year's Day of 1876 meant more than just the start of another year in the life of Cathy Williams, especially in regard to America's storied history. This was the start of a very special year (the long-awaited Centennial of the republic's birth from the forge of revolution against a powerful imperialist monarchy) for the United States, whose population had grown to 46 million in 38 states that spanned from the Atlantic to the Pacific.

This dynamic, young republic was gaining in strength and well on its way to becoming an industrial power. All of this national success was officially celebrated when President Ulysses S. Grant opened the Centennial Exhibition in Philadelphia, Pennsylvania, on May 10, 1876. National pride across America, including the western territories, swelled to new heights during the celebration of this Centennial year.

However, this was a most ill-fated year for the nation's greatest Northern cavalry hero of the Civil War, Lieutenant Colonel George Armstrong Custer. The hot afternoon of June 25, 1876 deep in the Montana Territory witnessed the most complete disaster suffered by American military arms in the nineteenth century, when Custer and his five companies of his 7th Cavalry troopers were wiped out to the last man by overpowering numbers of Sioux and Cheyenne warriors. He had made the mistake of attacking a massive Sioux and Cheyenne village in broad daylight of mid-afternoon with far too few bluecoats.

The flamboyant Custer finally met his match during a dramatic showdown along the Little Bighorn River. Here, deep in the heart of buffalo country below the Yellowstone River, Custer's legendary luck, that had played a part in the Civil War successes, ran out at long last. Custer's death and the systematic destruction of his five 7th Cavalry companies (he had divided his regiment to unleash two offensive efforts to hit opposite ends of the village) shocked the American people like no other military event in the nineteenth century.[182]

As a strange fate would have it, if not for the celebratory mood of the nation during America's Centennial, then the remarkable story about Cathy Williams' life would have remained untold to this day: something entirely lost in a misty past and absent from the pages of history. However, with the New Year of 1876, a greater sense of pride in the achievements of a young republic and its seemingly limitless destiny, including the course of westward expansion, was in the air, including at the frontier mining community of Trinidad.

For whatever reason, a reporter of the *St. Louis Daily Times* just happened to be in Trinidad. He was evidently just merely passing through the small town, while journeying along the Santa Fe Trail for some unknown purpose. But he was an opportunistic reporter who was always looking for ground-breaking news, especially a patriotic one for a major St. Louis newspaper for the advent of the year of 1876. He was a reporter of this "uncompromising Democratic newspaper" of the city located along the Mississippi near where Cathy Williams had first enlisted in the United States Army.

The *St. Louis Daily Times* had been established in St. Louis by three journalists from Dubuque, Iowa, in July 1866. As mentioned, this enterprising journalist was a true news hound with well-honed instincts and eyes that were always alert for any good story. Sometimes a fascinating story suddenly popped out when least expected, and this occurrence was about to happen once again for this reporter in the remote mining town of Trinidad along the quietly flowing river known as the Purgatoire.[183]

With the Centennial Year drawing closer, this *St. Louis Daily Times* journalist especially had his eyes open for a good story with a patriotic flavor to coincide with the New Year's arrival and America's one hundredth birthday. And when he least expected, this reporter stumbled upon a great story while in of all places, dusty Trinidad that seemed to be in the middle of nowhere. In this obscure river valley far from the larger towns of Santa Fe and Denver, he suddenly found a noteworthy story when least expected, thanks to freely-talking townsfolk. Proud of one of their own citizens, they told him about a remarkable life that actually had been a true western odyssey of a most unusual and non-traditional nature.

Indeed, a nearby woman had audaciously served for an extended period as a United States soldier during the course of western expansion, including in Colorado and nearby New Mexico. As these citizens rightly saw it, she had risked her life in helping to keep remote frontier towns like Trinidad safe from Indian attack, while serving as a Buffalo Soldier from 1866 to 1868. Evidently, some women and men (acquaintances and perhaps friends of Cathy) of Trinidad had informed the reporter about this black woman (now in her early thirties), who had served her country in the most unconventional manner. It is not known, but perhaps this journalist, eager to get a news "scoop" for the *St. Louis Daily* had passed around the word in town that he was looking for a good story of a patriotic nature.

As the reporter shortly realized, this was an amazing story that went well beyond his wildest dreams. Besides its obvious patriotic hues that involved arduous military service on the western frontier, including against the fearsome Apache, what made this story most intriguing to the reporter was the female warrior aspect. But this was also a fascinating story about personal commitment to America by a former female slave, who had faithfully served the republic since the early days of the Civil War.

Because of America's deteriorating race relations after Southern leaders had determined to keep former slaves (perhaps Cathy's own Missouri relatives, including her mother if still alive) in a subordinate place in society and economic life, despite the significant gains that blacks had achieved during the Civil War and the Reconstruction Period, then perhaps the publication of Cathy Williams' life story was intended to play a role in eventually helping to bid some of the nation's deepening racial wounds. Clearly, the reporter possessed a number of good reasons to tell Cathy's life story even beyond simply captivating a curious readership. However, this was not a politically-motivated story (to negate the greater possibility of an exaggerated or overly-embellished final product to delight partisan readers) because he wrote for an influential Democratic newspaper, and Republicans had freed the slaves in a righteous crusade to destroy the peculiar institution.
[184]

Making the reporter's job easier, this woman who had once wore a blue uniform with great pride lived nearby: almost certainly in the Latino community of "Mexican Hill," because the small frontier town was segregated (by choice and inclination rather than law). Cathy was obviously proud of her military service record that was almost without a disciplinary blemish for nearly two years. Fortunately, Cathy still possessed her military discharge papers. These official documents, of course, gave instant credibility to this seemingly outlandish story that seemed improbable at first glance. These dated papers were accurate in regard to exact details and official documentation that coincided with what the reporter had been told by townspeople about Cathy's faithful service as a Buffalo Soldier.

Realizing that he needed to conduct a personal interview at her adobe residence that was most likely located on the high ground of "Mexican Hill" above the river that meandered through the town in the green valley below the high ground, this newspaperman knew that he needed to learn the intimate details of Cathy's life story first-hand, but only if he first gained Cathy's confidence. After all, the reporter was white, just like Cathy's former slave-owners and haughty United States officers who had often looked upon her with contempt and disdain because of her color. Like a good newspaperman, he was conscientious and eager to verify the facts to the last detail.

By interviewing this former Buffalo Soldier in person, he would not have to rely on second-hand and perhaps exaggerated stories from those who knew Cathy. As he realized, obtaining information from others, even first-hand, was just too risky to ensure a story's correctness, because embellished accounts guaranteed a distortion of the facts. Clearly, he possessed a strong personal interest to getting to the truth of matters, and to make sure that this rather remarkable story was exactly right. If the stories that he had heard for this woman proved too unbelievable or false, then the reporter would simply walk away from the interview.

Therefore, the *St. Louis Daily Times* man knew that the key to ascertaining the truth was simply to get Cathy to tell him the full story of her life with an easy and relaxed candor. Thanks to a guide (evidently a friend or acquaintance of Cathy or maybe a Latino child who knew her) to lead the way to her home, he was determined to go straight to the direct source of information, and then judge for himself if the story was correct and true. As mentioned, Cathy Williams almost certainly lived in an abode house on "Mexican Hill," which was also known as the "Mexican settlement" that was located a short distance from the heart of town.

At this time, Trinidad only consisted of Main Street, with a few stores and saloons along the dusty thoroughfare, and Commercial Street, with a row of scattered houses for a distance of only about two blocks: both streets, which were transformed into rivers of mud during heavy rainstorms, were short and about equal length. Convent Street led to the small adobe Catholic convent and frontier church, which served the Latinos of "Mexican Hill" and Anglo Catholics in town. This modest Catholic Cathedral had been built in 1866, when Cathy had enlisted in the 38th United States Infantry.

Most importantly for the reporter and the St. Louis newspaper, this was exactly the kind of intriguing story that would make fascinating reading at the beginning of the nation's official Centennial celebration when patriotism was especially high: a tribute to a forgotten military veteran and remarkable woman, who had faithfully served her country with honor.

The fact that Trinidad's residents knew some key details of Cathy's story and spoke of it so openly to the reporter revealed that it was common knowledge, and was fully believed by those who knew her to be a good and truthful woman. Clearly, Cathy had talked about her life to her friends or clients—or both —for whom she washed and repaired clothing. Significantly, this common knowledge about Cathy's Buffalo Soldier record indicated that some of Trinidad's residents (white and Latino) also felt a measure of pride in her military service record on behalf of America.

Significantly, this pride in what she had accomplished against the odds superseded any lingering racism that had so often created such strong divisions among people: one fundamental reason why Cathy Williams loved the town and its relatively open-minded people. This situation most likely indicated that those who knew her story were lower class coal miners and immigrants from English speaking countries, including Ireland, rather than middle or upper class whites.

During this period, Cathy had almost certainly met a wild Ireland-born woman who was nicknamed "Crazy Ann," as she called herself with a sense of perverse pride. "Crazy Ann" survived in Trinidad by shady means in connection with active criminal elements, including perhaps even prostitution. Cathy was clearly part of the common people, mostly the lower and middle classes (white and Latino), especially the large Latino population of "Mexican Hill."

But as verified by her words and actions, the openness of Cathy Williams, who had freely told others about her life experiences as a Buffalo Soldier, also partly revealed that she was well-liked, if not admired to a degree, by the people of Trinidad. She was on very good terms with the people of the local community, which was necessary for conducting a successful small business:

additional evidence that she was part of the lower class (Latino rather than the white miners that would have included some Southerners, perhaps former slave-owners) community of the common people of Trinidad.[185]

For such reasons, this opportunistic reporter knew that he was about to get a very good true story for the *St. Louis Daily Times*. Ironically, the only periodical in town, the white newspapermen of the *Trinidad Enterprise* missed this great story that was right under their noses. It is not known but perhaps race or gender, or both, considerations might have played a factor in their failure to take notice of this remarkable story about one of their own townsfolk. After all and thanks primarily to the fact that this was the Centennial Year and patriotism was running high, the St. Louis reporter demonstrated open-mindedness (thankfully for us and the historical record in this case) to have aggressively pursued the story of the female Buffalo Soldier, or otherwise it would have been lost forever to the annals of American history.

As he wrote at the conclusion of the article in summarizing the facts to confirm the story's validity and his own devotion in making sure that he got this story exactly right, which appeared when printed in the January 2, 1876 edition of the *St. Louis Daily Times*: "In detailing the above the woman sometimes failed to recall dates and the names of places [she had never received as education because of slavery], but otherwise her narrative was smooth and well connected. The TIMES representative returned his thanks for the information and retired with the promise to give a truthful account of what he had been told."[186]

Ironically, Cathy Williams probably never saw the story about her remarkable life that was presented to the American public for the first time in the *St. Louis Daily Times* on the second day of 1876. As a tragic legacy of slavery, even if she had seen the article, Cathy would not have been able to read the words that told about the course of her life, because she was illiterate. But, of course, the possibility existed that someone, perhaps a friend, in Trinidad might have read the story to Cathy, after obtaining a copy of the January 2, 1876 St. Louis newspaper, if that was indeed the case in this remote southeast corner of Colorado.[187]

Despite the many hardships that she had suffered after leaving Buffalo Soldier service in October 1868, Cathy never doubted that she had made the right decision to depart the military, because her life in Trinidad had successfully met her personal and financial expectations. Unlike when serving in America's military establishment, she now continued to live her life on her own terms, without any officers or commanders arbitrarily dictating her fate and future with their endless orders and unbending rules, while manipulating her personal destiny on a mere whim. By departing military service before 1869, she had been spared possible participation in one of the darkest chapters of the Indian Wars on the Great Plains: the massacre of Sioux men, women, and children at Wounded Knee, in southwest South Dakota, on December 29, 1890.

The 7th Cavalry's commander, James W. Forsyth who was a West Pointer (Class of 1851), left a bloody legacy. He had ordered the firing on the defenseless Sioux at Wounded Knee in part to reap blood vengeance for Custer's death and defeat on June 25, 1876. Ironically, when she had served at Fort Riley, Kansas, during her first western frontier assignment, Cathy Williams had seen Major Forsyth. The major had reported to Fort Riley in the summer of 1866, just before Private William Cathay's arrival at her first assignment in the West.

In the end, Cathy Williams paid a very high price for her military service of nearly two years, including active campaigning. By 1890 at the time of the battle of Wounded Knee when she was in her mid-forties, Cathy was in overall poor shape physically. She suffered a number of aliments from her nearly two years of arduous service on the western frontier. As usual, Cathy had to continue to fight in a never-ending struggle for what was rightfully due to her, which was now well-deserved compensation for her military service.

This time she had to fight bureaucratic Washington, D.C. for her pension rights. As a sad fate would have it, the United States Government refused to acknowledge her faithful service of nearly two years and high sacrifice (mainly physical) on behalf of her country with a disability pension. Despite her longtime efforts for recognition of her "good" and faithful service to her country, Cathy's much-needed pension was unfairly denied to her primarily, because of the same old two enemies that she had fought against all her life: discrimination and prejudice because of gender and race. Therefore, as mentioned, she was denied what her male comrades had received for their Buffalo Soldier service.

By this time, Trinidad had "lost its frontier aspect," having grown to more than 9,000 people of all classes and colors. Cathy Williams was among those enterprising residents, who might have obtained their "land warrant" by this time. If so, then Cathy would have owned her own property in Trinidad to become a permanent pioneer on the western frontier: another fulfillment of a dream.

For such reasons and especially because of the best qualities of the "good people" of the isolated frontier community, Cathy's seemingly endless quest for a better place and a more fulfilling life had ended at Trinidad. It is not known how long she lived in the town that she loved like no other, or if she lived to see the arrival of the twentieth century and an industrial and glided age that had been unimaginable when she had been a lowly slave in Missouri so long ago.

Nevertheless, in the end, Cathy Williams had found a personally satisfying and permanent home close to her heart in Trinidad unlike so many other settlers, who had only journeyed to the western frontier in the hope of getting rich and returning back east in disillusionment. Unlike Cathy Williams who had literally found her long-sought place in the sun far from her native homeland, many others had departed the western frontier and returned disillusioned to where they had come. But this was not the case of Cathy Williams, who had made her lofty dreams come true.[188]

Part II

Chapter I: The Female Buffalo Soldier's Enduring Place in American Society and Memory

By the last decade of the twentieth century, the story of Cathy Williams had been embraced by black America for the first time, especially among young people in the major urban areas and a new generation of educators. The widespread awareness of the Buffalo Soldiers by a large segment of America's population first began in the 1970s with the increase of interest in fascinating aspects of ethnic history that had been long ignored by traditional historians. Black history of the West benefited immensely from this new development, allowing for the presentation of forgotten and untold narratives in America's saga.

On a national level, interest of the Buffalo Soldiers reached a high point when General Colin Powell, who had earlier initiated the Buffalo Soldier Project, officially recognized the service and sacrifice of the Buffalo Soldiers during the unveiling of a Buffalo Soldier monument at Fort Leavenworth (where this project had been initiated), Kansas, on July 25, 1992. Thanks to these key developments, the Cathy Williams' story gradually began to emerge for the dark shadows of this most neglected chapters of black history: the long-overlooked stories of African American women—the most forgotten players in America's story—who had risen up from slavery.[189]

Mirroring the popularity of the Buffalo Soldiers, including the story of Cathy Williams, in the military community in the United States and at military bases overseas, the degree that the African American community has embraced the history of the Buffalo Soldiers also became evident in the backlash that was directed against the 2003 satirical movie entitled *Buffalo Soldiers*. Not only was this movie not about black fighting men, but it also presented an especially cynical and negative view of the American military. The film's setting was the United States Army in West Germany, not long before the Berlin Wall fell in November 1989.

In this dark comedy and black satire reminiscent of Joseph Heller's anti-war classic *Catch-22*, American soldiers were depicted as behaving like common criminals of a black market drug cartel and crime syndicate. Worst of all, this film also perpetuated demeaning racial stereotypes about blacks (druggies and lowlifes), who were portrayed to represent the most negative aspects of inner city life.

Ironically, no mention was made to the real Buffalo Soldiers, from Cathy Williams' post-Civil War era to the Second World War. Consequently, the film's name was not only entirely inappropriate, but also damaging to the overall good name of the Buffalo Soldiers. The resulting angry backlash among history-minded blacks revealed the rise of an increased recognition of the Buffalo Soldiers throughout the African American community. As a result, a wave of indignation caused some blacks, men and women, to angrily respond to this controversial film.

Tara Phillips, who proudly identified herself as the "Granddaughter of a REAL Buffalo Soldier," contributed a highly-critical rebuttal in a blog about the movie's badly-misplaced name on the Amy Ridenour's National Center Blog (a project of the National Center of Public Policy Research) on Friday August 1, 2003: "My heart has been broken by this issue, particularly after hearing the review by [Roger] Ebert and [Richard] Roeper who also fail [like the film] to mention the history of the original Buffalo Soldiers. I do applaud, however Nancy Millar, a reviewer for JANE magazine who not only refuses to review the film, since it has nothing to do with the Buffalo Soldiers, but even goes on to reference, Cathay Williams, the only female Buffalo Soldier who disguised herself as a man so that she could fight. In 2003, the African-American experience is still forgotten . . . I IMPLORE you to take a stand. Artistic expression cannot justify the vilification of the honorable memory of these soldiers [and] most importantly, DO NOT PATRONIZE THIS FILM. It is an insult to our soldiers of the past and our soldiers of the present."[190] Of course, Cathy Williams probably would have almost certainly felt the same as Tara Phillips in this regard.

Indeed, Cathy Williams' story has also revealed the personal odyssey of a special kind of rebel, who fought against injustice in her own quiet way. In this sense, Cathy Williams was almost like a passive-aggressive activist, who outsmarted the system of the dominant power structure and high-ranking white male officials to get ahead in life by rising up from the lowly place that American society had unfairly ordained for her.

As mentioned, Cathy' novel strategy of disguising herself as a male was about the only means by which a former slave women could aspire higher in a strict patriarchal society with so many deeply-entrenched barriers based on gender and race: formidable dual obstacles that Cathy overcame in the most innovative way to provide a timeless example of the importance of an individual (male or female and regardless of color) maintaining flexibility and adaptability by thinking outside the box to circumvent society's greatest obstacles in order to gain greater advantages in life. Therefore, Cathy Williams' life story has offered a good many enduring positive lessons about how to succeed in overcoming formidable barriers of a discriminatory system and power structure by stealthy maneuvering in a clever way, while relying on a novel means to advance higher in life.

However, as could be expected, an inevitable backlash from some less enlightened Americans has also greeted the recent emergence of the Cathy Williams story. Some conservative white males have been less receptive to the possibility about Cathy's nearly two years of faithful service in the United States Army. Despite the undeniable facts revealed in her official military service record located at the National Archives, Washington, D.C., and other collaborating evidence, they have attempted to challenge the validity of her military service, but more because of racial and political rather than for historical reasons.

Ironically of course, if the United States was a black nation or a matriarchal society, little, if any, criticism toward the mere concept that Cathy Williams served in the United States Army for so long without detection would not be forthcoming. Unlike other countries–like Haiti and its ebony female revolutionaries who helped to win that black republic's independence–which have wholeheartedly celebrated black women as national heroines for their military roles, the United States has had no comparable black female military counterpart to celebrate. Therefore, the recognition of Cathy Williams today as a folk heroine has continued to be part of the internal dynamics of the ethnic community and an insular military culture in the United States outside of the mainstream.

Unfortunately, women of modern western societies have not possessed comparable opportunities to gain inspiration and pride in their own distinctive women warrior traditions (it is not known, but perhaps Cathy Williams had been partly influenced by a martial legacy, perhaps even a brave female family member who rebelled against slavery), because these roles failed to conform with the dominant values of paternalistic and patriarchal cultural norms.

Therefore, American women (white and black) have long lacked positive female military role models partly because such self-assertive examples have contradicted the stereotypical and traditional subordinate roles of women in society, especially submissiveness. In such western patriarchal societies unlike in much of Africa where many tribal societies have been historically female-based, an emphasis on a woman's courage, intelligence, and heroism in a patriarchal society have been long viewed negatively because they have posed a direct challenge to the status quo of a male-dominated society and long-existing value systems about gender.

In historical terms, this traditional denial of inspirational heroic and military roles for American females has been especially pronounced in regard to African American women partly because of the legacy of slavery and racism. Consequently, some of the most inspiring examples of spirited black resistance by men and women against slavery have long remained a closely-guarded secret in the South for fear that this information would inspire greater resistance among slaves. Disguising the high levels of slave resistance to slavery from the beginning, white masters went to great lengths to hide this truth, silencing the widespread black, including women, resistance to slavery. After all, such natural longings for freedom revealed far too much about the slaves' overall humanness (a natural love of liberty just like white Americans' revolutionaries of 1775-1783 and throughout the course of American history) that was deserving of equality like everyone else.

Indeed, black women in America have been rebellious since slavery first came to America, because the natural love of liberty always has been one of the greatest desires of human nature. The factors of gender and color, of course, made absolutely no difference in regard to this fundamental universal longing. However, the facts of black resistance to slavery, especially by women, have also been long hidden by popular racial stereotypes, especially the Southern myth of the docile "Sambo."

Because these many examples of rebellious slave women were deliberately silenced to hide the truth about grass roots resistance to slavery, African American women have long lacked inspirational role models of female resistance and warriors to provide positive images of heroism against racial oppression. Consequently, such examples of heroic black women have been sadly lacking in America's popular culture and in the history books.

This glaring lack of positive examples of self-assertive black women, especially in martial roles, has almost certainly played a part in making the lives of African American women more challenging in regard to self-esteem and pride. Of course, such positive female role models are extremely valuable in personal development and self-confidence of young black women, especially from low income neighborhoods in America's inner cities: a means for promoting a sense of well-being, healthy self-identity, and self-actualization. The dramatic story of Cathy Williams' life, therefore, helps to fill these voids in the lives of African American women, while meeting personal needs by providing a positive and inspirational role model for young women (black and white) today.

Popular Hollywood films and the glamorous lifestyles of stars and musicians, glamour models, modern media, and sensational romantic novels have failed to fill this crucial gap of providing truly positive role models for today's young black women. Unfortunately, these popular influences of America's popular culture have often offered exactly the wrong examples and messages to young black women to foster less than positive values. Modern media's most celebrated black women have today failed to provide the necessary moral examples of meaningful substance for the average woman (black and white), especially working and single mothers.

Such superficial examples offered today by modern media have often proved unworthy of lofty celebration compared to the many forgotten ennobling individuals who accomplished a great deal against the odds throughout the course of black history. However, the inspiring example of Cathy Williams, who struggled on her own and lived a rewarding life that she created for herself, has provided an exception to the rule.

Unfortunately, by the second decade of the twenty-first century, authentic positive role models for America's black women have been long misdirected to focus to the most superficial of personalities, models, and media darlings instead of individuals who have achieved real accomplishments of substance from hard work and personal sacrifice. Unlike for western pioneer women and a young Buffalo Soldier named Cathy Williams, who had been forced to struggle endlessly to survive in a cruel world, success has come relatively easy for today's most idolized women in American society.

Unfortunately, the fantasy world of Hollywood and the sensationalism-obsessed modern media have provided only a gapping moral void by too often failing to bestow today's African American women with meaningful role models of true substance and character required for overcoming life's challenges. Generating a remarkable measure of creativity and innovativeness upon Cathy Williams, times were so challenging that this young black woman had to go the greatest extremes just to ensure the most basic and decent existence, including even earning the right to fight for the country that had freed her in June 1861.

Clearly, today's cult-like celebration of personality according to the perverse priorities of a distorted TMZ culture has left a giant void in providing African American women with the best inspirational moral role model of a courageous black women (other than the usual Black History Month cast, including Harriet Tubman and others, who are routinely rolled-out by organizations and corporations on cue every February), who overcame almost insurmountable obstacles to provide powerful moral examples of true substance.

For many black women today, especially single mothers who continue to experience difficult economic times and personal situations, Cathy Williams' story has provided an inspiring example of the ever-lasting importance of never losing hope in the struggle for a brighter future. The author of the book *Our Black Year*, Maggie Anderson lamented a long-existing fear in an interview about her book during the celebration of Black History Month 2012 in part because of the lack of positive role models in the African American community: "My worst fear is that black people will always be the pitiable, ridiculed underclass . . . we're still stuck at the bottom."[191]

Significantly, this was a tragic fate that Cathy Williams refused to accept for herself because of her own hard work, determination, and willpower: key personal lessons about the importance of the strength of character that explained why her example is timeless and important to this day. In a striking paradox, virtually every culture (modern and primitive), nation, and people have long celebrated the heroic example of a female warrior except the United States.

In the annals of western history, Joan of Arc was the most famous of these women military heroines. Inspired by religious visions that convinced her that she had been chosen by God to save France, this young French girl achieved prominence after rising from humble peasant roots in 1429. In full armor and mounted on her warhorse, she led the French to one victory after another over the English invaders, convincing her people that God was on their side. The nineteen-year-old Joan was eventually placed on trial. She was given women's clothing to wear during the proceedings of a kangaroo court.

However, Joan shrewdly knew that it was important to wear men's clothing at her trial, because this apparel was an "outward sign of her uniqueness" and a distinctive identity, especially as a military leader who had inspired so many French fighting men. Joan was executed in public by burning on a pyre. She had effectively employed the appeal of religion as a political tool, but Joan had committed the greatest crime in a patriarchal society's eyes: she had transgressed far beyond the traditional cultural norms of a conservative and patriarchal society by dressing as a man and leading the way as a popular female warrior.[192]

In the Far East, the tradition of women warriors has been far more culturally acceptable and popular than in the West. In fact, these female heroines were part of a revered traditional world of the Japanese samurai. The fabled samurai brought the Japanese military art of combat to its highest level for a millennium and a half, beginning in the seventh century. Part of a respected legend well-known across the island, Japanese women became revered fighters of the Bushi military clans, which were inspired by ancient military traditions. Most of these warrior women hailed from families of substance and wealth. Fathers equipped their daughters to defend family, home, land, and clan. But these women warriors also marched in conquering armies that journeyed far from home to launch preemptive strikes.

Therefore, these highly-disciplined Japanese women became their people's and ancient land's defenders, relying on their own courage and the trusty "naginata" in combat. The "naginata" was a lengthy spear which these well-trained Japanese females swung at their opponents in a sweeping manner from side to side like a scythe. Making them more formidable in close quarter combat, samurai women also carried a dagger, the "kaiken."

In the annals of samurai history, female samurai warriors were famously known to "fight to the death" and against impossible odds in heroic fashion. Occasionally, in becoming cherished legends that have endured for centuries, because these brave "women fighters who alone or at the head of a group of fighters, managed to beat the enemy!"[193]

Cathy Williams' Military Legacy Resurrected in Bosnia, Afghanistan, and Iraq

Like Joan of Arc who had early provided an example of a western woman's courage and leadership qualities, Cathy Williams' legacy has been likewise revered in the African American community. The image of Cathy Williams has served as an inspiring role model to many African Americans by the twenty-first century, especially for young inner city women who have long needed such an uplifting example.

But fortunately and as mentioned, the American military establishment has celebrated Cathy Williams' legacy. In consequence, she had become a source of inspiration and pride to military women to this day. The best example of this development can be seen in the widespread utilization of the Cathy Williams story by the United States Armed Forces on both sides of the Atlantic. Consequently, Cathy's remarkable story has inspired a new generation of young women warriors, black and white, who have served in America's conflicts, including the War on Terrorism, in foreign lands far from home.

Cathy Williams' legacy has been enthusiastically embraced by the men and women of the United States military with considerable pride, fortifying them in their own courageous roles as America's defenders in far-away lands. Symbolically and most appropriately, the first official recognition of Cathy Williams' story in the United States came from within America's military establishment.

Indeed and most significant, Cathy Williams was a pioneer for all black women who have served with distinction in America's modern military. In many ways, this was a natural development because the United States military had long led the way for American society by integrating blacks into its ranks. And appropriately, black men and women have served in disproportionate numbers in all branches of America's modern military.

During the first decade of the twenty-first century, an estimated 200,000 women served in the United States military: around 14 percent of America's military, with nearly one-half of these having been African American women in uniform. In total, more than two million American women have faithfully served their country in the United States military.

For blacks and women in today's society and most importantly, the identification with Cathy Williams has extended far beyond her just having worn a military uniform from 1866 to 1868, embodying deeper personal, moral, and psychological meanings. Few Americans outside of the United States military establishment have been able to fully understand the kind of unique challenges and hardships encountered by American women (black and white) in today's military, especially in dangerous war zones overseas. And, of course, this situation was especially the case of Cathy Williams, who was the first black woman to have served in the United States military.

Ironically, like Cathy Williams, many of today's American women (black and white) have discovered to their surprise that the American military establishment and its overall conservative hierarchical structure, based upon traditional values, have only reflected many of the same inherent problems and prejudices that they have long encountered in American society at large: discrimination and prejudice stemming from long-existing divisions based upon sex, class, and color. To many American women in uniform even to this day, therefore, what they faced off the battlefield in the military establishment was often as much of a formidable opponent as the enemy on the battlefield.

In a strange paradox, this situation has brought the realization to victims of this patriarchal system and power structure that the real struggle for American women was much the same as before they had entered military service with the idealistic expectations of experiencing greater fairness in a new environment. Consequently, today's military women have closely identified with the personal struggles of Cathy Williams, both in and out of service, because she had been forced to fight against some of those same obstacles and prejudices, based on gender and race, that they have long faced. [194]

This warm embrace of Cathy Williams' historical legacy by the black civilian and America's military communities has been an inexplicable development to some conservative, traditional males, who have not accepted full equality for women. Consequently, the popularization of the Cathy Williams story has sometimes produced a reactionary backlash from angry conservatives and traditionalists, who almost seem to wish that her service to America from 1866 to 1868 had never happened.

Indeed, a surprising amount of criticism has been generated from some vocal members of the conservative community about the alleged implausibility of a young black woman and ex-slave serving capably for nearly two years in the United States military, despite the existence of ample documentation of Cathy's military service, medical records, and pension application records from official sources. Of course, this has been a false criticism because the undeniable facts of Cathy Williams' military service to America are not debatable, given the abundance of collaborating official documentation and other primary evidence, including located in the National Archives, Washington, D.C.

In stark contrast to politically-inspired unbelievers who have been largely conservative and traditional males, the young American men who have long served with honor in fighting America's wars overseas and beside military women have had no such doubts whatsoever about the inherent truths about the validity of Cathy Williams' military service to her country. Ironically, some African American men and women, who have died on the battlefield in defending America in Iraq and Afghanistan, went into their last fight with a sense of admiration in their hearts for what Cathy Williams had accomplished against the odds and what she personally represented to them.

While serving in the war against Islamic terrorists, some of these American service men and women (black and white) first learned about Cathy Williams' amazing life from military educators like Major Janice M. Gravely, United States Army. She presented an especially inspiring personal portrayal of Cathy Williams, reenacting the Buffalo Soldier experience to United States troops in Bosnia in the mid-1990s. Major Gravely's dramatic portrayals of Cathy Williams were videotaped by military personnel of the United States Public Affairs. These videos were later utilized for educating large numbers of additional fighting men and women about this forgotten heroine, who had proudly worn a United States military uniform. Major Gravely's portrayal of Cathy Williams was then continued by other female soldiers (officers and enlisted members) in the war zones of Afghanistan and Iraq. Here, Cathy Williams' military legacy was presented to a new generation of American fighting men and women in a dangerous wartime environment of a global struggle against terrorism.[195]

For an extended period, America's black soldiers, especially African American females, who served in Bosnia, Iraq, and Afghanistan, took comfort from the inspiring example of America's first female Buffalo Soldier. After all, she was the only African American woman who served in the United States military in the nineteenth century. What these young American women in uniform realized was the fact that Cathy Williams had enlisted for many of the same reasons that they themselves had joined the military: greater opportunity and the hope of a brighter future, a sense of adventure, patriotism, a professional career, and a desire to honorably serve their country.[196]

Consequently, as a model soldier who served America for nearly two years, Cathy Williams was a true pioneer for African American women in today's United States military. Significantly, this fact is now appreciated by larger numbers of women in the United States military. In truth, Cathy was the one who led the way for tens of thousands of black women to eventually follow in her footsteps in not only the twentieth century, but also twenty-first century. Therefore, Cathy Williams can be correctly viewed today as the "Mother" of all African American women, who have served with honor in America's military during one war after another. This increasing appreciation of Cathy Williams as an excellent positive role model for young women has been widespread among African Americans in the military and civilian communities in a rare dual appeal in the twenty-first century.

Capitalizing on her popular appeal at the grass roots level and understanding the inspirational qualities of the course of Cathy Williams' life to a new generation of young African Americans, the Hallmark Cards, Inc., Company, Kansas City, Missouri, capitalized on her inspiring example and colorful artistic image. The company obtained the rights for William Jennings' fine portrait of Cathy Williams for its "For a Special Graduate" (the heading at the card's top) Mahogany Card. This handsome Mahogany Card was on the shelves of hundreds of stores across America during the first decade of the twenty-first century. Significantly, this graduation card was distinguished by the words "The Story of the Female Buffalo Soldier" printed on the card's front bottom to nicely frame the Jennings' full-color painting. Inside this very visually-appealing card, a brief biographical sketch of Cathy Williams was presented to summarize her personal and military legacies.

Meanwhile, in the United States during the early years of the twenty-first century, a number of civilian women have also portrayed Cathy Williams in the blue uniform of a Buffalo Soldier, mirroring the portrayals of her by military women who served in major theater of operations during the War on Terrorism. In the northeast United States, the most widespread portrayals of Cathy Williams were performed by a talented former history and English teacher named Melodie Lynn Clark Thompson, of Cranston, Rhode Island. Like Major Gravely who inspired many military men and women about Cathy Williams in war zones overseas, Melodie Lynn Clark Thompson, also a New Englander, told audiences far and wide about this remarkable woman born and raised in America's heartland. A graduate of Wheaton College, Melodie (or Melody) performed her Cathy Williams' portrayal across the United States. She educated large audiences of a variety of government and

Department of Defense (DoD) agencies, including in Washington, D.C. (especially throughout Black History Month), during the first decade of the twenty-first century. As presented at the Smithsonian Institution, Washington, D.C., for Women's History Month (March) in 2002, Thompson's performance was entitled *Only A Woman: First Female Buffalo Soldier.*[197]

The overall impact of such dramatic performances (reenactments that were both biographical and historical) about the life of Cathy Williams had a widespread appeal, reaching thousands of individuals to inspire a new generation young women, especially African Americans, during the early years of the twenty-first century. In Melodie's words of October 2007 that described the overall experience of portraying Cathy Williams to people across America: "I have performed 'Only a Woman: The Cathy Williams Story' since February 2000. I can truthfully say, after countless performances in 10 different cities, from Rochester, NY to Columbia, S. Carolina, there is one aspect of audience response that has consistently been the same everywhere; and that is, the emotional impact. Something about [Private William] 'Cathay' touches people's hearts–and not just women. One of my most favorite memories is from Rochester, NY, where, after performing for St. John's College, an audience member came up to me and told me she would pay me out of her personal funds, if I would do the show later that day at her husband's school as a birthday present for him. A very unusual request, to say the least, but by the end of that later afternoon show, he was weeping . . . But I've seen the same laughter, consternation and eventually, tearful responses from all ages, all races and both genders . . . So what is it that 'gets to folks' about this 19th Century former female slave-turned-army private-in-male-disguise??

I would wager that it has something to do with her simple humanity–Something about her unassuming, tough exterior that silently screams her endearing vulnerability. Something about how far she seems from the audience's reality at first, but how close she becomes to their fears, their confusions, their tough times and survival instincts before it's all over. God knows, 'she' has certainly connected to my heart over the years . . . My most frequent return engagements have been to military bases and Washington DC Federal audiences. At these engagements, the hosts always set up a receiving line and/or a reception for me after the performance. More important than the accolades, are the sincere hugs and kisses of APPRECIATION that I get from the hundreds of attendees. They thank me over and over again for bringing them the story of Cathay. Despite the despicable conduct of her comrades towards her at the end of her tour of duty (1868), the onstage 'Cathay' is still able to somehow convey the kid of pride and dignity that military personnel admire and aspire too. I am always tremendously honored and humbled by this . . . I don't know how much longer I will be portraying Cathay Williams, myself, in the coming years [after 2007], but I am confident that her story will never end . . . ."[198]

A passionate and dedicated artist in love with her work, Melodie was not guilty of exaggeration in her astute analysis of the significance of the Cathy Williams story gained by large numbers of people from hundreds of portrayals. Because of her efforts and a good many other similarly dedicated educators, the heroic story of the Buffalo Soldiers, especially Cathy Williams, today holds a special place in the hearts and minds of large numbers of citizens in African American communities across the United States.

Modern Artwork Featuring Cathy Williams

More than a half dozen artists, black and white, who have painted portraits of Cathy Williams. John Jones, Charleston, South Carolina, has been one of the best of these modern artists. As mentioned, another talented artist who had painted Cathy is William Jennings, Kansas City, Missouri. In fact, he was the first artist to release an excellent portrait of Cathy Williams in full uniform, wearing knapsack, musket, and gear. Unfortunately, to this day, no photograph has been discovered of Cathy Williams. Therefore, no one today knows today exactly how she actually looked.

Artistic license, therefore, has inevitably come into full play for some of today's artists, allowing their imaginations to soar to considerable heights in creating their portraits of Cathy Williams. Cathy's military enlistment papers provided only the most basic information. On November 15, 1866, her height was described at five foot, nine inches and her color as dark, with black hair and complexion. Nevertheless, some artistic representations (although of excellent quality in overall artistic terms) of Cathy Williams have depicted a young woman of color of a relatively light skin tone. Naturally, such lightness of color (mulatto qualities) is indicative of white ancestry, while representing the long accepted traditional Caucasian standard of beauty.

Likewise, Cathy Williams is almost always depicted by artists in full uniform, and one that is usually unsoiled by rain, sun, and daily wear from months of service on the western frontier. Quite simply, these modern artists across America have presented an excessively pristine view of her imagined appearance, as if she had never undergone arduous campaigning in the southwest.

Therefore, the artist's representations of Cathy Williams have been glamorized and romanticized to an excessive degree to appeal to a wide commercial marketplace, the black and white communities. This development has been most obvious in these artists commonly portraying Cathy Williams as a shapely beauty, with striking model-like facial features that are light in tone. In general, African American artists have bestowed Cathy with dark features, while talented white male artists (as opposed to white female artists like exceptionally gifted Kathy Morrow, of Las Cruces, New Mexico, who has completed the finest and most accurate portraits of Cathy Williams) more commonly bestow Cathy with lighter features.

Of course, such extensive beautification (in regard to both traditional Caucasian-like features by mostly white artists and traditional black features by mostly African American artists) of the overall image of Cathy Williams has been the greatest distortion of all. Clearly, a young woman of such allegedly striking good looks could hardly have been successful in her disguise as a man for nearly two years of service in a United States regular regiment, when in close proximity with large numbers of male soldiers.

In truth, no documentation or primary evidence has revealed any hint of these alleged stunning good looks of this young woman in the prime of life. But this is not to say that Cathy Williams was necessarily homely or ugly. And of course, she certainly would have gone out of her way to appear as unappealing as possible to men, especially white officers, because her great secret had to be kept at all costs from 1866 to 1868.

Therefore, it would almost certainly seem that Cathy was of average or ordinary looks. Of course, these were physical qualities that would have been absolutely necessary for a successful ruse of serving in a Buffalo Soldier regiment for nearly two years. A veteran of the United States military, Marty Brazil, of Biloxi, Mississippi, has presented a very realistic portrait of Cathy Williams. Brazil created a fine ink sketch of Cathy Williams as a young

Buffalo Soldier. This is one of the best representations to what Cathy Williams actually looked like in part because the artist possessed keen insights about the American military experience. Knowing that she was tall and dark from her military service record, Brazil's portrait of Private William Cathay presented a sleek figure with little shape–almost without breasts and a nearly flat chest —in a United States uniform as worn by the Buffalo Soldiers in 1866-1867. His only error was in obviously depicting an overly tight-fitting uniform that was utterly impractical for her successful ruse, especially for an extended period of time.

However, he accurately presented Cathy Williams with an overall distinctive unisex or transgender appearance: the exact physicality and facial features that explained how she was able to serve for nearly two years in the United States military. Brazil correctly sketched the face of no ravishing beauty like other artists, who been only too prone to beautify in creating the popular myth and romanticized legend of Cathy Williams. Instead, he presented a very realistic and believable portrait of an ordinary, common-looking Cathy, who could easily be mistaken for a young male in uniform.

Most importantly, he also captured a distinctive look of subtle pride and simple dignity in the face and bearing of this young black woman, who was proud of the fact that she served as a "good soldier," in Cathy's words: an accurate source of pride supported by the facts and details contained in her official military service record at the National Archives, Washington, D.C.

Today's Cultural Impact of Cathy Williams

Unfortunately and as mentioned, some angry male traditionalists have reacted with indignation to Cathy Williams' story, as if hoping to silence some very obvious fundamental truths for racial, personal, and political reasons. In fact, some critics have even gone to outlandish lengths in attempting to denounce Cathy Williams' military service as an elaborate hoax: a military service that could have possibly occurred by this young woman, according to their biased reasoning and politically-driven agendas. They have made their prejudiced arguments with one-sided bias dominated by emotionalism, despite evidence of hundreds of white women who disguised themselves to serve in military ranks from the American Revolution to the Civil War.

Indeed, in the Civil War alone, an estimated 500 women on both sides successfully served disguised as male soldiers for extended periods, including during all four years of war. Most conveniently and as mentioned, these critics have entirely ignored the existence of a reliable body of solid evidence from official government military service and pension records, especially in Cathy's case.

More than ample primary documentation and official records have verified her own life story as revealed in the January 2, 1876 edition of the *St. Louis Daily Times*. As mentioned, this reporter at Trinidad also viewed Cathy's army discharge papers to verify her story. Sadly, these mostly right wing critics have seemed to be most disturbed by the fact that Cathy Williams was black. Clearly, issues of race and gender have continued to remain an excessive concern among many Americans, especially during the second decade of the twenty-first century with the rise of heightened racial tensions largely because of heated politics.

What certainly cannot be denied was that out of the more than 6,000 Buffalo Soldiers who served during the post-Civil War period, only one of these Americans was a woman, Cathy Williams. However, some criticism from distracters has been partly valid, but only in regard to aspects of Cathy Williams' life that often have been overly-romanticized and embellished by novelists.

Ironically, this relatively recent celebration of Cathy's life has been slightly misplaced, but only in the context that she had never deliberately attempted to become a role model or trendsetter for future generations. Her popularity today across black America certainly would have certainly astounded this humble woman of perseverance and faith. But the undeniable fact remains that Cathy Williams set an impressive precedent and inspiring example for large numbers of Americans today, especially African American women.

In summarizing the remarkable life of Cathy Williams, it is almost tempting to romanticize what she achieved in her life, especially from 1866 to 1868, adding to the layers of myth that have already be created by writers and artists. Perhaps historian Patricia Nelson Limerick in her work entitled *The Legacy of Conquest, The Unbroken Past of the American West* said it best, after scouring many accounts of white pioneer women, including a mother of seven children who trekked west and gave birth on the dusty Oregon Trail in 1853. She placed the overall experience of the female (black and white) experience in the "Old West" in a proper historical perspective:

"In endurance and stamina, Mrs. Knight was clearly the equal–if not the better–of the Kit Carsons and the Jedediah Smiths [and] The developing pictures of Western women's history suggest that Mrs. Knight, while perhaps braver than most women (and men), was no anomaly. Far from revealing weak creatures held captive to strong wills, new studies show female Western settlers as full and vigorous participants in history."[199]

Limerick's eloquent words are also valid in regard to Cathy Williams. Despite a most unconventional life, Cathy was very much of an ordinary, but extremely resourceful and resilient, young woman, who only attempted to survive a difficult life by overcoming the many barriers that lay in her path. Most of all, she refused to allow her dreams to die and fade away like so many other individuals (men and women) of less determination, despite facing an inordinate amount of obstacles. She struggled and persevered against the odds to succeed in life in the end, leaving behind an inspirational legacy that is truly timeless.

Indeed, Cathy Williams' life has provided us with an invaluable example of this truism that has applied as much to the unruly frontier of the "Old West" as to modern times: the ingenuity, smarts, and resourcefulness that have been required for a young person, especially a black woman on her own, to succeed in life against all obstacles. Then and today, success in life can perhaps only come in one's life from perseverance, determination, and hard work. Indeed, what was most significant about Cathy Williams' life was the fact that she faced far greater adversity and barriers than experienced by white female pioneers, whose lives were generally easier. Clearly, this was a highly disadvantageous situation for black pioneers that made Cathy Williams' ultimate success even more remarkable in relative terms, because the odds were far greater.

Large numbers of these stoic pioneering women (black and white) made their fair share of contributions and forgotten sacrifices in the settling of the West. These courageous women placed their hopes in the fulfillment of the American dream that could only be found by them in the ample opportunities provided by the West, which offered personal renewal and a fresh start in life. Here, in this seemingly unlimited expanse of the western frontier and its boundless promise, Cathy Williams literally reached out to secure her own destiny by embracing an opportunity to begin her life anew in a pristine land that offered a host of new possibilities, after she had ended her Buffalo

Soldier service at Fort Bayard.

Against the odds and in a true Horatio Alger story, Cathy Williams fulfilled her ambitions and dreams, which she never considered impossible or entirely out-of-reach from her grasp, although almost everyone else, black and white, believed otherwise. And what she achieved with an inordinate degree of perseverance and resourcefulness has provided us with an inspiring example that has well stood the test of time. Indeed, a good many examples have demonstrated that Cathy's story is still entirely relevant as an enduring lesson for today's youth, especially young females.

Therefore, Cathy Williams' life has inspired everyday Americans trapped at the lowest order of society's pecking order, especially in America's major urban areas, to this day. Caught amid the restrictive confines of second class citizen status, especially in America's inner cities, in a downward spiral of poverty, domestic abuse, and discrimination in a violent world, where survival of the fittest still dictates the course of daily life, a good many American women have been uplifted by the positive lessons of Cathy's unforgettable life.

Today, America's black communities, especially in major cities (such as Detroit, Michigan, and Chicago, Illinois), are in crisis with epidemics of economic downturn and broken families, while the gap between white and black Americans has continued to widen. The African American family has continued to be savaged by divorce, drugs, teen pregnancies, and poverty in crime-ravished inner city neighborhoods. The February 2, 2012 issue of *Rolling Out.com*, Washington, D.C., summarized the bleak situation in an editorial from the "Publisher's Page" entitled *A Civilization Under Siege*: 'The fact that 50 percent of African American students drop out, is a grave and dire matter [and] While the sun is on the horizon for so many other ethnicities, we have to identify and solve the problem in our own communities . . . We call our women names and denigrate them all the same, and then look for someone else to blame."[200]

Black communities of America's inner cities have still remained isolated from the mainstream of American society, existing as separate entities to mock the lofty Civil Rights' idealistic goal of full black integration into the mainstream to create a true multiracial society. Instead, African American communities, especially the inner cities, have remained isolated, failing to achieve significant gains compared to nonwhite immigrant populations, who had made the American Dream come true. Therefore, the racial and political divide between whites and blacks in America has widened by the second decade of the twenty-first century. This polarization of Americans along racial and political lines has left a deep chasm in an already fractured society that has continued to grow to this day.[201]

Long-sought solutions to these deep-seated cultural, societal, and economic problems of devastated black communities have not been found, because successive civic and government officials have blundered and wasted resources for generations. One of the most forgotten reasons for this overall decline has been due to the lack of true positive role models to inspire black youth. Even the African American past has largely failed to provide a sufficient number of lasting inspirational role models to fuel greater positive change.

Unfortunately, this situation has developed partly because only a few individuals of a standard historical cast of black heroes and heroines (only a relatively few inspiring examples thanks to corporate marketing priorities in the name of garnering greater profits) have been long presented to the American public as the best and only examples of black achievement, especially during Black History Month: the obligatory, ever-predictable small group of long-recognized black historical figures, Frederick Douglass, Harriett Tubman, George Washington Carver, Booker T. Washington, as if these relatively few individuals were the only African Americans, who made important contributions to America's story. Of course, this is still another enduring popular misconception and myth.

However, in still another striking paradox, these well-known black achievers have become mostly commercial products of America's corporate culture, because they have been deemed as palatable and more marketable for the reaping of greater financial gain through the promotion of their products to the American marketplace. Hence, the commercialization of a highly-sanitized and more acceptable history of these notable African Americans during Black History Month has been directed more at white consumers from whom the greatest profits can be gained by major corporations.

But the rather crass commercialism of only a relatively few African American individuals during Black History Month (recognition that has been regulated to a single month when, of course, twelve months might be more appropriate for recognition like the celebration of white history) actually does a great injustice, because hundreds, if not thousands, of other black woman and men made impressive and distinguished achievements that have been long ignored. Unfortunately, Black History Month has become big business for white corporate America at the expense of some of the most inspiring achievers in the annals of African American history.

In consequence, Black History Month has actually perpetuated the enduring myth that only a handful of black heroes and heroines are truly deserving of widespread recognition and celebration. Even worse, since the 1970s when these historical figures were resurrected with the rise of black awareness and the Civil Rights Movement, this well-worn cast of historical characters (despite their obvious overall worthiness) have lost much of their popular appeal, because they had always been routinely trotted out by major American corporations every February for public consumption and commercialism reminiscent of Christmas Season.

In addition and in general, these famous figures of black history have been primarily intellectual and political leaders, whose roles cannot always capture the popular imagination of the common people in general in quite the same way as hard-working, lower class individuals like Cathy Williams, who beat the odds by her never-say-die spirit. After all, Cathy was one of the ordinary people of the working class, and she was fated to struggle against the odds throughout her life. Cathy was quite literally, a person of the common people, because her life was best defined as embodying and symbolizing the everyday struggles of simple survival like so many Americans today.

Cathy Williams' legacy has continued to exist in a variety of unique forms to this day. In southern Maryland just outside Washington, D.C., the Cathay Williams Regiment of black female motorcycle enthusiasts was created in January 2007, because they were inspired by Cathy's life in the "Old West." They incorporated the life-lessons of the Cathy Williams story into their own personal moral code of conduct and honor. This "group of riding women who had a desire and yearning to form an all-female organization" rode their motorcycles (much like America's military veterans during the annual patriotic event on Memorial Day in Washington, D.C., known as Rolling Thunder) and lived by a strict military-like code of ethics based on honor and respect: "Live for freedom, justice, and all that is good; Show respect for authority; Never abandon a friend, ally, or noble cause; Always keep one's word of honor; Never betray a confidence or comrade; Avoid deception; Respect life and freedom; Exhibit manners, and Be polite and attention."[202]

As revealed in their organization's mission statement, these adventuresome Maryland women of color continue to "ride under the name of Buffalo Soldier in honor of Cathay Williams," and honor her memory and legacy.[203]

This unique group of African American women emphasized those admirable qualities that they lamented were too often missing in today's black community in an editorial entitled, *A Civilization Under Siege*, which feared the "Destruction of the Black Civilization."[204]

In 1989, the popular movie *Glory* detailed the distinguished role of the black soldiers of the 54th Massachusetts Volunteer Infantry during the Civil War, especially the courageous attack on Fort Wagner, Charleston, South Carolina, in July 1863. A new generation of African Americans suddenly gained inspirational heroes in these black soldiers, who had fought and died more than a century before.

And in February 2012, the George Lucas' movie entitled *Red Tails* accomplished much the same in regard to promoting greater general awareness about the history of the Tuskegee Airmen, although the Tuskegee Airmen's story has also enjoyed a long-overdue rediscovery since the 1960s. But the primary heroes of these popular movies, *Glory* and *Red Tails*, were males. As usual, black women, especially in the movie *Glory*, have remained glaringly absent in these historical films in part because American society has remained largely paternalistic in nature to this day.

Because a black woman did not play a supporting role in the movie *Red Tails*, a backlash resulted from politically-minded and socially conscious black women across the United States. *Clutch* Magazine featured an article on January 18, 2012 entitled, "Should Black Women Boycott 'Red Tails?'" What especially raised the ire of some black women was that one of the film's lead African American airmen characters enjoyed a passionate romance with a beautiful Italian woman: a situation that has been mirrored in the fact of many eligible black men in today's society having found female partners outside their race in America, leaving many African American women severely economically-challenged as single heads of families. One comment from a reader on the *Clutch* magazine website lamented how "black women are unloved by black men and Red Tails reinforces that fact."[205]

The title of another article, written on January 29, 2012, reflected the deep sense of outrage among many African American women in America, "Black Women Omitted from Movie 'Red Tails.'"[206]

D. Barbara McWhite, a black woman from northeast Florida, wrote an article entitled "Why I Won't Recommend 'Red Tails'" on January 31, 2002, and vented her indignation just after viewing the film: "I am tremendously disappointed that the only love interest in the entire movie was between the most elite and heroic black pilot and an Italian woman. My husband and daughter were likewise appalled . . . I cried at the end of 'Red Tails' . . . But I was unable to mourn the death of the best fighter pilot because I was still angry that his interracial love story was portrayed by the film's producers as the only love story worth telling. So I am unable to celebrate the movie. I won't buy the DVD nor will I recommend it to my family, and friends. I will not take my grandson to see it."[207]

Only recently, a black female history professor and scholar from the University of Michigan, Tiya Miles, almost gave up exploring the lives of African American slave women, when she became discouraged by a Southerner who worked at a highly-respected Georgia archives. This older gentleman emphasized to her that the story of black women was simply not an important topic for research. This young black scholar briefly lost some of her faith in her work because it was mocked and devalued. Tiya correctly emphasized how important aspects of American history cannot be fully appreciated without a fuller understanding of the role of black women.[208]

Here, lies a central dilemma for today's African American women–an overall lack of interest and focus on black women in American history, which has directly corresponded with the too common absence of African American female portrayals in historical films today. Throughout the past, black women have been too often left without a substantive female role model capable of generating greater interest in the ever-fascinating subject of black history.

Consequently, a more populist and overall appealing example is especially now needed to provide an inspirational example to today's black youth: an enduring moral lesson about the importance of perseverance and hard work for getting ahead in life by an average person from the lowest rung of society, especially rising on their own to accomplish what seemed virtually impossible at the time. At long last, a suitable inspirational and positive role model has emerged to fill this large void in the public consciousness: the remarkable life story of Cathy Williams.

Indeed and as mentioned, the saga of Cathy Williams has bestowed a host of invaluable life lessons about exactly what it takes today to succeed in life: old fashioned and too-often considered outdated values not unlike those of the Puritan ethnic (hard work, dedication, and sacrifice) that helped to create a dynamic America from the beginning.

However, the most obvious missing ingredient in the Cathy Williams story is the absence of the importance of a formal education. She was illiterate only because of having grown up as a slave in Missouri that had denied education to slaves. However, Cathy learned a great deal from the difficult school of hard knocks, and that informal, hard-earned education in slavery, the Civil War, and as a Buffalo Soldier provided invaluable lessons that served her well. Nevertheless and most importantly, Cathy Williams' determination and perseverance compensated for the lack of a formal education, allowing her to eventually achieve her lofty goals in life.

In overall terms, the Cathy Williams story has played a part in causing a resurgence of black pride to inspire a new generation of African American women, especially black youth: a fact fully realized by the savvy marketing people at Hallmark Cards, Inc. As mentioned, this belated recognition was fully revealed in Hallmark's release of its Cathy Williams graduation card under the Mahogany brand. The phenomenon of the popularity of Cathy Williams' story in the black community has revealed that her enduring legacy has played a role in filling a gapping void in the historical memory and popular consciousness for many African Americans, especially young women. Quite simply, the life of Cathy Williams has provided a much-needed positive black female role model and moral example warmly embraced by all ages and classes of African American women in urban and rural areas.

Today, the inspirational story of Cathy Williams in the African American community has left a deep imprint and lasting impact. Teachers in black schools routinely tell about her amazing life story and young children learn of the valuable life lessons glimpsed from her omnipresent struggle against the odds. Meanwhile, city and county libraries, book stores, government, including the Department of Defense (DoD), and local governments across the United States have presented programs and lectures about Cathy Williams to large numbers of Americans.

In addition, more than a half dozen re-enactors have portrayed Cathy Williams, including Loretta Hunter in the Washington, D.C., area, who wore the full uniform of a Buffalo Soldier, while giving lectures and acting-out presentations about her life. Therefore, the positive lessons of Cathy's life have been spread across the nation at the end of the twentieth century and the beginning of the twenty-first century to a remarkable degree. Americans of all colors have embraced her story and applied its life lessons to their own daily struggles in attempting to survive and get ahead in life against the odds.

In a February 11, 2008 blog, an African American woman in her thirties named Tami, from Indianapolis, Indiana, emphasized the enduring legacy of Cathy Williams with an easy eloquence and a clear historical understanding, which have partly explained the core popular appeal of the female Buffalo Soldier to a new generation of African Americans: "Next time you read a story about the trials faced by women in the modern military, think of Cathy Williams, the first recorded African American woman to serve in the United States Army . . . Imagine the fortitude it takes to march alongside soldiers in a time of war. Imagine the patriotism it takes to serve a country that believes you [are] a second class citizen because of your race and gender. Imagine the courage it takes to hide your femininity while you work alongside men in the brutal Western heat. Imagine the independent spirits it takes to live as a single woman in a time when women are powerless. Imagine the savvy it takes for an uneducated woman to run her own business, have her own money and a team of horses, too. Imagine having your accomplishments denied as you lie broken on your deathbed. Today, remember Cathy Williams."[209]

Because Cathy Williams was an ordinary woman and an average person of the common people, everyday women (black and white) across the United States have identified with and related to her lonely struggle on her own as a single woman against the odds. One troubled young African American women, who felt overwhelmed by life's seemingly endless challenges and her own day-to-day struggle as a single mother without adequate support and encouragement, read Tami's February 11, 2008 blog late that night, and responded immediately. She was frustrated by life's mounting responsibilities just before reading the blog.

No longer feeling completely defeated by life's stiff challenges, but revived by a new sense of purpose from reading about the inspiring example of Cathy Williams, she wrote at 3:40 a.m. on the morning of February 12, 2008: "Thank you for this post. It's 5:00 in the morning–been up since about 2:00 [a.m.] thanks to my 3 year old daughter's penchant for climbing into my bed and pushed me off the side in her sleep. Anyhow, I had the nerve to be sitting here feeling sorry for myself because I'm So tired and blah, blah, blah when you blessed me with this post. I tell people all the time that I would come back again and again as a Black women, and this story [of Cathy Williams] fills me with so much pride that I can hardly see through the tears to type this. It highlights the good of a blog like this. If people could only know who we really are, what we have survived, and the strength it took (takes) to do it they would know what an obscenity the prevalent and degrading images of us in popular culture and in our own communities is. Anyhow, thank you again so much."[210]

And this post came in the morning at 7:36 a.m. from Katrina, who wrote in response to Tami's emphasis on the great value of life's lessons in the Cathy Williams' story that can be derived by young women today, "Thank you for posting this."[211]

These examples have revealed the truth of the words of Cathy Williams re-enactor, Melodie L. C. Thompson, who faced her own set of unique challenges in life, while portraying Cathy Williams in an increasingly difficult personal situation, on October 12, 2007: "I don't know how much longer I will be portraying Cathay Williams, myself, in the coming years, but I am confident that her story will never end . . . ."[212]

Consequently, this book has been written in the hope that the legacy, life-lessons, and inspiring example of Cathy Williams will not be forgotten by a new generation of young Americans, especially women, of all races, because her story is truly universal and timeless. After the heightened interest in Cathy Williams reached a peak in the last decade of the twentieth century, her popularity has diminished thereafter in America's highly-disposable society and social media-obsessed culture that seemingly only celebrates the tawdry in a society that has become increasingly perverse. Consequently, the inspiring example of Cathy Williams is even more valuable today and needed more than ever before, especially in regard to the increasingly pronounced racial and gender divides that have torn apart the increasingly fragile fabric of American society during the early decades of the twenty-first century.

Ironically, Hollywood's excessive focus on sensationalizing the brutalities of slavery has become increasingly more graphic on the big screen, including the 2016 Memorial Day release of the second version of *Roots* that was far more graphically brutal than the popular original 1977 edition of the ground-breaking series about the trials of a black family in the ugly grip of slavery. Unfortunately, this emphasis on excessive white abuse of blacks (white Hollywood's longtime obsession with overly-graphic film depictions of brutality that have continued to escalate over time) is still another crass exploitation to reap greater publicity and profits by film corporations: unfortunately, little more than a self-congratulatory self-righteous exercise (validating an allegedly moral superiority of wealthy white elites over less enlightened whites of lower classes) by Hollywood's white liberal elite that has been cynically calculated to garner recognition and awards through this gross sensationalism.

But this entirely unnecessary (especially in regard to America's current highly combustible racial environment and greater polarization between black and white) portrayal of excessive black suffering in the most graphic way (interestingly, white Hollywood has not excessively focused similarly on the Holocaust's horrors, especially in an excessively graphic way—a striking double standard) that does absolutely nothing to enhance the self-esteem of millions of young black children in their formative years or to soothe growing racial antagonisms.

Worst of all, highly-impressionable young black children risk lifelong emotional and psychological scars (not to mention fueling early resentment, if not hatred, toward whites for historical racial sins) from witnessing such excessive violence of Nazi-like whites (as so graphically portrayed by white liberal Hollywood that seems obsessed with the brutality) against helpless black slaves, while threatening to additionally harm the already severely damaged race relations across America. Clearly, in overall terms, this is a high emotional price for black children have been forced to pay for the already-wealthy Hollywood elite to reap even greater profits under the thin veneer of presenting the so-called truth for educational purposes in order to bolster a smug self-righteousness in regard to racial matters.

In striking contrast to this excessive commercialization of "black pain" by Hollywood because of its disturbing obsessive focus on graphically depicting the worst of slavery's horrors to accumulate higher profits at the box office and to purge their own white guilt, Cathy Williams' story cannot possibly be more positive or spiritually uplifting by comparison. Significantly and as mentioned, the valuable timeless life lessons that can be derived from Cathy's many struggles can play a role in bolstering the self-esteem of young African Americans, especially females, while emphasizing positive qualities without engendering aspects of racial hatred and divisions like from the grotesque white-on-black abuse that has been overly sensationalized in the recent showing of *Roots* and other Hollywood productions.

After all, Cathy Williams' life has embodied an uplifting true story that now should be presented in a positive way by black Hollywood (not by the exploitative white Hollywood elite) for everyday black people across America: precisely the demographic that most needs to be inspired by the positive achievements of an ordinary young black woman of rare abilities. Such an uplifting example is much needed today rather than this almost perverse focus, if not neurotic obsession, of depicting the worst imaginable depths of black pain and suffering for greater sensationalism to garner recognition, higher profits, and awards for greedy Hollywood elites.

Most of all, the importance of Cathy Williams' story is about how a common woman of the lowest possible origins and burdened by the double handicap of her race and gender made her seemingly impossible dreams of a more rewarding life come true by her own efforts. By relying upon her own resourcefulness and intelligence, this single black woman overcame an inordinate amount of adversity and obstacles, rising up by her own strength of character and faith in a brighter future. Cathy's toughness and perseverance in the face of seemingly insurmountable barriers demonstrated the capacity of the human spirit to triumph over all manner of adversity in what was a remarkable success story.

In addition, the real lesson and legacy of Cathy Williams' life was that she succeeded on her own without a man, an occupational skill, an education, or personal connections to overcome the most formidable obstacles of a restrictive patriarchal society that sought to keep her in a subordinate role and relegated to the lowest rung for her entire life. By overcoming the day's most forbidden gender and cultural boundaries and barriers, she crossed a significant racial and gender frontier by serving as a Buffalo Soldier at a time when it was unimaginable for a woman (black or white) to do so. Against the odds, Cathy Williams succeeded by defying tradition and societal expectations by her own resourcefulness and flexibility: an unparalleled and notable achievement in her day.

Therefore, the dramatic story of the life of Cathy Williams has provided inspiration today to thousands of American women, black and white, when facing disadvantageous situations and seemingly no-win circumstances in modern society. The lessons of her remarkable life have offered a timeless example of what extremes of inventiveness and resiliency are required for common people, especially a single female, to succeed in life, despite the seemingly endless obstacles. While Cathy Williams' life can also serve as a less significant example of a symbol of female defiance to entrenched arbitrary authority, the most important lessons of her life are actually more comprehensive.

As mentioned, Cathy's story is truly an universal one for all people, places, and times, especially today when the challenges of the twenty-first century have become more formidable for young people: the struggle of a single individual on their own who managed to outsmart and rise above the arbitrary and oppressive societal dictates, based on racial and gender prejudice, which had been firmly set in place long before Cathy's birth to deny her full equality and a sense of personal dignity.

Clearly, the story of Cathy's life has provided a host of invaluable lessons about what it takes for any individual—male or woman —to succeed in life against the odds, revealing important universal truths that are still relevant and applicable to this day as they were in the nineteenth century: the undeniable reality that has emphasized how resourcefulness, determination, and perseverance are the true keys to getting ahead and succeeding in life. Most importantly, these are truisms that have not only transcended time and place, but also they are perhaps more important today than ever before.

Cathy's amazing success story about what was an outstanding example of individual perseverance and determination has revealed what extremes are often necessary for a woman in a restrictive patriarchal society to succeed in life in seemingly impossible situations and under the most challenging circumstances. She found her novel solution by defying the most fundamental traditions and dictates of a strict patriarchal society that was oppressive to a degree that it was unbearable for her. Therefore, the most radical and unorthodox solution was embraced for Cathy Williams to gain the respect, pride, and sense of self that were impossible for her to obtain in the civilian world and traditional society: disguising herself as a male to serve for nearly two years in the United States Army.

Fortunately, the fascinating story of Cathy Williams has gained greater acceptance because of the changing views of an American society that continues to be in flux today in regard to issues of gender and transgender identities and roles. Not long ago, the mere thought of a young woman serving for an extended period in the United States military was the most improbable and unrealistic of concepts to generations past. Ironically, this is an antiquated view still held today by some diehard male traditionalists and conservatives, despite all the evidence that have revealed otherwise.

After all, large numbers of American women (black and white) have served today with honor and distinction in the United States military, because of many of the same reasons that explained why Cathy Williams served on the western frontier: patriotism, career, honor, dignity, and the hope for a brighter future. Indeed, in overall terms, relatively little has changed in regard to explaining Cathy's core motivations in having decided to serve her country from 1866 to 1868.

Significantly, Cathy Williams was not only a western pioneer in the truest sense and on multiple levels, but also a ground-breaking military pioneer for all African American women, who serve today in the United States military with honor and distinction. However, to be fair to the historical record, Cathy actually only continued a longtime tradition of women warriors, disguised as males, going all the way back to ancient times.

In this sense, Cathy Williams' service in a Buffalo Soldier regiment on the western frontier was also part of an universal story of warrior women throughout the course of human history and in many societies around the world. But Cathy's most memorable contribution to American military history was the notable fact that she set an entirely unique historical precedent as the first black woman to have ever served not only in a Buffalo Soldier regiment, but also in a regular regiment of the United States Army.

Therefore, African American military and civilian communities, including elementary, high school, and college instructors and professors, have celebrated the triumphs of America's first and only known female Buffalo Soldier. Children and young adults in their formative years to aging Civil Rights marchers from the 1960s have been equally inspired by Cathy Williams' sense of determination and uncanny ability to overcome the odds in seemingly impossible situations.

In consequence, she has emerged as a popular role model in today's America from inner city schools of Los Angeles, California, to Washington,

D.C., capturing the imagination of many people in all walks of life. After all, the story of Cathy Williams, the first and only documented Female Buffalo Soldier in the annals of American history, has presented a host of new insights and understanding of not only the African American experience, but also in the history of warrior women in times of war that has extended back centuries.

Therefore, the story of Cathy Williams was timeless because it was most of all about a determined individual fulfilling lofty dreams and ambitions, despite the seemingly impossibility of her ever doing so. What was most remarkable and surprising was the fact that she succeeded in her ambitious plans of serving in the United States military, and got away with it for so long (nearly two years), which of course was a great compliment to her intelligence and resourcefulness. Clearly, Cathy Williams had dreamed big, and this called for taking a good many risks in her relentless quest for a better life both inside and outside of the United States military.

Today and as fate would have it, the final resting place of Cathy Williams is only known to God. She quite literally disappeared without a trace from the historical record, including from her beloved home of Trinidad, New Mexico, during the last decade before the twentieth century.

Unfortunately and as mentioned, Cathy was unfairly denied by the United States Government of what she was legally entitled to for her "good" service as a Buffalo Soldier for nearly two years: not only an invalid pension when she was older and in bad physical shape directly as the result of her arduous western frontier service, but also a decent burial and a rightful final resting place in a government military cemetery.

For her faithful service to America from 1866 to 1868, she was morally (but not legally since she was a female who should never have worn a blue uniform in the government's view and in legal terms) entitled to have been buried in a military cemetery with a government white marble headstone at Jefferson Barracks, Missouri, where she had enlisted in Company A, 38th United States Infantry, on Thursday November 15, 1866.

Instead, the last remains of Cathy Williams almost certainly now fill an unmarked pauper's grave somewhere on the western frontier, which was her adopted homeland that she loved and far from her native Missouri.

Clearly, the fascinating story of the remarkable life of Cathy Williams is a timeless one that can be rightfully seen as a celebration of the triumph of the human spirit. Perhaps the Cathy Williams Mahogany Card "For a Special

Graduate" from the Hallmark Cards, Inc., said it best in regard to the enduring inspirational legacy and uplifting example of America's only female Buffalo Soldier in inspiring countless young people across America to this day: "Your graduation day is a time to celebrate the woman you have grown to be—a woman of strength and character, of courage and conviction. Your life is a true reflection of the spirit and pride that have helped our people succeed through the ages. You are honored today, not only for all you have achieved, but for everything you have become."[213]

About the Author

PHILLIP THOMAS TUCKER, Ph.D., has won international acclaim as a ground-breaking "new look" historian. One of America's most prolific and accomplished historians, Dr. Tucker has authored highly original history and unique narratives to reveal long-silenced forgotten truths in updating the historical record for the twenty-first century.

Notes

[1] Cathy Williams Service Records, Records of the Adjutant General's Office, 38th Infantry, 1866-1869, National Archives and Records Administration, National Archives, Washington, D.C. Hereafter cited as Private William Cathy Service Records, NARA; "Cathy Williams' Story," *St. Louis Daily Times*, St. Louis, Missouri, January 2, 1876. Hereafter cited as *St. Louis Daily Times*, January 2, 1876; John W. Blassingame, *The Slave Community, Plantation Life in the Antebellum South*, (New York: Oxford University Press, 1972), pp. 19-103

[2] Booker T. Washington, *Up From Slavery*, (New York: Dover Publications, Inc., 1995), p. 11.

[3] "Letter from Frederick Douglass," *New York Weekly Tribune*, New York, June 6, 1846; *St. Louis Daily Times*, January 2, 1876; James Neal Primm, *Lion of the Valley, St. Louis, Missouri*, (Boulder: Pruett Publishing Company, 1981), pp. 17, 65, 137, 155-157, 187; Phillip Thomas Tucker, *The Forgotten "Stonewall of the West," Major General John Stevens Bowen*, (Macon: Mercer University Press, 1997), pp. 37-38; Private William Cathay Service Record, NARA.

[4] George M. Fredrickson, *The Inner Civil War, Northern Intellectuals and the Crisis of the Union*, (New York: Harper Torchbooks, 1965), p. 118; Nell Irvin Painter, *Creating Black Americans, African-American History and Its Meanings, 1619 to the Present*, (New York: Oxford University Press, 2006), pp. 112-113; *St. Louis Daily Times*, January 2, 1876.

[5] Fredickson, *The Inner Civil War*, p. 118; *St. Louis Daily Times*, January 2, 1876.

[6] *St. Louis Daily Times*, January 2, 1876; Stephen D. Engle, *Yankee Dutchman, The Life of Franz Sigel*, (Fayetteville: University of Arkansas Press, 1993), pp. 61-62; Private William Cathay Service Records, NARA.

[7]Washington, *Up From Slavery*, pp. 1, 9.

[8]Ibid., pp. 1, 5; *St. Louis Daily Times*, January 2, 1876; Engel, *Yankee Dutchman*, pp. 60-62.

[9]*St. Louis Daily Times*, January 2, 1876.

[10]Ibid.

[11]*St. Louis Daily Times*, January 2, 1876; Engle, *Yankee Dutchman*, pp. 60-62.

[12]Painter, *Creating Black Americans*, p. 109; *St. Louis Daily Times*, January 2, 1876; Frank McSherry, Charles G. Waugh, and Martin Greenberg, editors, *Civil War Women, The Civil War Seen Though Women's Eyes in Stories by Louisa May Alcott, Kate Chopin, Eudora Welty, and Other Great Women Writers*, (New York: A Touchstone Book, 1990), pp. 7-8.

[13]*St. Louis Daily Times*, January 2, 1876; Robert G. Tuck, Jr., "New Market's Native Sun: William Plummer Benton," *The Frederick News-Post*, Frederick, Maryland, July 16, 2012.

[14]Washington, *Up From Slavery*, p. 9.

[15]*St. Louis Daily Times*, January 2, 1876; Primm, *Lion of the Valley*, pp. 252-253.

[16]Jeffry D. Wert, *Custer, The Controversial Life of George Armstrong Custer*, (New York: Simon and Schuster, 1996), pp. 106-107; *St. Louis Daily Times*, January 2, 1876.

[17]Wert, *Custer*, p. 107; *St. Louis Daily Times*, January 2, 1876.

[18]Wert, *Custer*, p. 106; *St. Louis Daily Times*, January 2, 1876.

[19]*St. Louis Daily Times*, January 2, 1876; Judith Hick Stiehm, editor, *It's*

Our Military Too! Women and the U.S. Military, (Philadelphia: Temple University Press, 1996), p. 115.

[20]Engle, *Yankee Dutchman*, pp. 62-79; *St. Louis Daily Times*, January 2, 1876.

[21]Engle, *Yankee Dutchman*, p. 81; *St. Louis Daily Times*, January 2, 1876.

[22]St. Louis Daily Times, January 2, 1876; William L. Shea and Earl J. Hess, *Pea Ridge, Civil War Campaign in the West*, (Chapel Hill: University of North Carolina, 1992), pp. 1-283.

[23]Washington, *Up From Slavery*, p. 10.

[24]Clarene Lusane, *The Black History of the White House*, (San Francisco: City Lights Books, 2011), pp. 77-78, 81-86; *St. Louis Daily Times*, January 2, 1876; Henry Wiencek, *Master of the Mountain, Thomas Jefferson and His Slaves*, (New York: Farrar, Straus and Giroux, 2012), pp. 181-182.

[25]Lusane, *The Black History of the White House*, pp. 82-86; *St. Louis Daily Times*, January 2, 1876.

[26]Washington, *Up From Slavery*, pp. 2-3.

[27]*St. Louis Daily Times*, January 2, 1876.

[28]Bell Irvin Wiley, *The Life of Billy Yank*, (Baton Rouge: Louisiana State University Press, 1978), pp. 109-110.

[29]*St. Louis Daily Times*, January 2, 1876; Painter, *Creating Black Americans*, p. 117.

[30]*St. Louis Daily Times*, January 2, 1876.

[31]*St. Louis Daily Times*, January 2, 1876; Fredrickson, *The Inner Civil War*, p. 119; Lusane, *The Black History of the White House*, pp. 70-71; Painter, *Creating Black Americans*, pp. 112-113, 125; Duane G. Meyer, *The*

Heritage of Missouri, (St. Louis: River City Publishers, Limited, 1988), p. 400; John P. Burch, *Charles W. Quantrill*, (Vega: private printing, 1923), pp. 1-125.

[32]Painter, *Creating Black Americans*, pp. 117-119.

[33]Ibid., p. 118; *St. Louis Daily Times*, January 2, 1876.

[34]*St. Louis Daily Times*, January 2, 1876; Wayne C. Temple, editor, *Campaigning With Grant by General Horace Porter*, (New York: Bonanza Books, 1961), p. 438.

[35]Marguerite Merington, editor, *The Custer Story, The Life and Intimate Letters of General Custer and His Wife Elizabeth*, (New York: The Devin-Adair Company, 1950), p. 61; Wert, Custer, pp. 106-107; *St. Louis Daily Times*, January 2, 1876; Private William Cathay Service Records, NARA.

[36]Merington, ed., *The Custer Story*, p. 61; *St. Louis Daily Times*, January 2, 1876; Wert, *Custer*, pp. 106-107.

[37]Wert, *Custer*, p. 107; *St. Louis Daily Times*, January 2, 1876.

[38]*St. Louis Daily Times*, January 2, 1876; Wert, *Custer*, p. 107.

[39]*St. Louis Daily Times*, January 2, 1876; Private William Cathay Service Records, NARA.

[40]*St. Louis Daily Times*, January 2, 1876; Washington, *Up From Slavery*, pp. 1-2.

[41]Meyer, *The Heritage of Missouri*, pp. 316-317, 323-324, 340; Primm, *Lion of the Valley*, p. 186; *St. Louis Daily Times*, January 2, 1876.

[42]*St. Louis Daily Times*, January 2, 1876; Private William Cathay Service Records, NARA.

[43]*St Louis Daily Times*, January 2, 1876; Washington, *Up From Slavery*,

p. 12.

[44]Private William Cathy Service Records, NARA; Julia Stewart, *African Names, Names From the African Continent for Children and Adults*, (New York: Kensington Publishing Corporation, 1993), p. 66.

[45]*St. Louis Daily Times*, January 2, 1876; Private William Cathy Service Records, NARA.

[46]Frank N. Schubert, *Black Valor, Buffalo Soldiers and the Medal of Honor, 1870-1898*, (Wilmington: Scholarly Resources, Inc., 1997), p. 4.

[47]*New York Times*, New York, New York, May 12, 1861; Ron Chernow, *Alexander Hamilton*, (New York: Penguin Books, 2004), pp. 121-123.

[48]*New York Times*, June 14, 1864; Chernow, *Alexander Hamilton*, pp. 121-123.

[49]*St. Louis Daily Times*, January 2, 1876; Schubert, *Black Valor*, pp. 2-4.

[50]Schubert, *Black Valor*, p. 4.

[51]*New York Times*, July 11, 1868; *St. Louis Daily Times*, January 2, 1876.

[52]*St. Louis Daily Times*, January 2, 1876; Engle, *Yankee Dutchman*, pp. 61-62; Private William Cathay Service Records, NARA.

[53]Washington, *Up From Slavery*, p. 8; Blassingame, *The Slave Community*, pp. 200-201; *St. Louis Daily Times*, January 2, 1876; Private William Cathy Service Records, NARA.

[54]*St. Louis Daily Times*, January 2, 1876; Leckie, *The Buffalo Soldiers*, pp. 6, 9.

[55]Schubert, *Black Valor*, p. 168; *St. Louis Daily Times*, January 2, 1876.

[56]Stephen Crane, *The Red Badge of Courage*, (New York: Lancer Books,

1967), pp. 1-223; Jay Monaghan, *Custer, The Life of General George Armstrong Custer*, (Lincoln: University of Nebraska Press, 1959), pp. 202-281; Private William Cathay Service Records, NARA.

[57]*St. Louis Daily Times*, January 2, 1876; Private William Cathay Service Records, NARA; *Pennsylvania Gazette*, Philadelphia, Pennsylvania, February 24, 1773; Schubert, *Black Valor*, p. 5; Leckie, *The Buffalo Soldiers*, pp. 10-15; Deborah Gray White, *Ar'nt I a Woman, Female Slaves in the Plantation South*, (New York: W. W. Norton and Company, 1985), p. 118.

[58]Elizabeth B. Custer, *Tenting on the Plains, General Custer in Kansas and Texas*, (New York: Barnes and Noble, 2006), p. 264; Private William Cathay Service Records, NARA.

[59]*St. Louis Daily Times*, January 2, 1876; Private William Cathay Service Records, NARA; Meyer, *The Heritage of Missouri*, p. 323; Ann Griffiths, *Black Patriot and Martyr, Toussaint of Haiti*, (New York: Julian Messner, 1972), p. 16; Bruce A. Glasrud and Michael N. Searles, editors, *Buffalo Soldiers in the West, A Black Soldiers Anthology*, (College Station: Texas A&M University Press, 2007), pp. 101-102.

[60]*St. Louis Daily Times*, January 2, 1876; Private William Cathay Service Records, NARA; Schubert, *Black Valor*, pp. 8-10; Leckie, *The Buffalo Soldiers*, pp. 10-13.

[61]Washington, *Up From Slavery*, p. 1; Private William Cathay Service Records, NARA.

[62]*St. Louis Daily Times*, January 2, 1876; Private William Cathay Service Records, NARA.

[63]*St. Louis Daily Times*, January 2, 1876; Private William Cathay Service Records, NARA.

[64]Private William Cathay Service Records, NARA; *St. Louis Daily Times*, January 2, 1876.

[65]Primm, *Lion of the Valley*, p. 274.

[66]Ibid., pp. 275-276.

[67]Elizabeth Salas, *Soldaderas in the Mexican Military, Myth and History*, (Austin: University of Texas Press, 1990), pp. 1-66, 82-94, 120-122.

[68]David Geggus, editor and translator, *The Haitian Revolution, A Documentary History*, (Indianapolis: Hackett Publishing Company, Inc., 2014), pp. 33, 91-92, 177.

[69]*St. Louis Daily Times*, January 2, 1876; Ron Field, *Buffalo Soldiers 1866-91*, (Oxford: Osprey Publishing, 2004), pp. 11, 53; Stephen Berry, *House of Abraham, Lincoln and the Todds, A Family Divided by War*, (Boston: Mariner Books, 2009), pp. 55-56, 72-74.

[70]Francis Terry McNamara, *France in Black Africa*, (Washington, D.C.: National Defense University, 1989), pp. xiii, 6-9; Berry, *House of Abraham*, p. 55.

[71]Francis Lord, *Civil War Collector's Encyclopedia, Arms, Uniforms, and Equipment of the Union and Confederate Armies*, (New York: Castle Books. 1965), pp. 311-315.

[72]Ibid.

[73]Private William Cathay Service Records, NARA; *St. Louis Daily Times*, January 2, 1876; Field, *The Buffalo Soldiers 1866-91*, p. 53.

[74]*St. Louis Daily Times*, January 2, 1876; Benjamin Franklin Cooling, *Symbol, Sword, and Shield: Defending Washington During the Civil War*, (Shippensburg: White Mane Publishing Company, 1991), p. 168.

[75]*St. Louis Daily Times*, January 2, 1876; Field, *Buffalo Soldiers 1866-91*, p. 53.

[76]Tintype of Jacob Mullins, 8th Indiana, Ebay Dealer Fort Myers, Florida, mid-May 2016; St. Louis Daily Times, January 2, 1876; Compiled Service Records of Union Soldiers Who Served in Organizations from the State of Indiana, National Archives, Washington, D.C.

[77]Private William Cathay Service Records, NARA; Field, *Buffalo Soldiers 1866-81*, pp. 58-59; Lord, *The Civil War Collector's Encyclopedia*, 243-244.

[78]Field, *The Buffalo Soldiers 1866-91*, pp. 58-59.

[79]*St. Louis Daily Times*, January 2, 1876; Private William Cathay Service Records, NARA.

[80]William H. Leckie, *The Buffalo Soldiers, A Narrative of the Negro Cavalry in the West*, (Norman: University of Oklahoma Press, 1999), pp. 5-6; Schubert, *Black Valor*, pp. 4-5.

[81]Michael Lee Lanning, *Defenders of Liberty, African Americans in the Revolutionary War*, (New York: Citadel Press, 2000), pp. 63-86; Leckie, *The Buffalo Soldiers*, p. 6; Schubert, *Black Valor*, pp. ix, 4, 9; Jeffry D. Wert, *Custer, The Controversial Life of George Armstrong Custer*, (New York: Touchstone, 1996), pp. 145-230, 243, 318-355; *St. Louis Daily Times*, January 2, 1876.

[82]Lusane, *The Black History of the White House*, pp. 66, 70-71; Leckie, *The Buffalo Soldiers*, p. 9; *St Louis Daily Times*, January 2, 1876.

[83]Private William Cathay Service Records, NARA; Griffiths, *Black Patriot and Martyr*, p. 16; Leckie, *The Buffalo Soldiers*, pp. 8, 14; *St. Louis Daily Times*, January 2, 1876.

[84]Leckie, *The Buffalo Soldiers*, p. 8; David Nevin, *The Civil War, The Road to Shiloh, Early Battles in the West*, (Alexandria: Time-Life Books, 1983), p. 101; Shea and Hess, *Pea Ridge*, pp. 1-283.

[85]*St. Louis Daily Times*, January 2, 1876.

[86]D. Alexander Brown, *Grierson's Raid*, (Urbana: University of Illinois Press, 1962), pp. 5-232; Leckie, *The Buffalo Soldiers*, pp. 13-15; Paul Andrew Hutton, editor, *Soldiers West, Biographies from the Military Frontier*, (Lincoln: University of Nebraska Press, 1987), pp. 158-159.

[87]Leckie, *The Buffalo Soldiers*, pp. 14-15; *St. Louis Daily Times*, January 2, 1876.

[88]Leckie, *The Buffalo Soldiers*, p. 14.

[89]*St. Louis Daily Times*, January 2, 1876; Schubert, *Black Valor*, p. 12; Private William Cathay Service Records, NARA.

[90]Private William Cathay Service Records, NARA; Timothy D. Johnson, *A Gallant Little Army, The Mexico City Campaign*, (Lawrence: University Press of Kansas, 2007), pp. 9-271.

[91]Webb Garrison, *Amazing Women of the Civil War, Fascinating True Stories of Women Who Made A Difference . . . ,"* (Nashville: Rutledge Hill Press, 1999), p. 7.

[92]*St. Louis Daily Times*, January 2, 1876.

[93]*New York Times*, October 9, 1861.

[94]Ibid., May 2, 1863; *St. Louis Daily Times*, January 2, 1876.

[95]*Richmond Examiner*, Richmond, Virginia, December 12, 1863.

[96]Ibid; *St. Louis Daily Times*, January 2, 1876.

[97]*Richmond Examiner*, December 12, 1863

[98]*Memphis Argus*, Memphis, Tennessee, August 18, 1864; *St. Louis Daily Times*, January 2, 1876.

[99]*Memphis Argus*, August 18, 1864.

[100]*New York Times*, August 24, 1931.

[101]Private William Cathay Service Records, NARA; Glasrud and Searless, eds., *Buffalo Soldiers in the West*, p. 103; Primm, *Lion of the Valley*, pp. 161, 281; *St. Louis Daily Times*, January 2, 1876.

[102]Private William Cathay Service Records, NARA; Primm, *Lion of the Valley*, p. 230; Meyer, *The Heritage of Missouri*, p. 364; *St. Louis Daily Times*, January 2, 1876; Glasrud and Searless, eds., *Buffalo Soldiers in the West*, p. 103.

[103]*St. Louis Daily Times*, January 2, 1876; Private William Cathay Service Records, NARA.

[104]Private William Cathay Service Records, NARA; *St. Louis Daily Times*, January 2, 1876; Glasrud and Searles, ed., *Buffalo Soldiers in the West*, p. 103.

[105]Gayle C. Shirley, *More than Petticoats, Remarkable Colorado Women*, (Helena: Morris Book Publishing, 2002), pp. ix-x, 1, 3-4; *St. Louis Daily Times*, January 2, 1876.

[106]Shirley, *More than Petticoats*, pp. 3-4.

[107]Ibid., pp. 4-5; *St. Louis Daily Times*, January 2, 1876.

[108]Shirley, *More than Petticoats*, pp. 5-6; Auraria, Denver, Wikipedia, internet; Central City, Colorado, Wikipedia, internet; *St. Louis Daily Times*, January 2, 1876.

[109]Shirley, *More than Petticoats*, pp. 1, 3-9; *St. Louis Daily Times*, January 2, 1876.

[110]*St. Louis Daily Times*, January 2, 1876; Victoria Scott and Ernest

Jones, *Sylvia Stark, A Pioneer*, (Greensboro: Open Hand Publishing, LLC, 1991), pp. 15, 21-32.

[111]Private William Cathay Service Records, NARA; *St. Louis Daily Times*, January 2, 1876; Glasrud and Searles, eds., *Buffalo Soldiers in the West*, p. 103.

[112]*St. Louis Daily Times*, January 2, 1876; Private William Cathay Service Records, NARA; *Fort Riley, Its Historic Past*, (no date), pp. 2-4; David A. Dary, *The Buffalo Book, The Saga of an American Symbol*, (New York: Avon Books, 1974), pp. 1, 31-33; Glasrud and Searles, eds., *Buffalo Soldiers in the West*, p. 103.

[113]Private William Cathay Service Records, NARA; Milo Milton Quaife, editor, *My Life on the Plains, General George A. Custer*, (New York: Promontory Press, 1995), pp. 4-8; Glasrud and Searles, eds., *Buffalo Soldiers in the West*, p. 103.

[114]*St. Louis Daily Times*, January 2, 1876; Dary, *The Buffalo Book*, pp. 1,12-179; Eric Foner, *Forever Free*, (New York: Alfred A. Knopf, 2005), p. 185.

[115]Quaife, ed., *My Life on the Plains*, pp. 8-9.

[116]Merington, ed., *The Custer Story*, p. 190; Quaife, ed., *My Life on the Plains*, p. 354; Wert, *Custer*, p. 244; Libbie Custer to Rebecca Richmond, December 6, 1860, Kansas Historical Society, Topeka, Kansas; Monaghan, *Custer*, pp. 280-281.

[117]Libbie Custer to Rebecca Richmond, December 6, 1866, KHS; *Junction City Union*, Junction City, Kansas, October 21, 1866; *St. Louis Daily Times*, January 2, 1876

[118]Libbie Custer to Rebecca Richmond, December 6, 1866, KHS; *St. Louis Daily Times*, January 2, 1876.

[119]Private William Cathay Service Records, NARA; Libbie Custer to

Rebecca Richmond, December 6, 1866, KHS; Quaife, ed., *My Life on the Plains*, pp. 19-21; *Fort Riley, Its Historic Past*, pp. 3, 16-17; Junction City Union, October 21, 1866; Glasrud and Searles, eds., *Buffalo Soldiers in the West*, p. 103.

[120] Leckie, *The Buffalo Soldiers*, p. 6, 8; Wert, *Custer*, p. 243.

[121] T. J. Stiles, *Custer's Trials, A Life on the Frontier of a New America*, (New York: Vintage Books, 2015), p. 277; Wert, *Custer*, pp. 106, 236-237.

[122] Wert, *Custer*, pp. 237, 241-242.

[123] Stiles, *Custer's Trials*, p. 277; Leckie, *The Buffalo Soldiers*, p. 8; Merington, ed., *The Custer Story*, pp. 190, 204; *St. Louis Daily Times*, January 2, 1876; Wert, *Custer*, p. 244; *Junction City Union*, October 21, 1866; Libbie Custer to Rebecca Richmond, December 6, 1866, KHS; Private William Cathay Service Records, NARA.

[124] Wert, *Custer*, p. 106; Leckie, *The Buffalo Soldiers*, p. 61; Leckie, *The Buffalo Soldiers*, p. 8.

[125] Leckie, *The Buffalo Soldiers*, p. 8.

[126] "Libbie" Custer to Rebecca Richmond, December 6, 1866, KHS; *St Louis Daily Times*, January 2, 1876; Private William Cathay Service Records, NARA; Glasrud and Searless, eds., *Buffalo Soldiers in the West*, p. 103.

[127] "Libbie" Custer to Rebecca Richmond, December 6, 1866; *St. Louis Daily Times*, January 2, 1876; Private William Cathay Service Records, NARA.

[128] Bernard C. Duse, Jr., Alexandria, Virginia, to author, December 2, 2002.

[129] Schubert, *Black Valor*, p. 65; Thomas B. Marquis, interpreter, *Wooden Leg, A Warrior Who Fought Custer*, (Lincoln: University of Nebraska Press, 2003), p. 156.

[130]Schubert, *Black Valor*, p. 65.

[131]Ibid; *St Louis Daily Times*, January 2, 1876.

[132]Wayne Gard, *The Great Buffalo Hunt*, (Lincoln: University of Nebraska Press, 1972), pp. 4-9; Dary, *The Buffalo Book*, pp. 12-179.

[133]*St. Louis Daily Times*, January 2, 1876; Private William Cathay Service Records, NARA; Glasrud and Searles, eds., *Buffalo Soldiers in the West*, pp. 103, 106.

[134]Private William Cathy Service Records, NARA, *St. Louis Daily Times*, January 2, 1876; Glasrud and Searles, eds., *Buffalo Soldiers in the West*, pp. 103-104; Evan S. Connell, *Son of the Morning Star, Custer and the Little Bighorn*, (New York: Promontory Press, 1993), p. 126.

[135]Edwin R. Sweeney, *Cochise, Chiricahua Apache Chief*, (Norman: University of Oklahoma Press, 1995), pp. xiii, xix-xxii, 1-245; Donald E. Worcester, *The Apaches, Eagles of the Southwest*, (Norman: University of Oklahoma Press, 1979), pp. xiii-9; John G. Bourke, *On the Border With Crook*, (Lincoln: University of Nebraska, 1971), p. 17.

[136]Sweeney, *Cochise*, pp. xix, 246-254.

[137]Ibid; *St. Louis Daily Times*, January 2, 1876; Private William Cathay Service Records, NARA; Glasrud and Searles, eds., *Buffalo Soldiers in the West*, pp. 103-104, 106.

[138]Perry D. Jamieson, *Crossing the Deadly Ground, United States Army Tactics, 1865-1899*, (Tuscaloosa: University of Alabama Press, 1994), pp. 24, 36-53; *St. Louis Daily Times*, January 2, 1876.

[139]Jamieson, *Crossing the Deadly Ground*, pp. 37-38, 48, 51.

[140]*St. Louis Daily Times*, January 2, 1876; Phillip Thomas Tucker, *Cathy Williams, From Slave to Female Buffalo Soldier*, (Mechanicsburg: Stackpole

Books, 2002) pp. 163-166.

[141]*St. Louis Daily Times*, January 2, 1876; Tucker, *Cathy Williams*, pp. 166-170; Mary R. Lefkowitz and Maureen B. Fant, *Women's Life in Greece and Rome, A Source Book in Translation*, (Baltimore: The John Hopkins University Press, 2005), p. 129.

[142]*St. Louis Daily Times*, January 2, 1876.

[143]Ibid; Private William Cathay Service Records, NARA; Glasrud and Searles, eds., *Buffalo Soldiers in the West*, p. 104.

[144]*St. Louis Daily Times*, January 2, 1876; Private William Cathay Service Records, NARA; Patricia Nelson Limberick, *The Legacy of Conquest, The Unbroken Past of the American West*, (New York: W.W. Norton and Company, 1987), pp. 18-19; Glasrud and Searles, eds., Buffalo Soldiers in the West, p. 104; Jamieson, *Crossing the Deadly Ground*, pp. 36-38, 48-49, 51.

[145]Schubert, *Black Valor*, p. 168; *St. Louis Daily Times*, January 2, 1876.

[146]Schubert, *Black Valor*, p. 168.

[147]Jamieson, *Crossing the Deadly Ground*, p. 23.

[148]Ibid; *St. Louis Daily Times*, January 2, 1876; Mary Thomas, *Canadians With Custer*, (Toronto: Dundurn Publishings, 2012), pp. 87-89.

[149]Jamieson, *Crossing the Deadly Ground*, p. 23; *St. Louis Daily Times*, January 2, 1876.

[150]Worcester, *The Apaches*, pp. 10-11, 22, 29, 53-54, 98.

[151]Ibid., pp. 79-80; *St. Louis Daily Times*, January 2, 1876.

[152]Worcester, *The Apaches*, p. 98; *St. Louis Daily Times*, January 2, 1876.

[153] Worcester, *The Apaches*, p. 98.

[154] *St Louis Daily Times*, January 2, 1876; Private William Cathay Service Records, NARA; Tucker, *Cathy Williams*, pp. 141-181; Glasrud and Searles, eds., *Buffalo Soldiers in the West*, pp. 104-105.

[155] *St. Louis Daily Times*, January 2, 1876.

[156] Ibid; Private William Cathay Service Records, NARA; Glasrud and Searles, eds., *Buffalo Soldiers in the West*, pp. 102, 104-105.

[157] W. A. Graham, *The Custer Myth*, (Mechanicsburg: Stackpole Books, 2000), pp. 187, 202; *St. Louis Daily Times*, January 2, 1876; Private William Cathay Service Records, NARA; Glasrud and Searles, eds., *Buffalo Soldiers in the West*, pp. 104-105.

[158] Graham, *The Custer Myth*, p. 187; Private William Cathay Service Records, NARA.

[159] *St. Louis Daily Times*, January 2, 1876; Private William Cathay Service Records, NARA; Sarah Childress, "What We Still Don't Understand About Military Suicides," *Frontline*, April 3, 2015.

[160] Julie Wheelwright, *Amazons and Military Maids, Women Who Dressed As Men In Pursuit of Life, Liberty and Happiness*, (London: Pandora Press, 1990), p. 14; Private William Cathay Service Records, NARA.

[161] Private William Cathay Service Records, NARA; *St. Louis Daily Times*, January 2, 1876.

[162] *St. Louis Daily Times*, January 2, 1876; Private William Cathay Service Records, NARA; Fredrickson, *The Inner Civil War*, pp. 114-115, 122, 128-129; Lusane, *The Black History of the White House*, pp. 50-76.

[163] Private William Cathay Service Records, NARA; Schubert, *Black Valor*, p. 167; *St. Louis Daily Times*, January 2, 1876.

[164]Limerick, *The Legacy of Conquest*, pp. 48-50; Sally Roesch Wagner, editor, *Daughters of Dakota, A Sampler*, vol. 1, (Yankton: Daughters of Dakota, 1989), pp. xiii-xvii; *St. Louis Daily Times*, January 2, 1876

[165]Leckie, *The Buffalo Soldiers*, p. 9; Private William Cathay Service Records, NARA; *St. Louis Daily Times*, January 2, 1876; Wagner, ed., *Daughters of Dakota*, vol. 1, p. xvi.

[166]Leckie, *The Buffalo Soldiers*, p. 9; *St. Louis Daily Times*, January 2, 1876.

[167]Wagner, ed., *Daughters of Dakota*, vol. 1, p. xiii.

[168]Ibid., p. xvi.

[169]*St. Louis Daily Times*, January 2, 1876; Glasrud and Searles, eds., *Buffalo Soldiers in the West*, p. 105.

[170]Limerick, *The Legacy of Conquest*, pp. 49-50; Glasrud and Searles, eds., *Buffalo Soldiers in the West*, p. 105; *St. Louis Daily Times*, January 2, 1876.

[171]Private William Cathay Service Records, NARA; *St. Louis Daily Times*, January 2, 1876.

[172]*St. Louis Daily Times*, January 2, 1876.

[173]Ibid.

[174]Ibid.

[175]Ibid.

[176]Ibid.

[177]Ibid.

[178]Ibid; "The Early Days in Trinidad, Colorado," Sangres.com, internet; "Trinidad, Colorado," Sangres.com, internet; Sister Blandina Segale, *At the End of the Santa Fe Trail*, (Atlanta: Pathfinder Books, 2010), p. 68; Glasrud and Searles, eds., *Buffalo Soldiers in the West*, p. 105; Mark L. Gardner and Marc Simmons, editors, *The Mexican War Correspondence of Richard Smith Elliott*, (Norman: University of Oklahoma Press, 1997), p. 60.

[179]*St. Louis Daily Times*, January 2, 1876; Glasrud and Searles, eds., *Buffalo Soldiers in the West*, p.105.

[180]*St. Louis Daily Times*, January 2, 1876; "The Early Days in Trinidad, Colorado," Sangres.com, internet; "Trinidad, Colorado," Sangres.com, internet; Private William Cathay Service Records, NARA; Glasrud and Searles, eds., *Buffalo Soldiers in the West*, p. 105; Segale, *At the End of the Santa Fe Trail*, pp. 24-35, 59.

[181]*St. Louis Daily Times*, January 2, 1876; Segale, *At the End of the Santa Fe Trail*, pp. 28-29, 53; Casey Tefertiller, *Wyatt Earp, The Life Behind the Legend*, (New York: MJF Books, 1997), p. 255.

[182]Leckie, *The Buffalo Soldiers*, p. 8; Lally Weymouth and Milton Glaser, *America in 1876, The Way We Were*, (New York: Vintage Books, 1976), pp. 7, 12-15; Edgar I. Stewart, *Custer's Luck*, (Norman: University of Nebraska Press, 1987), pp. 306-463.

[183]*St. Louis Daily Times*, January 2, 1876; St. Louis Newspapers, An Ancestry.com Company, internet; Weymouth and Glaser, *America in 1876*, pp. 12-15.

[184]*St. Louis Daily Times*, January 2, 1876; Weymouth and Glaser, *America in 1876*, pp. 171-181.

[185]Segale, *At the End of the Santa Fe Trail*, pp. 28-29, 48, 237; *St. Louis Daily Times*, January 2, 1876; "Trinidad, Colorado," Sangres.com, internet.

[186]*St. Louis Daily Times*, January 2, 1876; Segale, *At the End of the Santa*

Fe Trail, p. 58.

[187]Ibid.

[188]*Fort Riley, Its Historic Past*, p. 20; *St. Louis Daily Times*, January 2, 1876; Private William Cathay Service Records, NARA; Glasrud and Searles, eds., *Buffalo Soldiers in the West*, pp. 106-111; Segale, *At the End of the Santa Fe Trail*, pp. 237-238.

[189]Tucker, *Cathy Williams*, pp. ix-x.

[190]Tara Phillips, "Mailbag Regarding Buffalo Soldiers," Amy Ridenour's National Center Blog, Friday, August 1, 2003, internet.

[191]BookPage, February 2011, Review of *Our Black Year*; *St. Louis Daily Times*, January 2, 1876; Private William Cathay Service Records, NARA; Geggus, ed. and trans., *The Haitian Revolution*, pp. 157, 177; Wheelright, *Amazons and Military Maids*, pp. 1-78; Stanley Elkins, *Slavery, A Problem in American Institutional and Intellectual Life*, (Chicago: The University of Chicago Press, 1974), pp. 1-139.

[192]*St. Louis Daily Times*, January 2, 1876; *Heroines, Remarkable and Inspiring Women, An Illustrated Anthology of Essays by Women Writers*, (New York: Crescent Books, 1995), pp. 33-37; Natalie Zemon Davis, *Slaves on Screen, Film and Historical Vision*, (Cambridge: Harvard University Press, 2000), p. 13.

[193]Robert T. Samuel, *The Samurai, The Philosophy of Victory*, (New York: Barnes and Noble, 2004), pp. 11-13, 15-17.

[194]*St. Louis Daily Times*, January 2, 1876; Linda Lowen, Linda's Women's Issues Blog, August 4, 2008; Judith Bellafaire, "America's Military Women–The Journey Continues," Women in Military Service for America Memorial Foundation, Inc.," internet.

[195]Major Janice Gravely to author, April 6, 2006 and August 28, 2007; *St. Louis Daily Times*, January 2, 1876; Private William Cathay Service Records,

NARA; Glasrud and Searles, eds., *Buffalo Soldiers in the West*, pp. 97-113.

[196]*St. Louis Daily Times*, January 2, 1876, Lowen, Linda's Women Issues Blog, August 4, 2008; Private William Cathay Service Records, NARA.

[197]*Only a Woman: Female Buffalo Soldier Cathay Williams*, Smithsonian Institution handout, March 1, 2002; Melodie L. C. Thompson to author, October 12, 2007; St. Louis Daily Times, January 2, 1876; Cathy Williams Hallmark Mahogany Card, Author's Collection, Upper Marlboro, Maryland.

[198]Melodie L. C. Thompson to author, October 12, 2007.

[199]Information from John W. Jones, Gallery Chuma, Inc., Charleston, South Carolina; Conversations with Marty Brazil, Biloxi, Mississippi; Limerick, The Legacy of Conquest, pp. 52-53; Cathy Williams Hallmark Mahogany Card, Author's Collection, Upper Marlboro, Maryland; Wheelwright, *Amazons and Military Maids*, pp. 1-160; Glasrud and Searles, eds., *Buffalo Soldiers in the West*, p. 111; Private William Cathay Service Records, NARA; Alfred F. Young, *Masquerade, The Life and Times of Deborah Sampson, Continental Soldier*, (New York: Alfred A. Knopf, 2004), pp. 3-320; Private William Cathay Service Records, NARA.

[200]Publisher's Page, A Civilization Under Siege: What Blacks Must Practice in Word, Thought and Deed, Rollingout.com, February 2, 2012; Limerick, *The Legacy of Conquest*, pp. 52-53; Private William Cathay Service Records, NARA; *St. Louis Daily Times*, January 2, 1876.

[201]Dinesh D'Souza, *The End of Racism*, (New York: The Free Press, 1995), pp. 1-17.

[202]Ibid; "Buffalo Soldiers Maryland–The Cathay Williams Regiment," internet; "Buffalo Soldiers Maryland—The Cathy Williams Regiment," internet; Kasai Rex, "The Problem with Black History Month," February 3, 2015, The Daily Good, internet.

[203]"Buffalo Soldiers Maryland–The Cathy Williams Regiment," internet.

[204] Publisher's Page, A Civilization Under Siege, Rollingout.com, February 2, 2012.

[205] "Should Black Women Boycott 'Red Tails?," *Clutch Magazine*, January 18, 2012.

[206] "Black Women Omitted From Movie 'Red Tails'," January 29, 2012, internet.

[207] D. Barbara McWhite, "Why I Won't Recommend 'Red Tails'," January 31, 2012, internet.

[208] Interview with University of Michigan History Professor Tyia Miles, "On Being" Program, American Public Media, Radio Interview, February 5, 2012.

[209] "What Tami Said," February 11, 2008, Online, internet; Cathy Williams Hallmark Mahogany Card, Author's Collection, Upper Marlboro, Maryland; Private William Cathay Service Records, NARA; *St. Louis Daily Times*, January 2, 1876.

[210] "What Tami Said," February 11, 2008, Online, internet.

[211] Ibid.

[212] Melodie L. C. Thompson to author, October 12, 2007.

[213] *St. Louis Daily Times*, January 2, 1876; Wheelwright, *Amazons and Military Maids*, pp. 1-20; Stiehm, ed., *It's Our Military, Too!*, pp. 60-133; Cathy Williams Hallmark Mahogany Card, Author's Collection, Upper Marlboro, Maryland; Glasrud and Searles, eds., *Buffalo Soldiers in the West*, pp. 106-111; Maureen Callahan, "White Hollywood only knows how to tell stories about black pain," *New York Post*, New York, New York, May 29, 2016.

Printed in Great Britain
by Amazon

28650123R00117

OFF LIMITS

WANTING HER COULD DESTROY US BOTH

PENNY DEE

Off Limits
Kings of Mayhem MC Series Book 5

Penny Dee

This book is a work of fiction. Any references to real events, real people, and real places are used fictitiously. Other names, characters, places and incidents are products of the Author's imagination and any resemblance to persons, living or dead, actual events, organisations or places is entirely coincidental.

All rights are reserved. This book is intended for the purchaser of this book ONLY. No part of this book may be reproduced or transmitted in any form or by any means, graphic, electronic, or mechanical, including photocopying, recording, taping, or by any information storage retrieval system, without the express written permission of the Author. All songs, song titles and lyrics contained in this book are the property of the respective songwriters and copyright holders.

Disclaimer: The material in this book contains graphic language and sexual content and is intended for mature audiences, ages 18 and older.

ISBN: 978-1713291602

Copy Editing by Elaine York at Allusion Graphics
Proofreading by Stephanie Burdett
Book design by Swish Design & Editing
Cover design by Marisa at Cover Me Darling
Cover image by Wander Aguiar :: Photography
Cover image Copyright 2019

First Edition
Copyright © 2019 Penny Dee
All Rights Reserved

DEDICATION

2019 has been a crazy hard year. This book is dedicated to all those who got knocked down and had to struggle to get up again. You're not alone. And we've got this. xx

NOTE FROM AUTHOR

Dear Reader,

Off Limits begins only a few months after Cassidy and Chance's bloody climax with Barrett Silvermane in *Hell on Wheels.* That book ended with an epilogue that takes place a couple of years after the events in *this* book. Timelines can get a little tricky when you write a series, especially if you write an epilogue that spans over a few years. So, I hope this clears up any questions you may have about when things take place. Thank you for continuing to read the Kings of Mayhem MC series. I hope you enjoy Chastity and Ruger's story as much as I enjoyed writing it.

Happy reading,

Penny Dee xx

PATH OF FAMILY

The Calley Family
Hutch Calley (deceased) married Sybil Stone
Griffin Calley
Garrett Calley (deceased)

Griffin Calley married Peggy Russell
Isaac Calley (deceased)
Abby Calley

Garrett Calley married Veronica Western
Chance Calley
Cade Calley
Caleb Calley
Chastity Calley

The Western Family
Michael 'Bull' Western
Veronica 'Ronnie' Western

KINGS OF MAYHEM MC

The Kings of Mayhem Motorcycle Club Original Chapter
Bull (President)
Cade (VP)
Ruger (SAA)
Chance
Caleb
Davey
Vader
Joker
Cool Hand
Griffin
Matlock
Maverick
Animal
Yale
Tully
Nitro
Hawke
Ari
Picasso

Caveman
Reuben (honorary member)
Prospect 1
Prospect 2

Employees of the Kings
Red (Chef, clubhouse housekeeper)
Randy (Clubhouse barman)
Mrs Stephens (Bookkeeper, administration)

OFF LIMITS

WANTING HER COULD DESTROY US BOTH

PENNY DEE

PROLOGUE

CHASTITY

Chastity 6 / Ruger 22

I dug the chalk into the concrete and concentrated hard on drawing the picture properly. I liked drawing on the driveway because it was so big, like a giant piece of paper. Drawing was my favorite thing to do in the whole world. Caleb said I was a good drawer, but Chance and Cade still teased me a lot, saying my pictures look like sticks and drunken rainbows.

Whatever.

Stupid brothers.

I changed my chalk, picking up a pink one to draw the nose and a yellow one for the whiskers.

I was drawing our cat Carburetor. He was a ginger cat with big paws and he loved me the best. For some reason he didn't like my dad. But that's probably because my dad wouldn't let him sleep on the end of the bed like I did... and because my dad could be a little scary sometimes.

When the screen door opened, I looked over my shoulder and saw a man step out onto the porch and light a cigarette. It was

Ruger. He was a friend of my Uncle Bull's. Today we went to church and watched his sister get buried and it was really sad because she was so young, and everyone was saying how terrible it was for someone so young to be taken so soon. She died last week when a car smashed into hers.

She was married to my Uncle Bull and now everyone says he is broken-hearted.

I watched Ruger step off the porch before I turned back to my drawing. Uncle Bull cried a lot when her coffin went into the ground. I had never seen him cry before and it really scared me. He was always so happy and kind. Always smiling, even if he had to wear those dark glasses all the time because he had something wrong with his eyes. They are a weird blue. Bright and light like there was a lamp on inside of them.

He loved Wendy.

That was her name.

She was young and pretty, and she was real nice, too.

But she was dead now.

"Whatcha doing, kiddo?" Ruger asked.

I looked up at him. He was standing next to me, looking down at my chalk drawings on the concrete. His long hair hung down past his shoulders and he had a bit of hair on his face. I liked Ruger. He had nice green eyes. They were kind and sparkled like shiny green stones.

"Drawing," I said, turning back to my picture.

"It's good."

I looked up at him.

"My brothers say I can't draw."

He raised his eyebrows. "They do?"

I nodded. "They say my pictures look like sticks and they can't figure out what they are."

"Well, now, that seems like a mighty unfair thing to say," he said, taking a draw on his cigarette. "I, myself, do not think they look like sticks. In fact, I think what we have here is some pretty amazing artwork."

Ruger spoke funny. He and Wendy came from a town far away from here—so far away it was in the very next state over from Mississippi, which I learned at school is called Louisiana.

I liked the way he talked.

"Really?" I asked, unsure. Ruger was nice. Kind. He was the same age as my eldest brother Chance. I had three of them. Brothers, that is. And they were all *way* older than me. So I knew when someone was pulling my leg. I squinted up at him. "What do you think it is?"

"That there picture?" He pointed at it with his cigarette burning between his fingers. "Oh, I know what it is… that there is some well-drawn, well-thought out—"

"Miss Chastity Ramona Calley, look at all that chalk all over your dress!"

Before Ruger could finish, my mom came storming down the driveway toward us. I looked down at the front of my dress and it was covered in pink and yellow chalk from where I had wiped my hands on it. There was also chalk all over my knees.

"It's okay, Mama, I'm creating *artwork.*"

I didn't really know what that meant, but Ruger had said it and I liked the way it sounded.

"Don't sass your mama, child," my mom said as she walked over to us. She took the cigarette from Ruger and puffed on it before handing it back. My mom was real pretty. The kind of pretty you saw on the girls in the magazines at Miss Tolliver's Hair Salon in town. She had long black hair like a raven's wing, and eyes like the bright blue sky. She was kind but could be mad if us kids misbehaved. "Now get inside, your uncle will be leaving soon and you need to say goodbye."

I whined. "Can't I have five more minutes so I can finish my picture, Mama?"

I gave her my best pleading eyes.

Well, that's what Chance called them.

And they worked too because my mama shook her head and gave me a half-smile. "Suppose another five minutes won't hurt none. You already gone and got chalk all over it, I s'pose there's no harm in a little more. Just don't you be talking the ear off Ruger now. It's been a hard day for your uncle for sure, but Ruger, as well. I'm sure he's feeling broken-hearted right now and just needs some quiet."

"She's good company," Ruger said kindly.

Mom smiled at him and then looked back at me. "Five minutes. No more."

"Yes, Mama."

When she disappeared inside, I looked at Ruger. "Is it true?"

"Is what true?"

"Are you broken-hearted?"

I watched him sit down on the edge of the porch. "I guess so, kiddo."

"Do you need some quiet?"

He smiled. "Nah, I like talking to you about your pictures."

He took another puff of his cigarette but he looked down and I could see he was sad.

"I'm sorry about your sister. Aunt Wendy was real nice."

He nodded but didn't say anything, and I noticed how the lump in his throat bobbed up and down as he thought about something. I felt bad for him because he looked so sad. So, I sat down next to him. I looked at the sugar skull ring on my finger. It was my favorite. My mom gave it to me for my birthday and said it came all the way from Florida. It was silver with blue stones in the eyes. My mom said they're called turquoise and were what you called semi-precious. I didn't know what that meant, but it sounded important.

I twisted the ring off my finger and placed it on Ruger's knee.

"What's this?"

"It's a happy ring."

"A happy ring?

"My mom says you can't be sad when you wear it. So, if *you* wear it you won't be sad no more."

When Ruger smiled, two dimples appeared on each side of his mouth and his teeth were very white.

"You're giving me your happy ring?"

"Yes. Because I don't want you to be sad."

I picked it off his knee and grabbed his hand, sliding the ring onto his pinky finger.

"Is it working?" I asked, looking up at him.

Ruger's eye widened and he smiled again. "Well, now, how about that. It works!"

"Really? You're not sad no more?"

He grinned. "Nope. Not one bit."

I grinned back, feeling really happy.

"But I can't keep it," he said.

My face fell. "Yes, you can. You have to because I don't want you to be sad, Ruger. You're nice."

He looked at me. He was thinking. And for a moment, I thought he was going to tell me he couldn't take the ring. But then he smiled at me and held his hand up to look at it on his finger.

"Well, how can I argue with that?"

I grinned. "You'll keep it?"

"How can I give it back when it works so well. See..." He pointed toward his smile. "It makes me real happy."

I threw my arms around his neck and kissed his cheek. Then, jumping off the porch, I picked up my chalk and kneeled against the concrete again. Thunder rumbled in the clouds above us and I wanted to finish my picture before it started to rain.

Ruger stood up and crushed his cigarette beneath his big motorcycle boots.

"See you around, Kitty Kat."

I looked over at him and squinted. "Why did you call me that?"

He nodded to the chalk picture of Carburetor, then winked at me before he walked away.

I couldn't help but smile.

Maybe I wasn't a bad drawer after all.

CHAPTER 1

CHASTITY

Let me get one thing out of the way right now.

I was a virgin.

Yep, you heard me right.

A virgin.

I know, I know. I bet you just asked yourself how the fuck a reasonably good looking twenty-two-year-old with a likable personality and an okay figure could still be a virgin. Believe me, it's a question I've asked myself a hundred times before.

I won't bore you with a poor-me sob story.

Or some plea about wanting to save myself for the right guy. Believe me, that wasn't the case.

I'm just going to give you the facts so you know exactly how this story started.

I'm an MC princess.

I was born into club royalty. The *club* being the biggest motorcycle club in the South, the Kings of Mayhem.

I'm the niece of the club's president, Bull Western.

Daughter of the infamous Garrett Calley and badass biker queen, Ronnie Calley.

And baby sister to the three Calley brothers: Chance, Cade, and Caleb.

Count that.

Three. Brothers.

Who all happened to be fierce, alpha biker Kings.

So, needless to say, finding a date in this town when I was growing up wasn't easy. Impossible, actually.

You date me and you're dating the club.

And there weren't lot of decent guys lining up to do that.

Actually, there were zero.

Nada.

Zip.

That's what you got for being me.

The only time I ever had any freedom with dating was in college where nobody knew anything about my involvement with the mighty Kings of Mayhem motorcycle club. Or whose daughter I was. Or whose niece I was. And I'll tell you something else, getting a guy to ask you out on a date is a lot easier without three alpha brothers hanging around.

I really wanted to lose my virginity before going to college because how awkward would that be? But let's just say that didn't quite work out because no one in this town was game enough to date me, let alone fuck me.

Not that there was anyone who turned my head or piqued my interest.

So, I left for college a virgin, ready to hand my V-card to the first decent college boy who was up for the task.

I met Joey the day I arrived in California. Tall. Good looking, Nice smile. Big, strong body straight off the field from football practice. Hair you could run your fingers through while losing hours beneath him. We fell quickly for each other. But Joey was from a religious family. His commitment to God and his faith meant no sex before marriage, which completely devastated my lose-my-virginity plans.

I admit, it was frustrating on many different levels. But even though we did abstain from the actual act of sex, we did satisfy each other in other ways when our make-out sessions got us hot and bothered. I mean, we were away at college and consenting adults. Fingers. Tongues. Hard but fully-clothed body parts. They all came into play. But Joey still wanted to wait.

When Joey asked me to marry him, I was ready to exchange vows on the spot and spend a month in bed with him. I was desperate to fuck and to be fucked. *I. Was. Ready.* But Joey wanted to do it right and ask my brothers for their blessings. He knew my father had been murdered during an altercation outside of a bar, but that was all he knew about it. I never went into detail. Never told him about the whole motorcycle cub thing.

Like I said, it tended to put guys off.

And I guess I thought it wouldn't matter once we got serious. I thought he would accept that part of me just as I accepted all of him.

But I was wrong.

So un*fucking*believably wrong.

When I brought Joey home to Destiny to meet my family, he flailed like a fish out of water. But it wasn't because he was so completely opposed to the MC world, or because it was in direct opposition with his religious views, it was because he didn't even try. He had my family and the club judged, sentenced, and hanged within minutes of meeting them. He thought he was better than them. *Than us.* And I saw a completely different side to him that I quickly realized that I didn't like. A prejudiced, *unattractive* side that didn't know compromise, or want to even entertain the idea.

We argued and he left early without asking my brothers anything.

He dumped me via text message the next day. Our worlds weren't compatible, he said, and I wasn't the girl he thought I was. We were done, he said, and I should move on.

Oh. And I should give back the promise ring he gave me... just because.

Broken-hearted and angry, I went to a bar in Destiny that very night to get drunk and finally get fucked. And boy, did I get drunk. Tequila shots. Beer chasers. But the fucked bit? Not a chance! No thanks to Mary-Jane behind the bar. She called my uncle who came to the bar with Ruger and hauled my drunk ass off the eager out-of-towner I was sucking face with.

So, there I was.

A twenty-two-year-old MC princess with her V-card very much in place. And no man in sight to take it from me.

Well... except one...

CHAPTER 2

RUGER

The bikini-clad ass grinding against my thighs was peachy and perfect, and the long blonde hair trailing down her toned and tanned back was silky and smelled like sweet shampoo. And her tits. *Fuck me.* They were fucking delicious. So perky and full. *And real.*

But I wasn't interested.

A lap dance wasn't why I was here, and I wasn't easily tempted when I was focused on business.

I glanced at Bull who was as equally disinterested in the sexy redhead shaking her luscious body on his lap.

We both looked over at our host who immediately realized trying to distract us with pussy wasn't going to work here.

Spider was the owner of the Slip 'n Slide, a shady strip joint on the outskirts of town. He was a real slimy character. The kind of guy who left you wanting—no, needing—a shower after he shook your hand. Lanky. Oily. Thinning hair. Leery eyes. Outlandish suits that were just plain bizarre. Like today's silver silk suit with dark blue palm trees plastered all over it. Yeah, that kind of guy.

With a jerk of his chin the girls left us, and as soon as the doors closed behind them, Spider lapped on the charm.

"Not your flavor? No problem. There's plenty more where they came from. Or would you prefer we just got down to business?"

Spider owed the Kings of Mayhem for a favor we extended him years ago. Since then, Bull had kept him in our back pocket because he was a good set of eyes in the shadows. He had his ear to the ground and the pulse of the seedy side of town running through his veins. He knew all the shady comings and goings in the county. It was real bottom-feeder stuff, but sometimes it proved valuable.

Like now.

"When you called you said you had some information about Roger Toombs," Bull said.

Roger Toombs was the number-one suspect in the disappearance of Kayla Jenkins, a twelve-year-old girl who went missing seven years earlier. You didn't live in Destiny and not know the heart-churning story. She disappeared while playing in her backyard while her mom, a hardworking single mother, was inside fixing supper. Despite never finding her body, it didn't take long for law enforcement to piece it all together and find Roger Toombs.

The piece of shit had previously attempted to coerce young girls into his van.

Unfortunately, a series of perfect catastrophes meant Roger was never charged with her abduction, even though he was clearly responsible. When the law couldn't get him, Kayla's mom approached the Kings of Mayhem with three-hundred dollars in crumpled bills and a white gold watch with a diamante missing from the face, as payment. She wanted justice for Kayla. And she wanted us to get it for her.

I was visiting from New Orleans at the time. It was the anniversary of my sister's death, and back then I liked to ride out to Destiny and spend it with Bull if time permitted. I was sitting at one of the barbecue tables at the clubhouse when Donna Jenkins arrived, looking red-eyed and at the end of her rope. I listened to her story, empathizing with her heartbreak and wanting nothing more than to pull every tooth from Roger Toombs's mouth. One. At. A. Fucking. Time.

I became her contact in the club. The person she would call and spill everything to when the days got particularly long or particularly hard, and it wasn't long before I was promising we would get justice for her beloved daughter.

But Toombs disappeared before we could get to him. He skulked away in the dead of night and we later found out that he was hiding out in South America. But he also had an elderly mom in town, and we always suspected he would sneak back into the country to see her one day.

Apparently, today was that day.

Prior to Kayla's disappearance, Toombs was a regular at the Slip 'n Slide, which was known as The Slippery Pole back then. Spider was under explicit instructions to let us know if he heard any murmurs through the seedy underground grapevine if Toombs was back in town.

"You boys sure you don't want a dance. It's on the house. The drinks, too. Got to look after my friends. So, what do you want? Name your poison. We got Jack, Jimmy, and Johnny. All the J's. Or... or perhaps you want something a little more?"

Spider was a weasel. And he was stalling.

Bull leaned forward and removed his dark glasses, fixing his supernatural blue eyes on our host. Bull had an acute eye condition that forced him to wear dark glasses all the time. It also gave him eyes the color of a Hollywood demon, which unnerved a lot of people. He was a big guy. Fierce and formidable, and his otherworldly glare only added to his intimidating presence. Add to that a dangerously low voice with dark undertones. "Roger Toombs. Where is he?"

"Ah, shit, Bull," Spider whined reluctantly. "He's in one of the peep show rooms."

I stood up with a rush. "You mean he's here?"

Spider looked nervous. "Now before you boys get all excited, I don't want no trouble like the last time."

The *last time* involved Bull, Matlock, and me shooting up one of the private rooms when we came to question a patron about his involvement in the assault of Matlock's sister. The idiot decided to pull a weapon, so we pulled three and put him in the hospital.

I stormed over to Spider. "That piece of shit murdered a little girl and you're worried about us messing up one of your rooms? Where is he, Spider? Tell me now or I swear to God I will push all those stinking yellow teeth of yours so far down your throat you'll be shitting enamel for weeks."

Spider shoved his hands up to placate me. "I know, I know. He's scum. But come on, Ruger, it costs me a lot of money when you guys come in here and question my customers."

I grabbed him by the scruff of the neck and shoved my gun under his chin. "I don't think you heard me right, Spider. *That piece of shit murdered a little girl*. Now... so I don't kick in every single motherfucking door in this joint, I repeat, where the fuck is he?"

Spider stammered. His eyes danced over my face, weighing how far he could push me before I shot him. Would I? Or wouldn't I? He didn't know me well enough. I might just be crazy enough to do it.

He sighed. "He's in cubicle four."

I let him go and brushed past him.

He looked at Bull nervously. "I did the right thing, Bull. We're good, right?"

Bull gave him a couple of hard pats to the cheek. "Just as well you did, Spider. You certainly wouldn't want us finding out he was here and you didn't tell us. Then we'd definitely not be *good*."

I stormed out of the room and down the dark corridor in the direction of the peep show rooms. Muted music pulsed through the walls, its heavy, muffled beat pounding in time with my heart.

I thought about little Kayla Jenkins and the photo of her I still carried in the breast pocket of my cut.

I thought about her mom, Donna, and her anguish of not knowing the whereabouts of her daughter's remains.

I thought about the charm bracelet with the twelve little silver charms—one for each of her birthdays—that her mom said she never took off her wrist.

I thought about Roger fucking Toombs and all the shit I was going to do to him for all the things that the justice system allowed him to get away with.

"Before you go kicking in any doors, can I suggest you stop and think about this for a moment?" Bull asked calmly behind me.

"I don't need to think about anything. I've had seven years to think about this moment."

"Then you want to make sure it goes down smoothly."

I turned to look at my president. "He's going to confess and he's going to tell me where he buried her body, so her poor, broken-hearted mother can lay her baby to rest."

"I agree. So let's stop and take a breath."

I glared at my president, my rage itching to come face to face with Toombs.

"Don't kill him in here. Rough him up, sure. Hell, make him piss his pants. Make him bleed a little. But you find out from him where Kayla is, and then you do whatever you gotta do, you understand me, brother?"

Sometimes my emotions got the best of me. For a calm guy, it was a little unusual. But coming face to face with scum like Toombs did that to you.

I found cubicle four and kicked the door in.

Roger Toombs jumped up with his cock in his hand. Behind him, on the other side of the glass, a redhead was fucking a blonde with a strap-on.

One look at us and the hard cock he had been jerking off went flaccid in his hand.

He knew me and I knew him.

I walked over to him and pulled the curtain down to block his view.

From this moment forward, Roger Toombs was never going to know a single moment of pleasure ever again.

He was only going to know me.

And the pain I could inflict on the wicked.

When Donna Jenkins answered her front door, she knew.

She took one look at my face and the realization seeped into her tired blue eyes. Her chin quivered, and with a sigh, she released the deep breath of pain she had been holding on to for seven long, painful years.

It was finally over.

There would be no trial.

No sensationalized headlines.

No passionate debates between a prosecutor and defense attorney.

Kayla's story would not be heard in a courtroom.

It was now buried with the man who ended her life seven years ago.

As far as the authorities were concerned, Toombs was still on the run. Not that they were looking for him anyway. But the truth was, his story ended in a shady copse outside of town after leading me and Bull to a musty old suitcase hidden deep in the woods near the river.

Kayla's remains were already at the crematorium and in the capable hands of Hamish McGregor, the crematorium director and a long-time friend of the Kings who helped us out from time to time.

"Thank you," she whispered.

I held out the silver charm bracelet and dropped it into her hand.

Finally seeing her daughter's charm bracelet after all these years, she started to cry and my heart cracked open, spilling blood into my chest.

With a sob, she hugged me tight and kissed my cheek. "God bless you."

I wasn't a crier but it was all I could do to hold back my own tears.

I nodded, my face stiff as my emotion caught in my throat.

Seven years and it was done.

I hugged her tight, and as the sun began to sink into the horizon, I said goodbye to Donna Jenkins and steered my bike for home.

CHAPTER 3

RUGER

I had a house on the outskirts of town. A renovated 1950s bungalow with a huge veranda and a saltwater pool in the back. I had used all my savings to buy it when I'd moved to Destiny and patched over to the original chapter of the Kings of Mayhem nine months earlier.

I also had a room in the clubhouse. It wasn't a fuck pad. It wasn't for entertaining. It was more for convenience than anything. Because sleeping off liquor in the clubhouse was a hell of a lot more comfortable than sleeping it off in a jail cell, or in a hospital bed if I wrecked my bike on the ride home after a night of drinking. But I was rarely there, preferring the peace and quiet of the little house on Neroli Street.

As I drove into the driveway, the sun was hitting the horizon and the stars were already visible. Summer was here and it lingered in the warm night air.

Inside, the little house was hot and stuffy from being locked up all day. I pulled a cold beer from the refrigerator, popped the cap and took a long, cool drink, savoring the quenching hit only the very first mouthful could give you. Taking it outside, I sat on the deck overlooking the pool and let the balmy summer evening engulf me.

I loved it out here. It was the one place I knew I could still my mind from the chaos. Somewhere I could sit in fucking silence and decompress from all the shit I saw and did as the sergeant-at-arms for the Kings of Mayhem.

Some days I sat under the stars for hours. While others—if the day had been particularly brutal— I stripped out of my clothes and dove into the watery depths of my pool, just to find the silence beneath the water and let it surround me. It was something I did a lot lately. Swimming naked, to drown out the noise of my world and the things I had to do to survive in it.

The move to Destiny had been a life-changer for me. A new start after a long and tumultuous time in my home town. I had left New Orleans and patched over for one reason, and one reason only.

Astrid.

For three years our turbulent relationship had spun us in circles, rudderless and wild. It had been a bad relationship, machine-gunned with jealous outbursts and meltdowns because she was possessive and needy, and a special kind of crazy.

We fought like dogs and made up like rabbits.

It was the same old scene every time.

Fight. Makeup. Fuck. *Repeat.*

Yet, like a fool I kept going back for more because at the end of the day, Astrid was crazy hot and my dick could hands-down out-debate my common sense every single time.

It was a vicious cycle, one that was never going to end well.

The last time we fought she hit me with a fucking baseball bat. Gave me a fucking concussion and broke my thumb. When she visited me in the hospital afterward, she cried and told me she loved me. Begged for my forgiveness. But when she left, I left, too. *In the opposite direction.* I hopped on my bike and rode to Destiny. I needed for us to be done. And for that to happen, I needed to be gone.

Why? Because when it came to Astrid, I couldn't help myself.

Case in point: when she turned up on my doorstep six months ago looking so fucking fine and smelling so fucking good, I couldn't resist it. We fucked all night, right through to dawn. But just like I knew it would, my regret showed up with the rise of the sun the following morning. Sex with Astrid was like devouring a tall glass of milk on a hot day only to find out it was curdled with the last mouthful. I told her to go and to never come back. She agreed and I haven't heard from her since.

There had been no other women since her. I was done with fucking around. In my youth, I'd surrounded myself in pussy, but it all stopped when I met Astrid, and despite the amount of pussy on offer, I never cheated on her with another woman. It wasn't my style. I liked fucking. *I liked fucking a lot.* But I wasn't a total bastard.

Not that there was much happening in that department.

Since moving to Destiny, I was pretty much living like a monk. I wasn't into club girl pussy and I'd been so busy with club business lately, there really wasn't much opportunity to meet anyone.

Plus, I wasn't the type of guy who was looking for anything long term.

Despite being with Astrid for three years, I was never in love with her. My faith in love and the *happy ever after* was rattled by the divorce of my parents when I was just ten years old, and by the string of failed romances my mom paraded in front of me and my sister in the years that followed.

Then I completely lost my faith in it when my sister Wendy found her once-in-a-lifetime love in Bull, only to die in a car wreck three months after her wedding.

Bull didn't often show his pain about losing the love of his life. But when he did, it was usually only to me. And every single time, I was grateful I'd never been in love just so I would never know the soul-crushing agony of losing it.

Yeah, yeah, some people would call that cowardly. You know, the whole *it's better to have loved and lost than to have never loved at all* bullshit. But the simple truth? I was thirty-eight, almost thirty-nine, and my heart was intact and scar free.

And I had every intention of keeping it that way.

Yet tonight, drinking my beer alone, there was an ache in me I couldn't shake. An ache that had nothing to do with my responsibilities in the club, or sending a child killer to hell. It was an ache for the touch of a woman. For the soft, velvety comfort of a female body. And maybe a little more than that. It was the idea of having someone to share all of this with, the good and the bad, and all the fucking ugly that came with being with me.

But there was no one—and there wouldn't be—because I would fight that ache.

I would fight it with everything I had because I wasn't sure I knew how to end a man's life with my bare hands and then come home and touch a woman the way she deserved to be touched with those same hands.

So, for now, while my fucking dance card was empty and I was trying to still the mayhem in my head, my right hand would have to do.

 CHAPTER 4

CHASTITY

Well, goddamn!

I stared at the mess in front of me.

Who knew how much damage a burst water pipe could do to your apartment?

The carpet squelched beneath my shoes as I surveyed the destruction.

"So?" I looked at the apartment super. "What happens now?"

"What happens now is that you move out for the next few weeks until we get this fixed."

"Next few weeks? Are you kidding me? Why is it going to take so long?"

"Believe me, kid, if I could get it done sooner rather than later I would. But the damage to both yours and the upstairs apartment is extensive. I've got the perfect storm happening here. Broken pipework. Water damage. Cracked brickwork and soggy drywall. Not to mention the threat of black mold with this goddam heat. And then there's the inspection we'll need to get on the repairs."

"Meaning?"

"Meaning you need to go pack yourself a suitcase."

"Great," I mumbled, walking away and wondering where the hell I was going to live for the next few weeks.

As I walked through my apartment, I surveyed the damage and considered my options. My mom's was definitely a no-go. According to my oldest brother Chance, she and Ari were hot and heavy, and when he was staying there following his release from hospital, he had to endure some pretty enthusiastic noises coming from their room at night.

So the ick factor totally ruled out Mom's house for me.

My next option was my Uncle Bull's. But he was so fiercely protective of me it would be like living with a chaperone. No, worse. My father. And it would probably be a nightmare for him anyway. He'd become so preoccupied by my whereabouts and wellbeing it would turn him into a bull with a sore head.

Pun totally intended.

My brothers' places were also out. They had families of their own. While Honey and Caleb were busy with their growing brood, Cade and Indy had her mom staying with them because she had sold her house and was waiting for her new home to become available.

And with the wedding only weeks away, Chance and Cassidy's house was wedding central. So, me moving in would be an added strain on an already chaotic river cottage.

That left my handful of close friends, but they simply didn't have the room.

I walked into my bedroom. The damage was less in there, but the smell of damp carpet and mildew was already beginning to permeate the air. I pulled a suitcase down from the closet and started packing, while my feet continued to squelch in the soggy carpet.

I needed a place close to campus *and* my casual job at Wax-It. I was part-time at Humphrey University, or Hum-U, as most people called it, and was finally only weeks away from graduating.

After Joey and I had broken up, I'd caught a bad dose of laryngitis, and that coupled with Joey parading a new love interest around campus, made my decision to take a year off school a no-brainer. I moved back to Destiny and took some time off to figure out what I wanted.

It took me a few months but I'd finally made a life-changing decision.

I wanted to be a paramedic.

So, I was finally back at college.

Zipping my suitcase closed, I was still no closer to solving my temporary living arrangements, so I gave in and rang my uncle. He was an overprotective man but he was also one hell of a problem solver.

He answered on the third ring.

"So if I told you my apartment was uninhabitable for the foreseeable future, what would you tell me to do?"

"First, I'd want to know why it was uninhabitable. And secondly, I would tell you to pack a bag and then to hold tight until I got there."

"What if I told you my bags were already packed and I was ready to go?"

"Then I'd tell you I would be there in fifteen minutes."

Twelve minutes later, I heard a truck pull into the driveway, and as I zipped up my case, my uncle Bull and Ruger appeared in my room.

Instantly, my heart went to my throat. Because, before we go any further, I should probably explain that I have a major crush on Ruger.

Okay, *major crush* was probably an understatement.

To be completely honest, I have an undeniable longing to get naked with him.

I know, the guy is a hundred years older than me and was more of an uncle than a friend, and more of a father figure than a confidant, but tell that to my poor heart. It has a mind of its own, or so it seemed, and lately whenever I see him my pulse picks up speed and my skin flushes. I reverted to being a teenager who lost her ability for speech.

Not to mention her IQ.

And since I was being really honest, the truth was, I was fantasizing about seeing him naked more and more.

Yeah. A lot more.

Like right now, as he walked into my waterlogged bedroom looking like fifty fucking shades of sexy, all broad-shouldered and thick muscles in his Kings of Mayhem cut over his white t-shirt and black slacks.

He was six-foot-something of pure sex on a stick.

Whatever the hell that meant.

"You're staying with me," my uncle said, taking in the sodden carpet and water-stained walls.

I finally tore my eyes off Ruger to look at him. "Um, not a good idea."

He raised an eyebrow at me. "Why not?"

"Well, because ..."

"Give me one good reason."

"Because I would drive you crazy. And God knows you'd drive me crazy."

I was pretty sure I was the only person on the planet who could make the formidable president of the Kings of Mayhem look hurt.

But one blink and it was gone.

"Then tell me where you're going to stay, Sherlock?" He folded his arms across his broad chest.

I shrugged. "Well…"

I'm pretty sure my uncle went through my options and came up with the same zero options I had.

"She can stay with me," Ruger said, appearing in the doorway. While my uncle and I had been talking, Ruger had busied himself by checking out the rest of the apartment.

Now he was back, waving an invitation for me to come live with him.

My heart dislodged itself and took flight in my chest.

I looked at him. "Really?"

"Sure, why not? I've got the room. And it's closer to Hum-U than here. There's also one hell of a security system, too, so you know you'll be safe."

I looked at my uncle who, by the look on his face, didn't seem to hate the idea.

I considered it. Ruger was right. His house was closer to campus, which would help with the travel time between home, work, and school. It also had a pool. A big, sparkling saltwater pool that was going to be heavenly when the sultry Mississippi summer really ignited.

I looked back at Ruger.

It also had a really good view.

"Okay, if you're sure…"

I couldn't say I wasn't excited by the idea of living with him.

Not that anything could ever happen.

My uncle had made it clear to every member of the Kings of Mayhem that I was strictly off limits. And by *made clear*, I mean he let them know that if any of them laid a finger on me they'd lose their balls.

Besides, Ruger would never see me as anything more than an almost niece.

"That's settled then," he said with a delicious grin. "You'll move in with me for a few weeks."

I grinned back at him.

Sure, Ruger was an unreachable dream. Like me, he was completely off limits and in the no-go zone. But it didn't mean I couldn't look.

And it certainly didn't mean I couldn't fantasize.

I grinned to myself as I followed him outside and threw my suitcase into his truck.

The summer just got a helluva lot hotter.

# CHAPTER 5

CHASTITY

"So where did you ending up staying?" my boss Simone asked.

We were standing out in front of Wax-It. Ten minutes earlier, the fire alarm had gone off in the small strip mall where we worked and everyone had piled out onto the street while the fire department investigated the cause. Now we had to wait for them to declare it safe before we could go back inside.

While we waited, Jane, the hairdresser at the salon, stood with us, smoking a cigarette with one hand and fanning herself with the other.

It was hot.

Stinking hot.

The air was heavy with heat, and without the blast of air conditioning, we were sweltering on the sidewalk.

"With my uncle's best friend," I replied, using a salon brochure to fan myself. "His name is Ruger."

Jane's eyes lit up. "Ooh, is Ruger a biker, too? Is he hot? I bet he's hot. He's hot, isn't he?"

That was Jane, always asking the important questions first.

"No. He's like, a hundred years old," I said, downplaying how attractive my new roomie was. It was an automatic defense mechanism I learned as a teenager. Because if high school taught me one thing, it was how far girls would go to meet one of the Kings of Mayhem. Like pretending to be my friend just so they could hit on my uncle, or my brothers, or any other King they set their sights on.

It made you guarded.

It made you wise.

Not that Simone or Jane ever showed any sign of using me to gain access to any of the guys. Simone was busy juggling both a girlfriend *and* a boyfriend, and Jane was happily married to her high school sweetheart. Not that marriage stopped her from appreciating other men. She had a strict *look but no-touch* policy. And believe me, she looked a lot.

"Ruger sounds sexy. It just rolls off the tongue. *Ruger.*" She began to purr his name. *"Ru. Gerrrr."*

Simone rolled her eyes and fanned herself as she leaned against the wall.

Simone was fun, almost six-foot with a halo of black curls and flawless dark skin, while Jane was four-foot nothing with bright blonde hair and skin as clear as porcelain. They were complete opposites. Simone was straight up and called it like she saw it. While Jane was flighty and a little batshit crazy.

And I loved them both dearly.

"He has a nice house and it's close to work and school, so it made sense to stay there until my apartment is ready," I explained.

"Bet it helps that he's easy on the eyes, too," Jane added, dragging on her cigarette.

"Speaking of easy on the eyes—hot mechanic, six o'clock," Simone said, straightening as she gave us a *check out what's behind you* look.

Jane and I swung around.

Two weeks earlier, a gorgeous new mechanic had started at the workshop across the parking lot. Tall. Good looking. Strong jaw. Nice blue eyes. Inky black hair.

When we made eye contact, he winked at me and I couldn't help but smile back.

"Girl, that tall glass of water sure has got eyes for you something bad," Simone said as she turned back to look at him.

"What?" I shook my head. "That's crazy talk."

"It's true," Jane added. "When you drove in, McHottie over there couldn't drag his eyes off of you. He watched you climb out of your car and didn't look away until you were all the way inside. You should go over there and ask him out."

I turned to look at her. "I'm not doing that."

"When was the last time you went on a date?" Simone asked.

"I do date, okay."

"Sure, you date plenty... if you're a nun," Jane said.

Simone gave me a look. "Honey, if you don't climb back in the saddle, your little red wagon is going to grow cobwebs."

"My little red wagon...?"

Jane let out a giggle. "Seriously, Chastity, you need a bit of — "

Jane's words fell away and both her and Simone's jaws dropped open as they stared at something behind me.

"What on Earth has gotten into the two of you?"

Puzzled, I swung around, and when I did my mouth fell open, too. "*Oh!*"

Across the parking lot, McHottie had undone his overalls and they hung off his hips, displaying a body of golden, muscular perfection as he walked out of the workshop.

I think the three of us swallowed at the same time, our eyes riveted to him as he sauntered out into the sun and tipped a full bottle of water over himself.

"*Sweet baby Jesus!*" Simone muttered.

"I don't think Jesus had anything to do with that," Jane replied, unable to tear her eyes away from him. "That boy is all sin. Every single inch of him."

"And I bet there are a lot of inches," Simone added.

Mesmerized, we watched him shake off the water, the move sending a spray of diamonds glittering into the sunlight. He reached up and ran his hand over his wet hair and down his neck. When he lifted his face, our eyes met across the concrete and he grinned at me. I licked my lips, my mouth suddenly dry. His grin was pure cockiness. He knew he was hot. But it was also pretty sexy because damn, he was *fine*. He wiped the water from his lips with the back of his hand and winked at me, before disappearing inside the workshop.

For a moment, my friends and I said nothing. We just looked at each other.

It wasn't until the fire chief appeared and told us we could go back inside that we even moved.

"What in the name of all things holy was that?" I asked.

"*That*," Simone said with a conspiratorial grin. "Is your next boyfriend."

Jane crushed her cigarette beneath her high heel and laughed. "Boyfriend? Hell, I think at this point Chastity will be happy just to play with his womb broom."

I almost choked on my own breath. "Womb broom? Red wagon? Seriously, where do you guys come up with these?"

Inside the salon, a fireman assured Simone it was a false alarm. Kids had smashed open the alarm and run off. It was an expensive prank for everyone because Simone had already sent out a group text canceling the afternoon appointments.

"You both might as well go," she said. "Make the most of this beautiful afternoon."

"Are you sure?" I asked.

"You don't need to ask me twice," Jane said, already picking up her purse and throwing it over her shoulder. She planted quick kisses on our cheeks as she breezed past us. "I've got a husband at home who owes me a back rub and I plan on cashing in on it."

We watched her leave, her platinum blonde hair glowing in the sunlight as she climbed into her old Volkswagen Beetle.

Two minutes later, Simone shooed me out the door and I found McHottie waiting for me outside.

Leaning up against the wall, he straightened when I walked out and then sauntered over to me.

And holy hell, up close McHottie was even McHotter.

Blue eyes heavily fringed with long, dark lashes sparkled down at me. Although his hair was swept off his handsome face, it fell over his forehead like he had just ran his hands through it.

"Hey there," he said. When he smiled, a dimple pressed into his cheek. "I saw you were leaving, thought I'd try and catch you before you got away."

He had a very thick Alabamian accent, which somehow made him even sexier.

I didn't know what to say. Because basically I was useless when it came to this kind of thing.

Fortunately, he was clearly used to women losing their ability to speak around him, and he didn't wait for a reply. His eyes sparkled down at me as he offered me his hand. "My name is Peter."

I shook it. "Chastity. Nice to meet you."

He smiled. He had almost perfect white teeth, except for one at the front that was slightly chipped. Which I liked it because it meant he wasn't completely flawless.

"*Chastity.*" He rolled my name on his tongue. "Well now, that's a real pretty name. Tell me, what do pretty girls with pretty names do for fun in this town?"

I laughed at his cheesiness, but felt my cheeks redden under his sparkly gaze. I wasn't easily flustered around men. Hell, I grew up with a clubhouse full of some of the crassest ones. But the way this guy looked at me had my blood zipping through me.

"We go to bars with men who buy us drinks and show us a good time."

My response seemed to surprise him. Intrigue him, even. "Is that so." His eyes never left mine. "What time should I pick you up?"

"That depends." And mine never left his. "What night are you taking me out?"

"How about tomorrow?"

"Tomorrow at seven would be perfect."

Our locked gaze lingered for a bit longer. Then he licked his lips and blew out an appreciative breath. "Goddamn."

He handed me his phone and I added my number to his contact list.

"Tomorrow at seven, it is," he said, taking his phone back.

"I'll be waiting."

His eyes swept over me. And when he walked away he cast a smoldering look over his shoulder before disappearing into the workshop.

I grinned and pushed back a surge of uncharacteristic excitement.

I had a date with a boy.

A *very cute* boy.

Time to dust off that v-card, or at least I hoped so.

CHAPTER 6

RUGER

I never planned on inviting Chastity to live with me.

But the kid needed a break.

The last two years had been hell on her and her family, and I kind of had a soft spot where she was concerned.

As it turned out, having her as a roomie was nice. She was good company and brought a nice energy to the house. For the first time ever, my refrigerator was filled with food and my bathroom was littered with a female artillery of makeup and skincare items.

She was also easy to be around. I had known her since she was a kid, but I'd never taken the time to get to know the young woman she had grown into. And I had to admit, I was enjoying it more than I would've thought.

She was smart.

Interesting.

Funny.

And gorgeous inside and out.

Not that I wanted to notice how gorgeous she was. She was Bull's niece and totally off limits... I also had no intention of breaking that rule.

Plus, I was a million years older than her and had no desire to be one of those guys who hooked up with a pretty young thing he had nothing in common with. Although, I had to admit, Chastity and I had more in common than I thought, considering our sixteen-year age gap. Like our combined love of gumbo and jambalaya, and a mutual obsession with eighties horror movies.

She was cool and I liked her.

But she was completely safe from me. I was in the middle of a self-imposed dry spell from women until I figured out a few things in my life, and I had no interest in going where Bull warned all Kings to never tread.

When I arrived home, Chastity's car was parked in the garage but she wasn't inside. Although, Three Dog Night's *"Joy To The World"* was pumping out of the speakers when I walked in. That was another thing I loved about sharing my house with Chastity. She was always playing music. None of the new shit or Top 40 crap. No. She loved the classics like Zeppelin, the Stones, the Eagles, Creedence Clearwater Revival, and other classic bands from the same era.

Stepping out onto the patio, I found her outside sunbathing by the pool.

"Hey, roomie!" she called out.

"You're kidding me," I mumbled under my breath, caught off guard by her tiny bikini and the way it barely covered any of her body.

I walked over to her.

Jesus Christ. Animal was on his way over and Chastity was lying there practically naked. I stole another look at her on the sun lounge, her hot pink bikini bright against her tanned, flawless skin. Appreciation flared in my chest, but I quickly vanquished the observation before it went any further. When I handed her a towel, she lifted her sunglasses and looked puzzled.

"What is this for?"

"Animal is on his way over."

"So?"

"So . . . you need to cover up." When she continued to look puzzled, I explained, "Animal by name, *animal by nature.*"

Animal was the craziest of my club brothers, and crazy enough to not listen to his president.

She rolled her eyes and sighed as she snatched the towel from me. Standing up, she wrapped it around her tiny waist and headed for the house.

"Where are you going?"

"To put on my nun's habit."

I watched her walk away, deliberately not noticing how her long, dark hair fell down to her waist, or the way the late afternoon sun bounced off her golden skin.

I ran a frustrated hand over my head, irritated at myself.

I wasn't a creeper.

I wasn't a dirty old man.

But it was hard to forget that she looked so damn fine in that barely-there bikini.

Even harder to forget was the way my body reacted to seeing her in it.

CHAPTER 7

CHASTITY

I sat rigid in my seat and stared at the paper in front of me, the big FORTY-NINE written in red at the top and seeping into the paper like a stab wound.

"Not your best work, Miss Calley," my biology professor, Dr. Lincoln, said before moving on to the next desk.

My heart sank. A forty-nine wasn't a pass. Hell, a forty-nine declared you barely showed up to the party.

Fuck.

I needed to pick up my game. Focus more. Get in some extra study time.

Lincoln dismissed the class and I gathered up my stuff and shoved it into my bag.

"How did you do?" The good-looking guy with dark hair asked when I stood up and started to make my way down the aisle.

His name was Bryce and we had been friends since class started. Sometimes we went for coffee after class, but it was purely platonic and always just to discuss our mutual course.

"I totally crashed and burned." I showed him my grade and he winced. "You?"

"I did okay." He shrugged non-committally. I glanced at the paper in his hand and saw the ninety-two.

"Holy shit!" I said, taking it from him and staring at the grade like it was the Holy Grail. "You nailed it!"

But again, he downplayed it. "I guess I was just lucky."

"Lucky? A ninety-two is not luck, Bryce. It's damn near genius."

He looked sheepish. "You know, if you need a study partner..."

We had been talking for weeks now, but this was the first time he had offered to help me study. Although, judging by the way he was looking at me, it wasn't just studying he was hoping for.

But I was already going out with Peter and didn't need the distraction of another cute boy asking me out. And Bryce was definitely the type of guy who could distract you. Good looks. Big brown eyes. Crooked but cute smile.

"You will be the first one I ask, believe me."

I handed him back his paper.

"You want to go for coffee today?" he asked. "I can go over a few things with you so you can get it right in your head."

"That sounds really good, but I can't, I've got plans."

As a thank you for saving my ass by giving me a place to stay, I wanted to cook Ruger dinner, and I needed to stop by the market to get supplies on the way home. When he used to visit us when I was a kid, he loved my mom's corned beef. So this morning I had called her and written down the recipe. But I wasn't much of a cook, so I wanted to allow myself plenty of time to get things right before he got home from the clubhouse.

Bryce hid his disappointment behind his cute smile. "Sure, maybe another time, then."

"Definitely."

"Perhaps we could swap numbers and you could give me a call in case you have questions. Or want to grab coffee." Again, he gave me that cute, crooked smile.

"Sounds good."

We punched our numbers into each other's phones.

"There," he said, handing my phone back to me. "Don't be afraid to use it."

"Thanks." I threw my bag over my shoulder. "I'd better go, I'll see you in class next week, okay?"

With another cute smile, he walked off and I couldn't help but admire his cute butt in his jeans as he walked away. He was just cute all over. Smart and attractive. A very dangerous combination.

I grinned to myself. It was true.

When it rained, it really did pour.

CHAPTER 8

RUGER

"Really? We're back here?" I said to Bull after we pulled into the alleyway behind the Slip 'n Slide.

It was late morning and in the bright light of day, there was no hiding just how seedy the club was from the outside. Garbage from a nearby dumpster festered in the heat and the stink was thick in the air around us.

When Bull said he needed me to follow him to an appointment, I didn't realize we'd be paying our sleazy Spider friend a visit.

I made it a point of trying to avoid people who gave me an immediate urge to punch them in the face.

"I got a call from the mayor's office this morning. Seems we have a new resident in town."

The Kings of Mayhem MC had a lot of allies in this town. The mayor's office was full of them, including our new mayor, Sallie Holloway. Who was also secretly keeping Bull's bed warm.

"Who?" I asked, climbing off my bike.

"Someone bought Eagle's Nest."

"The vineyard?" Eagle's Nest was a winery just out of town. "Who?"

"Gimmel Martel. You ever heard of him?"

The name wasn't familiar. "No. You got a feeling about him?"

"I've always got a feeling about wine tycoons buying into this town," Bull said, opening the back door to the club.

Inside, the stench of stale liquor, cigarette smoke, and sex was thick. The lunchtime trade was already starting. Men in suits. Men in tennis shirts and shorts. Men with tight cotton shirts and comb-overs. Men whose wives had no idea they were here. They drank beer and watered-down whisky as a woman wearing nothing but a thong and a cowboy hat danced on stage.

Spider lounged at the bar. Today's suit was red and brown plaid. When he saw us, he came over.

"What can I do for my favorite bikers?" he asked, rubbing his hands together. "Blonde? Brunette? Maybe a feisty redhead? What tickles your fancy today, gentlemen? Perhaps you prefer something with a little more of an *international* feel? German, perhaps? Claudia is a lovely chick. Great tits. Even better ass."

"Gimmel Martel. What can you tell me about him?" Bull said, ignoring the offer.

Spider glanced around, suddenly nervous at the mention of the name. He adjusted his collar and his shadiness went from ten to a thousand in a matter of seconds.

"Follow me," he said with another nervous glance around the club.

He led us through the scattering of empty tables to his office in the back. It was just as seedy as his club, and once inside I couldn't help but wonder how much body fluid was drying on the surfaces.

"So you've heard," he said, walking behind his desk.

"Yeah. *We've heard*. The question is, why didn't we hear it from you?" Bull asked.

"I just heard about it myself."

"Yeah, I find that hard to believe, *Spidey*."

"It's true. I swear. I mean, I heard rumors but nothing concrete. Not until this morning."

"What can you tell us about him?"

"Word on the street is that he's into some pretty heavy shit with the Saljav cartel."

I looked at Bull but he remained motionless despite the mention of the Saljav. They were a fierce and greatly feared cartel that ran out of Central America. They were ruthless killers who showed little restraint and no mercy. Not someone you got into bed with.

If you did, chances were you'd wake up with more than a horse's head lying next to you.

"This *word on the street*... how reliable is it?" Bull asked.

"Pretty fucking reliable." Spider looked serious. "I have to be honest with you, Bull, the idea of those freaks being even remotely involved with anyone in this town scares the fuck out of me. You know they were behind the Lobo limousine incident, right?"

Lobo was a small town in Central America. So small it wasn't even on a map. One morning last June, a limousine rolled down the town's main street and came to a stop by slowly crashing into a streetlight in front of the police station. Inside were the decapitated bodies of several people, their shoes off and their heads in the trunk.

The incident made the news all around the world. It was a message to anyone who dared to fuck with the Salvaj.

This is what happens to our rivals.

"What is Martel's involvement with the cartel? How does he benefit from aligning himself with them?" I asked.

Spider's shifty eyes shot to mine. "It's your basic import-export deal. Martel has the real estate and transportation, and they have the product. It's so simple it's almost unbelievable."

"And you're absolutely sure about this?" Bull asked.

"Yeah. I've heard it from more than one source." He shook his head. "If I hear anything else I will contact you. But fucking keep my name out of this, Bull, because I don't want my head to end up on a spike and sent to my mother in the mail."

Outside the club, we talked as we walked to our bikes.

"You think it's reliable information?" I asked Bull.

"Despite being a slimy sonofabitch, he's never let us down before. But we need to investigate it. Find out for ourselves if Martel really is involved with the Saljav, and if he is, how far does his involvement go and what the fuck does that mean for Destiny?" He climbed on his bike. "I want to pay Gimmel Martel a visit. Ask him myself."

We started our bikes and the sound of two barking Harleys rumbled through the alleyway.

"That's our next move?"

Bull nodded. "Tomorrow, we'll pay him a visit. Welcome him to our town ... Kings of Mayhem style."

After I left Bull, I headed for home.

Earlier, Chastity had texted me asking if I would be interested in having dinner. A thank you for letting her stay with me.

It was thoughtful but not necessary. I was enjoying the company.

When I pulled up to the house, Chastity's car was in the driveway and all the lights were on. As I approached the front door, I was greeted by the distinct smell of something burning.

Inside, she was chopping salad vegetables at the kitchen counter, while Roky Erickson sang about a *"Creature With An Atom Brain"* on the stereo. The sharp aroma of burnt food was thicker inside, but apparently, she didn't notice it.

"Hey, is everything okay?" I asked, dumping my backpack on the kitchen table.

She looked up and smiled. "Sure, why do you ask?"

"It smells like something is burning in here."

"It does?" She looked surprised but then her features smoothed and she waved it off, returning to chopping up bell peppers for the salad. "It's just dinner. It's a new recipe I'm trying."

I glanced at the electric skillet on the kitchen counter. It was definitely ground zero.

When I walked over to it and opened it, I had to contain my laughter.

"Um, Chastity? What the fuck is this?"

She looked up. "Corned beef. Why?"

I stared at the charcoal lump smoldering in the pan.

"Wait... it's not meant to look like that!" She shrieked, as she peered over my shoulder. "And where are my onions and carrots?"

I looked at the black lumps next to the hunk of burned meat, suspecting they were the missing onions and carrots in a charred disguise.

Chastity raced to the notepad by the telephone and started to read out what she had written down.

"Fill pan with water, a splash of vinegar and cloves. Add onion, carrots, and meat. Cook for several hours until meat is tender."

I lifted the meat up with a roasting fork. "I think we passed tender a few hours ago. We're well and truly into rigor mortis now."

She squinted as she held the notepad closer so she could see what she had written. "Oh crap! I think *pan* was meant to say *pot*. I was supposed to do it in a pot. Not a pan!" She threw the notepad down on the counter. "See, this is why I don't cook."

I dropped the meat back into the electric skillet, and when the fork fell away, the meat was bright pink inside. I wanted to laugh, but Chastity looked so disappointed.

I walked over to her. "How about you keep going with the salad and I make us some pasta."

"You cook?"

I winked at her. "I'm a man of many talents. Grab me a can of tomatoes out of the pantry."

Within half an hour, the offending corned beef was disposed of and two plates of steaming pasta marinara sat on the kitchen counter. I grabbed a couple of beers, flipped the lids off and handed one to Chastity. Because it was hot, we sat out on the deck overlooking the pool and ate our dinner.

"This is so much better than hot pink corned beef," Chastity said, slurping pasta through her plump lips.

"It was a pretty impressive color. And those carrots and onions..." I teased.

She blushed but laughed. "Talk about epic fail. Although, I don't know why I'm so surprised. After today it's a wonder I didn't burn the damn kitchen down."

"What happened today?"

She reached for her beer. "I flunked my biology exam."

"Damn." Chastity was a smart girl. I didn't think she could fail at anything. Except, maybe cooking. "Do you get to retake it?"

"No. So I have to nail my next one, or I risk flunking the class."

"When is your next exam."

"In a couple of weeks."

I took a sip of my beer. "Do you need help?"

"Desperately," she said. "I asked Indy but she is on nightshift for the next four nights. And there is this guy in my science class who offered to help me study. But if I'm really honest, I'm not sure how much studying he'd like to get done."

"He likes you?"

"I think so. But I can't afford the distraction right now. Not with my exam only a few weeks away." She took a sip of beer and then picked up her fork again. "Besides, I've got a date with someone else."

My eyes shot to hers. "You have a date?"

She gave me a sheepish look, and I couldn't help but notice how long her lashes were. "Yeah, tomorrow night…"

I ignored the strange bite in my gut. "With who?"

"Some guy who works at the mechanic workshop near Wax-It."

I tried to think of any mechanics who worked out that way, but couldn't think of any. "A mechanic, huh?"

She chuckled. "You say that like mechanics are trouble."

"Yeah, well, most of the ones I know *are* trouble."

"That's because most of the mechanics you know are caught up with biker business."

The way she said it struck a nerve and I couldn't understand why. I narrowed my eyes and focused on getting my pasta onto my fork.

"Anyway, this guy seems nice. He's new in town. Moved up from Mobile a few weeks ago." She started twirling her pasta with her fork. "Which is great, by the way."

"Oh yeah, why is that?"

"Because it means he doesn't know anything about me or who my family is, or anything about the club."

Again, a weird sensation tightened in my gut. "If a guy doesn't accept you or where you're from, then he isn't worth your time."

I knew her ex-boyfriend had dumped her because of her family roots being so deep in the Kings of Mayhem MC, and I knew it hurt her badly.

"I know, but it tends to put people off. It's easy for you guys. Girls drop their panties in a heartbeat to get close to a King and don't try denying it. My entire life I've watched girls lose their minds over my brothers and other club members. But it's different for us girls. Guys are easily intimidated."

"Then clearly they're not for you." I picked up my beer and took a swig. "You want to date a guy with balls."

"I'm pretty sure Peter has some balls." She grinned at me. "And believe me, I plan on finding out."

I choked on my beer. "What the fuck?"

"Sorry, is that too much of an overshare?"

"Yeah, that was too much of *everything*."

She shrugged. "I don't know if you've noticed, *roomie*, but I don't see a lot of guys lining up at *your* front door to date me. So I intend on taking full advantage and seeing where it goes."

The idea of her *seeing where it goes* with a mechanic in town made me frown.

I tried to think of a suitable response, but I was suddenly distracted by a drop of marinara sauce on her bottom lip, followed by the swipe of her tongue as it peeked out to lick it away.

As she flicked her long, dark hair over her shoulders, alarm bells went off inside me and my stomach roiled with guilt.

Because in my head I was the one licking the rich sauce from her lips.

Suddenly frustrated, I pushed my food away as I forced the thought from my mind.

I wasn't interested in Chastity

I didn't think of her that way.

Not at all.

But obviously my self-imposed dry spell decided it was time to fuck with me and make me think that I did.

CHAPTER 9

RUGER

The following morning, Bull, Chance, Cade, Maverick, and I rode out to meet Gimmel Martel at Eagle's Nest.

Eagle's Nest was a majestic, antebellum home rising out of a lush green lawn at the end of a long white driveway. Surrounded by grapevines for as far as the eye could see, it was a massive property oozing opulence and old Southern charm. It was palatial. Extravagant. And as out of place in Destiny, Mississippi, as a pope in a brothel.

When we pulled up to the celebrated vineyard, we were stopped by six-foot security gates and men dressed all in black. It was to be expected. Six men roaring up on Harleys was a notable threat.

What wasn't expected was being let through with little interrogation.

It meant only one thing.

Martel was expecting us.

We parked our bikes by a statue of David. *Yep. The naked Italian guy*. Right here in Destiny.

Maverick found it fascinating, while Cade and Chance looked confused by it.

At the top of a broad set of concrete steps stood the man we came to see. Gimmel Martel. Wine importer. Business tycoon. Probable drug mule for the lethal Salvaj cartel.

He wasn't a tall man. Next to a six-foot-six Maverick, he was downright tiny. But for what he lacked in size, he more than made up in pompous charm. His French accent was thick. His aloof arrogance thicker.

"Ah, the legendary Kings of Mayhem. Welcome, welcome. To what do I owe the pleasure?"

Bull stepped forward, removing his glasses to expose his otherworldly eyes.

"We were just in the neighborhood. Thought we'd drop by, do the neighborly thing and introduce ourselves."

Bull was as intimidating as fuck. But Martel was unfazed.

"I see. Well, it's a pleasure. Welcome to my home. Please, if you will join me in the parlor so we can get better acquainted." He extended an arm and gestured for us to step inside the grand foyer.

If the outside of Eagle's Nest was magnificent, then the inside was plain over the top. Everything was excessive. From the parquet flooring and luxurious velvet window dressings, to the ornate furniture, plush Turkish carpets and gilded artwork lining the timber paneled walls. The ceiling was high and painted, and a massive chandelier of wrought iron and crystal hung over the grand, sweeping staircase.

As we followed Martel through the foyer to an opulent room off to the side, our footsteps echoed through the house.

"Killer acoustics," Maverick whispered, impressed. To drive home the point, he started to whistle until Bull threw him a dark look.

Martel led us into the parlor which was as over-exaggerated as the rest of the house. Gilded alabaster walls. Renaissance artwork as tall as me. French décor I hadn't seen the likes of since I'd left New Orleans.

Martel spoke to his servants, one of whom I suspected was a bodyguard, in French. He asked one to bring us a bottle of Syrah but *not the good one.* Which caught my attention. He had no idea I was fluent in his native tongue and could understand every word. Which became more apparent when he added, *I'm sure these rednecks wouldn't know a good bottle of wine if it had a voice and could introduce itself.*

To which his staff laughed.

I planned to say nothing. After all, my knowledge of his language without him realizing it, was an asset. But when he referred to us as assholes in French, asset or no asset, it was time to put him in his place.

In perfect French I asked, *"Would you prefer this discussion take place in French, Mr. Martel?"*

His head snapped to me, taken back by my flawless enunciation.

Then I added in Latin, *"Or perhaps you would prefer Latin?"*

And because I was enjoying the flash of discomfort on his smarmy little toad face, I also threw in some of my mother's native tongue and asked, *"Or are you familiar with the language of the people of Denmark?"*

With a tight jaw, Martel held my gaze as he weighed the situation before finally replying, "English will suffice."

We stared at one another for a moment longer. And it was in that moment his mask slipped and I could see the monster beneath the façade. Gimmel Martel was never going to be an ally of the Kings of Mayhem.

And he knew I knew it.

He drew his eyes from me, and like a light switch, his demeanor was again kind and welcoming.

"Please, have a seat," he said to Bull.

But Bull didn't move. "We're fine standing."

"Of course. I, on the other hand, have had a rather demanding morning. I was just about to enjoy a cigar… can I tempt you to join me?"

"Not today."

Martel held up a Gran Habano. "You mind?"

"By all means."

We all watched as he took his time lighting his cigar before sitting back and crossing his legs. Sweet smoke clouded about his head. "So, gentlemen, how can I help you?"

Bull was indulging him.

For now.

"I'm going to cut to the chase," he said. "I've heard *things*. Rumors about your little wine importing scenario being a front for something a little more *unsavory*. Less legal, if you will. More likely to piss off someone you don't want to piss off. Someone like *me*, for instance."

If Martel's forehead wasn't so shiny and stiff, and obviously full of Botox, it would've wrinkled with confusion. He looked slightly confused. Perplexed. Innocent.

Like a liar.

"I'm afraid I don't understand."

Bull had a short wick at the best of times. And this guy was going to burn it down quick if he kept up this act.

"Let's just say, there's been mention of you working with our friends over the border… powerful friends… to help shift their merchandise."

Martel looked surprised.

"Are you talking about a *cartel*?" He suddenly burst into laughter as if it was the funniest thing he'd ever heard. "Oh please, you have a very strong imagination, my friend. That's what TV shows and movies are made of... not real life."

He laughed again, but when Bull didn't move a muscle his laughter slowly faded.

"I assure you, I am merely a man who likes his wine. I import it for the enjoyment of others, and grow my own merely for personal pleasure. A hobby, if you will."

He looked relaxed. Like a man without a care in the world. Although, his body slightly stiffened when Bull sat down in a gold velvet wing-backed chair across from him.

"Boy, that's a relief to hear," he said, faking a smile that was as unnerving as his demonic eyes. "Because I'd hate for us to have a problem here."

"A problem?"

Bull's smile vanished as he dropped the niceties. "If I discover you're lying to me and Eagle's Nest is a façade for bringing drugs into my town, I'll fucking burn it to the ground. Do you understand me?"

The two men stared at each other.

"I think it's time you left," Martel said calmly.

Bull said nothing as he rose. But his eyes remained on Martel as he walked toward the door.

I, on the other hand, decided to give him a farewell in French. *"Today, we came here as a courtesy. But you put a hair out of place in this town, and next time, we'll bring war."*

You could cut the tension in the room with a butter knife.

Thankfully, Martel didn't stick his turtleneck-wearing thugs on us and we made it out alive.

Outside, Yale stared at me in disbelief.

"Dude! *You* know French?"

I gave him a look. "My father was French, my surname is La Montagne and I'm from New Orleans. The chances were heavily in my favor, *mon ami.*"

Yale still looked surprised. "*Fuck.* I didn't even know you had a surname."

Yale wasn't the smartest tool in the shed.

I raised my eyebrow at him and kept walking to catch up to Bull.

"Martel is lying," I said.

"I know."

"He thinks he's got us fooled."

"Good, it means he'll fuck up."

I slid on my sunglasses. "So, what do you want to do about it?"

Bull climbed on his bike. "We wait and we watch. And when he makes a move, we take him down."

CHAPTER 10

CHASTITY

On Saturday night, Peter picked me up for our date, and when he arrived, he took one look at the black dress I was wearing and whistled.

He looked good, too. Black button-up shirt over well-fitting chinos, cleanly shaven with black hair tousled and falling over his forehead.

He took me to a bar in town called The Salty Fish. It was usually a popular place on a Saturday, but tonight it was quiet because of a college football game over in Humphrey.

We sat in the dark booth toward the back of the bar, in the corner, where a glowing Miller Lite sign barely made a dent in the shadows.

"So, tell me how a good-looking girl like yourself is single?" he asked after the waitress left with our order.

The question was cheesy, but he asked it with the cutest grin on his face and it came across as more endearing than anything.

"I had a long-term boyfriend in college, but when I came back to Destiny we broke up."

It was only a half-truth. I just didn't feel like explaining the reasons behind it. I had moved on from Joey. He wasn't *Joey who dumped me by text message* anymore. He was just *Joey, some guy I used to know*. He made sure of that when he replaced me within a month of ending our engagement.

"And no one since?"

I shook my head. "No. I've been busy trying to finish college while working part-time."

He nodded. "I get it. I had to juggle finishing high school and working at my daddy's workshop in the afternoons and on the weekends. Then there was football."

That explained the athletic body and impressive abs.

"Did you go to college on a football scholarship?" I asked.

"Nah. When my mom walked out on us I had to quit school altogether and go and work for my old man."

"I'm sorry," I said, feeling bad for the assumption.

"It's okay, I did alright. I've been fixing cars full-time for almost six years now and I'm good at it." He grinned at me across the table. "I've been told I'm pretty damn good with my hands."

He winked when he said it and I smiled, but I wasn't really feeling the sexual innuendo he was throwing my way. Peter seemed nice and he was definitely easy on the eye. But our conversation had slowly become stilted and forced. Without warning, my mind drifted back to last night when I was sitting with Ruger out under the stars. We had talked for hours, about everything and anything, and with every passing minute I had felt a subtle pull in his direction. It felt like we could talk forever and would never run out of things to say.

But this, now... it was obvious Peter and I had little in common.

I cleared my throat as if it could somehow clear the thoughts of Ruger from my mind. Not to mention the butterflies brushing up against my insides when I thought of him.

The waitress brought over our order of burgers and fries, plus a beer for Peter and a Coke for me.

"Do you have brothers and sisters?" I asked, grabbing a fry and popping it into my mouth. Peter's gaze dropped to my lips before he replied.

"Nah, it's just me and my old man. What about you, do you have brothers and sisters?"

I wondered if Peter's boss had filled him in on who I was, but decided he must have no idea for him to have even showed up for our date.

"Three older brothers." Again, his eyes watched my lips. "But no sisters."

As an awkward silence fell between us, I sipped my drink and picked at my burger, while searching for things to talk about.

"What made you move to Destiny?" I asked.

He smiled lazily. "Got into a bit of trouble back in Alabama after my old man died. Went off the rails. Did some stupid shit. My uncle lives out by the watermelon fields and invited me to stay with him so I could start fresh." He took a swig of beer while I wondered what *stupid shit* he did back in Alabama that required him to *start fresh* in another state. But he gave me a reassuring look. "I've put that all behind me now."

It didn't matter. I had already made up my mind that a second date wouldn't be happening. We were definitely missing that spark that warranted another night out and really didn't have anything in common. So I was grateful when he paid the bill and suggested we head home.

"Let me walk you to the door," he insisted as we pulled up in front of Ruger's house.

Ruger's bike was in the driveway, but I knew he wasn't home because his truck wasn't in its usual spot next to it. But he had left the porch light on.

"Well, thanks for dinner," I said as we reached the door.

Peter turned me to face him and I knew he was going to kiss me when I saw the look on his face. I laughed nervously, suddenly wishing I had said goodnight to him in the car instead. I thought we were on the same page. When he abruptly suggested we leave the restaurant I thought it was because he felt the same lack of interest as me.

Instead, he bent his head and went in for the kiss. But as soon as his lips touched mine, I knew it wasn't *his* lips I wanted to feel there.

I broke it off and stepped back, ready to say goodnight.

But Peter didn't seem to notice my lack of interest. Instead, he grinned at me. "How about I come in for a nightcap."

I hesitated long enough for him to push the door open and walk in. A little annoyed at his cockiness, I walked in behind him, certain more than ever that this guy had to go. Our date was done. We were done. The whole thing had been a bad idea. "Listen, I'm actually pretty tired. Can I have a raincheck on that nightcap?"

But Peter ignored me and moved into the living room as if he owned the place. I followed him closely, and when he stopped suddenly, I slammed into his back. Without warning, he swung around and smashed his lips to mine.

"Okay, that's enough," I said, pulling away from him. "I think you'd better go."

He looked at me, frustrated. "You're kidding, right?"

I frowned. I didn't appreciate his tone.

"No. I'm not. It's time for you to leave."

His face darkened and a nasty glint came over his eyes. "You're a fucking cock tease, you know that?"

My eyes darted to his.

"Excuse me?" I asked, taken back by his sudden change in demeanor.

"You heard me," he said darkly. "You've been creaming those panties wanting me to touch you all night, and when I finally do, you play hard to get."

Creaming those panties. What the fuck?

I recoiled further away from him.

"You need to leave," I demanded.

But he ignored the warning. Instead, he walked toward me, predatorily.

"Why? Is your pussy too good for me?" He grabbed at me, and when I struggled, he wrapped his arms around me so I couldn't move. "Come on, baby, you know you want to do it with me."

He kissed me, this time thrusting his tongue into my mouth until I was gagging.

"I said no!" I yelled, ripping my mouth away from his. I elbowed his ribs and his hold on me broke. "Now get the hell out of my house."

When I shoved him in the chest, he hit me so hard across the face, my head whipped to the side. Momentarily paralyzed by the sting, I quickly regained my senses and shook it off. Anger tore through me. No man did that to me. Feeling furious, I pulled back my arm and punched him right in his filthy mouth.

But if I thought it was enough to deter him, I was wrong. A dark heat raged in his eyes as he wiped the blood from the corner of his mouth and smiled.

"I knew you MC bitches liked it rough." He stalked toward me, and before I could move out of the way, he pushed me backwards so I lost my footing and fell onto the couch. Quicker than I could blink, he was on top of me. And he was hard. I could feel it against my thigh as he blanketed me. Pushing me around had turned him on.

"Get the fuck off me!" I demanded.

"Don't be a tease, baby. You know you want it. You've been watching me with those fuck-me eyes for weeks now." I struggled violently beneath him. "Yeah, baby. Keep struggling. I like a bitch with a bit of fight in her. It fucking makes me so damn hard."

Just as I was about to knee him in the balls, his weight disappeared off me and a growl reverberated around the room. As I looked up, Ruger threw Peter up against the wall and held him there by his throat, his eyes wild with rage.

Peter tried to fight back, but he was no match for Ruger's strength and struggled in his grasp. Blood flew in the air as Ruger smashed his fist repeatedly into his face.

Christ. He was going to murder him.

"Stop!" I yelled and Ruger's fist paused mid-flight. I stumbled to my feet and went to his side. "You'll kill him."

Compared to Ruger, Peter was a skinny runt. He couldn't take the type of pounding he was being given.

"He was forcing himself on you," Ruger growled. "Someone needs to teach him a lesson."

"And you have. But no more. Let him go. You'll end up killing him, and he's not worth the prison time."

Ruger looked at Peter, who was barely coherent at this point, and smiled menacingly. "Can't send me to prison if they can't find the body."

Peter looked terrified, even peed his pants, the stain spread across his light-colored chinos as Ruger held him pinned to the wall.

I placed my hand on Ruger's arm. I needed to soothe the rage out of him. To calm the storm in those bright green eyes. "Let him go."

He did as I asked and Peter dropped to the floor in a bloody, whimpering mess.

Ruger hauled him to his feet, his eyes blazing with rage. "Just so you know, *I am* going to kill you."

Panicked, Peter took off out the front door but tripped on his way down the steps and fell into a heap on the grass. Scrambling to his feet, he scurried across the lawn to his car, where he gunned the engine and sped off into the night.

"Are you okay?" Ruger asked gently.

I nodded. I was rattled, but I was okay. "Thank you."

His thumb tenderly caressed the swollen skin of my cheekbone. "Did he do this?"

When I nodded, his eyes darkened and his jaw tightened. He hissed in a deep breath. "Let me go after him and finish what I started."

"Like I said, he isn't worth it."

Ruger didn't think twice, he pulled me against his chest and wrapped his arms around me. The strong pounding of his heart against my cheek filled me with comfort and I softened against him. It felt good to be in his arms. Warm and comforting. It felt right.

He ran his hand threw my hair and kissed the top of my head, and it was the balm I needed.

"Just so you know," I murmured against his chest. "I was totally about to kick his ass."

I felt him chuckle, heard the throat rumble in his chest. I knew I should end the embrace and step away, but the gentleness in his touch was soothing and I wanted to stay this close to him for a little longer.

It was Ruger who pulled away.

"I have no doubt you would've handed him his ass." His eyes sparkled as he looked down at me.

Something passed between us. Something warm and unmeasurable.

But in a heartbeat it was gone.

And as I looked him in the eyes, I began to wonder why I even went out with Peter in the first place.

When the man I was really interested in was right under my nose all along.

CHAPTER 11

RUGER

In chapel the following day, Bull brought the club up to speed about Gimmel Martel. It wasn't unusual for Bull to explore someone's past as much as he had with Martel. Someone with his connections, wealth, and power had the potential to poison this town and in order to protect our interests, Bull made sure any new face, business, or corporation entering the county was fully vetted.

But it was hard to focus.

I was distracted by Chastity and how she had gone on a date.

And how that date had forced himself on her.

My hands fisted beneath the table when I thought about it. My knuckles were red. My bones glowing with the bruises you got when you pounded them into a raping asshole that you caught trying to sexually assault your roomie.

But it wasn't just the attack that had me wound up.

For some damn reason, the idea of her dating at all appealed to me about as much as nails down a blackboard.

Clearly, I was feeling protective of her. It was normal. I'd known her, her entire life. So when she went on a date it only made sense that I would feel... *jealous?*

Not jealous.

Protective.

And with good reason. I had half a mind to hunt down the asshole and finish what I had started last night. Despite Chastity's pleas for me not to.

I frowned and tried to focus on what Bull was saying. He had moved on from Martel and was discussing the marijuana fields and this year's crop, which was being distributed by the Knights. Once upon a time, they had been our rivals. But a profitable supply and distribution deal between the clubs had made us allies, and the last few years had been lucrative for both of us. This year we were going to triple our return on investment.

But my mind kept shifting back to last night and how good Chastity had looked. How *beautiful* she was. Her eyes. Her hair. The way that dress hugged her luscious curves.

All the things I shouldn't be noticing. Yet couldn't stop thinking about.

Jesus Christ, she was just a kid.

Not to mention, Bull's niece.

I shifted uncomfortably in my seat.

I told myself my reaction came from a shift in our friendship. Which was to be expected when you shared a house together, right?

But the idea of her dating. I didn't like it.

Not one bit.

And now I needed to work out why.

Was it because she was Chastity and no man would ever be worthy?

Or was it for more selfish reasons?

CHAPTER 12

CHASTITY

The day after my disastrous date with Peter, I had classes in the morning and then a shift at Wax-it until four o'clock. Thankfully I didn't see Peter, because according to Simone, he had called his boss and quit with some excuse about moving back to Alabama. It didn't surprise me. If I were him, I would, too. He had poked the Kings of Mayhem bear, and he knew it. His best chance at not living a life where he had to look over his shoulder everyday was to leave town.

And let's face it. The only reason he was still breathing was because I had stopped Ruger from going after him, and showing him what a real man thought of a man who forced himself on a woman.

Finishing up at the salon, I climbed into my car and drove home with the windows down because the air conditioning was acting up. It was one of the hottest days of the summer so far, the heat was thick in the air and I had been fantasizing about Ruger's pool since lunch time.

When I arrived home, Ruger was in the driveway washing his bike.

Shirtless.

"How much do you charge?" I asked as I climbed out of my car. "Mine could use a wash."

"I don't come cheap," he replied, standing up from washing the motorcycle wheels, and dear God, I almost choked on my own breath.

My eyes swept up the length of him. Yeah, he was sixteen years older than me, but he had the body men my age would kill for.

Wide, rounded shoulders.

A broad, chiseled chest.

Arms you couldn't wrap two hands around.

Tattoos covering his arms and his chest, and across his impressive six-pack. When he moved, his abs rippled beneath his taut, perfect skin.

"Do I get a roomie discount?" I asked, trying desperately to tear my eyes off that ridiculously sexy V disappearing beneath his belt.

"I'll tell you what, two pairs of hands are faster than one. How about you help me with my bike and I'll help you with your car."

He threw a soapy sponge at me, and it sent water spraying across my stomach. Soap suds soaked into my shirt and dripped onto my thighs.

I tracked his eyes as they slid up and down the length of my body, and noticed how his jaw tightened before he looked away. Goosebumps rippled along my skin. That look. His eyes. I bit down on my bottom lip. It was unmistakable. He had just checked me out, and it had unnerved him.

"I'll get another sponge," he said, turning away.

He walked into the garage and took a second sponge off one of the shelves, picking up a second bucket near the door as he walked back out to the driveway. I watched as he effortlessly picked up the bucket full of soapy water and poured half of it into the second bucket. He was big. He was strong. And he did everything with ease.

When he crouched down to clean the wheels of his bike, I squatted down across from him to clean the other one.

I stole a glance at his knuckles. They were red and swollen from repeatedly coming into contact with Peter's face.

"He left town," I said, looking at him over his motorcycle.

"Who?"

It was hard not to notice the way his shoulder muscles rolled and pulled with every swipe of the sponge.

"Peter," I said.

He paused, only briefly, but then kept washing the wheel. "Wise move."

I couldn't help but feel bad for getting Ruger involved.

"Turns out he didn't have any balls after all."

He lifted his head and his eyes met mine. "Men who force themselves on a woman very rarely do."

I bit into my lower lip. "I know you don't believe me, but I *was* going to kick his ass."

He didn't reply, but a ghost of a smile tugged at his lips.

When we were done with his bike, he hosed it off and dried it with a cloth, gently wiping away the drops of water on the shiny paintwork as if he were caressing a woman's body. Instantly, heat flooded my veins. It was just a piece of machinery. A hunk of metal and chrome. But his hands swept over it with care and respect, and the tenderness of a lover.

Of course, my mind instantly went to where it shouldn't. If he touched his bike like that, how did he touch a woman? I imagined it was with infinite tenderness. His hands were big, strong, and I would bet he could make any woman writhe with pleasure beneath them.

I glanced down at his boots. His feet were big. His body was big. His hands were big. What were the chances that his cock was big, too?

My breath left me in a gasp and he looked over at me, his sparkling green eyes questioning.

"You okay?"

My cheeks flushed.

I was standing there picturing him naked, and every inch of me felt hot with desire. I struggled to swallow. "I think I'll start on my car."

He joined me and we were both silent as we cleaned my beaten-up Dodge. I had lost my ability to talk because I couldn't get the crazy images of a naked Ruger out of my head. But I wasn't sure what had caused his silence.

I glanced over at him. He looked like he was lost in thought. Like he was trying to figure something out. It was probably club business, I decided, and he would never confide in me about it so I let the silence linger between us.

Without warning he aimed the arc of water at me, soaking me head to toe.

It shocked me out of my thoughts and I grinned wickedly across at him.

The move meant war.

I dunked my sponge in the bucket and threw it at him, hitting him in his rock-hard chest. Water and bubbles gleamed on his flawless body, the white suds in deep contrast to his smooth, tattooed skin.

It was on then.

Water flew through the air and soap suds rained down like snowflakes as we fought our battle and chased one another around the car.

As I ran toward the sponge laying on the hood of the car, I slipped, but Ruger's strong arms caught me.

To right myself, I pressed my palms against his chest. It was hard like stone but infinitely warm. His eyes darkened and his lips parted. Immediately, the muscles between my legs began to throb, stimulated by the look of raw need on his face.

I struggled to swallow. "Thanks."

He smiled but it didn't reach his eyes. Heat radiated from him, and I could see his pulse pounding against his throat. "You're welcome."

The seconds ticked by excruciatingly slow. My breath caught in my chest. Against me, his body felt powerful and protective. And the scent of him. It was pure man.

He cleared his throat and let me go, and the sudden absence of his body against mine made me shiver. I took a step back, surprised by the tightening of his jaw and the frown on his face.

"I think we're done," he said, looking away and picking up the bucket and sponge.

And just like that it was over.

Ruger walked away and I was left standing there wondering what the hell had just happened.

CHAPTER 13

RUGER

Jesus Christ, I was in hell.

In the bathroom I stripped out of my wet jeans and stood naked at the sink. I leaned against the porcelain, my fingers gripping the edge until they were white-knuckled.

"What the fuck is wrong with you?" I asked my reflection in the mirror.

My cock was hard and my body was jacked up and tight with tension as images of Chastity all wet and soapy tormented me. I squeezed my eyes tight to send them away, but there was no escaping them.

The way her sopping wet t-shirt clung to her body and her tight, perky nipples. The way the soapy water slid down her firm, wet thighs. The way her bee-stung lips glistened when she ran her soft, pink tongue across them. Her juicy ass and long legs as she bent over and searched the water bucket for the sponge.

Frustrated, I stepped into the shower and stood under a stream of warm water, the tautness in my shoulders slowly easing as I soaped up my body and refused to think about Chastity.

Or her luscious body.

And the things I wanted to do to it.

I wasn't meant for her in that way, I reminded myself.

My place in her life was like that of an uncle. A friend. *A protector.*

Fuck.

I thought about our past. I had watched her grow up. I was there when she was born and the day she started her first day of school, for crying out loud. I was there after her father died and again when she started high school, watching as she stumbled through the awkward teenage years trying to figure out who she was.

Hell, I was there for almost every milestone, including the day she left for college.

Now I was starting to see her in a different light and it made me feel like a creep. I shouldn't be noticing her perky breasts and the way her nipples pressed against the fabric of her shirt. And I definitely, shouldn't be wondering how those juicy lips of hers would taste, or how that luscious body of hers would feel under mine as I made love to her. But I was and it was making me hard every time I did.

I'd never been tempted to do anything about it. But now I was stroking my cock, and as hard as I tried, I couldn't get her out of my head. *Those succulent lips. Those lusty eyes. The way her ass swayed as she walked. The way she smiled at me.* My lips parted and a moan escaped me. This was happening whether I liked it or not. I was jerking off to a woman I had no business fucking with. But tell that to my cock. I closed my eyes and thought about her and the smooth flesh of her throat. About her flawless skin. About the slim contours of her arms and the way her tongue ran over her lips as she thought about something. The feel of her hand on my arm. On my chest.

Her lips wrapped around my cock as she bent her head to fuck me with her mouth.

I groaned and my stroking picked up speed. I was going to come. How couldn't I when all I could see in my mind's eye was Chastity kneeling before me with her lips closing over the head of my cock? With a husky groan, my orgasm tore out of me and I came in throbbing waves into the stream of shower water. It was my first release in days, and it just kept coming. I pressed my free hand against the glass and moaned with ecstasy until it slowly receded.

Breathless I dropped my head back and let the shower wash it all away.

My cum.

The sin of wanting her.

The images of her in my head. *Naked.*

My groan echoed around the bathroom. What the fuck was wrong with me?

I ran a hand across my head.

I'd hoped jerking off would get her out of my system.

But the moment I thought of her again I knew there was no chance. The need to hold her. Kiss her. Fuck her. It was still there.

There was no denying it, I was drawn to her and powerless against it.

And I was totally screwed.

Obviously, I needed sex.

And I needed it with something other than my hand.

It was time to get back in the saddle and start dating again.

I needed the distraction. Something to stop me from noticing Chastity.

The way she looked.

The way she smelled.

The way she walked into the kitchen wearing nothing but a tank top and a tiny pair of shorts.

I was a grown man, yet I was walking around with fucking wood whenever she came in wearing those shorts. Or her bikini. Or the tight black skirt she had to wear to work.

Let's face it. She could walk in wearing a fucking burlap sack and it would make me hard.

So the clear and obvious answer here was to go on a date.

I had known Jenny for a few months. She worked for the supply chain who kept the clubhouse kitchen stocked. Every month she would come in and go over an order with Mrs. Stephens, the club's housekeeper and events coordinator, and our conversations got longer and longer with every visit. I knew she was interested in me. She was sweet and clearly a classy lady, and when she flirted it wasn't over the top or a blatant invitation to take her to bed. She was funny and kind, and definitely the type of woman you could see as a permanent fixture in your life.

In a desperate move, I broke my *no women* ban and asked her out on a date.

Much to my club brothers' surprise.

But not Chastity's.

When I told her, she didn't say much. Just smiled and wished me luck before wandering out of the room. It was those moments of clarity that told me I was delusional and a fucking douchebag for ever suspecting there was a mutual attraction between us. Chastity wasn't interested in me.

So in order for me to make everything right in the universe again and get back to being a grown-up and not a love-struck creeper, I was going to take a beautiful woman out to dinner and see what happened.

Which was hopefully a lot of physical fun.

When I picked Jenny up for our date, she answered the door looking beautiful in a silky red dress, heels, and her hair pulled up into a messy blonde bun. She smiled brightly and it was a pretty smile. I'd always thought she was attractive, but tonight was the first time I noticed just *how* attractive she was.

"You look great," she said, taking in my black slacks and fitted black shirt.

"And you look beautiful." I gave her a chaste kiss on her smooth cheek and caught a breath of her subtle perfume. Her eyes glittered up at me and I caught the glint of appreciation there.

I took her to a restaurant in Humphrey. An upscale restaurant called Les Fleur.

It was a nice place. The type of place where waiters smoothed down the table linen between courses, and the head waiter ruled over the room expecting nothing but impeccable standards from his wait staff.

For a weeknight it was busy and the gentle murmur of dinner conversation mingled with the sounds of silverware against china plates as the waiter led us to our table.

I hadn't been on an actual date in years. I had worried it would be awkward. That our conversation would be stilted, followed by long pauses of silence as we struggled to find things to talk about. But it wasn't awkward and we talked easily, about everything. In fact, it was so easy, appetizers came and went, followed by main entrees and dessert, and before I realized it was late and the dinner crowd was thinning.

"Well, that was amazing," she said with a big smile. Her eyes sparkled. "Shall we go back to my place?"

I knew where this was going. And it was exactly what I was after.

Sex.

With something other than my hand.

With a beautiful woman who was clearly into me.

With someone who wasn't the niece of my best friend.

I walked her to her door and we lingered beneath her porch light. She made the first move. Leaning up, she pressed her lips to mine and I responded by holding her to me as I kissed her back. *I want this.* I kissed her harder and she melted into me with a whimper. *I want this.* I was exactly where I wanted to be. I wanted to kiss her until I couldn't think of anything else. I wanted to take her inside and spend the next few hours in her bed. *I really do.* Except... who was I kidding?

My head and heart were saying two different things.

In fact, one was lying.

The kiss died and she pulled back to look at me.

"I'm sorry, did I misread the signs?"

"No, not at all."

A small smile curled on her lips and heat filled her expression. "Want to come inside for a nightcap?"

I should want to.

But unfortunately, I didn't.

Christ, what was wrong with me?

"I should get going," I said, to both of our surprise.

She looked up at me, her wide blue eyes searching my face. "I thought we hit it off really well. Did I miss something?

I felt like a tool.

"I'm sorry." I brushed her cheek with the back of my hand. "I had a really good time tonight. You're a beautiful woman, but tonight made me realize I'm not really ready for this."

"Are you giving me the *it's not you, it's me* line?" she asked good-naturedly.

I smiled at her. "No, definitely not."

She slid an elegant hand across my zipper. "It doesn't have to mean anything."

But I gently pulled it away. "As much as I would love to take you up on that offer, I'm not going to. You deserve better than me going in there and taking that from you when I'm not sure about it." I smiled at her. "So I'm going to walk away. And I'm going to go home and take a cold shower."

That wasn't true. I wasn't even remotely aroused. But I didn't want her knowing that. And she seemed to appreciate the white lie. She smiled and stepped back.

"You know, if ever you do decide you're ready for something more than dinner, call me?"

I gave her a smile. Jenny was a classy lady and I hoped she found someone who deserved all the good she had to give.

"You can count on it."

She blew me a kiss goodbye and I made my way down the porch steps and walked quickly to my truck.

Because if I were being honest.

I just wanted to get home to Chastity.

CHAPTER 14

CHASTITY

"Chastity."

My name was a gentle whisper slowly filtering into my brain and gently pulling me out of my deep slumber.

My eyes fluttered open and immediately focused on Ruger's green eyes sparkling down at me.

I smiled sleepily.

"There she is," he said with a beautiful smile.

Feeling groggy, I sat up. I had fallen asleep on the couch.

While he was on his date, I had tried to study. But it was impossible to concentrate knowing he was out with another woman. Every minute ticked by with excruciating slowness.

What were they doing?

Where did he take her?

Was she pretty?

Was he going to fuck her?

I had given up trying to study. Instead, I celebrated my pity party for one by watching reruns of *Breaking Bad* and eating Milk Duds until my stomach ached.

Sometime between Walt and Jesse cooking meth in the desert and Jesse trying to dispose of a corpse while Walt's wife confronted him about selling marijuana to her husband, I fell into a restless sleep.

I looked at the clock on the wall. It was just after nine-thirty. He was home early. *This is a good sign.* But then I wondered if the date had gone exceptionally well and he had already taken her home and slept with her.

"You're home early," I said admiring his black slacks and tailored, button-up shirt he was wearing. "The date didn't go well?"

He sank down on the couch next to me and reached for my feet, pulling them onto his lap. "It was okay."

"Just okay?" I raised an eyebrow at him. "Where did you take her?"

"Les Fleur."

"That fancy place in Humphrey where you basically have to kill someone to get a reservation?"

He grinned. "Well, the food *is* worth it."

"Hmph," I said, trying to ignore how good he looked dressed up.

"What does hmph mean?"

I shrugged. "I didn't take you for a fine-dining kind of guy. You must like this girl."

"She's nice." Again, he downplayed it, so I threw a cushion at him.

"If she's nice, what are you doing home at nine-thirty?"

"Your exam is in three days, isn't it?"

"Yes, but stop trying to change the—wait, are you saying you came home to help me study?"

The smile he gave me poured warmth into my soul.

"Sure. But if I'd known you were here being a big ol' lazy bones on the couch, I might've stayed out with my date." He gave me a wink and my heart rolled over in my chest.

Ruger had cut his date short to help me study.

"Well don't just sit there, girl, go get them books and let's do this!" he said, reaching for his glasses on the table and slipping them on. Ruger was a good-looking man, but wearing glasses took his sexiness to a whole new level. It was badass biker meets handsome nerd.

The effect was ridiculously hot.

Feeling happy, I grabbed my books from the kitchen table, and for the rest of the night we sat on the couch, me cross-legged and Ruger with his long legs stretched out in front of him as he quizzed me on medical microbiology and infection control. Not an exciting topic, but Ruger plowed ahead with the questions anyway, seemingly getting into it and patiently going over the correct answers when I got them wrong.

Books lay scattered on the couch beside us and across his lap, and as the hours passed us by, I couldn't help but wonder why he left a beautiful woman to come home and study with me. But at the same time, secretly loving that he did and hoping there was something a little more than friendship involved.

I woke up with a pain in my neck. At some point while we studied, we had both fallen asleep. As the fog of sleep slowly lifted, I remembered Ruger making us coffee to help keep us awake because my eyelids had grown heavy and I couldn't stop yawning. The coffee had been strong.

But clearly not strong enough.

Groaning, I sat up and looked over at my roommate asleep at the end of the couch. He looked relaxed, his lashes long and dark against his cheeks, his perfectly full lips slightly parted, his dark brows even.

He's beautiful.

His glasses had fallen onto his chest. Worried he might break them, I pulled them off and placed them on the coffee table.

But the move woke him. Slowly, his eyes opened and immediately found mine.

"Hey," he said, his voice hoarse with sleep.

"Hey," I whispered back.

He sat up looking crumpled and sleepy.

I gestured to his glasses on the table. "Sorry, I woke you. I didn't want you breaking them."

"It's okay. I can't believe we fell asleep."

"I know, right? With biology being so exciting and all."

He smiled sleepily and I had an overwhelming urge to kiss him.

But I licked my lips and pushed the thought away.

On the TV, *The Princess Bride* was just beginning, and when Ruger realized, he groaned.

"You've seen it?" I asked, surprised.

"Seen it? I can practically recite it."

"You?"

"Only a billion times."

Ruger was a constant surprise to me. "Tell me, how does a big bad biker come to know *The Princess Bride* so well?"

"It was my sister's favorite movie and she used to watch it over and over until my eyes and ears bled. Our father gave her the video for Christmas." He gave me a sideways glance. "Videos were what we had before DVDs, by the way."

I gave him a fake glare. "Oh, you're hilarious."

Then Ruger went and quoted the movie and my heart burst like confetti in my chest.

"When I was your age, television was called books."

He grinned at me. That delicious, panty-melting grin that was never far from my mind, and I laughed.

But when our eyes met, slowly our smiles faded and the air around us grew heavy in the silence that followed.

Neither of us moved. Neither of us spoke. Suddenly, it grew very hot. My lips parted and his eyes dipped to them. In his throat, his Adams apple struggled to move as he swallowed deeply. He lifted his gaze and it locked to mine, and it was unmistakable what I saw there. *Desire.* My heart pounded like a drum as I held my breath. *Kiss me.* It was a mantra in my head. *Kiss me.* Because more than anything, I wanted to feel his lips against mine.

The air around us was so thick, I could barely breathe. Time had stopped. The moment stretched out.

Until he cleared his throat and abruptly broke the spell. "I should go to bed."

I swallowed thickly. My mouth dry. My mind scrambling for something to say. "Yeah, I guess it's late."

It was all I could think of to say.

And it sounded so lame.

But I was fighting both shock and disappointment at the same time.

Shock about the level of desire I saw in Ruger's eyes.

And disappointment because he seemed intent on doing nothing about it.

A cold awkwardness replaced the heat in the air as he pulled his big body to his feet. "I'll see you in the morning. Good night, Chastity."

When he was gone, I let out a shaky breath.

Disappointment flooded my chest.

I had fallen for Mr. Untouchable.

And it was in that moment I truly realized what had been there all along.

What I had originally thought was a crush had somehow morphed into something much, much more.

CHAPTER 15

RUGER

I escaped to my room.

Why?

Because I was seconds away from taking Chastity's face in my hands and kissing her senseless.

And who knew what would've fucking happened after that?

I was officially in the danger zone.

I tried not to read too much into it. But I kept thinking about her eyes. There was no denying the want there. Like she was silently begging me to kiss her.

And I had been tempted.

Lord, how I had been tempted.

Feeling antsy, I ran a frustrated hand through my hair and raked my fingers down my face. My body was tight with need, my head crazy with thoughts of kissing her until we were both breathless, before taking her right there on the goddamn couch.

I groaned with searing frustration.

It was one thing to jerk off to the one woman who was completely off limits to you. But to actually consider taking it further and actually touching her was complete insanity.

Hello, douchebag.

I squeezed my eyes shut and pinched the bridge of my nose.

I wanted to take a swim. To let the cool saltwater wash it all away. The need. The want. The tight longing in my chest. But I couldn't leave my room and risk running into Chastity again because there was only so much a man could take in one night. So I opted for a cold shower instead and knocked back two shots of Tennessee whisky to help me sleep.

Thankfully, the next day I had club business to keep me distracted.

Over the last week, our surveillance of Eagle's Nest confirmed our suspicions that Martel was up to something more than making wine. For the last two days, several trucks had come and gone from the vineyard and our intel told us there was much more than wine onboard.

Bull decided it was time to send a message.

We watched and waited for another truck to come and go.

We tracked the truck the moment it left the gates of Eagle's Nest, and followed it by drone as it made its way through back roads. Ten minutes out of town, as it entered a long stretch of highway heading toward the state line, it was met with a massive oil tanker blocking the road.

Our massive oil tanker blocking the road.

As soon as the truck came to a stop, I descended on it. Even though he was armed, the trucker gave little resistance. Clearly, his payroll didn't cover protecting his load from a bunch of hijacking bikers.

Maverick unlocked the back, and as our eyes adjusted to the darkness, the cargo slowly came into view. It looked innocent enough. Crates and crates of wine, all stamped with the familiar Eagle's Nest logo.

With Joker's help, I unloaded a solitary crate onto the dusty roadside, and cracked it open. Rows of wine bottles gleamed in the afternoon sunlight. Exactly what the manifesto declared should be in there.

Bull walked around the crate, examining it, not saying a thing, thinking, studying, before crouching down and yanking on one of the pieces of timber. With a crack it gave way, revealing a secret compartment filled with bags of white powder.

Just as we suspected, Martel was cutting cocaine in the cellar of Eagle's Nest and then shipping it out to distributors.

Bull held up a bag of blow.

"Sonofabitch," he growled. He looked at Joker who was reading the truck's manifesto on a clipboard. "Where is it headed to?"

"Over the state line. A small town just out of Baton Rouge."

"It's probably where the cartel have set up shop to distribute," I said.

Bull stalked over to the truck driver.

"You give your boss a message from me. Tell him we have his truck. Which means we have his coke. And if he wants it back, he knows where to find me."

"How do I get back to town? It's a good ten miles back to Eagle's Nest."

Bull gave him a cold look. "Start walking."

Maverick drove the truck back to the clubhouse while we provided security in the front and behind. Once inside the hallowed halls of the clubhouse, it would be temporarily safe from law enforcement and anyone else who would be interested in a semi-trailer full of drugs.

After arriving back at the compound, Bull called an emergency chapel.

"What does this mean for the Kings of Mayhem?" Griffin asked, when all my club brothers were finally present.

"It means we just poked the bear to make it react," Bull replied.

"And what happens when he comes looking for his coke?" Cade asked.

"He can have his truck and his drugs. But he has to earn them back by leaving town. Gimmel Martel and his special brand of business will kill this town. And I ain't taking that lying down."

"And if he doesn't leave town and decides to retaliate instead?" Caleb asked.

"Retaliation would be a declaration of war." Bull looked around the table. "And if it's war he wants, then it's war I'll give him."

After chapel broke, I debated hanging back at the clubhouse. The adrenaline of the day had me jacked up, and only a few shots of bourbon would help me come down.

I debated it. There was a lot going on in my head that I needed to untangle. I should drink with my brothers and have a good time, forget about it for a few hours.

Or I could quiet the chaos in my head by sinking into my pool and shut out the world in the underwater cathedral where it was peaceful and calm. And silent. *So fucking silent.*

Joker, Maverick, Cool Hand, and Matlock were keen to keep drinking.

But the need to lose myself in my watery solitude won out, so I climbed on my bike and headed for home.

CHAPTER 16

CHASTITY

It was official.

I was dying.

Well, according to the fever I had and my inability to swallow the gargantuan lump of coal that had taken up residence in my throat. I groaned as I attempted to sit up in bed and reach for the glass of water on my night stand. Everything ached. My head, my body, hell, even my damn hair hurt.

Last night I had gone to bed feeling fine. Now I was in the seventh realm of flu hell. Which wasn't surprising, considering Mrs. White came into the salon with a bad cold the day before and coughed all over me when I was waxing her mustache. It was only ever going to be a matter of time before I got the funk.

After draining my glass of water, I moaned again as I lay back down on my damp pillow and let my fever carry me away into a deep, feverous sleep. Fractured images that didn't make sense floated in and out of my brain. I wanted Ruger and, in my delirium, it became my obsession.

Through broken sleep I pictured him naked. Felt his skin beneath the slow glide of my tongue, along the velvety skin of his stomach. Heard his husky rasp in my ear as he buried his face in my neck and took me in every way possible in his bed. *I want you.* I felt the pulse of an orgasm throbbing through me as he made me come.

A few hours later I woke up feeling slightly better and with the need to get out of bed. The aches were gone, but I felt drained, lethargic, and God help me... aroused.

Very aroused.

Deciding Ruger's saltwater pool would do wonders for me, I slipped on my bikini to go for a swim. Ruger would be at the clubhouse, so I had the house to myself.

Heading into the kitchen, I was about to open the back door when something out of the window caught my eye.

It was Ruger and he was rinsing off in the outdoor shower.

Naked.

Like he'd just stepped out of my fevered sleep.

I froze, unable to move as I drank him in. I could see all of him. His body. His bare ass.

His cock.

I swallowed thickly and bit down on my lip, utterly fascinated by the view.

By his nakedness.

By his broad shoulders.

By his thick biceps and how they moved and flexed as he soaped up his gleaming skin.

My eyes were riveted to him, mesmerized by how fucking beautiful his body was. Spellbound by the way the shower water rolled through the dips and grooves of his six-pack in glistening rivulets, and snaked down the soft trail of hair to his big cock. It was long and thick, and swayed when he moved.

Despite never actually touching one, I knew what an erection looked like. But this wasn't one. This was relaxed. *And it was so fucking big.* I licked my lips and willed him to touch it and soap it up. I wanted him to stroke it. I wanted him to make it hard. I wanted him to start breathing quicker as he slid his hand up and down the length of it and made himself come.

My lips parted with a gasp. I was so tight with need I was about ready to snap. Weeks of longing came to a head. My stomach started to spasm and lust made me reach down and slide my fingers beneath my bikini bottom.

Just one brief touch.

I was wet, *soaking wet*, and watching him in all his naked glory was making me wetter. I flinched at my own touch but imagined it was Ruger and his beautiful cock which made my body cream and pulse with pleasure.

I gasped. This was going to happen. A brief touch wasn't going to work here. I needed something to give in me before I went crazy with want. A release. Something to put an end to the insane desire.

He turned to face the stream of water and dipped his head back, rivulets of water trailing down his broad, muscular back. His ass was rock hard and flawless, his legs powerful and strong, everything about him was driving me wild.

My eyes fluttered as pleasure began to swell at the very beginning of me. I'd never felt a man there, but I was ready to come at the thought of him running his cock through the wet folds of velvet flesh and around my aching clit.

My heart gathered speed in my chest and my breathing became ragged as I watched him turn his back to the stream of water and his cock swung back into view.

I licked my lips, my fingers slick as they teased my clit. I started to pant, watching his cock and wanting it inside me.

It was the thought of him pushing into me that unraveled me. I started to come and had to bite down on my lip and press my hand to the wall as a delicious, warm bliss spread through me. My pussy pulsated against my fingers, wanting more, aching to be filled by all of him as it throbbed with my climax.

Breathless, I fell against the wall and let my gaze fall to the man who had me burning with a fever.

He turned off the shower and picked up a towel, wrapping it around his narrow hips as he headed for the back door. I realized there was no way I could face him after I'd just made myself come watching him take a shower, so I willed my boneless legs to work and ran back to my bedroom where I pretended to be asleep. I would wait a while and then wander out, disheveled from sleep. If he were still home, I would pretend I'd just woken up and do everything in my power to not think about him naked, or how much I wanted him to touch me and make me come again.

CHAPTER 17

RUGER

The beautiful brunette grabbed me by the cock and pressed her luscious body against mine. Before I could stop it, her lips were on mine, her tongue sliding into my mouth, her big breasts pressing into my chest.

We were in my bedroom at the clubhouse where she had taken me by surprise when I'd walked in.

She pushed me backwards until I was on the bed and she climbed on top, moaning against my mouth as she started to grind her barely dressed body against my lap. Her lips tasted like vanilla and cherry, and felt glossy as they moved enthusiastically over mine.

It was my birthday.

And clearly my club brothers thought I needed to get laid.

Hence the hot escort.

But it wasn't going to happen.

I mean, I appreciated the gesture, but I had no desire to participate.

I didn't want a party to celebrate my thirty-ninth birthday. But when I had arrived at the clubhouse, one was already in full swing. After a few tense weeks, my brothers were hell-bent on having some fun, and my birthday was the perfect outlet.

Tonight, things were going to get wild.

And if the beautiful woman climbing all over me had her way, she was about to get wild with me.

I ripped my mouth from her and gently pushed her away.

"Okay, you need to take it easy," I said. "This isn't going to—"

She cut me off with her lips and thrust her tongue into my mouth again, trying to coax a response from me. But she wasn't going to get one.

Again, I pushed her away. "This isn't happening."

She leaned back and looked surprised. "What do you mean?"

"This… you and me… "

She looked wounded by the rejection and I felt like an ass.

"Look, you're gorgeous. You really are. But I don't want—"

"Are you saying you don't want to fuck me?" She raised an eyebrow at me.

And I had a feeling she wasn't used to being told no.

"I'm saying I wasn't expecting this."

She leaned closer and grazed my ear with her lips. "When they told me it was for you, I told them I'd do it for free."

Again, I gently pushed her away. I needed to keep her at arm's length to avoid another lip assault. "And that's really kind of you, but I don't want to fuck you."

Her brows slammed together and she gave me a dark look as she climbed off my lap. "Fine. But just so you know, they insisted on paying me, and I don't do refunds."

And here I thought she was doing it for free.

"I'm sure that will be fine."

She gathered up her belongings but paused to look over at me. "You want to know something? I was really looking forward to it. You're a hottie, Ruger. All the girls at The Den think so." The Den was the brothel the Kings of Mayhem owned.

She walked over, and in a surprising move, planted a kiss on the top of my head. "Whoever she is, I hope she realizes how lucky she is."

"What do you mean?" I asked, surprised.

She smiled. "The girl you're in love with."

I chuckled. "No, no... you've got the wrong—"

"Deny it all you like. But I know the look of a guy who's pussy-whipped, it's written all over your handsome face. Happy birthday, Ruger. Go home to your girl."

And with that, she left the room and closed the door behind her.

I waited for a moment, sitting on the end of the bed with my head a mess, before I got up.

In the bathroom, I brushed my teeth and gargled with mouthwash to get the taste of vanilla and cherry out of my mouth.

She was wrong.

I wasn't in love.

I wasn't.

Leaning over the sink, I took a deep breath and exhaled slowly.

Since last night, thoughts of wanting to kiss Chastity had simmered beneath every conscious thought.

I groaned.

Hell, who was I kidding.

It wasn't just thoughts of kissing her invading my every waking moment. Because I didn't just want to kiss her. I was aching to touch her, and it was slowly killing me.

Being my birthday, she had sent me a couple of text messages, but my responses had been short and non-committal because I needed to catch a breath and untangle the mess in my head. And that meant staying as far away from her as possible.

But as it turned out, that was worse.

Because when I wasn't near her, I was wishing I was.

Fuck. I needed to get out there and have a good time.

The way I saw it, tonight I had a choice. I could get shitfaced with the boys. And hell, it was my birthday. I *should* get that drunk with my brothers and have a good time. Even if the thought of waking up in the dead of night, hungover and filled with the ache of loneliness in my clubhouse room was as appealing as a knee to the balls.

Or I could go home, and sleep in my bed, knowing the girl of my dreams was sleeping only yards away from me in another room.

One of them was pure torture.

And it wasn't the one involving a painful hangover.

I stared at my reflection in the mirror.

"Well, birthday guy, what's it going to be?"

Leaving my room, I made it through the throng of people celebrating my birthday without me, and climbing on my bike, I headed for home.

It was late when I got back to the house. The porch light was on, so I knew Chastity was home. There was no point trying to pretend my chest didn't fill with warmth knowing she was inside. I was getting tired of fighting what I really felt. It was easier to recognize it and then accept I was a sonofabitch for feeling it.

Inside, the house was still but the kitchen light was on and I figured Chastity was probably in bed. I tried to be as quiet as I could and sat down at the kitchen table to take off my boots.

That's when I saw the cupcake on the kitchen counter with a candle sticking out of the icing. I got up and walked over to it, warmth spreading through me. Chastity had done this for my birthday.

"I was going to surprise you."

Her voice came from behind me. I swung around and there she was, standing in the doorway, dressed in a pair of tiny shorts and a flimsy tank top that did nothing to hide her flawless body. My mouth went dry as a million different, yet equally carnal, scenarios rushed into my mind.

You really are a dirtbag.

"It's late. You didn't have to get up," I said, doing everything to calm down what was happening behind my zipper.

"But I did... to do this." She smiled as she came into the kitchen. Picking up a lighter from the table, she lit the candle on the cupcake and held it up.

"Happy birthday, Ruger."

Our eyes met over the lit candle.

"Thanks, Chassy."

I blew out the flame.

"Did you make a wish?" she asked.

I did.

I wished that I could have her. That there was a place for us in this world. That I could do all the things I fantasized about doing to her. That I could kiss her. Touch her. *Make love to her.*

"If I tell you, it won't come true."

Her eyes held mine.

"If you tell me, it just might."

In that moment, I knew. My suspicions hadn't been the fantasies of a sex-starved man. The way she was looking at me and the tone of her voice... she was taking us one step closer to the danger zone.

It was up to me to pull us back.

But it was impossible not to notice the desire in her eyes. She wanted me to touch her. To kiss her. And I was more than fucking tempted. I was fucking *aching* for it.

Worst of all, I was running out of strength to fight it.

Her lips fell open with a raspy breath as tension tightened in the air around us.

She took a step closer and my pulse quickened.

She licked her lips and it was all I could do not to groan.

She slid her elegant fingers up my chest and laced them around my neck.

My breath left me as lips sweeter than nectar brushed against mine.

Her mouth was so warm and tender, her tongue velvety smooth and so sweet, it was more than I could fight.

Fight this.

But I was powerless against it.

With a moan, I pulled her to me and seared my lips harder to hers. In a dizzying fog, I realized what I was doing. I understood the line I was crossing. But dear God, it was too damn hard to resist. Our kiss deepened. It was fierce, and hard, and demanding. It was also so fucking out of this world, my mind spun on its axis.

Using every ounce of strength I had, I broke it off.

She looked up at me, slightly dazed, her eyes hooded and full of lust, her beautiful lips parted and wet.

"I've got an early start tomorrow," I said, fighting the urge to kiss her again. But her lips were so plump and ready for the taking, I couldn't help myself. With a growl, I kissed her again, deeply, breathlessly, my heart pounding, my cock thickening. I was getting lost in her. This was going too far. But goddamn, I couldn't stop. Without breaking our kiss, I slumped on the chair and she slid her thighs over mine to straddle me.

She whimpered against my lips, her pussy grinding over my groin as she rocked against the hard outline of my cock. I clasped her luscious ass against me, enjoying the friction and wanting nothing more than to rip those tiny shorts off and bury myself deep and hard into her.

I had finally lost my mind.

But dear God, if this was insanity, then sign me up and give me the t-shirt because I couldn't stop.

It was the sudden shrill of my phone that broke the spell and brought me crashing back down to Earth.

I looked at it vibrating on the table. It was Bull. But I didn't answer it. How could I when I had his niece rubbing her sweet pussy over me? When she was kissing me into a frenzy and I was moments from tearing off her panties?

When it stopped ringing, I looked at Chastity. We had crossed the line.

And we had enjoyed every step.

But the spell was broken, and as reality crept back in, the air around us cooled.

Nothing more was going to happen tonight.

Or tomorrow.

Or ever.

I knew where my moment of weakness was. Now I just had to make sure I didn't get close enough to it again.

"I'm sorry," she whispered.

I cupped her face. "You don't ever have to say that to me."

My phone vibrated with a message and we both turned to look at it.

Bull.

"I'll let you get that," she said softly, climbing off my lap. "Goodnight, Ruger, and happy birthday."

I watched her walk away, raw lust pounding through my veins. "Good night, sweetheart."

I raked my fingers down my face as regret began to trickle through me.

I couldn't let that happen again.

Because going there with Chastity was breaking all the rules.

And she could easily be the ruin of me.

CHAPTER 18

CHASTITY

He was gone when I woke up. The little house was still but the aroma from his early morning coffee still lingered in the air. Disappointment wove its way through me. I'd hoped we could talk some more before he left for the clubhouse, but he'd obviously left earlier than usual.

I needed to talk to him about what happened last night. The kiss. Did it mean anything to him when it meant everything to me?

I spent the morning at Wax-It before heading over to the clubhouse a little after three where I was meeting Cassidy, Indy, Honey, and Daisy for a bridesmaids' get together. With the wedding only a couple of months away, there was still a lot to organize.

Driving there, my stomach was in knots at the thought of seeing Ruger. Knowing we'd kissed. Knowing what it felt like to have his lips rolling sensually over mine. Remembering the hard outline of his erection in his jeans.

Every part of me ached to feel more.

When I arrived, he was nowhere in sight. But the girls were all gathered in one of the booths.

When I sat down, Indy's face was planted on the table.

"What's wrong with you?" I asked.

She turned her head to look at me, her cheek still resting on the tabletop.

"I'm pregnant."

My face lit up with happiness. "You're having a baby?"

She grinned at my enthusiasm and sat up. With an excited squeal, I threw my arms around her neck.

"I'm going to be an auntie again."

"And again and again," Cassidy laughed, rubbing a palm over her swollen belly.

"Especially if Caleb and Honey have anything to do with it," Indy joked as I released her.

"Don't drag me into this," Honey said. "I'm enjoying not being knocked up for once, thank you very much." She pointed at us. "And don't you ladies go wishing it on me, or I swear to God it will probably happen."

Honey had just given birth to twin boys. She also had a daughter under the age of two. She and my brother Caleb had a one-night stand and managed to get pregnant despite their use of copious condoms during the night.

"Because you two are like fucking rabbits," Indy said.

"No more than anyone else." Honey pulled the straw out of her drink and sucked the soda off the end of it.

Cassidy and Indy both gave her a pointed look.

"What? We have our dry spells," she said.

"Sure you do. When was the last time you two did it?" Indy asked.

Honey looked at her watch. "About an hour ago."

"Case in point," Cassidy said.

Honey looked sheepish. "What can I say? I can't keep my hands off my husband."

Apparently, Caleb and Honey had an astronomical amount of sex.

Which is exactly what a sister wants to hear about her brother and his wife.

I tended to tune out these conversations, so I was relieved when Cassidy changed the subject.

"Who are you bringing to the wedding as your plus one?" she asked me.

I shook my head. "No one."

"You're not seeing anyone?" Indy asked.

"Don't sound so surprised. Did you forget who I'm related to?"

"I know... it's just, we were so sure you'd met someone."

I looked at the three of them.

"Why?"

"Because you've been walking around all dreamy-eyed and love-struck for the past week," Honey explained. "We were sure you'd met a guy."

I shifted uncomfortably.

I hadn't met a guy.

I'd just fallen even further for the one I wasn't allowed to have.

I thought about the kiss.

Thought about Ruger's hands on my hips and the sensual way his mouth moved over mine, and my heart tightened.

I was just about to say something when Cassidy's friend, Daisy, joined us in the booth.

"Okay, so I think I've found the dresses. What do you guys think?"

While Indy, Honey, and I were bridesmaids, Daisy was Cassidy's maid of honor. It was a responsibility she'd thrown herself into with wild enthusiasm. She came to these meetings armed with a folder full of things to do, buy, decide, and choose.

In charge of finding us some decent bridesmaid dresses, she was determined to pick the best damn bridesmaid dresses Destiny had ever seen.

She pushed a photo across the table. It was a picture of four women wearing the same dress color, but all of them different styles. One was strapless, one was backless, one showed a lot of boob, while the fourth was off the shoulder.

All four were stunning.

"I was thinking these, in black. Now I've called the designer and they can have them done in two weeks. They just need to take our measurements, so I made an appointment for Saturday. What do you ladies think?"

Her suggestion was met with approval all around the table.

"Yay!" She grinned excitedly.

Cassidy leaned over and kissed her friend on the cheek. "Thank you for being such an incredible maid of honor."

Daisy waved her off. "One day you'll return the favor... if I ever find Mr. Right in this godforsaken town."

"Who are you bringing to the wedding?" Cassidy asked.

Before she could answer, Chance, Bull, Maverick, and Ruger walked into the clubhouse. Immediately my heart took off in my chest. All four of them were huge men. I'm talking *mountain man* huge. And it was no surprise people turned to look at them when they walked in. But it was Ruger who had the biggest presence about him. Big and muscular, he looked like a Viking ready to take on a foe. His size commanded attention and it was no wonder women were only too willing to drop their panties for him.

Being fucking gorgeous helped, too.

I licked my lips and told myself to stop looking, but I couldn't tear my eyes off him.

"So, I was thinking about asking Ruger," Daisy said.

My eyes darted to her.

"Ruger?" I spoke before I could stop myself.

"Yeah. I mean, why not? The guy is hot. Look at him."

"He's fucking hot," Honey agreed. "If I weren't with Caleb, I would climb that man like he was a tree and I was a hungry bear."

We all looked at her.

"What? Just because I'm on a diet doesn't mean I can't look at the menu." She shrugged.

I turned back to Daisy. "I didn't realize you were interested in him."

"Are you kidding me?" She sighed dreamily. "Every time I see him I have this unreasonable urge to lick him. You know what I mean?"

I glared at her.

Yeah.

I knew what she meant.

It was like my unreasonable urge to punch her in the face at that very moment.

"You should ask him," Indy said to her.

"I agree," Cassidy added.

I looked at Honey expecting her to do the same. But Honey was already looking at me. And she knew. I could see it in her eyes. She goddamn knew I was in love with Ruger.

"You know what," she said, shifting her gaze to Daisy. "I think you should keep your options open."

I wanted to kiss her. To throw my arms around her neck and thank her.

But more than that, I had a sudden urge to confide in her.

Honey wasn't the judgmental type. Her easy-going nature naturally aligned with Caleb's laid-back attitude. They were a good fit.

If any of my brothers were going to be okay about me and Ruger dating, it would be Caleb.

Chance and Cade would probably get all protective and alpha-ish about it.

And my Uncle Bull would be even less forgiving.

Not that there was anything going on. Just the fantasies of a love-struck roomie.

I looked across at Ruger and thought about all the things I wanted to do with him. *To him.* I was desperate to feel his lips on me again. To feel his body so close to mine that I was engulfed in the masculine warmth that was pure him. I wanted to feel him on top of me and nestled between my legs. I wanted to feel him push into me. To fill me. To make me come with his powerful body.

"Why don't you go over there and ask him?" Cassidy suggested, but before anyone could reply, she let out a deep breath and ran her hand over her belly. "Boy, this one is active today."

"Are you okay?" Honey asked.

"Yeah, she's just active, is all."

We all looked at her.

"Wait, you said *she's* active. Are you telling us you're having a girl?" Daisy gasped.

Realizing she'd let the cat out of the bag, Cassidy tried to calm the sudden excitement around the table.

"Don't say anything! I only just found out this morning. Chance doesn't even know!"

"How are you going to tell him?" Indy asked.

"He's going to be so excited!" Honey added.

"I don't know, I was thinking of getting him naked, and just when he thinks the night can't get any better, floor him with the news."

Indy picked up her glass of iced water to toast the idea. "Spoken like a true Queen of Mayhem."

When I didn't raise my glass like my sister-in-laws because I was so distracted by Ruger standing over at the bar looking every possible shade of sin (and because I distanced myself from all conversations that included any of my brothers being naked), Honey nudged my foot under the table.

"I'm sorry, cheers..." I grabbed my ice water and we clinked glasses, although I was only vaguely aware of what was going on.

Ruger had my head screwed on back to front.

But only Honey seemed to notice.

I told myself to stop staring, but it was impossible. And when our eyes met across the room, I felt my heart damn near fly out my chest. He gave me a wink and turned away to talk to Bull and Maverick, like we hadn't kissed and I had almost made myself come by grinding against his lap the night before. But a couple of times his beautiful green eyes glanced over in my direction, and every time they did, excitement zipped through me from my head to my toes.

I couldn't wait to get home. I wanted to talk to him about what happened. About the kiss and what it meant. That it wasn't a mistake, that it was everything, and how I wanted more. Heat pooled between my thighs as I thought about kissing him and how it would feel to lie beneath him as he kissed me hard and pressed that strong, muscular body into mine. And then I thought about his cock. I already knew it was big. *Thick and long.* And if there was one thing I was certain of, his was the cock I wanted to take my virginity with mind-blowing orgasms.

I watched him disappear outside with my uncle, and a few minutes later their bikes roared out of the parking lot.

After another round of conversations about dresses, the cake, and Cassidy's update about the guest list and who had RSVP'd, I decided to head home.

But as I made my way to my car, Honey caught up with me.

"Okay, what's going on with you and Ruger?" she asked.

Despite wanting to confide in her, I wasn't quite ready to admit anything yet, not before I'd spoken to Ruger. Was the kiss a one-off? Or was something starting between us?

"What do you mean?" I asked, rummaging through my bag for my keys.

She dangled them in front of me, a knowing look on her face. "You left them on the table."

I took them from her. "Thank you."

"You're crushing on him, aren't you?" It was more of a statement than a question. "You want to tell me about it?"

I licked my lips.

"I already know the answer, Chassy. When he walked into the room, your energy changed and you couldn't keep your eyes off him. He distracts you. And if I'm as smart as I think I am, you distract him."

"Really?"

I couldn't hide my surprise. Or how happy her observation made me. Which was exactly what she was going for. She raised an eyebrow at me and then smiled.

"So, it's true, you have a thing for Ruger?"

The jig was up. There was no point in denying it.

"Just don't say anything to anyone," I pleaded. "I don't even know if it's anything or—"

"You mean something has already happened?"

Again, there was no point denying it. I was sure it was written all over my face.

"We kissed."

Her eyes widened. "You kissed—when?"

I glanced around the parking lot to make sure no one could hear.

"Last night, when he came home... things got intense." I thought about the moment before our lips met. How the air had crackled with electricity and how I had desperately wanted him to kiss me. And then I thought about that moment when it was too late to turn back, the kiss was going to happen, and the look of pure desire on his face right before our lips brushed together. "I'm in love with him."

Honey's eyebrows disappeared beneath her dark fringe. "In love?"

"I know it's crazy. But something's changed between us, and just the idea of him lights me up inside. I see him, and all I want to do is kiss him and touch him, and be around him."

Honey's surprise softened to understanding and she gave me a gentle smile. "Sounds like love, alright. So, what are you going to do about it?"

"We haven't spoken since he broke off the kiss. But I'm going to talk to him tonight when he comes home."

"What are you going to say?"

"What else can I say? I'm going to tell him I'm in love with him."

CHAPTER 19

RUGER

I lied to myself. Said it meant nothing. That holding her in my arms didn't feel like heaven. That the feel of her body on mine wasn't exhilarating and desirable. That kissing her hadn't brought me back to life after months of solitude. That resisting the urge to make love to her wasn't damn well killing me.

But it was bullshit. Because it meant everything whether I wanted to admit it or not.

I was at war with myself. I wanted her. I ached for her. But it was wrong. So fucking wrong. I'd known her since she was a kid. She was my friend. My *close friend*. Wanting her like this was not just wrong, it threatened to destroy our friendship.

Not to mention, destroy the bond I had with Bull.

I knew I had to face the consequences of the night before. Of kissing her.

And loving it.

So, as I rode home, I thought about what to say to her. She wanted more. She wanted me to touch her. To kiss her. To make her moan. And I was hard at the thought. But I would let her down gently. Tell her it couldn't go any further. That I was too old for her. That it was a mistake, and we should pretend it never happened.

She was a smart girl. She would see the sense in my argument. And she would agree with me because, by now, she was probably already questioning why she'd even let me kiss her in the first place.

Yet the moment I walked in the front door and found her standing at the kitchen counter making coffee, the points that had seemed so clear in my head as I had ridden home, vanished like a puff of smoke.

One look at her and the world fell away.

I paused in the doorway and looked at her across the room. Our eyes locked and I could see the emotion ripple through her expression. Hope. Expectation.

But she knew what was coming because it was written all over my face.

Slowly, her expression fell. "You're going to tell me it was a mistake, aren't you?"

I saw her shoulders drop and I let out the deep breath I had been holding. "You know it was."

She pressed her palms against the countertop and looked away for a moment before fixing her gaze to mine. "You don't believe that."

She didn't give me a chance to reply. Instead, she closed the distance between us.

"Chastity..." My voice was coarse, my throat dry. But she didn't stop. When she reached me she rose up on her tiptoes, and without a word, pressed her lips to mine.

I couldn't deny it anymore. All I wanted was to kiss her. To lose hours tasting those sweet lips. To sink my cock into her, right to the hilt, and thrust into her luscious body until we were both panting and damp with sweat, and trembling with ecstasy.

Instead, I closed my eyes and took a breath before gently pushing her away.

She deserved more than this.

Hating myself, I ran a hand through my hair.

"Please don't push me away," she pleaded, hurt. She was trying hard to hold back her tears.

Fuck.

In all the years I'd known her, I'd never seen her cry. Even when that bag of dicks, Joey, broke up with her via text message.

Guilt rattled through me.

Because I didn't want to be the one to make her cry.

And because I was aching to kiss away her pain.

Before I could stop myself, I took her face in my hands.

Tears glittered in her long lashes as she looked up at me.

"Please don't cry, angel," I begged, pressing my forehead to hers. "I can't stand seeing you cry."

She softened against me. "Why won't you let this happen?"

"Because I'm not for you," I whispered.

"But you could be."

Her lips were close. *Too close.* With a slight tilt of my head I could brush them with mine and capture her mouth in a deep, lingering kiss. Overwhelmed by the urge, I swallowed thickly and closed my eyes against the thought, despite every fiber of my being begging me to give in and do it.

To take her face in my hands and kiss her until we were both breathless.

To kiss the smooth flesh of her throat, all the way down to her breasts.

To touch her.

To peel her clothes away from her and spend the next week worshipping her beautiful body in my bed.

"Angel—" I breathed the word, but she cut me off with her sweet lips. And before I knew it, her mouth was on me again, her tongue tangled with mine in a tantalizing dance.

A groan escaped me. There was only so much a man could take. I'd wanted her for too long. Fought the urge for what seemed like a lifetime. But I was no match for the temptation of her mouth moving sensually over mine.

In one maddening moment, I gave in, cupping her face in my hands and kissing her fiercely. I walked her backwards and pinned her to the wall, my body reacting to the sweet touch of her lips and the way she was kissing me back. She murmured and it was like music to my ears, luring me away from what I should be doing, and tempting me with everything that I shouldn't.

The kiss deepened and she softened in my arms, her lips and tongue driving me wild. I couldn't stop now. Hell, a fucking freight train couldn't stop this now.

I lifted her up into my arms and carried her to my bed. Gently lying her down, I crawled over her and nestled between her legs. When she felt the ridge of my cock pressing against her jeans, she moaned with desperation. She wrapped her long legs around my hips and began to grind against me, her little murmurs making me crazy.

"Are you sure about this?"

"Yes," she moaned between kisses, her legs tightening around my hips as she rubbed herself against me.

My cock thickened to almost painful levels, punching against the zipper of my jeans. I kissed her harder, grinding against her soaked panties.

"I want you to be my first," she whimpered against my lips.

Her words hit me like a hammer. I froze and pulled back.

Be my first.

She looked up at me from the pillows, her beautiful face flushed with desire, her hooded eyes heavy with lust, her sweet lips kiss-swollen and wet.

"You're a virgin?"

She nodded. "Yes."

Suddenly the gravity of what I was doing slammed into me.

A virgin.

With a huff I let out the deep breath I didn't realize I was holding.

Chastity was still a virgin.

And she was offering it to me.

If I was that level of asshole, I would keep going.

But that's the thing, I wasn't a dick.

Taking her virginity wasn't an option for me.

This. Us. What was happening... yeah, it wasn't going to happen.

I pulled away and climbed off the bed, raking my hands through my hair as I paced the floor.

"What's the matter?" she asked, sitting up.

"We can't do this."

"Why?"

I couldn't miss the hurt in her voice. *Fuck.* The last thing I wanted to do was hurt her even more. But this... this was insanity.

That little bit of information had suddenly changed everything.

She looked up at me, her large blue eyes wide and confused. "You don't want to have sex with me?"

Christ, if only she knew what those words alone did to me. I was so fucking hard for her it was making me see stars.

I sat down on the bed next to her.

"I'm too old for you, baby girl. You don't want to do this."

She huffed out an angry breath. "This again? You're really going to start with the age thing? It didn't matter two minutes ago when you were grinding up against me."

That memory alone was enough to make me want to rip her panties off.

"You're a virgin," I said.

"So? You were too once upon a time."

I gave her a pointed look. "Losing your virginity should mean something. It should be special."

"And you're saying this isn't special?"

"No, that's not what I'm saying."

"That's *exactly* what you're saying."

"No, it's not."

"What, then? If it's special, then what's the problem?"

"The problem is that you should be with someone special for your first time."

"I thought I was."

"I care too much about you, angel."

"That doesn't even make sense. If you care about me so much, let it be you who takes my virginity."

I raked my hands down my face. She wasn't going to make this easy.

"One of us needs to be the voice of reason here," I said.

She swallowed deeply, her face open and full of pain.

"Why is it such a big deal?" she asked.

"Because it's a big decision. And if it isn't, then it should be."

"Don't I get a say?"

Tears sprung to her eyes and she looked away. Sitting down next to her on the bed, I gently placed a finger beneath her chin and turned her beautiful face back to me. "What are we doing, sweetheart? You know this isn't for us."

She turned away and I cursed myself for letting this happen. For letting this get so far.

I reached for her hand. "I'm too old and grumpy for such a beautiful young thing like you, Chastity. You should be with someone your own age. Someone who isn't as jaded and weather-beaten as me."

"You're talking as if you're an old man. You're thirty-nine."

She tried to pull her hand free, but I held onto it.

"You should be dating guys your own age. Not climbing into bed with a dusty old biker."

She looked at me, her beautiful eyes full of rejection. "I don't want you because of how old you are, or what you are, I want you because of *who* you are. Age shouldn't matter. And it doesn't, not to me."

She bit her lower lip and it was all I could do to not take her beautiful face in my hands and kiss her seven ways to Sunday.

"Surely there is a nice guy... a nice, *younger* guy, out there."

"I'm sure there is, but I'm not interested in him."

"How do you know?"

"Because I'm interested in you," she said softly.

I pushed a lock of hair behind her ear.

"It's just a crush," I said. "For both of us. And if I let anything happen, then we'd end up regretting it."

She dropped her lashes and I could see the hurt on her face.

"You're a beautiful girl, Chastity. I bet there's a hundred guys lining up to date you."

She looked away. "You sound like Bryce."

"Bryce?"

"A guy in my science class. He's asked me out a few times."

"Maybe you should go?"

I hated the words the moment they left my mouth.

I didn't want her to go on any dates.

But I had to do the right thing here.

"You're young. Explore your options. Have some fun. Go on a date with this guy... Bruce."

"Bryce," she corrected me.

"Bryce." I nodded, hating him already. "You'll probably be thanking me soon."

Her jaw tightened. But she didn't say anything more.

It broke my heart to hurt her, but finding out she was a virgin was a game-changer. I was old school. Don't get me wrong, I've popped a few cherries in my lifetime, but in my youth, not as a thirty-nine-year-old man to a woman almost seventeen years my junior. There was no shame in the age gap. But this was Chastity we were talking about. She deserved so much more than me.

Walking away, I disappeared into the bathroom and took a cold shower. When I came out, dressed and ready to head out for the night, her bedroom door was closed and I could hear the muffled sound of music through the door.

I debated checking on her, but thought better of it. She needed time to think without me around. So I walked away, slipped on my cut, and with an ache in my chest, left for the clubhouse.

CHAPTER 20

CHASTITY

My humiliation lasted all through the next day and into the next, gathering speed and size like a violently spinning snowball.

After deciding that maybe Ruger was right and perhaps I should go out with Bryce, I messaged my science buddy and accepted his dinner offer.

I agreed to the date because I was hurt and humiliated, but also because what if Ruger was right. What if all I had was a crush?

Maybe I needed to *explore my options* to realize this was nothing more than some stupid crush I'd held onto since I was a teenager.

Maybe dating someone else would help me get over it and see things for what they were... just a fantasy.

But even as I got ready for my date, my heart was a lump in my throat and I knew it was pointless.

Because what I felt for Ruger wasn't a crush.

My feelings ran a lot deeper than that.

Bryce was nice. I liked him.

But he wasn't Ruger.

I slid a velvet choker around my neck and stood back to survey my reflection in the mirror. I wore a simple summer dress with peasant sleeves, a hemline to my thighs and a neckline low enough to show just a hint of my boobs. The outfit was on point. But my shoes were the real show-stealers. Smoking hot stilettos that made my legs go on for miles.

The kind Ruger would like.

I frowned in the mirror.

Not that he'd be here to see them. He had barely been home in the last couple of days. He was making a point of being wherever I wasn't. He was overreacting and it was breaking my heart. I didn't want it to be this way. Two nights ago we were kissing passionately and about to make love.

Now he was avoiding me completely and I was going on a date with Bryce from college.

Bryce was a nice guy, but completely opposite to what I was attracted to. Preppy with model-like looks. He didn't have that *thing* that made me weak in the knees.

Not like Ruger. He didn't just make my knees weak, he made me want to get on them.

But he had made things perfectly clear.

He didn't want me.

And if I liked it or not, I was going on this date.

CHAPTER 21

RUGER

It had been a long day. I'd barely slept the last couple of nights because all I could think about was Chastity and how I'd broken her heart. The look on her face. The tears she was fighting back. Her flushed cheeks. *The way she rubbed her pussy against me as I grinded into her on my bed.*

Last night, the memory had tortured me until all I could do was jerk off so I could get some goddamn sleep.

When I woke up, I was in a bad mood.

Today, she was going on a date with some kid from college named Bryce.

I only knew this because I overheard Ronnie talking to Caleb and Honey about it at the clubhouse yesterday.

I knew I should be happy about it. After all, it was what I told her to do.

You wanted this.

Yeah, right. I wanted her to go on a date with Bryce about as much as I wanted a bullet in my brain.

As a result, I walked around all day like a moody sonofabitch, taking it out on the prospects and anyone else who irritated me.

Finally, after dealing with club business all day, I rode home.

I told myself I was going home to make sure this Bryce character wasn't a dick. To check him out, not because I saw him as some kind of competition, but because I wanted to make sure she wasn't climbing into a car with Ted Bundy, or another Peter.

When I pulled up to the house, a strange car was parked in the driveway.

It was a Volvo. Clean. Tidy. No garbage scattered on the seats. No beer bottles or cigarette packets discarded on the floor. Solid tires. No scrapes or dents in the paint work.

Bryce.

The hair on the back of my neck began to prickle.

Was this kid a fucking saint or what?

Feeling my stomach churn, I bounded the steps to the front door and mentally braced myself for what I was going to encounter inside.

I had already spent the day torturing myself about this fucking date. I kept telling myself it was a good thing, but was no closer to accepting it.

And nothing could prepare me for actually coming face to face with Chastity and her date.

Or how good she looked.

When she saw me, she stopped and paused, and we stared at each other for a moment, the air tight with tension.

I drank in every inch of her. Her pouty red lips. The tangled bun of dark hair and the stray curls falling around her beautiful face. The way the little black dress clung to her luscious curves.

The way Bryce stood there looking like the cat who got the fucking cream.

Jealousy burned through me. I glared at him, my hands fisting at my side.

Chastity glanced at me and she knew, *she fucking knew*, this was killing me inside. But if I thought she was enjoying the pain she was inflicting on me, then I was wrong, because when our eyes met she didn't look satisfied, she looked heart-broken.

And guess what, sunshine, you're the ass who broke it.

With gritted teeth, I watched Bryce slip her jacket over her shoulders and wipe a stray strand of hair from her face.

It took every ounce of restraint to not go over there and pull his hands off her and kiss her like she'd never been kissed before.

There were a million things I wanted to do, but nothing more than taking her to my bed and burying myself so deeply in her until the ache in my chest vanished. I wanted to feel her surrender beneath me. Wrap her legs around me. Moan my name against my lips.

Awkwardness was as thick as smoke in the room. Obviously, Chastity felt it too because she escaped to her bedroom to get her purse, leaving me alone with her date.

I told myself I wasn't going to say anything to him. That it wasn't my place. Chastity was twenty-two years old and could date whoever she wanted. But one look at the good-looking kid in the chinos and well-fitted shirt made me prickly with jealousy.

He smiled and I wanted to punch all his perfect white teeth down his throat.

"You must be Ruger," he said, sticking his hand out. "Chastity has told me all about you."

I doubted that very much.

Reluctantly, I took his hand and gave it a nice, firm pump. "You must be Bryce."

He grinned but it faded when I didn't let go of his hand and instead stepped closer to whisper in his ear. The next few words out of my mouth were said on impulse and with violent warning.

When I stepped back, the kid had gone white. I should feel bad saying what I said, but my conscience was no match for my jealousy or the fierce protectiveness I felt sweeping through me.

Unable to stand it another moment, I turned and stormed out. This was fucking killing me.

I rode to the clubhouse. I was going to get drunk. And I mean, I was going to get *fall-down* drunk.

I played pool with Maverick. But it was hard to focus when Chastity was out with another man.

She had looked like every man's dream tonight.

Yeah, everyman's wet dream.

I had no doubt Bryce would be itching for a taste, despite my whispered words of warning in his ear before I left. He was probably pressing his body up against hers while I was here shooting pool and talking shit to Maverick.

Rage spiraled through me at the thought. And instead of shutting it out, I began to obsess about it. About him pulling her against him as they danced just so he could rub his college-boy erection against her tight body. Him running his hands up and down her tiny waist and settling on her ass. Him taking her lovely face in his hands and kissing her...

My hands curled into fists, and without thinking, I pounded them against the pool table.

"What the fuck is wrong with you?" Maverick asked. "You've been a moody sonofabitch all fucking night."

"Nothing."

Maverick shook his head as he lined up his shot. "You're a bear with a sore head, buddy." He sank his last ball into the corner pocket. "And come to think of it, I've never seen you lose your cool. Makes me think it's got something to do with a woman."

"Who are you? Fucking Columbo?" I asked as I took a shot and missed.

Maverick looked confused. "Who the fuck is Columbo?"

"The TV detective. Jesus, where were you raised... fucking Mars?"

"Peach Grove, Georgia. So pretty close." He chalked his pool cue and leaned down to take his shot. "So you gonna tell me who's got your panties in a twist?"

Sure. I've got a hard-on for our president's niece. You know, the girl we've all been warned to stay clear of? Yeah, well, I want to take her in my arms and kiss her until we're both out of oxygen and dizzy with lust. I want to peel the clothes from her body and make love to her right through to dawn. I want to make her come. I want to make her scream my name. I want her to be mine and mine alone. So what did I do about it? I made her go out on a date with another guy, and now I'm here obsessing about it like a fucking psycho. No, worse. Like a fucking teenager.

I threw the pool cue onto the table when Maverick sank the black ball.

It was no use.

Tonight, was a nightmare. Nothing was going to stop me from thinking about Chastity.

"Want another game?" Maverick asked.

Just as Maverick began to rack up again, the door to the clubhouse opened and Cool Hand stumbled in with his wife Heidi and a couple of her girlfriends. Ready to party, the four of them made their way over to the bar and started doing tequila shots.

One of Heidi's friends, a gorgeous blonde in a tight pink dress and legs for miles, kept glancing over her shoulder at me. I knew the look and could see the invitation in her eyes. After another couple of drinks, she walked over to me and offered to take my mind off things for the rest of the night.

She handed me a shot of tequila and licking her lips, came in for the kill.

CHAPTER 22

CHASTITY

So in true tradition that was my dating life, the date sucked.

After a *really* uncomfortable yet thankfully brief encounter with Ruger back at the house, we took Bryce's car to a Mexican restaurant in town. The drive was awkward and the conversation stilted. Bryce was normally a friendly guy, chatty and outgoing, but during the drive he was quiet and preoccupied. Like he wanted to be anywhere but in the car with me.

I chalked his behavior up to nerves until it carried on through dinner. He was distant. Fidgety. Almost strung out as he kept eyeing the front door.

Finally, when the waitress offered to bring us another drink and Bryce all but begged her for the check, I decided to confront him.

I waited for the waitress to leave before turning to him.

"Okay, enough is enough. What's going on here? You've been asking me out for weeks, and now that we're finally on a date, you're acting like you'd rather get a root canal than be here with me. What happened?"

Surprised, Bryce took a swig of his drink. "It's nothing. Really."

"Sure. That's why you look like you're expecting an assassin to walk through those doors any minute now."

He swallowed slowly, and it was while I watched his Adam's apple bob up and down that it suddenly occurred to me.

Ruger.

My face darkened and my blood began to boil.

I fixed my eyes to his. "What the fuck did Ruger say to you?"

Bryce drained his drink and then ordered another before leaning his arms on the table and telling me exactly what happened.

Infuriated, I walked out of the restaurant and took a cab home.

I was pleased when I saw Ruger's bike *and* truck in the driveway because it meant he was home, and I wanted nothing more than to tell him exactly what I thought of him and what he had said to Bryce.

This stupid little thing between us. Yeah. It ended now.

Stomping up the porch steps, I flung open the front door and stormed inside, surprising my annoying roomie who was sitting at the kitchen counter drinking a beer and flipping through a motorcycle magazine.

In that moment I hated him.

Truly hated him.

Because he looked so damn gorgeous and I could feel the overwhelming ache for him through the heat of my anger.

He paused his beer bottle mid-way to his lips when I started yelling.

"Who the hell do you think you are?"

He put his beer down. "What the hell?"

I stomped toward him. "Don't you *what the hell* me, Ruger. Exactly what are you doing?"

"I have no idea what you're—"

"Bryce! I'm talking about Bryce. First you tell me to go on a date with him. So, I do. But then you tell him to keep his hands to himself unless he wants a smack down."

My blood was boiling. But it was nothing compared to the rage I felt when a small, sexy smirk hit Ruger's lips.

He thought this was amusing.

"What fucking game are you playing with me?" I cried.

His smirk slipped and he frowned. He rose from the stool he was sitting on and opened his perfect mouth to say something, but I wasn't done yelling at him.

"You want me, but then you push me away. You tell me to go on a date, but then intimidate the poor guy I go on a date with. What the fuck is wrong with you?" I stepped closer and shoved a pointed finger in his chest. "What, you can't have me so nobody can, is that it?"

"I'm not playing any games," he said, which I ignored because that was bullshit.

"Yes, you are. And you play dirty."

"You need to calm down," he said.

Which of course only made me madder.

"Don't you dare tell me to calm down!" I shoved him in the shoulder. "Where do you get off threatening my date?"

"I didn't threaten him."

"Bullshit. I think the term was, *you touch her and I will hammer you so hard in the nuts you'll be wearing your ball sac as a hat.* Or how about my personal favorite *I have a gun and I know where you live. If you think I won't put a bullet in that college-boy vagina of yours, then you have another thing coming.*"

I glared at him, but again, a smirk twitched on his stupidly perfect lips.

"Fuck you, Ruger. I liked him."

The smile left his mouth in an instant, so I knew my words had gotten to him.

"If you don't want me, let me fucking go."

I turned to leave. I was going to pack my bags and stay at my mom's for the night, then work out where to stay until my apartment was ready.

But Ruger grabbed my wrist.

"Don't," I yelled and yanked my wrist free. Tears stabbed my eyes and my traitorous chin decided it was time to quiver in front of the one human being I didn't want to see me cry. "It's so easy for you to forget about our kiss and how good it felt, isn't it? Well, it's not for me! But I'm done. Do you hear me? I'm fucking done."

I went to turn away, but the ferocity in his voice stopped me.

"You think this is easy for me?" He growled. "You think seeing you with some preppy chino-wearing douchebag doesn't kick me straight in the balls? You think it's his arms and not my arms I want you in?" He took an intimidating step toward me, towering over me, his eyes fierce, the emotion rampant on his face. "You think every ounce of me isn't begging me touch you? To take you in my arms and kiss you until you've forgotten every other man you've ever known."

My heart hammered in my throat. The way he was looking at me. His words. The rapid rise and fall of his chest. I could barely breathe for all the desire rippling through me.

"You think I haven't thought about peeling every item of clothing from your gorgeous body and spending the night making love to you until neither of us can take it anymore?"

I licked my lips as he came a step closer. We stared at each other, the air around us crackling with tension.

"If you think I don't want you, then you're goddamn blind, Chastity."

It happened so quickly, I didn't have time to think it through. One minute I was pushing him away and yelling at him, the next my lips were crashing against his in a kiss so sizzling hot it made me dizzy.

In an instant he had my face in his big hands, turning my anger to mush as his mouth sensually and powerfully took command of mine. My argument vanished like smoke, replaced by a need to have everything with this man. His tongue. His kiss. His body. His hands roaming my body like they were doing now.

Breathlessly, I pulled away to look at him. He was panting, his lips wet with my kiss, his body hard and pressed up against me so I had nowhere to move. His beautiful green eyes drifted over my face, the pads of his thumbs gently caressing my cheeks as he caught his breath.

His eyes met mine. "This isn't a game. Not to me."

"Then, what is it?" My voice was nothing more than a whisper.

He licked his lips and I watched the glide of his tongue sweep over the delicate skin with a hunger to taste more. My body felt more alive than it had in days. Weeks. Months. Hell, it had never felt as good as it did when Ruger had his pressed up against me.

"This could be the ruin of me," he finally said.

"Or it could be the best thing that ever happened to the both of us," I replied.

I felt the outline of cock flinch against me, and I knew then that this was going to happen. That we were about to break all the rules.

And that when we did, there would be no turning back.

CHAPTER 23

RUGER

My resolve had crumbled.

I accepted that now.

The moment I had turned down Heidi's friend's invitation, I knew I was done fighting what I felt for Chastity. I knew I would go home and wait for her to come back from her date and confess everything. Knew I was going to lay everything on the line.

I had to put an end to the never-ending nightmare.

But this... this I wasn't expecting. The anger. The confrontation The want in her eyes as we laid our emotions bare.

Desire tore through me, and before I could stop, I was kissing her like a man starved. My body had a mind of its own, and dear God, I was losing my mind with wanting her.

"I want you so badly," she moaned, her hands twisting in my t-shirt.

My blood burned with lust, my cock thickening at the thought of ripping off those panties and burying my face between her thighs. I yanked her back to me and slammed my mouth to hers, holding on tight to her arms as I kissed her senseless. I couldn't take it anymore. The aching. The need. The craving. Not being able to be in the same room as her without wanting to touch her. I was addicted to her. And I couldn't resist my addiction anymore.

She whimpered and softened against me as I kissed her hungrily, my hands moving up to tangle in her hair. The world be damned. I couldn't fight this anymore.

Her hands slid between us to rub the hard ridge of my cock, and it was all I could do to stop myself from tearing her clothes from her body and taking her right there and then.

But she was a virgin.

She needed a soft touch for her first time.

And I was going to make sure that was exactly what she got.

"Please don't push me away again," she pleaded between our kisses.

There was no way in hell I was pushing this angel away.

Ever again.

I was a strong man.

But not strong enough to fight this.

I held her face in my hands. "Are you sure you want this?"

She looked up at me, her deep blue eyes bright with lust. "So badly."

The desire in her words pushed me over the edge. I lifted her off her feet and kissed her greedily as I walked her to my bedroom and set her down beside the bed. She looked up at me, her face flushed, her chest rising and falling as she undid her dress and let it slip to the floor.

Holy. Mother. Of. God.

Her body was magnificent, and the white bra and panties she wore were a stark contrast against her flawless tan.

She was fucking perfect.

I am going to hell for this.

She went to take her bra off, but I stopped her, preferring to do the task myself. With one flick of my fingers, her bra came undone and slid to the floor, revealing a perfect pair of breasts. I swallowed thickly, wanting to jump right into devouring her perky pink nipples with my mouth and tongue, but enjoying the torture of prolonging it as I undressed her.

I dropped to my knees, peeling her panties from her and sliding them down her long, slender legs. She shivered beneath my touch as my fingers trailed along the smooth slopes of her thighs, and a gasp fell from her parted lips as my tongue followed suit.

"Oh, Ruger," she moaned as I planted kisses across her stomach and up to one breast. Christ, she was so soft and creamy. This was worth every second of eternal damnation.

When I slid my lips over one tight nipple, she moaned and reached for my belt.

"I want to see you," she rasped.

I stood back and lifted my t-shirt over my head, and her eyes danced with desire as she took in my bare chest and abs.

My belt and jeans were next to go, and then finally my boxers.

She bit down on her bottom lip, and a small gasp escaped her when she saw my cock.

Walking toward her, I took it in my hand and gave it a couple of teasing strokes and her eyes sparkled with lust.

When I reached her, I took her in my arms and kissed her gently.

"Let me touch you," she whispered against my lips.

Her gentle hand slid up my cock and a tremor ran through me. Christ. I'd spent a lot of time fantasizing about her touching me, but nothing could prepare me for it.

"You're so hard," she breathed. She started to stroke me and my breath caught in my throat. This woman was driving me crazy with her touch, her smell... her fucking *everything.*

Her thumb rolled over the pearl of pre-cum on the crown and dragged it down my shaft in a tantalizing move that made me slick and so damn aroused, I wasn't sure how I was going to make this last.

I groaned. "Lie down on the bed for me, baby."

I was dying to be inside her. But I was going to take my time. I didn't want to hurt her. I wanted her ready for me. All creamy and supple for when I pushed into her sweet pussy. I was going to make her come. And then I was going to take her virginity.

"Relax, angel," I whispered against the warmth of her throat as I kissed a trail down her neck to her chest, taking a puckered nipple between my lips and gently suckling her. She writhed beneath me, sighing and parting her thighs. I kissed the soft swell of her stomach and the tight dip of her navel, slowly making my way down to the tiny patch of hair between her open thighs.

"Don't stop," she breathed, reaching behind her to hold onto the headboard.

I smiled and pushed her legs further apart, exposing her completely and enjoying the view. Her pussy was fucking perfect. Smooth and pink. I leaned down and parted the soft folds with my tongue and she trembled against my lips, her gentle moans falling around us as I swirled and licked at the sensitive nub of nerves.

She was so creamy and delicious, and it was taking everything I had not to bury myself in her. Instead, my tongue licked over her clit and trailed over the most sensitive parts of her before shallowly penetrating her. She cried out and squeezed my shoulders, her thighs quaking, her hips reaching upward to meet every lick of my tongue into her pussy. Her flesh was like velvet as I tongued her deeply. She gasped again and scrunched her fingers into the bed sheets, my name falling from her sweet lips in desperate, whispered breaths. My cock ached, needing her touch. Needing her body. But this moment was for her.

She started to pant. "Oh God, Ruger... oh God ..."

Her toes dug into the mattress and her pussy quivered against my lips. She arched her back and came with a cry, her fingers gripping my shoulders, her body trembling as she came on my tongue.

I groaned. I was so fucking hard it was almost painful. She looked up at me from the pillow, her cheeks flushed with pleasure, her dark hair swirling around her perfect face as she struggled to catch her breath. She was fucking beautiful.

When she smiled up at me I felt something inside me change. Something hard and unforgiving suddenly softened and let go.

I rose up to my knees and took my cock in my hand. I reached for a condom and she watched me slide it on. Nothing about this moment was wrong. Here, with her, there was only right.

Leaning down, I covered her body with mine.

"Are you sure?" I asked.

I searched for any sign of doubt, but saw nothing but desire in her lust-heavy eyes.

She nodded. "I want this. More than anything."

My thumbs brushed her jaw, and my eyes remained on hers as I settled between her firm thighs, and with one smooth stroke pushed into her tight pussy.

She squeezed her eyes closed and there was a flicker of discomfort on her face as I broke through her innocence and took her virginity from her.

Slowly, I pulled back.

"Look at me," I whispered.

She opened her eyes, and again I pushed into her, this time all the way. Her lips parted with a moan of both pleasure and pain.

"Is this okay?"

She nodded and then sighed as I started to rock into her, again and again, careful not to hurt her. It was hard not to let go and fuck her. To do what my body was urging me to do. To quicken my pace and go deeper and deeper. Because this wasn't about me. This was all about her. But goddamn, she was so tight and swollen, it was absolute torture not to give in and thrust harder and deeper into her firm body.

I wanted to make her come while I was inside of her. But I knew the chances were slim. She would be sore. Tender. So I took it slow as I made love to her, and kissed her deeply until I couldn't hold back any longer. My head dropped to the warmth of her throat, and I came, moaning her name against her slick skin as I pulsed deep inside of her.

When my breathing evened out and the ecstasy slowly receded, I gently pulled out of her.

"Are you okay, baby? Did I hurt you?"

She smiled up at me, her beautiful blue eyes sparkling like stars. "It was perfect."

I leaned down and kissed her before climbing off the bed and taking care of the condom in the bathroom across the hallway.

Stealing a glance in the mirror, I thought about my best friend, and then about Chastity's brothers and how they would react when they found out about us. I was too old for her. I knew it and so did they. But I had claimed her. Taken her virginity. And I had no intention of backing away now. Let them try to come between us and I would fight them until my last breath.

This angel was mine. And mine alone.

When I walked back into the bedroom, I paused to take in the image of her. She was in my bed, all naked and tanned, and it was exactly where she fucking belonged.

I joined her and pulled her to my chest, falling in love with the warmth of her body against mine and the feel of her satiny flesh covering me.

"No regrets?" I asked.

She brushed her lips against my chest. "Not one."

She fell asleep in my arms, and the last thing I thought before I closed my eyes was how I'd never felt so content in my fucking life.

CHAPTER 24

CHASTITY

The following morning, my eyes fluttered open and it took me a moment to realize where I was. When it slowly dawned on me, I smiled. I had finally done it.

V-card. Consider yourself blown to smithereens.

I stirred in Ruger's arms and felt the warmth and heaviness of his body as he shifted in his sleep. I was sore. And I had bled just the tiniest bit. But I felt so fucking amazing that I didn't care.

I had lost my virginity to my crush.

And now I was waking up in his arms.

Surrounded in his warmth, I turned to face him. I stole a few minutes to admire him as he slept. He was beautiful. I took in the full lips, the long lashes and the dark eyebrows, and my stomach flipped. This man. This broad-shouldered beauty had done things to me that no man ever had. He made me orgasm with his tongue, then took my virginity with such tenderness, it turned me on just thinking about it. I started to throb and let my hand slide between us to where his hard cock rested against his belly.

I wrapped my fingers around it and he stirred, moaning as a small smile tugged at his lips.

"If you keep doing that, shit's gonna get real."

He chuckled and opened his eyes, and I was momentarily taken back by how green they were in the early morning light.

"Hey, beautiful," he said, kissing me softly. "Are you okay? Sore?"

I wasn't sore. I was wet.

Aroused.

Ready.

He had fucked my virginity out of me. And now I wanted more.

I shook my head and smiled up at him. "Last night was incredible."

He smiled and it was stunning. "*You* were incredible," he said sleepily, brushing a kiss to the tip of my nose.

As I continued to stroke and tease him, he moaned and his eyes closed again.

His lips parted with a ragged breath. "That feels real good, baby."

His fingers were warm as they slipped between my thighs. He moaned when they slid easily into me because I was so slick and ready for him.

He nuzzled his lips to my throat. "Are you sure it's not too soon?"

I whispered in his ear. "I want you to fuck me."

It was all he needed. He reached for a condom on the bedside table, rolled it on and settled himself between my legs. With one push he was inside me again. It stung, but I was so damn turned on it passed quickly and all I could feel was the pleasure of him stroking into me.

It was warm and gentle. Both of us still hazy from sleep.

"Goddamn, you feel amazing," he rasped in my ear.

I was caged in big arms and the bulk of a muscular body. And completely lost in him as he made love to me.

He slowed his pace and started to grind slowly, so the friction lit up my clit like a sky on the Fourth of July. The swell of an orgasm rose like a wave and I moaned, licking my lips and raising my hips to meet every shallow grind of his pelvis against me. I felt it coming at me. The surge of pleasure. The eruption of bliss. And it hit with so much force it felt like I was free-falling off a cliff into the unknown. I cried out and gripped his broad shoulders.

"Yeah, angel, come for me. Come all over my cock." He pushed hard against my clit, prolonging my orgasm with the pressure. "Fuck you make me hard, baby. So fucking hard."

His dirty talk. His cock. The shallow grinds and thrusts, they kept me lost in space for just a few moments longer before I slowly drifted back down to Earth.

I sank into the mattress like a ragdoll, boneless and so fucking happy I couldn't keep the stupid grin off my face.

He paused above me. *In me.* He looked down into my face, his eyes heavy with lust, his lips wet, his expression full of heat.

With one hard jerk he thrust up into me again, his big cock hitting my womb and igniting a new throb in my swollen clit. I gasped. Another thrust. Then another. He stayed pressed into me after the fourth and started to grind against the swollen bundle of nerves again. *Oh God.* I was about to come again.

My eyes flicked open with surprise. "Oh my God... Ruger..."

He thrust into me again and continued with the delicious grinding until my second orgasm rushed through me, deeply and more intense and so powerful my muscles were not my own. They convulsed violently against him, squeezing him, gripping him, coaxing him into his own climax.

It was all he could take. He pumped into me, once, twice, three times before his dark eyebrows almost slammed together and his face shimmered with euphoria. I felt him pulsate in me, his big cock throbbing against the sides of my pussy as he came. He cried out my name and moaned, consumed in ecstasy and lost in bliss as my body milked him of every last drop.

He shuddered and stilled, his breath raspy, his big arms shaking as they held his muscular body above me.

Coming down, he blanketed me in his bulk and I was lost in his warmth, my body heavy with contentment.

When his breathing evened out, he rolled off me, pulling me to his chest with his strong arms and pressing a kiss to the top of my head.

While I felt my heart fill with love, I whispered a silent promise to him that I was his and his alone.

CHAPTER 25

RUGER

We took a shower together and kissed under the stream of water.

I had places to be. People to see. Shit to get done.

But fuck it.

Fuck them.

I didn't want this moment to end.

I had fallen into a big vat of *what the fuck have I done,* but I didn't want to climb out because I knew the moment we left my house, this could be over.

And I didn't want it to be over.

I wanted to lose myself in her for the day and work out what the fuck we were going to do.

Was something real happening between us?

I already knew there was.

But could it survive what was going to happen when people found out?

Her brothers were going to hate it.

And her uncle was going kill me.

None of which worried me. But I felt a fierce protectiveness toward Chastity and what she was going to have to go through. All because of me. All because I couldn't keep my hands off her.

She pulled away from our kiss. Christ, she was beautiful. Water ran in gleaming rivulets down her gorgeous body, trailing diamonds along her tanned skin.

She had me so hard it was painful.

Her eyes dropped to my cock jutting up between us. She looked up at me through dark lashes, and lust shimmered across her face as she reached down and touched me. I flinched, my feet rooted to the spot as she took me in her hands and dropped to her knees.

Knowing what she was going to do and knowing she'd never done anything like that before, I said her name.

"Chastity—"

But she cut me off by sliding her luscious lips over the broad head of my cock and sucking me in to the warmth of her sweet mouth.

Fuck.

Me.

Swirling her tongue over the polished skin, it flittered as she tongued the eye, then slid beneath the rim with one torturous lick, making me see fucking stars.

I slammed a palm against the wet tile wall and groaned.

"Fuck, baby, that feels so good…"

Looking down and seeing my cock disappear between her pouty pink lips was almost enough to send me over the edge.

"You like this?" she asked, looking up at me as she licked me from base to crown with her velvety tongue.

I groaned and my knees went weak.

Mind. Fucking. Blown.

Her cheeks hollowed as she sucked me in again and again, and the teasing of her mouth was sheer agony.

"That's it, baby, fuck me with that beautiful mouth."

In response, she drew the full length of me in until my engorged head hit the back of her throat. My groan reverberated around the shower. *This woman. She was driving me wild.* Warmth and wetness tightened around the length of me as she dragged her mouth back along the thick shaft again. It felt good. Too good.

"You're killing me," I moaned.

I bit down on my lip as an overwhelming sensation exploded across my cock.

"I'm going to come," I breathed desperately, giving her time to pull her mouth away. But she didn't. Instead, she tightened her mouth around me and sucked harder, her tongue swirling and torturing me until I couldn't fight off my orgasm any longer.

My palms pressed harder against the tiled walls as I gave in to the ecstasy, and my cock pulsed into her mouth with my powerful release. Lost in euphoria, I dropped my head back as she lapped up everything I had to give her.

When she released me, I drew her to her feet and cupped her lovely face in my hands.

"You are incredible," I said, looking into the vibrant blue of her eyes.

Two dimples appeared on either side of her mouth as she smiled. "You're only now working that out?"

I smiled and kissed her with so much passion I stole the breath from her. This was right. Being with her felt right. There was no room for fear or caution. My head was no longer at war with my heart. I didn't need to worry about falling.

Because I had already fallen in love with her.

CHAPTER 26

CHASTITY

After the shower I pulled on one of Ruger's t-shirts and sat in the kitchen while he made me breakfast. The view was pure eye candy. Ruger shirtless and in a pair of black pants with a belt hanging low on his hips, and his broad, muscular back to me as he flipped pancakes at the stove.

My body reacted accordingly.

Now that he'd taken my virginity, he had opened the door to a sexual awakening I was ready to dedicate hours to exploring.

With him.

He flicked off the stove and turned around, revealing a six-pack that flexed and released as he slid pancakes onto the two plates on the countertop. I watched him pour maple syrup over the two stacks and wondered how long it would be before he would make love to me again.

He slid a plate across to me.

"These look good," I said, hungrily digging into them.

He grinned and it was so beautiful I felt love bloom in my chest. This man was everything. I was in love with him and it made me giddy. I was so happy I wanted to scream it from the rooftop.

In time.

"So, what happens now?" I asked, pushing pancakes through the maple syrup.

"I think we need to take a breath and think about how this is going to work," he said soberly.

"I don't need time or space to think about this. I know what I want. I want all of you and everything that comes with you."

He smiled again, and just as it did before, love flared in my chest making me warm and happy. When he leaned down and scooped up his pancakes, his thick arms bulged at the shoulders and biceps.

"I think we need to be upfront and tell Bull—"

"No!" I said, a little too forcibly.

He stopped chewing and raised an eyebrow, but didn't say anything.

"I mean, can we keep this quiet for a bit?"

He put down his fork. "If you're worried about how he's going to react—"

"I already know how he's going to react. He'll hate it. He'll lose his shit, and once he's finished killing me, he's going to kill you." I pushed my plate away. The idea of telling my uncle had killed my appetite. "But that's not why I want to wait."

"Why, then?"

I leaned forward on my arms. "Because I want to enjoy this for a while. The moment we tell anyone about this the whole club will have an opinion about it."

A tiny smile hinted on his lips because he knew I was right.

He brushed a strand of hair from in front of my eyes. "I'm going out of town for a couple of days with your uncle. Let's take that time to think about how we're going to do this." His eyes sparkled and his voice softened. "But we need to tell him, Chassy. What we're doing, it's breaking all the rules—"

"They're stupid rules."

"Regardless, we have to be tell Bull. I don't want him finding out by accident."

"I understand. But I just need some time. The club has owned everything of mine since I was born. My family. My friends. Hell, it has influenced everything in my life. I just want this one thing to be mine... just for a while."

I could see he understood by the look in his eyes. "Fine. We'll wait until I get back from Gulfport, but then we tell him."

I nodded. I would follow Ruger's lead.

He had more to lose because of this, and God knows I wasn't ready to lose him.

CHAPTER 27

RUGER

It was hell walking into chapel a few hours later and not being able to talk to Bull about Chastity. But I respected her choice in taking some time to enjoy what was happening between us without any speculation and judgment from other people.

And part of me thought she was right. As soon as people knew, it would become a topic of conversation and everyone would have an opinion. Not that I gave a fuck about people's opinions. That concern had left me years ago. What I did care about was having my time with her invaded by the club. I wanted to get to know her. Work out what was happening between us.

There was no doubt I was getting lost in her.

And it was the worst fucking time to lose my head over a chick.

But that was the thing. She wasn't just some chick.

She was my best friend's niece.

The woman I had fallen for.

And she was all I could think about.

At chapel, I was preoccupied. Mentally, I was at home with Chastity, naked and exploring every inch of her delectable body with every inch of my tongue. I was packing a serious boner. Even after keeping me up all night with her tight pussy, I was still aching for more, and the ache was distracting me from the task at hand.

The timing was crap. Bull needed me to focus. Especially as we discussed our scheduled meet up with Martel. He had reached out. Wanted to negotiate the return of his drugs. It was time to flex our muscle, and Bull needed my experience now more than ever.

Yet all I could see was Chastity.

My growing addiction.

Thankfully no one picked up on my distraction because I had one hell of a poker face.

"Okay, let's get this business with Martel over and done with." Bull looked around the table. "Chance, Cade, Caleb, Maverick, Matlock, and Ruger, you come with me to the hangar."

Martel's truck was secured in a hangar in a secret location. With that amount of cocaine in the back, we couldn't afford to keep it at the clubhouse for too long. The local police were allies, but the ATF were something different altogether. If they decided to raid our clubhouse, we would be doing serious prison time.

Bull rose to his feet. "Joker, Davey, Nitro, Hawke and Cool Hand, I want you on Martel detail. I want eyes on him from the moment he leaves Eagle's Nest. Vader, Animal, and Yale, you stay here with the prospects... I don't want the clubhouse to be empty while this goes down. I don't trust this asshole. He knows we'll be arriving with serious manpower and may try to send his own message by blowing up the goddamn clubhouse."

The bark of Harleys roared into the afternoon as we left the compound and headed toward the hangar. We were picking up the truck and taking it to the abandoned drive-in out near the watermelon fields. But Martel wasn't getting it. Not until he left town. It was here solely as proof that his drugs were exactly as he had sent them.

Martel arrived at the drive-in only minutes after us, in a Rolls-Royce flanked by two black SUVs.

"I see my truck is intact," he said, tugging on the cuffs of his suit as he stood across from Bull. "You won't mind if I have my men check the cargo?"

"Not as long as you don't mind my men watching them do it," Bull replied.

Martel nodded to two of his bodyguards who followed Maverick and Chance to the back of the truck and climbed in to inspect the crates.

"I took you for a smart man," Martel said. "But this isn't the move of a very smart man."

Bull looked unfazed. He didn't care for what Martel had to say, but he humored him anyway. "How so?"

"You're a businessman, Mr. Western. There is a lot of money to be made here. Think of your club. Your town. Lives can change. We could bring so much money into this county it would make your head spin. This region is untouched. It's an untapped resource. No one has any distribution veins running through anywhere near here. Hell, even in this state. If you let this happen, *I* can make your wildest dreams come true."

It was a theatrical speech. Polemic and over the top.

But it fell on deaf ears.

Bull stepped forward, towering over Martel as he leaned in. "You listen to me, you fucking drug dealing piece of shit. The reason it's an untapped resource is because I made it that way by squishing bugs like you whenever they lift their head out of whatever dumpster they've been hiding in. Your *business* isn't welcome here. No cartel bullshit in this town, in this county, or in any Kings of Mayhem territory. That integrity is not for sale.

Now pack up your fancy French labels and find somewhere else to peddle your blow."

Martel looked slightly rattled. Sweat began to drip down his temple.

"You're making a big mistake," he said. "Think about the money. The possibilities a business deal between us could bring to everyone involved."

"This isn't up for negotiation," Bull said darkly. "Now get out of my town."

He turned and began to walk away, but Martel called out to him. "My associates won't appreciate this. Considering the consequences this will have, what would you like me to tell them?"

Bull only half-turned back and looked over his shoulder. "Tell them to go fuck themselves."

And so the line in the sand was drawn.

When Bull walked away, Martel watched him leave, a storm cloud darkening his usually smug and arrogant face. He didn't like being told no, and Bull had just served it up to him in abundance.

"You'll regret this," he called out.

But Bull ignored him and kept walking away. We climbed on our bikes and didn't give him another glance as we rode away, taking his truck and cocaine with us.

He would get it back when Bull was certain he was leaving town.

Back at the clubhouse, we met in chapel.

"What are the chances the cartel is going to come looking for blood?" Chance asked, clearly echoing the thoughts of every King sitting around the table.

"There is always that possibility. But the cartel isn't going to flex its muscle based on Martel's call. They'll reach out."

"By putting our heads in a burlap sack," Joker said grimly.

"No, they will make contact first. But I have a feeling that's not going to happen."

"What do you mean?" Cade asked.

"I received some information a few days ago. Ruger and I are going to check it out in Gulfport. And if my sources are correct, then the cartel's not going to be a problem." He looked at us around the table. "Relax, gentlemen, I think the only chain we rattled was Gimmel Martel, and if we fear that piece-of-shit weasel, then we need to hang up our cuts and walk away."

By the time chapel broke, the mood was lighter. But I didn't hang around for the aftermath, and ignoring the curious glances of my club brothers, I tore out of the compound and headed for home. Tomorrow, Bull and I would leave for Gulfport and I planned on spending as much time with my girl as possible before we left.

Chastity was waiting for me, wearing nothing but one of my t-shirts over a tiny pair of panties, and my heart lit up in my chest when I saw her. I picked her up and kissed her wildly as I walked her in my arms to my bedroom.

I couldn't help but feel like I was walking the plank toward an agonizing end.

But damned if I cared.

I was so addicted to her; I'd walk through my worst nightmare to keep her with me.

Bull and I rode to Gulfport.

After a night of burying myself so deep inside my girl, it was hard to ride beside her uncle knowing he had no idea I had crossed the boundaries of trust.

Guilt tightened in my chest. My loyalty to Bull was in direct conflict with my promise to Chastity to keep our involvement on the down-low. Every fiber of my being wanted to come clean. To confess. To tell him I had broken his one rule about Chastity, but that I would keep breaking it because damn, I was into her. I had no idea if what we had would last. Hell, I didn't even know what it was.

What I did know was that I hadn't been able to stop thinking about her since I'd left her lying in my bed this morning, her creamy body spread out, naked and smooth.

My cock thickened with lust at the memory.

But I had to focus.

We were in Gulfport to find out all we could about Gimmel Martel and just how involved with the Salvaj he was.

"He's not," said the scantily clad woman as she leaned down and poured bourbon into two crystal tumblers on the table in between us.

We were at an exclusive establishment called The Opium Den. It was the kind of place you didn't show up to without an invitation. You had to be recommended by a patron to gain entrance to the hallowed halls. It was an upmarket sex club where guests could choose the BDSM poison of their choice.

Like all men, our cultured friend had a weakness. And apparently, his was a dominatrix called Madam Triple X.

Thanks to our spidey friend back in Destiny, we had managed an appointment with the very popular Madam Triple X.

She had agreed to talk to us, for a fee, of course. Her clients' confidentially was of the utmost importance, but clearly for sale if the price was right.

Tall, with the body of a goddess, she didn't exude the viciousness some doms made a profitable living from. Her voice was calm. Smooth. Almost gentle. And very, very addictive.

"How well do you know Martel?" Bull asked.

"Well enough that I can make him come on command," she said very matter-of-factly. She straightened and gestured to the bourbon. "Please, gentlemen, enjoy."

Smoothing down the front of her PVC corset, she sat down across from us and crossed her long legs. She exuded a sexual energy that was as potent as it was apparent.

"And he talked to you about his involvement with the Salvaj?" Bull said, ignoring the bourbon.

"He thinks he's very secretive. But there's a certain amount of vulnerability when you're indulging in your pleasures. I overheard him talking once. Heard him mention the Salvaj. It piqued my interest. So I questioned him while I tortured him. *Just the way he likes it.* And he eventually admitted to me that he used the Salvaj name as a shield, but wasn't actually involved with them at all."

"Then what happened," I asked.

She looked at me. "Then he came."

The look on her face was pure heat.

Pure seduction.

"You're sure?" Bull questioned her.

"That he came? Oh, I can assure you he did."

Bull's eyebrow went up. "I mean, about the Salvaj."

She looked almost amused. "I have a diverse clientele, Mr. Bull. From wealthy businessmen and rock stars, to teachers, doctors, and the political elite. I most assuredly know when someone is lying."

She looked at the thirty-thousand-dollar Patek Philippe on her wrist and stood up. "Now, if you gentlemen don't mind, I do have another client due here in fifteen minutes that I need to prepare for."

We both stood.

"Just one more question," I asked. "Why are you telling us this?"

"Because you asked," she smiled seductively. "And you offered me the right amount of money."

By the look she gave us, I was certain she was telling us the truth.

In the end, we were gone for longer than two days. But it was worth it. By the time we left Gulfport, Bull was satisfied Gimmel Martel had as much involvement with the Salvaj as we did.

Zero.

Finally heading for home, a peacefulness washed over me like warm water.

I had missed my girl and I couldn't wait to see her.

But an ache tightened in my chest.

Tomorrow I would tell Bull about us.

And nothing would ever be the same between us again.

CHAPTER 28

CHASTITY

I was waiting in the clubhouse when Ruger and my uncle returned. I couldn't wait to see him and I knew he would come to the clubhouse first, so I made an excuse to be there at the same time as they arrived.

When he saw me, his face lit up and my heart turned to mush.

"Chastity, what are you doing here?" my uncle asked. He looked tired, actually, they both did.

"I came to see Mrs. Stephens about something, but she isn't here." It was a white lie. I was here for one reason only.

Because of the big man standing next to my uncle looking so fuckable that the muscles between my legs were pounding.

I was dying to touch him, and judging by the look on his face, the feeling was mutual.

"She only comes in on Tuesdays and Thursdays. You want me to call her?"

I shook my head. "No, it wasn't that important. It can wait."

My eyes met Ruger's and I could see how desperately he wanted to kiss me.

"Well, I'm beat. I'm going to grab a couple of things from my office and then head home." My uncle brushed a kiss across my cheek as he walked past.

While he disappeared into his office, Ruger and I acted like we were friends, not lovers, chatting easily at the bar but sitting a safe distance apart. And it was torture. I hadn't seen him in days, and it was all I could do not to touch him.

But when Bull left a few minutes later, and we were finally alone in the bar, we both gave in to our needs and went for each other.

With a groan, he gave me a searing kiss.

I pulled away to whisper in his ear. "I want you to fuck me in your clubhouse bedroom."

My words did things to him, I could see it written all over his face.

"Don't fucking tease me, girl." He growled in a husky, low voice. "I haven't seen you in days and I'm fucking dying for a taste."

"Baby, I haven't even started teasing you yet," I whispered.

He groaned and exhaled roughly as he stepped away from me. Desire and lust were rampant in his bright green eyes. "I missed you, baby."

I lit up inside. "I missed you, too. So much." I tugged him by the hands. "Now about that room."

I glanced around. The clubhouse was empty now, but before long it would be full of people. We would have to be sneaky, and we would have to be quick. It was dangerous coming here in case someone saw us. But knowing we could be busted made for added excitement.

As we disappeared around the corner, he pulled me to him and planted a searing kiss on my lips. I groaned against it and melted into his chest. I couldn't wait for him to take me on his bed in every way possible.

"You're such a bad girl," he growled.

"You haven't seen anything yet," I replied.

My hand slid to the front of his jeans, to the outline of his already hard cock, and I rubbed him through the fabric. My pussy pulsed, and I was so turned on I could barely stand.

"You touch me like that and things are definitely going to happen." His voice was low and guttural.

"That's what I am counting on." I gave him another teasing rub, and his face shimmered with arousal.

"I'm going to do such bad things to you on my bed," he warned.

I raised an eyebrow. "Best you lead the way, then."

He grabbed my hand and we almost ran down the hallway toward his room. We were both so turned on you could feel it in the air around us.

He paused at the doorway to kiss me again, this time long and slow, before we tumbled into his bedroom and came to a very sudden halt.

Because there, sitting on his bed, was a very pregnant woman.

She stood up when she saw us, her eyes bouncing from him to me, and back to him.

I remembered her. It was Astrid. His ex-girlfriend.

She was beautiful. Blonde and well put-together. And closer to his age than me.

A bad feeling started to tingle in the base of my spine. Especially when Ruger let go of my hand.

"Ruger," she said his name affectionately.

"Astrid," he said her name with no affection.

I just stared at her.

"What are you doing here?" he asked.

She ran a hand over her round belly, and the dread I felt was like ice water in my veins.

"I hope you don't mind. One of your biker friends said I could wait for you in here." She smiled and sighed. "I had to see you."

All the air left the room.

"Well, here I am."

There was more belly rubbing and I started to feel sick.

"Do you think we can talk?" She looked at me and then back to him. "Alone?"

"Whatever you have to say, you can say in front of Chastity."

A flicker of irritation gleamed in her eyes but then she smiled, and nodded.

"I wasn't going to tell you. I wasn't going to come here. But you deserve to know."

I held my breath.

Please don't say it.

Please don't tell him you're pregnant with his baby.

In the end she didn't have to.

Because Ruger did.

"Are you telling me it's mine?" He gestured to her big stomach.

She smiled and blinked back a sudden onslaught of happy tears. "Yes."

And just like that, my world crumbled beneath me.

"No," I breathed. And both of them looked at me.

She closed the steps between them and took his hand, placing it on her stomach. The baby must've kicked because she started to laugh between her tears. "Did you feel that? Did you feel your son kick?"

His son.

I looked at Ruger. Yeah, he felt *his son* kick. I could see the barely disguised emotion on his face.

"My son?" he asked in disbelief, his dark brows drawn together.

She nodded through more tears. "Yes, Ruger. Your son."

I stepped away from them, barely capable of breathing.

I was gutted.

"Congratulations." The word left my lips with an edge of bitterness. Again, they both looked at me.

"Chastity…"

I couldn't stand another moment of it. Not only had my world suddenly changed in a matter of seconds, I also felt like I was intruding on a deeply intimate moment.

I had to get out of the room.

"I'll leave you both to it."

Ruger tried to stop me. "Chastity, please don't leave…"

But I was already out of the room, although not far enough that I couldn't hear her say, "Let her go, Ruger. We have a lot to catch up on."

Tears blinded my eyes as I fled the clubhouse, somehow not running into any of my brothers or other Kings, and drove away from the compound with my heart breaking into a million pieces.

Fuck my life.

She's pregnant with his baby.

CHAPTER 29

RUGER

She's pregnant.

And she assures me it's mine.

"Remember that night I visited you a few months back?"

I did.

"You made love to me all night." She smiled and closed the door. Taking my hand in hers, she pulled me to her so her pregnant belly hit the hardness of my stomach. "That night we made a baby, Ruger."

It was bittersweet. Finding out I was going to be a father. But at the same time, possibly losing the woman I had fallen in love with.

Things were too new between us to handle something as monumental as an ex showing up in my room pregnant with my baby.

Not for me.

But I knew this would throw everything for a loop.

I knew my mind should be solely focused on the woman in front of me who was allegedly carrying my baby. But half of it left with Chastity when she fled my room and now I was distracted with worry.

I quickly texted her.

> **Me:** *Baby, you didn't need to leave.*
> **Me:** *Text me when you get home.*

Astrid huffed with irritation.

"Ruger, please. We need to talk about this."

"I agree."

"Then if you agree, put down the phone and give me your full attention."

Astrid was the jealous type. Not to mention demanding.

But she was right. I needed to focus all of my attention on this. We had a lot to talk about.

"Whatever you need, I'll give it to you. My son will never go without."

"What about a mother and a father who are together?"

I looked at her, caught off guard. "What?"

"We were always good together. Three years is testimony to that, surely."

Was she crazy? Our three years together was like a sick carnival ride of fighting and great make-up sex.

"The last time we argued you gave me a concussion and broke my thumb with a baseball bat." I shook my head. "That's not healthy, Astrid."

"I know I used to get a little crazy. It was only because I love you so much, Ruger. But since you've been gone I realized how much of a jealous psycho I was and how it pushed you away. But I've changed. I guess you can say I've grown up." She rubbed her stomach. "And now we have a son to think about."

I had always wanted kids.

It was Astrid who had stalled having them. Which, in hindsight, was a good thing because when our relationship spiraled out of control it would've been hard to leave if there were kids involved.

But now she was here and we were having a baby.

I thought about Chastity and my heart felt heavy with regret. The last thing I wanted to do was hurt her.

I glanced at my phone. Half an hour had passed and she still hadn't replied.

Despite Astrid's disapproval, I fired off another text message.

Me: *Baby, please.*
Me: *Let me know you're okay.*

I wanted to go after her. But given the circumstances, I owed it to Astrid to stay and work this out.

When I asked her if it was possible for someone else to be the baby's father, she turned on me, her emotions going from 0 to 100 in seconds.

"What are you suggesting? That I'm some whore like that slutty young thing you just brought to your room? Really, Ruger. I thought you preferred grownups."

Hearing her talk about Chastity like that detonated my protectiveness.

"You speak about her like that again and I'll throw you out of here until you can find some manners. Do you understand me?"

Her eyes flared with fight and I could see her weighing her options. Fight me or stay with me.

"I'm sorry. I just didn't expect you to replace me so soon."

That was typical Astrid. She fought with guilt trips.

"I've known that *woman* my entire life. She's nothing but an angel."

The image of Chastity kneeling before me in the shower with my cock sliding in and out of her succulent lips flashed across my mind's eye, and then vanished.

"What do you want from me, Astrid? You want me to be a good father to this kid, you know I will be. Whatever it takes. But you and I, we're not together."

"Come back to New Orleans with me. Your son is due in two months. Spend some time with me, *with us.*" She grabbed my hand and put it on her belly again. "You'll see how good it can be."

I pulled my hand away.

"My life isn't with you in New Orleans, anymore. That chapter's done."

"I agree, but a new one is just beginning." She kept stroking her belly. "Come back for a few weeks. Don't we owe it to our son? Best-case scenario, you fall in love with me again. Worst-case scenario, we can at least tell our boy that we tried."

She fixed me with eyes filled with sincerity.

"We at least owe him that, don't we?"

CHAPTER 30

CHASTITY

I felt numb. No. I felt like shit. I barely remembered the drive back to Ruger's house, and the moment I stepped in the front door, I burst into tears.

She's pregnant.

I went to the kitchen and started to make coffee but slumped at the island counter and let my tears rain down my face.

She's fucking pregnant.

And now we are over.

I was a realist. What Ruger and I had was brand new, there was no way it could stand against a pregnancy with his ex-girlfriend of three years.

When I was in California, one of my guy friends had a one-night stand with a girl who worked at the local Chuck E. Cheese. Two months later she told him she was pregnant. He had no interest in her and she really had no interest in him. But as the pregnancy progressed, they grew closer and their one-night stand became a friendship, which eventually led to them falling in love and getting married. Three years later they were still crazy for each other and expecting baby number two.

Also, Reina, one of the part-time hairdressers at work, started dating a guy she met at a bar over in Humphrey. When they were two months into the relationship, his ex-wife announced she was pregnant and he decided to go back to her, leaving Reina devastated.

And who could forget my own brother, Caleb. He and Honey had fallen crazy in love with each other after their one night together resulted in her pregnancy. Now they were hopelessly in love and married with three kids.

So, me and Ruger... I wasn't going to hang around and let that shit happen to me. The best defense was attack. End it now and minimize the pain.

Another wave of tears coincided with my phone vibrating with another message from him. I read it, deleted it and turned my phone over. I didn't want to hear or see him. I needed space so I could process this clusterfuck.

When his bike tore into the driveway an hour later, I was neck-deep in a well of despair. And when he burst through the front door, I hurriedly wiped the tears from my cheeks. Not that I could hide my red, swollen eyes. The moment he saw them, his face softened with pain.

"Baby, please ..."

He came toward me but I put my hands up to stop him. "Please, don't."

"Chastity—"

"Is it true? Is she having your baby?"

He took a step back.

"She visited me seven months ago and we spent a night together."

"So, it's yours."

He thought for a moment and then nodded. "The timing is right."

I looked away, unable to speak because a lump lodged itself in my throat.

"We can get through this." His voice was calm, steady, which was in direct contrast to mine.

"You were with her for three years and now she's having your baby." I shook my head, fighting another wave of tears. "You'll go back to her."

"No, I won't. I don't want her. *I want you.*"

"You say that now." My chin quivered.

"Don't do this. Don't push me away because you're frightened. We've overcome so much already. This is something we'll get through."

"Will we? How?" A flicker of anger lit up inside me. "Tell me how we survive you and her wandering down memory lane together while she grows your baby inside her. It's only a matter of time before you realize you want her back. The woman you loved for three years. The woman giving you a son."

He took a step toward me.

"What we have is bigger than all of that. What I *feel* for you is bigger than all of that." Despite my resistance, he took my hand. "I never loved her. But I love you."

I shook my head. He was wrong. It was only a matter of time.

I pulled my hand away. "We don't have a chance against this."

"*You're* not giving us a chance," he said.

"No, I'm not giving you a chance to hurt me when you decide to go back to her."

"So you're ending this?"

Pain shot through my chest.

"Yes." Again, my chin quivered and my lips trembled as I said the words I never expected to say. "This isn't going to work."

His face registered the anger and pain. His nostrils flared and he exhaled a rough breath of air. He turned away and then swung back, his silver rings glinting as he ran a frustrated hand through his hair.

"You're scared. But I'm not letting you end what we have because you're scared."

I stood up. "It's not about being scared, it's about being realistic."

He took a step closer, but I stood my ground as his bright eyes blazed with green fire.

"I fucking love you, do you hear me? I'm fucking head over heels in love with you. I don't want this to be over."

"You don't get the choice."

"And why don't I? I'm all in, Chastity. You and me."

"You need to leave."

He took another step toward me so we were almost touching. "I'm not going anywhere until you calm down and we talk about this."

"We have talked about this. You confirmed she's pregnant with your baby and I've told you it's over. The end."

I was fully angry now.

Angry because his beautiful ex-girlfriend showed up pregnant.

Angry because he was the one who knocked her up.

Angry because even standing there with my heart shattered into a million pieces I wanted to melt into him and lose hours kissing his beautiful mouth.

"You need to go," I demanded. Even though I had no right. This was his house. But I couldn't go home to mine. It was still uninhabitable. "Please, just give me time to process this."

But he just stood there, his bright eyes sparkling across at me as he searched my face and tried to figure out his next move.

"I'm all yours," he said roughly. "Do you understand me?"

My tears started to flow down my cheeks. I couldn't say anything.

He looked at me, standing completely still as he asked, "Don't you want me anymore?"

Of course, I wanted him.

I wanted him more than I wanted to fucking breathe.

He reached up and cupped my face in his hands and I felt weak and powerless because he was so damn beautiful. My heart ached and my body begged for him to touch me. My gazed dropped to his mouth, making my heart pound in my chest.

"Tell me you don't want me," he demanded.

But I couldn't. His mouth. Those lips. I was desperate to taste them. Even for one last time.

"Tell me we're through."

I struggled to swallow, mesmerized by his handsome face so close to mine.

"Tell me you don't want me to touch you right now..."

I couldn't.

"Tell me you don't want me to kiss you..."

He moved closer and I licked my lips.

"... to carry you into that bedroom and make love to you..."

My lips parted.

"Tell me you don't love me—"

He closed the space between our mouths and kissed me, his lips taking command as his tongue lusciously coaxed mine into participation. And for a moment I surrendered into him, kissing him back and whimpering against the deliciousness of the kiss. It was everything and more. *He* was everything and more.

I knew I should let go, but instead I twisted my fingers into his shirt and held him to me, enjoying the heat and strength of his big body up against mine. He groaned and our kissing found new levels of need and desperation as we both gave in to the urgency of the moment. His palms pressed into my cheeks and I could feel the hard, rigid outline of his erection and I wanted him. I wanted him so bad I could barely stand it. He breathed my name, desperately, over and over, and begged me to tell him it wasn't over. And more than anything in the whole world, I wanted to tell him that it wasn't because I was so fucking in love with him it hurt to even think about not loving him. But then I remembered Astrid and the baby, *his baby*, and I pulled away so damn quick I almost fell over. I steadied myself against the kitchen counter.

"You need to go," I panted.

"Chastity—"

"Please!"

His eyes blazed across at me and his chest rose and fell heavily.

"Fine, I'll go. But this isn't over." He crossed the room to the front door, but turned back to me before walking out. "This. You and me. We're not done."

And then he disappeared outside, slamming the door behind him.

CHAPTER 31

RUGER

Gutted, I left Chastity and climbed on my bike. It was torture knowing she was ending it, but I wasn't going to give up. I would give her the space she asked for and the time she needed to process everything, but we weren't done. Not by a long shot.

She was scared. And I was going to break my back showing her she had nothing to be scared about. But in the meantime, she needed time apart and I was willing to give it to her, despite my overwhelming need to be close to her.

My life was better with her in it as my girl.

And I wasn't giving up on that.

On us.

I steered my bike in the direction of the back highway leading out of Destiny toward Humphrey. I was going to ride to clear my head and let the hypnosis of the highway help calm the chaos taking place in my mind. But when I felt my phone vibrate against my chest I pulled over, hoping it was Chastity.

But it wasn't.

It was Astrid.

And she was crying.

"It's the baby," she sobbed into the phone. "I'm in the hospital."

Alarm detonated inside of me.

"What happened? Are you and the baby okay?"

Is my son okay?

"It's been a complicated pregnancy, Ruger. That's why I wanted you to come back to New Orleans, you know. Less stress. It's been hard. I miss you. I need you." She sniffed back more tears. "I need your help. *We* need your help."

"Is the baby okay?"

"He's doing okay. For now. But they're keeping me here overnight."

Relief spread through me.

"Where are you? Destiny General or St. Vincent's?"

"St. Vincent's."

"I'm on my way."

Twenty minutes later I was navigating the corridors of the maternity wing of St. Vincent's Hospital. When I found Astrid's room, she was sitting up in bed, her eyes red and swollen from crying.

As soon as she saw me, she started to cry again.

"What happened?" I asked.

"She started to have contractions," came a voice from across the room.

I looked up and came face to face with Astrid's sister, Thea.

Thea and I had never gotten along. She hated me. Except for that one time when she tried to stick her tongue down my throat and begged me to fuck her at a barbecue their uncle threw for Fourth of July a few years back. I never told Astrid about it because I figured we'd all done shit we regretted when we were drunk. And Astrid would never forgive her.

Since then, Thea had always treated me with contempt and never failed to put me down in front of her sister.

Now her eyes narrowed when she saw me.

"But they're okay now?" I asked Astrid.

"No thanks to you," Thea said.

The bitch couldn't help herself.

But I simply ignored her.

"Do they know what caused it?" I asked.

"The doctors said it's stress," Astrid said.

"And she needs to keep her stress levels low," Thea added. "I told her not to drive out here and do this. Not while she is so emotional and so far along in the pregnancy. But I was never able to stop her from doing crazy things when it came to you."

"Thea—"

"It's okay, Astrid. I'm not going to drag his balls across hot coals..." She threw daggers at me with her cold blue eyes. "... this time."

Again, I ignored my ex-girlfriend's sister.

"The stress caused the contractions?" I asked Astrid.

She nodded. "The doctor said I'm sensitive to stress. Because the pregnancy has been so problematic... if I get too stressed I could go into premature labor and... Ruger, our son could die."

She started to cry. Like *really* cry.

I was used to Astrid's crocodile tears. She could flick a switch and out they'd come. But these were genuine because our baby's life was in danger and she was scared.

Hell, I was scared.

I squeezed her hand.

"What can I do to help?" I asked.

Astrid looked up at me with wet eyes. "Come back to New Orleans with me, Ruger, and be there when your son is born."

CHAPTER 32

CHASTITY

Crying made me sleepy.

I fell face-first onto my bed, closed my eyes and let sleep take me as far away from reality as it wanted to take me.

Anything to not be feeling how I'm feeling.

Something woke me up two hours later. I stared up at the ceiling, disoriented, tired and with the awful realization that I'd just fucked up more than I ever had in my twenty-two years.

As I lay there, my eyes slowly focused on the slow turning ceiling fan, and I began to see things more clearly.

When I realized how immature I'd been, I sat up with a rush.

Finding out Astrid was pregnant with Ruger's son had sent me reeling.

Now I'd gotten my bearings, I could see how childish I had been.

I quickly reached for my phone and saw Ruger had tried calling me only moments earlier. I hastily called him back and was relieved when he answered almost immediately.

"So that was an epic fail," I said lamely, my voice hoarse with sleep.

"Chastity—"

I cut him off. "I behaved like an immature brat and I'm sorry. I was caught off guard and I reacted poorly. You deserve better than that—*we* deserve better than that."

He paused and I held my breath, praying he wasn't going to tell me I had been right and we should take a break while this mess played out.

"Baby," he said.

"Yes?"

"I'm outside."

I stood up. "You're what?"

I started to walk out of my bedroom, but then ran to the front door and pulled it open. He stood on the other side, his phone pressed to his ear. When he saw me, we both shoved our phones away and I fell into his arms.

He lifted me off the step and kissed me hard before letting me go.

I was so relieved to see him. "I'm sorry I freaked out."

He rubbed his thumbs across my cheeks. "I meant what I said, baby, I'm all in. You and me, it's what I want."

"It's what I want, too. We'll figure this out."

I was so thankful I hadn't lost him.

Inside, he kissed me again and I melted into him, comforted by the heat of his powerful body. When he broke off the kiss, he ran his fingers through my hair and fixed me with his green eyes. He didn't say anything. But I could see everything in his eyes. He was as relieved as I was.

"I really love you," I whispered.

With a growl he lifted me up into his arms and took me to his bedroom where he spent the rest of the afternoon showing me just how relieved he was.

CHAPTER 33

RUGER

I was lost in a flood of relief and bliss. In true Chastity fashion, she was being amazing about the situation, and I couldn't be more grateful for my amazing girl.

Or love her more than I did right now.

We were naked, our bodies entwined and slick with the heat of our lovemaking. She was warm and supple against me, her body softened by the orgasms she'd had beneath me only minutes earlier. She rested her cheek against my chest as I trailed gentle caresses up and down her back.

Shafts of dusty gold light spilled into the room through the high windows, creating a warm, hazy glow around us as we slowly came down from our highs.

"What are you going to do?" Chastity finally asked.

Her voice was hoarse and smoky.

"She wants to go home to New Orleans."

I watched her swallow. She knew what was coming.

"She wants you to go with her, doesn't she?"

I nodded. But I had already made up my mind that I wasn't going, so it wasn't going to be an issue.

"I told her that was an impossibility."

Chastity was silent for a moment, but then sat up. Her lashes dropped and she stared at the quilt she was absentmindedly picking at.

"You have to go," she finally said.

"What? No."

She looked at me and I could see the determination in her eyes. "There is a right or a wrong thing to do here, Ruger. The wrong thing would be to stay here while Astrid took care of a problematic pregnancy on her own in a city that's a state away."

"This is her trying to get me back."

"Of course, that's a factor. But so is the threat to your son. You have to go or you'll never forgive yourself if something happens."

"The baby isn't due for two months."

Two months without Chastity would be torture.

"Two months we can do for the sake of your son coming into this world safely."

I looked at my girl, my heart relieved she wasn't going anywhere, but my brain already forecasting the problems ahead for us if I went to New Orleans.

"Let me tell Bull," I said.

"Are you kidding me? No way."

"He needs to understand the situation."

"Oh, he will and you'd better believe you'd be riding out of Destiny minus your balls. Don't add fuel to the fire. Don't make this any worse than it already is."

She had a point. Telling Bull now might be more unwise than I thought.

"We'll do it your way. But when I get back, I'm telling him, baby. I'm not messing around. I want you. And I don't want to scurry around like frightened mice."

She looked pensive. "If we get through the next two months, I'll tell him myself."

The look of doubt on her face made me frown. I took her hand. "There's no doubt for me that we will. I love you. And unless you decide you don't want me, then I'll be coming home to the only woman I want."

I told Bull about Astrid and the baby the next day.

It was the worst timing in the world. The tension with Martel was continuing to rise and the club needed their sergeant-at-arms. But family came first. Bull insisted I go and make sure my son made it safely into the world.

Plus, there was a situation unfolding in New Orleans, and Bull thought it would be good to have me there. I would be his eyes and ears. As president of the original chapter, he was like the High Priest of all fifteen Kings of Mayhem chapters. He had a stake in everything and always made sure to have every base covered.

Astrid and I were due to leave in two days.

But until then, I was going to do everything in my power to show Chastity that I was her man and that no matter what happened, I wouldn't let her down.

CHAPTER 34

CHASTITY

Ruger and Astrid left early Sunday morning.

I didn't see them go. Ruger slipped from my bed after waking me up with his body, a thousand kisses, and a mind-blowing orgasm. The kisses were because he loved me, he said. The orgasm was to remind me how good it was going to be when he got back. I smiled and laughed, and did everything you're supposed to do when you're trying to show your boyfriend that him moving interstate with his ex-girlfriend who was pregnant with his son didn't really break your heart. I didn't want him to go and I knew if I told him, he wouldn't. But that wouldn't be fair on him. This was about family. *His son*. Ruger deserved to be there. To play a part in him coming safely into the world. And this was the only way.

But the truth was, I hated it.

I knew Astrid wanted him back. And no amount of reassurance from Ruger was going to calm this awful niggle that something was about to go terribly wrong.

But I had to trust him.

We didn't stand a chance if I didn't.

Not in our world.

I also knew a thing or two about regret. If he didn't go and something happened to his son...

So when they left, I refused to cry. Two months and he'd be back.

I tried to keep myself busy, and between school and my job, it wasn't difficult to do. I took my biology exam and nailed it, earning an impressive ninety-four and putting myself in the top five percent of the class. Bryce didn't sit with me anymore. And he wasn't interested in keeping up with our coffee dates either, despite accepting my apology for our disastrous date. I felt bad about it until I saw him walking around campus, hand in hand with another girl from our class, and realized things had worked out better for him too.

Ruger rang every night before turning in, and then again, first thing in the morning. And when he could, he would ride home to see me and we would spend hours wrapped in each other, making every second count before he had to leave again. He was living at the New Orleans chapter clubhouse—his old home— and was busy with club business, following up on a few things for Bull while he was there. He saw Astrid every day, but only to check in or to take her to a doctor's appointment, which was reassuring and comforting.

But even so, despite what he said, I couldn't shake my sense of foreboding.

Slowly, the days turned into weeks, and then the weeks into a month.

I was relieved when six weeks after Ruger left, my best friend Emma flew into town for an overnight stay. She had been traveling throughout South America for weeks, and our communication had been limited.

"Wow, nice digs!" she said, taking in the comfortable living room of Ruger's house. "When you told me we'd be staying here, I was surprised. I can't believe your apartment still isn't ready to move back into."

The truth was, the super had called me just after Ruger's departure, to tell me I could move back but I didn't want to. While he was away, it was nice falling asleep in Ruger's bed, surrounded by his things and the scent of him still lingering in his sheets.

More than anything, I wanted to confide in Emma. And I would. In time. But I wanted the time to be right.

"Oh my God! Who the fuck is this?" she asked, looking at a photo of Ruger and his grandma on the wall. Knowing she wasn't into old ladies, I figured she was talking about Ruger.

"That's Ruger," I replied, trying to sound nonchalant.

"The guy who owns this place?"

"Yes."

"Is he single? Because if he's single, then, girl, you need to hook us up!"

"He isn't single," I said, directing her toward the couch. "Now sit down and let me get you a drink."

I loved having Emma around. She was one of the nicest people I knew and she had me in stitches with laughter all evening. We drank margaritas and ate homemade quesadillas as she filled me in on what her free-spirited ass had been up to during her travels.

"You know who I ran into the other day?"

"Who?"

"Joey."

"Joey!" Ugh. My ex-boyfriend.

The one who dumped me after he met my family and learned about the motorcycle club.

"A-ha. And he was with his *wife*."

"Wife?"

Emma nodded. "She's pregnant, too. And I mean, she's about to pop that baby out."

"Wow, so he finally found his *Mrs. Right.*"

"I don't know about that. He looked totally miserable."

Part of me wanted to be glad—*the childish, immature part*—because of the way he had treated me.

But it was hard to hold a grudge. Because if he hadn't dumped me, *we* could be married and I would've never known the intensity and the sheer magic of loving Ruger.

At the end of the day, Joey did me a favor by dumping my ass.

"What about you? Any potential *Mr. Right* on the horizon?" Emma asked, looking at me over her margarita glass. When I didn't answer fast enough, her eyes widened. "Oh, you need to fill me in, girl. I can see it written all over your face. You're being plowed like a soybean field before planting season."

Emma grew up on a farm in Iowa.

When I went to deny it, I couldn't, and my face broke into a big grin.

"I knew it!" She put down her margarita glass. "I'm going to pee and when I get back, I want to hear all about it."

While she went to the bathroom, I looked at my phone. Lately, Ruger's nightly phone calls were coming later and later. It was already ten o'clock, and he still hadn't called.

Feeling slightly inebriated thanks to a pitcher of margaritas, I wondered if it was because he was out with Astrid, enjoying a quiet dinner somewhere, laughing about old times and wondering if he wanted to make new memories with her.

Jealousy prickled at the nape of my neck. And the alcohol wasn't helping. It was wearing down the walls between logic and emotion, making me question the things I thought I had found peace with.

It was also making me impatient.

When there was a harsh knock at the door, it almost made me jump out of my skin. I glanced at my watch. It was late.

Who would be visiting Ruger at this time of night?

Jumping up, I checked the peephole, and standing on Ruger's front step was a blonde lady.

Of course, there was.

Wearing a trench coat and high heels, she impatiently puffed on a cigarette before banging on the door again.

"Can I help you?" I asked as I pulled open the door.

Her eyes swept over me and then she scoffed. The bitch actually scoffed, before taking another puff on her cigarette.

"So you're the latest," she said, an evil smirk curling on her bright red lips.

Her mean eyes fixed to mine and gleamed with venom.

She glared at me.

So I glared back. "I repeat, can I help you?"

Her face was familiar, but I couldn't put a name to it.

"I wasn't going to come here, but I think my sister deserves better than what she's getting. So here I am."

"Congratulations. But who are you and what the fuck are you talking about?"

"Astrid is my sister."

My chest tightened. Right. That was why she looked so familiar.

"And...?"

"And ... I'm here to tell you to back off."

I gritted my teeth. So not only was I dealing with one woman trying to end my relationship, now I had to deal with her sister, as well. Fucking fabulous.

"You know he's fucking her, right? As we stand here, they're off playing happy families. And so they should. They're about to have a baby. So, I'm here to let you know exactly what's happening and to tell you that it's time to let go."

Usually, I would have some witty retort or a sarcastic response. But her words got to me exactly where she meant them to...right into my vulnerable heart. They struck a nerve and fueled my paranoia, rendering me speechless. Not that she was going to give me much of a chance to reply. Instead, she continued to career headfirst into her vicious attack.

"As much as I think he's a pig and he should die a slow and painful death, there's no denying when two people are meant to be together." She blew smoke at me. "You should probably quit while you're ahead."

Before I could reply, a voice came from behind me.

"Okay, I've heard about enough of this!" Emma stepped between me and the she-beast standing on the porch. "Listen to me, you psychopathic nightmare. You need to go, and you need to go before I shove that cigarette all the way down your goddamn throat. Am I making myself really clear? Now get on your tricycle and ride yourself off this porch and out of our faces for good. And don't even think about bringing your raggedy-ass back here."

Without waiting for a response, she slammed the door on Thea and turned to me.

"Are you okay?"

I nodded.

"Good," she said. "Best you make another pitcher of margaritas and then tell me what the fuck that was all about."

CHAPTER 35

CHASTITY

There was a good reason I stopped drinking margaritas years ago, and it was currently banging on my skull as I drove Emma to the airport the next morning. Following Thea's late-night visit, we'd sat up till late, drinking another pitcher of margaritas, while I explained everything to her.

Armed with the facts, Emma assured me I had nothing to worry about. That it sounded as if Ruger was in for the long haul with me, and was only fulfilling his parental obligations with Astrid.

"If you ask me, that man only has eyes for you," she said.

Saying goodbye to her at the airport was hard. I missed seeing her every day like we used to in college. She was my voice of reason. A confidante I missed dearly.

Before driving back to Destiny, I sat in the parking lot and tried ringing Ruger. Last night he didn't call until almost midnight, but I had missed his call because... well, because margaritas. After two pitchers, I had well and truly passed out by the time my phone rang.

Now I was desperate to hear his voice. His late-night call made my stomach ache and my head buzz with questions. Why did he call so late? What had he been up to all evening?

I tried not to let my paranoia get to me. I trusted him. I loved him. And I reminded myself that it was me who told him to go to New Orleans.

But I knew Astrid wanted Ruger back, and the visit from her sister last night was further proof of it. I wondered which one had come up with the idea. The classic divide and conquer plan of attack. Astrid would try to wear down the object of her desire while her sister delivered a paralyzing blow to the baby daddy's girlfriend.

When my call to Ruger went to voicemail, I threw my phone on the passenger seat and started the drive home.

As I drove along the quiet stretch of highway between Humphrey and Destiny, a county sheriff's car sped up behind me and turned on his lights.

Pulling over, I looked in the rearview mirror and watched a sheriff's deputy climb out of the patrol car.

Confusion tingled at the base of my spine.

I wasn't speeding. My car was registered. There was no reason for him to pull me over.

Instinct told me to drive away.

But lately my instincts had been so skewed by paranoia and the upheaval of Ruger leaving town, I ignored them.

But something was off, and when the deputy appeared at my window, that feeling only got stronger. I felt his eyes burning into me from behind his mirrored aviator sunglasses.

I wound down the window and handed him my license and registration. Which he wasn't interested in taking.

"Climb out of the car, please, ma'am."

I looked at him, puzzled by his demeanor.

"Would you mind telling me what the problem is, officer?" I asked.

"Just climb out of the car, lady."

I didn't like his behavior. Or his abruptness.

Or the fact that he was acting like I was a wanted felon.

"Not until you tell me why you've pulled me over."

The air between us snapped with tension.

Something is wrong.

"I said climb out of the goddamn car," he growled.

Every nerve and fiber told me not to do as he said.

Every cell of my being screamed at me to flee. But I ignored them because there was still a part of me that wondered if this was all about a broken tail light or something innocent, and that Dirty Harry was just a hard-assed cop who didn't like to be questioned by the people he pulled over.

I opened the door and stepped out, but immediately realized my mistake when he took an intimidating step toward me and backed me up against the vehicle.

He removed his sunglasses and I didn't like the ice water in his eyes. Or the way they lingered over my breasts as he looked me up and down.

"Step away from me, officer," I said.

Instead of taking a step back, he took a step closer until I was wedged between him and the patrol car.

"Or what? You going to yell? You going to scream? Look around us, *Chastity*, no one is around to hear you."

Anger and fear collided in me. He knew my name. And he was right. The road was unusually quiet.

I had stepped into a very bad situation. But I refused to let him intimidate me.

This was something to do with club business.

My mouth felt like it was filled with sawdust. "What do you want?"

He licked his lips and I saw the malice and heat in his eyes.

"Oh, baby, there's a lot I want from you." His hands found my hips. "And I'm just dying to take it. But how about we start with the basics. I've got a message for your uncle. A message from people high up in the food chain, so to speak." He shoved his hand between my thighs. "Tell him to stay out of Gimmel Martel's business or things are going to get real ugly."

I gritted my teeth.

"Get. Your. Hands. Off. Me." I demanded.

But he just laughed and put his hands on my hips again.

"Such a tough little girl. Got yourself some mouth on you." Lust shimmered across his face and he licked his lips. He slid his hands upwards from my hips to my waist. "You should put that mouth to better use, and I have some real good ideas."

I wasn't going to let him get away with what he was doing.

Deputy Monroe had crossed the line.

He was trying to intimidate me.

Had just assaulted me.

Why? To send a message to the club.

My heart pounded and I wanted to scream. But there was another part of me, one born from being raised in the club, that took over.

"You want to send a message to the club?" I asked.

"Oh yeah, I'm going to send a *big* message," he leered.

I drew in a deep breath, summoning everything I had ever learned over the years, listening to my brothers, my uncle, Ruger.

My eyes met his. "Well... let me reply on their behalf."

Being up so close to Deputy Monroe, one thing had become very apparent.

Deputy Monroe was bogus.

The uniform. The badge. The hat. They were all fake.

But the Glock in his holster definitely wasn't.

You didn't grow up in an MC and not know how to tell a fake gun from a real one.

When he decided to get handsy again, I grabbed it from his holster and shoved it under his chin.

"What the—" he growled.

"If you think I won't use it, then I promise you that will be your last mistake," I warned, jamming the muzzle harder into his jaw bone. My blood buzzed with adrenaline and pounded through my veins. Feeling the rage of him putting his hands on me, I turned us around so his back was against the car. "Now open the door and get in."

He paused, his cold eyes glaring into mine, before he reluctantly turned and opened the door.

But I wasn't nearly done with him.

Because he had been so handsy and thought he could cop a feel, I slammed the door on his hand.

He yelled with pain, his eyes almost bulging out of his head.

"Oops, my bad," I said as I opened the door again.

"You fucking bitch!" he yelled, gripping his now broken hand.

I leaned toward him, my eyes fixed to his as I drove my knee up into his balls.

Again, he roared with pain and crumpled over.

"You... fuck..." he wheezed.

I pressed the end of the Glock into his shoulder, forcing him to straighten. "Don't you know it's bad manners to put your hands on a woman without being invited?" I gestured to the car. "Now get the fuck in."

As he lowered himself into the driver's seat, I grabbed the handcuffs from his fake tactical belt. I slid them onto his wrist, the one attached to his black and blue hand, then snaked it through the steering wheel.

"You're going to pay for this," he growled.

Penny Dee

"See, that's where you're wrong." I waved the gun in front of his face. "Because I've got the gun and you're handcuffed to the goddamn steering wheel."

His nostrils flared and sweat dribbled down his temple. "You fucking whore."

I pressed the Glock into his cheek. "Call me any more names and I'm going to shoot you in the face. *Repeatedly.*"

And I wasn't kidding.

Maybe I was in shock. Or maybe it was hardwired into my DNA. Whatever it was, this asshole had pressed my last button. I knelt down and whispered in his ear, "How does it feel, *Deputy Monroe*? You just got your ass handed to you by a girl."

He was angry.

But he was defeated.

I held his angry gaze as I pulled out my phone and called my uncle. I didn't say much. Only that he needed to pick up the piece of shit who was currently handcuffed to a patrol car on the highway between Humphrey and Destiny, because apparently, the bag of dicks had a message for him.

Oh, and just so you know, he copped an uninvited feel on the side of the road.

What Bull would do to him afterward would be something I would never be told.

But knowing how fiercely protective the Kings were, I knew it wasn't going to end well for him.

When I spoke to my uncle later, he lost his shit over the encounter. I was not to go anywhere without an escort. I was to carry a weapon on me even in the goddamn shower. And if anyone tried anything like that ever again, I was to put a bullet in them.

"Are you going to tell Ruger?" I asked before I could stop myself.

"No, I'm not telling him. I don't need our sergeant-at-arms dealing with this. I'm going to handle it myself. Anyway, he's neck-deep in personal shit in New Orleans with his girlfriend."

"Ex-girlfriend," I reminded him, a surge of anxiety shooting up my spine.

"Yeah, right. That relationship is like a mind-fucking carousel. They fight and break up, then get back together so often it gives me a chronic case of whiplash. If he's not back with her, then it would be a fucking miracle."

His words broke my heart and filled me with a sudden fear that he may be right.

And it was a reminder that my uncle had no clue about us. That he didn't know who Ruger had become to me in the last couple of months. What we had done. What I had given him that I would never be able to give to any other man.

Before I asked Bull, I already knew I wouldn't tell Ruger.

But when I heard his voice later that night on the phone, all of a sudden, the fact that I couldn't tell him made me angry.

Instead, I went looking for an argument. I knew what I was doing. I was taking it out on him. And he had no idea why. Only that I was being difficult. He didn't know that a man had rubbed his hands down my body and slid them between my thighs. That he had assaulted me. Threatened me.

Suddenly, it was all too much.

The absence.

The distance.

Astrid and the baby.

The fact that he wasn't here with me when I needed him more than ever.

I gripped the phone tighter and let everything unravel in one giant meltdown before hanging up on him and throwing my phone against the wall.

There was only so much one girl could take in a day. And I had reached my limit.

CHAPTER 36

RUGER

The next morning, I woke up unsettled from the argument with Chastity the night before. I was tired. Flat out, beat-down tired. And last night I had barely slept, thanks to my brain choosing the lonely hours between midnight and four AM to obsess over every facet of our fight.

When I woke up I checked my phone, but there were no missed calls or messages from Chastity.

My fingers hovered over the screen as I debated calling her, but thinking better of it, I threw my phone on the bed and took a shower instead.

She had unraveled on the phone. Made accusations. Questioned me. And I could hear it in her voice... I was losing her.

Under the stream of warm water, I soaped up my body and tried to shake the after-effects of her words. Despite being haunted by them, my cock was hard and needy, so I stroked myself until I came, hoping the hit of oxytocin would ease the tension tightening my skull. But it didn't. Because I had a feeling I had just been dumped.

Chastity hadn't come out and said it, but there was no doubt in my mind that my girl was dumping me. She had grown wary and she was done. And could I blame her? You didn't ride off into the sunset with your pregnant ex-girlfriend and expect the girl who owned your heart not to have a problem with it.

I felt trapped between a rock and a fucking hard place.

When I stepped out of the shower my phone pinged with a message and I launched for it, hoping it was Chastity.

But it wasn't.

It was Astrid.

Astrid: *Dr Halidad had a cancelation. She can see us at 2pm.*

I had a couple of things to take care of at the clubhouse and Bull wanted me to pay a visit to a few contacts while I was still in town. So the timing was perfect. I could get it all done and be back in time for the appointment.

I wrapped a towel around my hips before I flicked her back a response.

Me: *I will pick you up at 1:30*

Astrid: *I look forward to it* ☺

Astrid: *Oh, and promise me you'll stay for dinner at my place afterward.*

Lately, she had tried to get me to stay for dinner, and so far I had been able to avoid it. For me, it was important to keep the boundaries clear. I wanted the lines in the sand to be stark and unmistakable.

Me: *I have plans*

Astrid: *:(*

Astrid: *Relax. It's only to say thank you. Not every offer is an attempt to rekindle our relationship. This will be a lot easier if you didn't think everything was about trying to get back with you.*

She did have a point. If we were going to co-parent our son, we had to learn how to do it without reading into things.

Me: *Dinner sounds good.*

When I picked her up for the appointment, she was standing on the porch waiting for me. Since arriving back in town, the club had loaned me a pickup to use so I could take Astrid to appointments. Despite some guys taking their old ladies on the back of their bikes right up until the birth of their baby, there was no way I was risking anything happening to her or our son.

She smiled brightly when she saw me, and I was suddenly overcome with a peaceful calmness. Maybe she was being honest and wasn't interested in getting back together. Maybe all she wanted was for us to be able to raise our son together without any drama.

We shared a smile, and for some reason it felt like everything was going to be okay.

"Everything is looking good," Dr. Halidad said as we sat across from her in her office. She was a highly recommended obstetrician. When I'd found out about the baby, I'd asked Teeth, one of my club brothers from the NOLA chapter, to do a little investigating and find a good doctor. He and his wife had six kids. They knew what they were looking for.

"But if he doesn't turn up for the show in the next couple of days, I'd like to induce him."

"Is there anything I can do to encourage him to make an appearance?" Astrid asked.

Dr. Halidad smiled. "If you're into old wives' tales, there are plenty. Eat spicy foods, have intercourse—but I think that one may have been made up by the husbands." She winked at me.

"There's no truth to it?" Astrid asked.

Dr. Halidad crossed her legs. "While orgasms can cause your uterus to contract, and sperm does contain prostaglandins, the jury is still out. It's definitely not a given." She smiled at us and sat back in her chair. "But it's certainly fun to give it a go."

Astrid looked at me.

I looked back.

Yeah. Sex wasn't going to happen.

"I think he's ready to meet his mom and dad, so I'm going to go right ahead and book you in to be induced on Thursday."

Thursday was only two days away.

Astrid reached across and grabbed my hand. "Can you believe it, Ruger?" Her face was bright with happiness. "Only two more days and your son will be here. Can you believe it?"

I couldn't.

And the sudden realization that I was about to meet my son filled me with a happiness like I had never known.

After the appointment, I dropped Astrid home so I could take care of some club business for Bull. When I finished up at the

NOLA clubhouse, I tried ringing Chastity, but the call went straight to voicemail.

Frustrated, I took a quick shower before heading back to Astrid's apartment in the French Quarter.

Inside, Astrid had set the table and poured us wine.

"Dr. Halidad said it's okay to have a glass," she explained.

She looked nervous.

"Are you okay?" I asked.

She smiled. "Yeah, I'm good. It's just... it's really happening now. In less than two days, we're going to be parents."

I understood where she was coming from. The idea was crazy. And if I was really honest, I was a little nervous about it, too. I took her hands in mine.

"Everything is going to be okay, I promise."

We sat down to eat. Astrid had ordered in a feast from the delicatessen on Peters Street, including the caprese, which she knew was my favorite.

We talked easily as we ate, but as I poured myself another glass of wine, I noticed she was looking nervous again. When I quizzed her, she started to rub her belly.

"I guess as it gets closer I'm wondering how this is all going to work," she said.

"How do you mean?"

"With us, Ruger. You and me."

"Astrid—"

"I know... please, hear me out." She cut me off. "I'm not suggesting anything other than you and I spend as much time as possible with our son when he arrives. Maybe you can move back permanently. It will be hard to have a relationship with him when you live a state away."

And there it was. The reason for tonight's dinner. Astrid was trying to get me to commit to something I just wasn't willing to commit to yet. My priority was making sure my son arrived safely. After that, we would figure out how it all worked. But we would figure it out with Chastity.

I stood up. "It's late. I should go."

"Please, don't." She awkwardly rose to her feet. "I'm sorry. I don't mean to push the subject. But he'll be here soon and I think we should have some kind of plan, don't you?"

We had a plan.

"I should really go. I'm beat."

I wanted to call Chastity. Hear her voice. Tell her I loved her. *Beg her not to give up on me.*

"You've had a few glasses of wine. You can sleep here."

"I'm fine. I've only had a couple of glasses."

She stopped me when I went to pick up my keys from the kitchen counter. "I didn't say anything earlier, but I've been feeling strange since this afternoon."

I swung around. "Strange? How do you mean?"

She smiled broadly. "I think I might be in the early stages of labor."

There's nothing like those words to kick your ass into action.

"Are you kidding me? Then we need to get you to the hospital."

"No, no. Not yet." She laughed at my reaction. "It could be false labor. It's really nothing yet. Just a few twinges. No pain." But her laughter faded and she looked at me with big, pleading eyes. "Please, will you stay? I'd feel so much better if you were here."

I looked at her swollen belly where my son was growing. If she was right and she was in the early stages of labor, it would be better for me to be here in case things escalated during the night.

"Sure. I'll take the couch."

"Thank you," she said softly.

She got me a pillow and blankets, and I settled onto the couch for the night. I heard her moving about upstairs, heard the shower and then the soft hum of the hairdryer before my eyes grew heavy and I fell into a deep sleep.

It was the gentle caress of lips that woke me.

I was dreaming I was back in Destiny at the clubhouse. Chastity was there and she was kissing me and dear God, it was so good to see her. To touch her. To kiss her. I wrapped my hands around her jaw and kissed her hungrily, wanting her so badly my cock was almost punching through my jeans. She echoed my own thoughts.

"I want you so bad. Make love to me," she breathed in my ear.

She pressed her hands against my cock sending a surge of desire tearing through me and ripping me out of my dream.

My eyes flicked open.

But it wasn't a dream.

And it wasn't Chastity who was kissing me.

It was Astrid.

She was leaning over me, her mouth moving against mine as her hand rubbed my cock.

Well, fuck.

"Stop!" I pushed her away, gently because she was pregnant, but hard enough to let her know I meant business. "What do you think you're doing?"

"What does it look like I'm doing?"

She rubbed me again, and the pleasure swirled through me. I pulled her hand off me.

"This isn't going to happen," I said. But she didn't listen and I had to move away to stop her from grabbing my crotch again.

She frowned and rose to her feet.

"I love you, Ruger. We're a good fit and we can make this work. Your son will be here soon and we can be a family. Let's make the most of the time we have left and spend it reconnecting."

She untied her robe and let it slip to the floor. She had nothing on underneath and stood before me naked, flawless, and *very determined*. In the dim light, her round belly glowed like a large shiny orb.

I stared at her like a dumbass.

"I want you and I know you want me. I want you to touch me, baby. I want you to make love to me." She took my hand and started to guide it to the mound of hair between her legs, but I yanked it away and sat up.

"Okay, this stops now," I said, swinging my legs over the side of the couch and standing up. "This isn't going to happen, I thought you understood that."

I was an ass for not seeing this coming. Astrid had always used sex as a way to reconnect after a fight. It was in her nature to think everything between us could be fixed by a night of fucking in her bed.

I picked up my keys and wallet off the coffee table, and shoved my cut over my hoodie.

But if I thought she was going to give up easily, then I was a stupid fool. Astrid wasn't the quitting kind. She stepped toward me and fixed me with her big eyes, touching me on the arm and making sure her belly brushed against mine.

"Look me in the eyes and tell me we're through." She took my hand and pressed it against her breast while her other hand rubbed the front of my jeans. "Look me in the eyes and say you don't want me, and I will walk away."

Once upon a time, the look she was giving me now would see me throwing her over my shoulder and carrying her to the bedroom where I would spend the next few hours buried inside her, making her moan my name over and over again. But those days were long gone. I knew it. And now I needed her to understand it, too.

I took a moment to look her right in the eyes because I wanted to be sure that I had her full attention.

"You and I, we had our chance and it didn't work out. We're over, Astrid. So, no, I don't want this." Her hand left my jeans. "You're a beautiful, special woman, but my heart wholly belongs with someone else now. Do you understand me?"

Her other hand released its hold against mine and I pulled it away from her breast. I could see the pain in her eyes, and as much as I wanted to comfort her, the best thing I could do was walk away. I bent down and picked her robe up off the floor.

"Does this have something to do with that girl?"

Just the thought of my girl filled my chest with warmth.

"It has *everything* to do with her."

"Do you love her?" she asked with a slight tilt of her chin and eyes glittering with tears.

I slid her robe around her shoulders. "Very much."

Her shoulders slumped but she nodded, giving up the fight. "She's a lucky girl."

"I'm the lucky one." I gave her a small smile. "I'm going to head back to the clubhouse. Are you going to be alright?"

She nodded. "I'm sorry."

I headed for the front door, determined to get back to the clubhouse for some shut-eye. "I'll come by tomorrow at ten and take you to your doctor's appointment."

I had just opened the door when I heard her gasp. When I looked up, she was standing a short distance away with wide eyes and her hands to her face.

"Oh my God!" She looked at me startled. "My waters just broke."

CHAPTER 37

RUGER

After nearly twenty hours of labor, the baby was still no closer to coming, and Astrid was exhausted. There were complications, they said, and they would need to perform a cesarean section.

I paced the waiting room while Astrid was in surgery. I checked my phone, over and over, wanting desperately to hear from Chastity but getting nothing but radio silence. I typed her a text but deleted it, then typed her another one, but deleted that, too. My head was a tangled fucking mess. Part of me wanted to tell her that we weren't done, that we would never be done. But the other part of me was pissed at her for not already knowing that.

I had turned into a fucking teenager.

No. You've fallen in love and it's made you batshit crazy.

With a frustrated growl, I shoved my phone into my cut and raked my fingers down my face. I had to focus on Astrid and my son coming into the world. But I felt torn in all directions.

Finally, after an hour, a nurse appeared to tell me the surgery went well and both mother and baby were doing well. Elation flooded my veins as she led me to the babies' room to introduce me to my son. *My son.* But when she took me over to him, I stopped in my tracks and my chest tightened.

Confused, I shook my head.

"Are you sure this is baby La Montagne?"

The nurse nodded. "Absolutely. I helped deliver him myself."

I stared at my son in the crib.

Now, either my Viking forefathers came to America by way of the Orient, or this kid wasn't mine.

My heart dive-bombed to my stomach.

Feeling duped, I walked back to the maternity ward, unsure how I felt.

No.

I knew how I felt.

I was fucking gutted.

My son.

He never existed.

And I looked like a fucking fool.

Emotion burned in me, but I bit it back. This ended now.

Astrid was sitting up in the bed when I walked in.

"How are you feeling?" I asked, my jaw tight.

"Tired and sore, but I'll be okay." She looked down. "Did you see him?"

Pain flared in my chest. "Yes, I've seen him."

She looked up. "So you know?"

I nodded. "My question is, did you?"

The way she hesitated told me she did.

"I thought there was a chance he was yours. I mean, I *hoped* he was." She frowned as she picked at the hospital blanket pulled up to her waist. "I met Lee when I got back to New Orleans after visiting you. I was so miserable about saying goodbye to you. It was just one night. When I found out I was pregnant, I thought about you. About us. I guess I convinced myself it was your baby." She sniffed back her unshed tears. "I thought by the time he was born you'd realize how much you missed me, *us*, and that it wouldn't matter whose baby it was. I thought we could find each other again."

I was angry, but relieved. Angry because Astrid had manipulated me again, and relieved, because it was no longer permanent. I was no longer tied to her.

Although, none of it compared to the disappointment of learning he wasn't mine. I wanted kids, I knew that now. But I wanted them with the right woman, and that certainly wasn't Astrid.

It was all so bittersweet and I needed time to process it.

"I love you." She took my hand. "Just because he isn't yours biologically doesn't need to change things. We can be a family."

Astrid hadn't changed a bit.

She was still manipulative and selfish, and she always would be.

I gave her a small smile despite the glow of anger in my chest because here was where it ended.

The manipulation. The lies. The dysfunctional bullshit.

It was done.

I pulled my hand free and reached up to wipe a lock of her hair from her forehead. "You need to tell whoever Lee is that he is a father now. Give him the opportunity to do the right thing by you and your boy."

She stared at me for a moment, fighting back her tears and biting her lip, before sighing and resigning herself to the fact it was over. "This is goodbye, isn't it?"

I nodded.

"Will I ever see you again?"

No. She would never see me again.

And I would never forgive her for the time I lost with Chastity. The woman I was desperately in love with and who had probably given up on me in my absence.

"You and your son are going to be just fine," I said. "You take care of yourself."

A lone tear spilled down her cheek, but she hurriedly wiped it away with the back of her hand. "Thank you."

Leaning down, I pressed a kiss to her forehead before I turned toward the door and walked away for good.

Outside, I climbed on my bike and took off into the darkness of an early Louisiana morning.

I was headed for home.

And I was going to get my girl back.

CHAPTER 38

RUGER

I rode through the darkness and arrived home just as dawn began to break on the horizon. Punching in the alarm code, I entered the house quietly. It smelled like home. Like comfort. *Like her.* And it felt so good to be back. I walked to our bedroom and saw her sound asleep, curled up with my pillow, her long lashes fanning her smooth cheeks. She looked like an angel. *Perfect.*

I knelt next to the bed and whispered her name, my heart aching to touch her.

Her lashes fluttered open, and in the pale light of dawn, her big blue eyes slowly focused on me.

"Am I dreaming?" she asked, her voice husky and raw.

I smiled. God, she was beautiful. How the fuck had I survived the past few weeks without her?

"No, baby, you're not dreaming," I said.

"I miss you," she whispered sleepily.

I wiped a lock of hair from her face. "You won't ever have to miss me again, baby."

"Promise?"

I smiled. She was still half asleep. Still heavy with dreams and slumber. And so fucking gorgeous it made my chest hurt.

Suddenly, the drama of the last thirty-six hours and the lack of sleep, hit me in the face. I was exhausted.

But not too exhausted.

I had something more pressing than sleep I needed to do.

Ached to do.

I pulled off my clothes and slid beneath the blankets and into the warmth, bringing my girl to my chest and kissing her tenderly.

"Don't break up with me, baby," I whispered against her lips. "I won't ever leave you again."

She stirred against me and curled her warm body toward me.

"Tell me you're still mine," I pleaded, my hand sliding between her warm thighs where she was already wet and ready. "Tell me you still want me."

She moaned as I slid my fingers between her dewy lips and began teasing her.

"That feels so good," she murmured, her eyes closed.

I brushed her lips with mine. "Tell me…"

Her big blue eyes opened and I saw them fill with lust and pleasure as my fingers teased her clit. She trembled against me and her lips parted as she took in a raspy breath.

"You have no idea how much I missed you," I whispered.

She said nothing but her eyes told me everything. She was still mine. She still loved me. And if I kept doing what I was doing, she was going to come.

I pressed harder against her clit, swirling her creaminess around it and giving it enough friction to build the tension in her. Her body woke up and her breathing quickened.

"Show me you're still my queen."

She bit down on her bottom lip and it was all I could do to hold back from driving into her sweet body.

She started to come and rocked against me, moaning my name as she trembled and clenched her thighs.

"You're so fucking beautiful," I said as she shuddered and came, her pussy quivering against my fingers. I kissed the moan from her lips and didn't stop until she softened beneath my touch. "Tell me what you want from me, and it's all yours."

As she sighed contently, her big blue eyes found mine. "What I want is this." Her fingers whispered a trail down my belly and began stroking up and down the length of me. After weeks of going without it, her touch set me on fire. "I've shown you that I'm still yours. Now show me, you're still mine."

I flinched as she rolled her thumb over the crown and dragged my slickness down the length of the shaft.

"Let me get a condom," I said coarsely.

She shook her head. "No. I want to feel you. *All* of you."

"Are you sure?"

She brushed her lips to my ear. "I want to feel every inch of you. *Naked.*"

With a growl, I rolled her onto her back, fully prepared to show her exactly that. Taking my cock in my hand, I teased her soaking wet pussy with just the head, penetrating her shallowly and then pulling back again. She whimpered and bit down on her lip, looking up at me with lust-heavy eyes, begging me to push inside of her. It was a tease for her, but it was torture for me because her tight pussy suckled at the thick head, trying to pull me in, to cocoon me, and it was driving me insane. I wanted to drive deep into her. Give her all of me. But I wanted to tease her first. I wanted to hear her tell me she wanted me. Because fucking hell, I wanted her like I'd never wanted anything.

Two months.

Two fucking months with only stolen moments with her.

Two fucking months with just my hand and a head full of fantasies when she wasn't around.

But I wanted to hear her say it first.

Wanted to hear her say she missed me as much as I missed her.

Call me a narcissist, but I needed to know she was still mine.

That the last few weeks hadn't cooled her want for me.

"Please..." she whimpered. "I need you inside me."

Her words hit me right where I needed them to and I slid my cock into her, hard and slow, so she could feel every inch entering her pussy, and fucking hell, it was all I could do not to come. She was so wet. So tight and warm. I felt engulfed by her and the pleasure was immeasurable.

I pulled back and then slid back in again, driving in deeper this time, making her gasp. Her body surrendered beneath me as I kissed and caressed her, my cock filling her, my pelvis grinding against her, my hands tangling with hers as we made love. It was slow and purposeful. Two bodies moving in perfect synchronicity. Two hearts lost in the moment.

She moaned as I rocked into her, biting her lip in that distracting way, bringing me close to losing it. With a cry she shuddered, and her pussy clenched violently as she started to come again. She clawed at the bed beneath her, her thighs tightening around my hips.

I dropped my head to kiss her, to steal her moans from her mouth, wanting all and everything from her.

"Come in me," she pleaded breathlessly. "I want you to fill me with all of you."

Fuck.

She was too much.

I had gone without this for too long.

I started to come. I grabbed her ass and thrust harder into her tight pussy, my mind spinning as my orgasm consumed me. And for the first time in my life, I almost passed out from the pleasure. It was blinding. Dizzying. Like nothing I had ever known, and I cried out her name as I collapsed against her, moaning into the warmth of her smooth throat.

Nothing.

No one.

No other woman had ever made me come like she did.

Every. Single. Time.

CHAPTER 39

CHASTITY

He was back.

And I had no intention of letting him go.

Not for the next twenty-four hours anyway.

He woke me up at dawn and spent hours making love to me before falling into a deep, heavy sleep. I left him alone and spent the day on an assignment. The day had started warm and sunny, but by lunchtime it was cold and overcast, and by suppertime it was raining hard.

As night fell, I slid into the bed next to Ruger's naked body and felt safe and warm as he slowly started to wake up and wrapped me in his arms.

"I've missed you, baby," he murmured, his eyes still closed.

I twisted in his arms so I could press a kiss to his lips. "I've missed you, too."

Outside, it was dark and rain continued to rattle against the window.

In here, with Ruger, I felt content and happy.

"Will you tell me what happened in New Orleans?"

I didn't want to sound needy. But there was a part of me that needed the reassurance that nothing had happened between him and Astrid.

We hadn't talked since he'd returned.

Basically, it had been sex and sleep in the twelve hours he'd been home.

Hell, I didn't even know why he was back. When I had first asked him, he'd been more interested in kissing me and getting me out of my clothes than offering any explanation. Then he had fallen into his coma.

Now a million scenarios were racing through my head.

Had she had the baby? If so, why wasn't he still in New Orleans with his son?

Or was she still pregnant and he simply came home because of our fight?

Alarm tingled at my spine. Or had something happened and he came back to clear his conscience?

"Ruger..?"

He opened his eyes. "She had the baby."

I was surprised. "She did? When?"

"About an hour before I rode out of New Orleans and headed for home."

I frowned, confused. "What about your son—"

"Turns out he's not my son."

His words stunned me.

"What do you mean?"

He rolled onto his back and rubbed his eyes with his palm. When he turned to look at me, I could see he was still tired.

"After she visited me that one night nine months ago, and I told her that it was over for good, she went out with girlfriends, got drunk and spent one night with a guy. Some guy she knew through friends. Turns out this kid is the father. Not me."

I stared at him, my mouth agape.

"Did she know?"

"Yeah, she knew. Not for certain. As she said, she knew there was a small chance it could be mine, so she clung to it and hoped it was true."

So many emotions snaked through me. Anger. Relief. Empathy, because I could only imagine how Ruger felt, thinking he was going to be a father only to find out he wasn't.

I traced his beautiful mouth with my fingertips.

"Are you okay?"

He gave me a small, tired smile. "Yeah. I'm good."

I didn't want to push the subject. He probably hadn't fully processed it. But when he was ready to talk about it, I would be there to listen.

Until then... we had weeks of catching up to do.

We made love again, then ate supper and shared a bath where he filled me in on what happened in New Orleans, and I brought him up to date with what had happened in his absence.

But I didn't tell him about what happened with the fake deputy.

Because the moment I did, our reunion would be over and he would go after Martel with guns a-blazing.

CHAPTER 40

RUGER

Things happened pretty fast when I got back. There was no time to explain to Bull about Astrid and the baby not being mine. When I walked into the clubhouse, he was preoccupied with the Martel situation and his focus told me there was no time for personal conversations. He didn't even ask if Astrid and the baby were okay. Which was unusual for him. Family meant everything to Bull. It came first. But right now, his mind was focused on Martel and the unfolding situation.

So, I knew shit was serious.

Of course, when I learned what had happened in my absence, I understood why.

And my head almost burst with fury.

One of Martel's men had assaulted Chastity.

"Wait, someone hurt Chastity?"

A rage as red hot as hell ripped through me. The thought of someone laying a hand on her made me want to break some balls.

Why had no one told me?

Why hadn't *Chastity* told me?

"And no one thought to tell me?" I growled.

"You were out of town. You had your own shit to deal with," Bull said.

I was blinded by my wrath. Mind blown by a need to protect my girl.

"I don't give a fuck if I was out of town, you should've told me!"

Bull didn't know my feelings for Chastity went any deeper than she was family. He didn't know I was in love with her. That the idea of someone touching her made me white-hot with fury. It was another one of those moments where withholding that information made things harder.

"What happened?" I demanded.

Bull explained how one of Martel's thugs pretended to be a deputy sheriff and pulled her over. When he attempted to intimidate her, my kickass girlfriend got his gun from his holster and shoved it into his chin, followed by a knee into his ball sac and a door slam to the hand.

If I weren't so enraged by it, I would probably be turned on by my sexy ass queen.

"I'm going to find this fake deputy and I am going to put a bullet in him," I raged. The thought of him touching my woman, *assaulting her*, poured heat into my veins. And it mingled with the guilt that I hadn't been here to protect her. "He needs to be dead."

"He's been dealt with accordingly," Bull said. He stood up. "No, this shit stops now and it stops with Martel."

"Then we need to go pay that motherfucker a visit," I seethed. I was going to let Martel know who he was fucking with.

And then I was going to crush him.

I expected resistance when we arrived.

Instead, the fancy gates parted and we were allowed up to the main entrance.

Martel waited for us on the steps looking as if he didn't have a care in the world.

Looking smug.

I looked at the two thugs standing beside him and wondered if either of them were involved with what happened to Chastity, and my hand itched over my gun. Bull glanced in my direction. Despite his sunglasses, I knew he was looking at me, giving me a silent reminder to keep my cool. I gritted my teeth, fighting every fiber of my being that screamed at me to put a bullet between Martel's eyes.

"Friends!" Martel opened his arms as if asking a question. "No truck?"

Bull smiled calmly. "You know you're not getting that truck back until its driving your drug-dealing ass out of town."

Martel's smile barely wavered. "Then we find ourselves in an interesting situation, gentlemen. An impasse, if you will. But I'm sure we can reach some reasonable compromise."

"You lied," Bull said, a twitch in his jaw. "We don't compromise with liars."

"Please, let's not discuss business on the porch like common folk. Join me in the parlor and let us settle this over a pinot noir and brioche."

I'd had about enough and stepped forward. I was prickling to make him pay for what he ordered to be done to Chastity.

"Fuck you and your parlor, you whiny little toad. You're a dead man, do you understand me. I'm going to crush you like the slimy critter you are. I'm going to personally skin your hide and wear that smug little smile of yours as a hat. And I'm going to enjoy it, you psychopathic fuck!" I leaned in. "You come after our loved ones and its war."

Martel grinned, amused by the emotion and the obvious torture on my face.

"I see," he said as I stepped back. "That was very descriptive, thank you, Mr. La Montagne."

His use of my last name made me want to set fire to him. But by the look on his face he knew I was motivated by something a little more than Chastity being family. I had to rein it in before Bull came to the same realization.

As I took a step back, Bull stepped forward and removed his glasses. Bright with emotion, his unholy eyes glowed with warning.

"You came after my niece." He leaned closer, and in a low and dangerous voice, added, "If you wanted to see the mad Bull, then know that you've unleashed it."

Martel's smile slipped, but he quickly recovered. "Duly noted."

We turned away. We were done. As we descended the steps and walked to our bikes, Bull replaced his sunglasses.

"Next move?" I asked

Bull slid his legs over his bike.

"We burn it," he said, looking across at the grapevines. "We burn it all to the ground."

We waited until it was dark before we descended.

From the shadows we took out Martel's men and drove the truck full of cocaine into the field of Martel's prized Syrah vines.

And when it was in position, we set it alight and stood silhouetted against the raging inferno and watched as the truck, the grapevines, and Eagle's Nest all burned to the ground.

CHAPTER 41

CHASTITY

It was late when Ruger got home, and the moment he walked in I knew he was furious. The look on his face told me everything.

"You know, don't you?" It was more of a statement than a question.

"Know what? That my girlfriend was assaulted by a piece of shit thug who works for the drug dealing asshole we currently have over a barrel? Or the fact that she didn't tell me someone pulled her over and assaulted her on the side of the road?" He strode over to me and took my face in his hands. "Are you okay? Did he hurt you?"

I was momentarily taken back by the emotion in his eyes.

"No, he didn't."

"Are you sure?"

His eyes searched my face and I could see how tormented he was at the thought.

"Yes, I'm fine." I put my hand on his arm. "He didn't hurt me. I was able to disarm him before he could do anything."

Ruger let out a shaky, angry breath. "I want to kill him."

"I think Bull has already taken care of the situation."

He pulled away from me. "I should've been here. Why didn't you tell me?"

It was hard to miss the hint of blame in his tone. He wasn't just angry at *Deputy Monroe.* He was also angry at me for not telling him.

"You had enough on your plate," I said calmly.

His eyes burned into mine. "Nothing is more important to me than you. Do you understand me? Nothing."

While his protectiveness lit a fire in my heart and made me want to tear his clothes off his big body, it could also be a little tiresome being treated like I couldn't handle things myself.

You couldn't be a part of an MC family without having some grit. It wasn't all status and titles. If you were going to be a motorcycle club princess, you had to back it up with some lady balls. And since I was a Calley, I pretty much had that covered. But occasionally the men around me forgot I could hold my own and they needed reminding.

Like right now.

"It was nothing I couldn't handle."

"How can you say that? Do you know what these guys are capable of? Anything could have happened to you. *Anything.* Do you know what that does to me? You should've told me and I would've come home."

"And done what?"

"Break every bone in his body before I put him in the ground."

"It got handled."

My response seemed to fuel his anger rather than dampen it.

"No, it wasn't handled because that piece of shit is still walking around!" He gritted his teeth and ran a hand through his hair. "Granted, he's missing several fingers, but he's still breathing."

Right. So Bull took the asshole's fingers, good to know.

"He touched you. Do you know what that makes me want to do to him?"

I'd be lying if I said the look on his face didn't turn me on.

That the emotion on his face didn't make me wet.

That the way his chest heaved with the anger possessing him made me throb with need.

Finally, his mood began to thaw. "Baby, the idea of him touching you..."

I didn't want to talk about it anymore.

What was done, was done.

In the distance I could hear the sound of fire engines. Coupled with the faint acrid aroma of petrol coming off Ruger's cut, I wondered where he had just come from, and if he was responsible for whatever the fire engines were traveling to.

I slid his cut from him, and although his anger still lingered in him, he put up little resistance when I led him to the bathroom and peeled the rest of his clothes off his body.

Pushing him into the shower, I stood back and let my clothes drop to the floor. Heat and lust flared in his eyes, and his impressive cock thickened and swayed as he watched me.

Inside the shower cubicle, I lathered up his body, wiping the soapy sponge up his strong legs, over his powerful thighs, and up to his hard cock. He flinched, and water dripped from his parted lips as his breathing quickened.

Inspired, I brushed my fingers across the thick column of flesh on my way up to his pelvis and enjoyed the thrill when he shivered beneath my touch.

Next, I soaped up his abs and his rock-hard chest, before I stood behind him and washed his broad shoulders and down his muscular back.

When I was done, he returned the favor and soaped up my body, his big hands sliding the bubbles across my skin with infinite tenderness. He was gentle. Loving. And in the silence, I could feel his desperation and torture, and knew it was because he was terrified of losing me.

"Ruger..." I breathed his name. But he cut me off. He caught me by the nape of my neck and drew me to his mouth. His kiss was slow and full of emotion, and his powerful body trembled. When he pulled away, he dropped his forehead to mine.

"I love you," he said, and I could see the torment in his eyes. He was still angry but it was nothing compared to what he felt for me. "Please don't keep anything from me again."

"I won't."

His thumbs brushed my cheek. "You're my queen. Trust me when I tell you that."

After our shower, he led me over to the bed where he made love to me slowly. It was excruciatingly exquisite, every movement deep, every breath hot, every brush of our lips purposeful and full of promise. We spent hours lost in one another. Our mutual cries of pleasure filling the air around us and thrusting us further into a realm of pleasure where only he and I existed.

Sometime near midnight, I collapsed, throbbing and exhausted, on the bed, and he fell behind me, wrapping me in his big arms and cocooning me in his warmth.

I sighed with utter contentment.

This man.

He was everything.

And it was about time everyone knew.

Ruger left early the next day and I had a shift at Wax-It in the morning, followed by a get together with Cassidy and the rest of the bridesmaids, so I didn't see him until I arrived at his house later that evening.

When I walked in, he was removing two beers from the refrigerator. He was dressed in nothing but a pair of boxers, and the sight of his hard-muscled torso lit fires all over me.

When he saw me, he swept me up in his arms and kissed me.

"Already stripped down to your boxers, I see," I joked between kisses.

"I'm all about good time management, baby," he said, walking me to his bedroom as he kissed me.

"I can see. So, this is what you have planned?"

"The beers are cold, the pizza is ordered, and my beautiful woman is finally here ... now the fun can start."

He started to undress me.

First my shirt and then my bra. Heat filled his eyes as he secured his velvety lips to one nipple. I moaned and dropped my head back, enjoying the swirl of his tongue on the taut, sensitive flesh.

"I've been thinking about you all day," he said, sliding his tongue over to the other nipple. "And it's made me horny as fuck. I've been waiting to do this for hours. Fuck, your nipples are perfect."

Next to go were my boots and my jeans, and when I was down to just a pair of white panties, he pushed me onto the bed and dragged them down my legs, making me shiver when his fingers ran along the soft skin of my thighs.

Pushing my legs apart, he buried his face between my thighs and delivered a mind-shattering orgasm within minutes of licking, sucking, and penetrating me with his tongue.

Gasping for breath and desperate for more, I rolled us until he was on his back and I was sitting on top of him. "Two can play at that game."

He cocked a sexy eyebrow at me. "Game?"

"Tongue play," I said, my eyes full of the heat left behind by my orgasm. "I'm going to fuck you so hard with my mouth, you're going to see stars."

"Oh fuck, Chastity…" he breathed, desperately.

But just as I was about to peel off his boxers, the doorbell rang.

"Leave it," he begged. "Tell me more about mouth fucking me."

I laughed. "It'll have to wait, or the pizza will get cold."

"Fuck the pizza." He anchored me to his hips. "I've got better plans for that beautiful mouth of yours."

I leaned forward to plant a brief kiss on his lips. "Pizza. Then you get your orgasms. And trust me. You're going to need your strength."

I kneeled back and his gaze dropped to the giant erection pressing at the front of his boxers. "Maybe you should answer the door, considering I'm armed with this."

When I brushed my hand over the bulge and started to rub it, he raised an eyebrow at me. "I'm seconds away from sacrificing our pizza," he warned.

I laughed and untangled myself from him.

As I pulled on one of his t-shirts, the doorbell rang again.

I scooted through the house, humming to myself because I was high on being with my man.

But when I opened the door, dread shot up my spine and burst across the rest of me.

Because it wasn't the pizza delivery guy standing on Ruger's doorstep.

It was my uncle.

Surprise collided with confusion on his face. "Chastity, what are you doing here? I thought you had moved back to your apartment."

His eyes swept over me. I shifted nervously. Ruger's t-shirt barely reached my thighs.

In the worst timing in the world, Ruger walked into the room, shirtless and in his boxer shorts, flicking through the money in his wallet, ready to pay the delivery guy. He came to a halt when he saw Bull, and their eyes met across the room. In that moment my uncle put two and two together.

"You sonofabitch!" He launched through the door and ran at Ruger, thrusting him up against the wall. "What the fuck? That's my niece! Tell me now… tell me goddamn now that you're not fucking around with her."

Ruger held Bull's fierce gaze. He was calm. "I won't lie to you, brother."

In response, my uncle snarled and his fist connected with Ruger's jaw, and then again in the mouth.

And then it was on. All hell broke loose. My uncle threw punches while Ruger did his best to deflect them. He didn't throw any punches of his own. He wasn't going to hit his best friend, but he sure as hell wasn't going to let his best friend keep hitting him.

"You goddamn motherfucker," my uncle boomed. "She's just a kid."

"I'm not a kid," I yelled at him.

Stupidly, I threw myself into the melee trying to stop the fight.

Unfortunately, Bull's elbow collected with my cheek and dropped me to the floor like I was a house of cards. Stars danced before my eyes as pain seared a burning path into my brain. I cried out.

"Chastity!" Ruger shoved past my uncle and crouched next to me.

"Get your hands off her," Bull growled, storming over to us and dropping down beside me.

Ruger ignored him. "Are you okay?"

I nodded, rubbing my cheekbone. "Yeah, I'm fine."

Ruger's hands were tender as they pulled mine away from my face so he could survey the damage. His eyebrows slammed together, so I guessed it wasn't good.

Bull also looked concerned as his bright eyes inspected the gigantic bruise I suspected was forming around my cheekbone. "I'm so sorry, sweetheart."

"It was an accident," I assured him. Bull would rather cut off his arms than hurt me. Even through his anger he would be feeling devastated about hitting me in the face with his elbow.

"I'll get you some ice," Ruger said, rising to his feet.

As he went to the refrigerator, Bull watched him then glared at me. "What the fuck are you doing with him, Chastity?"

"Following my heart," I replied, glaring back at him.

I could see my answer annoyed him because he rolled his eyes and shook his head with frustration.

"He's too fucking old for you."

"He's only sixteen years older."

"Exactly. Too old. Especially when you're so young."

"I don't care," I said through gritted teeth.

Ruger returned with an icepack and gently placed it on my cheek. I winced.

"Sorry, angel," he said softly.

Bull growled as he stood up, hating the tenderness in Ruger's words.

"Come on, Chastity, we're leaving." He tried to pull me to my feet, but I yanked my arm away and stood up by myself.

"I said no, Uncle Bull. I'm staying here with Ruger."

"The hell you are."

"I'm not leaving with you. This is where I belong. With him. Can't you see, I'm in love with him."

Surprise rippled across my uncle's face, and for a moment his face softened. But then he looked at Ruger again and his expression grew fierce.

"She's my niece. You've known her since she was a baby, you sick fuck."

"That might be true, Bull. But she's not a child anymore. She's an adult. A grown woman, and I'm fucking in love with her."

"In love with her? Are you fucking kidding me? Do you forget how long I've known you? How many hearts I've seen you break apart when a woman no longer holds your interest? If you honestly think I'm going to stand by and watch you do the same thing to my niece, then you are fucking delusional."

"Chastity isn't like any woman I've known. I mean it, Bull, I love her." Ruger's sparkling green eyes found mine. "And I want to spend the rest of my life with her."

Despite the tension in the air, love lit up in my chest.

I want to spend the rest of my life with her.

It was the first time he'd ever said anything like that.

"You know that's not going to happen," Bull replied angrily.

"That's not your choice," I said to him.

"No, it's his." He pointed at Ruger. "And I'm telling you now, kid, he's going to break your heart. Why do you think he's gotten to be this age without a wife?"

I fixed my uncle's fierce eyes with my own. "Because they weren't right for him."

"And you are? Christ, kid, he's going to be an old man when you're still young." Anger bounced off him as he shook his head in disbelief. "He got another woman pregnant, for fuck's sake! Is that what you want? A guy who knocks up one woman and takes off after a woman sixteen years younger than him?"

"It didn't happen that way!"

"Oh, it didn't, huh?"

"No, when we got together we didn't know about Astrid and the baby."

Fury burned bright in my uncle's eyes. They darted to Ruger. "Exactly how long have you been messing around with my niece?"

I didn't give Ruger a chance to answer and yelled at my uncle. "Why can't you be happy for me?"

"Because you're making a mistake." He glared at Ruger again. "A big fucking mistake."

"That's your opinion."

"Yeah? What do you think your brothers will say about it?"

"They'll understand—" Ruger said.

My uncle cut him off. "Don't you fucking talk to me. You stay out of my way or I swear to God, Ruger, I'll gut you and cut your goddamn balls off."

But Ruger wasn't easily intimidated by my uncle. Or by anyone.

"This is happening, Bull. Whether you fucking like it or not."

My uncle's nostrils flared. "We'll fucking see about that."

He stormed out and slammed the door behind him, the bang sending a shockwave rippling through the room. Less than a minute later, Bull's Harley took off down the street.

I went to Ruger and he pulled me to his chest, wrapping his big arms around me. He pressed a kiss into my hair.

"You okay, angel?" When I nodded, he released me and guided me over to the couch, and handed me the icepack. "Keep this on."

"Where do you think he's gone?" I asked.

"I'm guessing straight to your brothers."

I grimaced. They weren't going to take this well.

"Hey, it's going to be okay." He rubbed my knee. "At least we don't need to hide it anymore."

I put the icepack down and crawled over to him. Climbing onto his lap, I slid my thighs on either side of his hips and kissed him slowly and softly, careful to avoid the cut on his lip.

"Good, because I want all those hot babes at the clubhouse to know that you're mine." I laced my fingers behind his neck. "And I want every boy in town to know that I'm Ruger's girl, and Ruger's girl only."

Love gleamed in his beautiful eyes. He smiled up at me and I fell in love with him all over again. This was right. This was how it was meant to be.

"People will have opinions," he said.

"Fuck them and their opinions."

"And we're going to get a lot of resistance."

I looked him in the eye. "I know."

"Are you ready for it?"

"As long as we're together, I don't care. We'll show them they're wrong."

A small smile tugged at the corner of his swollen lip where Bull's skull ring had torn the skin.

He reached up and brushed his thumbs along my jaw as he inspected the bruise forming on my cheek. "Does it still hurt?"

"No." I ran a delicate finger along his cut lip. "Does this?"

Our eyes met and locked. The air grew thick between us.

"No."

Beneath me, the ridge of his cock pressed against my panties.

"Did you mean what you said to my uncle. About wanting to spend the rest of your life with me?" I asked, a pulse taking up between my thighs. When I shifted so I could rub against the growing bulge behind his shorts, lust shimmered across his face.

"Every damn word," he said hoarsely.

I pressed harder against him, enjoying his thickening cock rubbing against my clit. I started to rock gently against it, dragging my teeth over my bottom lip as pleasure swirled through me. Being with him like this and knowing he saw a future with me lit me up like sunshine.

Not to mention, made me so damn wet.

I knew we had more pressing matters to deal with. My formidable uncle knew about us, and it was only a matter of time before my brothers did, too. But I needed the distraction. And so did Ruger. I needed to stop him from riding off after my uncle, because if I was completely honest, I had no idea what they would do to each other.

And I could see he was moments away from doing just that.

I reached down and took the outline of his cock in my palm.

"Tell me this is mine," I whispered. "Tell me this belongs to me."

"It's all yours, baby," he rasped.

My fingers slid beneath the elastic of his shorts and eased them down over his hips, allowing the giant shaft to spring free.

Curling my fingers around him, I started to slide my palm from root to head, and he licked his lips and started to pant.

"You like this?" I asked.

He looked up at me through hooded lids. "I like everything you do to me."

"Likewise," I said, smiling wickedly at him as I guided his hand beneath my soaked panties. When he felt how wet I was, his eyes unfocused and raw need rippled across his face.

"Oh fuck, Chastity..." he said desperately.

He swallowed thickly as I continued to stroke him while holding his fingers to my slick clit.

"You like that?" I breathed. "You like how wet you make me? How hungry my body is for you?"

He groaned, his eyes hooded, his lips wet as they parted with another moan.

"You make me so hard, baby. So fucking hard."

He bit down on his lip as I started to rock against his fingers, summoning my orgasm with his hand on my pussy and my free hand jerking him.

"Give me your pussy," he demanded.

I pushed my panties aside and pushed the broad cock head through the slippery skin before slowly sinking down onto him.

Heat and pleasure filled me as I took every inch of him inside.

He groaned. "Fuck, your pussy is so fucking perfect."

With a moan I started to ride him, my hips rocking back and forward, slowly and deliberately, my body clenching him tightly. Tiny pulses of pleasure flittered through me, making me whimper as the pleasure began to rise.

"You look so damn hot riding my cock, baby."

I bit down on my lip and pushed my hands upwards to my breasts, dropping my head as sweet bliss came at me from all directions.

"Ride me hard," he rasped out.

In this position my clit received all the TLC it needed, and the friction was mind-blowing.

My orgasm gathered quickly, then surged forward and crashed through me in a wave of blinding pleasure. I cried out, unbridled and lost in a dizzying ecstasy.

"That's it, baby, come for me. Come all over my cock."

I whimpered, my body turning to jello. He grabbed me by the hips and drove his cock deep into me, thrusting hard and groaning, his eyebrows snapping together and then releasing as his orgasm hit with full force. His beautiful lips dropped open with a desperate gasp.

I couldn't take my eyes off him. I needed to watch as he came undone beneath me. Needed to see the raw emotion of his face as his orgasm tore into him.

"Fill me with your cum," I moaned, loving the look of ecstasy hijacking his beautiful face. "Give me all of it, baby."

His eyes lost focus and he cried out.

"Chastity!" My name tore from him with an animalistic cry, and with a jerk and shudder he pulsed into me, his face lost in ecstasy as he filled me.

Slowly the air stilled and our panted breaths filled the space around us as we both came down from our high. I collapsed against him and enjoyed the warmth of his naked chest against my skin and the wild pounding of his heart against my cheek. Filled with love, I melted into him.

The rest of the world be damned.

This man was everything.

CHAPTER 42

RUGER

It was hard to shake my fight with Bull.

For twenty-two years we'd been best friends.

I was fifteen, almost sixteen when my twenty-year-old sister fell in love with him and brought him home. Since then, I'd looked up to him. Admired him. Wanted to be like him. And as I grew up, he became my best friend. The man I stood next to when he finally married my sister. The man I held in my arms as he wept over her sudden death only three months after their wedding. The man I disarmed when he'd taken his gun to Stockade Hill to end the soul-crushing pain of losing his wife. The man I'd sworn to always stand beside no matter how fucking stormy the weather got.

For twenty-two years I'd never failed him, and it gutted me that now we were at odds.

But it wasn't my involvement with Chastity that burned us. I could and never would regret what we had together. What really twisted the knife in was how Bull didn't think I was good enough for his niece. Yeah, I got the age difference thing. Yada fucking yada. But to fucking stand there and tear me down in front of her. To reveal what he really thought of me. Yeah, he was pissed at me and we all say shit when things are heated, but fuck, it was obvious he thought I was some kind of douchebag when it came to this woman.

Of course, I had fucked my fair share of women. But I was never an asshole to them. I didn't lead them on. Didn't fucking rough them up or hurt them. We fucked. Lost ourselves in each other, physically, so the fuck what? And that all stopped with my three-year relationship with Astrid.

And let's not fucking forget that since moving to Destiny I'd basically been living like a fucking monk. Despite my one night with Astrid and a couple of go-nowhere dates, I hadn't been with anyone.

I wanted to have it out with him. Let him get it out of his system. Let him do his worst. Talk to him about it like I should have months ago.

But no matter what, he needed to know I was in love with his niece and there wasn't a damn thing he could do about it.

I braced myself for the showdown at the clubhouse the next day. But when I arrived, Vader told me chapel was canceled because Bull had left town for the day.

"What for?" I asked.

I was sergeant-at-arms. Where my president went, I went. If there were any new developments with club business, I knew about it. I was Bull's lieutenant. His second set of eyes.

His protection.

Vader shrugged. "Didn't say. He stormed in here like a fucking tornado, banged around in his office for a bit, then left."

"Do you know where?"

"No. When Joker asked him what was happening, he told him to fuck off and mind his own business. Since then, no-one has heard from him and no one knows where he is."

Not no one.

I knew where he was.

Twenty minutes later, I rode through the cemetery gates and parked next to Bull's Harley in the parking lot. It was a five-minute walk through the massive graveyard to Wendy's grave where Bull sat in front of her tombstone, a bottle of Jack Daniel's in his hands.

I stopped a few yards away from him.

When he spoke, he didn't turn around. "Come any closer and I'll fucking kill you."

I could hear the emotion in his voice.

And the Jack Daniel's.

One thing I'd learned early in life was the futility of trying to reason with a drunk man. But I had to at least try.

"I love her," I said matter-of-factly, my voice almost alien in the lonely quiet of the graveyard. "I know you don't approve, and it kills me that you don't. But you need to know that it won't stop me from loving her."

He said nothing. So I continued. Because he needed to know exactly how it was.

"And if you ask me to choose... I *will* choose her over my brother."

Bull slowly pulled himself to his feet and turned around. His glasses were off and his piercing eyes were heavily shadowed from lack of sleep and too much whisky. He came toward me, his steps slow, his body affected by liquor, a darkness sweeping over him.

"You're not my brother," he seethed in disgust. "You stopped being my brother the moment you touched my niece."

He was angry and he was drunk, but hearing him say those words was like a giant kick in the balls.

"The one woman I told you to stay away from and you went ahead and did it anyway. The one woman who was off limits to everyone. And you did it anyway. The one woman you knew was like a daughter to me. And you did it anyway." His emotions started to get away from him. "The one woman I trusted you not to touch. AND. YOU. DID. IT. ANYWAY."

I didn't care who you were. Michael Western was a formidable man. And like this, he was fucking scary.

"I fell in love with her," I said calmly.

"Love? LOVE?" He yelled. His eyes lit up with fire. "Are you fucking kidding me?"

He pulled out his gun and pointed it at my head. Adrenaline pounded through me but I refused to be intimidated.

"No, I'm not kidding you. I'm in love with her."

He tightened his grip on his gun as he took a step toward me. "Is that what you tell yourself so you can sleep at night? Is that what gets you through knowing you're a sick sonofabitch who likes young girls."

"She's twenty-two. She's a woman. Not a girl."

He might have a gun pointed at my head, but I wasn't going to let him brand me with that kind of bullshit.

"You've known her since she was born."

My eyes narrowed. "Is that what you truly think of me? That I was a sick fuck lusting after her since she was a kid. Are you fucking serious? I don't care how angry or fucked up you are right now, Bull, both you and I know that is not the case here. I fell in love with the woman, not the child. So you accuse me of that shit again and I swear to God, you'd better pull that trigger before I get to you."

The air between us crackled with tension.

"I should kill you right here, right now."

"For what? For loving Chastity? For wanting to protect her? For wanting to give her everything?" I took a step toward him so his gun was only inches from my forehead. "For treating her like the queen she is?"

"She wasn't meant for you!" He hissed, his eyes wild. "*This life* wasn't meant for her."

I grabbed the end of his gun and pressed it against my forehead. "Then shoot me, Bull. Fucking put me out of my misery, then. Because I love her and if she's not meant for me, then I might as well be dead. So you want to punish me, go right ahead. Put a bullet in my brain and this all goes away. What are you waiting for? Do it. DO IT!"

Our eyes locked and I could see the fury in his. A fury that came from his very soul. And I could see it, the want to end this, a need to punish me, the desperation for this to be done.

His finger trembled on the trigger, while his lips curled into a snarl before parting in a cry of anguish.

Frustrated at his inability to pull the trigger, he stepped back and fired rapid rounds into the sky. They rang out across the cemetery, causing a flock of birds to take flight from the poplar trees.

He glared at me. And I glared back, my pulse pounding in my ears.

"This isn't finished," he growled, taking a few unsteady steps backward. He stumbled over to the bottle of Jack Daniel's laying on the grass and picked it up, while I remained rooted to the spot.

"You shouldn't ride drunk," I said calmly, like he hadn't just had a gun pointed at my skull.

But he just looked at me and said nothing as he brushed past and disappeared up the hill and out of view.

CHAPTER 43

CHASTITY

I was surprised when I didn't hear anything about it the next day.

No phone call from my mom.

No interrogation from my brothers.

No gasps of surprise from my sisters-in-law.

No rant from my uncle.

I waited. All through class and then through a three-hour shift at Wax-It, expecting some kind of fall out. But nothing happened.

Just a weird radio silence.

But when I saw Ruger later that afternoon and he told me what happened at the cemetery, it all made sense.

Bull was obviously keeping it to himself while he processed it.

"What do we do now?" I asked.

"The wedding is tomorrow, let's focus on that and then worry about Bull and his reaction."

Chance and Cassidy were getting married at Lannister Farm, a stunning bed and breakfast just out of town. Once upon a time it had been a massive apple farm and cannery, but as progress had swept through the county, the farm had been broken up into separate parcels of land. Now, the remaining farmhouse and apple grove were a popular place for weddings and weekend retreats.

Later, I was due to meet Cassidy and the other bridesmaids there. We were having a girls' night on the farm before the wedding the following day. At Bull's command, Chance had organized security to pick us up and take us to the venue. Apparently, he had put a lot of security in place for the event.

"Don't mull over it tonight when I'm gone," I said as we sat on the couch.

"I didn't plan to."

"Yes, you did."

"And how do you figure that?"

I pushed my fingers into his hair and kissed him. "Because I know you."

Heat filled his eyes. "Oh, you do, do you? Exactly what is it that you know about me?"

Kneeling before him, I pushed up his t-shirt. I loved the feeling of his warm skin beneath my palms as I brushed them across his thick abdominal muscles and upward to his broad chest.

The look he gave me made me wet. It was raw. Uncontrolled. *Pure.*

It was also a challenge.

"I know that about now you're hoping I'm going to undo your belt buckle and fuck you with my mouth."

His breath caught between his lips.

"I know that by now your cock is hard and ready for me to suck it."

I leaned in and slid my tongue over a nipple, and as I kissed his warm skin, his pulse throbbed against my lips. Slowly and teasingly, I undid his belt buckle and slacks.

"I know I can make you come just by using my tongue."

I worked my way down his smooth chest to the hard muscles of his stomach, dragging my tongue over the dips and grooves of his six-pack and enjoying the way they trembled beneath my lips. His belly was warm, his skin radiating heat as I moved lower, the tip of my nose brushing through the soft trail of hair leading down to his cock. His arousal jutted upwards between us, the broad head gleaming with slickness, the thick column hard and veined.

I flicked out my tongue and licked the shiny crown, and he expelled a hiss of breath. But when I slid my mouth over the entire head and teased the rim with my wet tongue, a loud, tortured moan ripped out of him.

"Where'd you learn to do that, girl?"

"You," I managed to reply with my mouth full of him. I closed my lips over him again and sucked, and he almost lost it. He grabbed a fistful of the couch beneath him and groaned.

"Fuck!" he rasped.

Pulling my mouth free, I looked up at him and wrapped my fingers around the slick shaft. "I know what you like because you tell me with your moans ..." Flattening my tongue against the crest of his cock, I dragged it slowly across the sensitive flesh, and Ruger responded with a desperate moan. "By the way you tremble beneath my touch..."

My wet lips closed over the head and gently suckled, and he flinched and shivered.

"By the way your voice gets smoky and coarse when I use my tongue..."

Slurping him into my mouth, I sucked him tighter and teased the rim with my tongue until he groaned out my name.

"You're going to make me come, baby… "

I didn't want him to come yet. Not until I got my fill of him.

Pulling back, I rose to my feet and pushed him backwards on the couch, then climbed over him to slide my thighs on either side of his hips.

A tremor rolled through him as he moaned. "What are you doing to me, baby?"

I looked him in the eyes as I fixed him to me and very slowly sank down on his cock. He breathed out a groan as I began to ride him, long and slow, my pussy hungrily sliding up and down his hard shaft.

"This," I said. "This is what I'm doing to you. And I don't plan on ever stopping."

# CHAPTER 44

RUGER

I arrived at Lannister Farm just after two-thirty and found the apple farm crawling with hired security. Bull had ensured that there was ample protection to keep out any threat from Martel or anyone else.

If this was New Orleans, our president would have locked down the club and enforced a ban on events until the threat had passed. But not Bull. He would not retreat in fear. He was notorious for insisting life went on as usual, even when tensions between the Kings of Mayhem and other parties were in the red zone.

The ceremony was set to take place in a garden full of flowers and surrounded by a lush green hedge. When I walked in, Chance was standing beneath an archway of blossoms and lattice work, looking relaxed and happy in a black suit and a rich blue tie. Cade and Caleb stood beside him, each dressed in the same suit but with black ties.

I sat in a row with Maverick and his girlfriend Autumn, and a dateless Joker.

Just as I sat down, Bull walked in wearing the same suit as Cade and Caleb, and was pushing Griffin down the aisle toward the archway. Dressed the same as the others, Griffin was the fourth and final groomsman.

As usual, Bull had on his glasses, but as he stood with his nephews and Griffin, I knew he was scanning the growing crowd looking for me. When he found me, his jaw set and I could feel the burn of his glare across the heads of the guests sitting between us.

He stared at me and I stared back at him.

It was ridiculous.

In the two decades we'd been friends, I had never seen him act this way. He was a man of action. If he felt wronged by you, you felt the weight of his power either through pain or consequence. But the man standing under that floral archway murdering me with his eyes was behaving like a petulant child. I expected a beat down from him. Hell, I expected two. What I didn't expect was him keeping his distance like I had the fucking plague.

I planned to confront him. Because at the end of the day, he needed to know that I was in love with Chastity, and I didn't need his blessing to continue.

As the music started, an excited murmur rippled through the crowd, and the love of my life appeared at the edge of the aisle, followed by Cassidy's friend Daisy, then Honey and Indy, and finally, Cassidy.

They all looked stunning, but none more than Chastity. Dressed in a backless black dress, she was so fucking beautiful it almost hurt to look at her.

I watched her walk slowly down the red-carpeted aisle, taking in her curves and the way her nipples pressed against the silky fabric. Her hair was up and diamonds dripped from her ears. When she saw me, her ruby-red lips parted into a big smile.

I could count the number of weddings I'd been to on one hand. My sister's wedding to Bull, which seemed like a lifetime ago, and three of my club brothers in New Orleans, including Hot Potato, our treasurer, who got so drunk before his vows he vomited on his bride's dress and then went on to nail not one, but two of the bridesmaids in the restroom. It wasn't a good start to the marriage, but it was a good sign of things to come. They were divorced within the year.

But this wedding, there was something special in the air. I had seen Chance's relationship develop with Cassidy first hand, and I knew it would be a cold day in hell before this one went up in smoke.

Fuck. I was getting sentimental in my old age. Falling in love with Chastity had made me soft.

Throughout the ceremony, I couldn't keep my eyes off her, my head full of ideas of a future with her. I had meant what I had said to her in the shower, she was my queen, and the sooner I made it official, the better.

With the ceremony over, we all stood and clapped as the bridal party made their way down the aisle. But as Bull walked past, he stopped next to me. "Just so you know, I'm still going to kill you."

I didn't miss a beat and continued to clap. "And I look forward to you trying."

The air snapped between us before he walked off.

Maverick leaned over. "What was that about?"

I grinned to myself. "That, my friend, was the beginning of the thaw."

Maverick shrugged and went back to clapping as the rest of the bridal party passed. And I continued to grin to myself. While Bull's threat was genuine and there was a good chance I was going to feel some kind of physical pain along the way, it was indicative he was ready to face what was happening between me and Chastity.

And that was a good sign.

The reception was held next to where the ceremony took place, and while the bridal party was off having photos taken, I went to the bar. I wasn't in the mood for small talk. I was ready to sit back and watch.

I glanced around at the wedding guests. At my club brothers and their families. At the laughter and smiles all around me, at the strong sense of happiness and love in the air, and my heart glowed in my chest. These people, they were my family and I wanted them all to know that I was the luckiest fucking man in the world because the most amazing, beautiful, vibrant goddess was in love with me, and I was head over heels in love with her.

Fuck.

I sounded like a Hallmark card.

But I was at the mercy of what I felt for her.

I was in love.

Hell, I was fucking drunk with it.

Caleb joined me at the bar and clamped a hand on my shoulder. "So, it's true. Our sergeant-at-arms has gone and lost his head over a girl."

I raised my bourbon to my lips and took a mouthful, using the time to work out how Caleb felt about me and Chastity. He seemed pretty easy going about it. But then again, that was Caleb.

"You okay with that?" I asked.

He shrugged. "She's a grown woman. Old enough to make her own decisions."

"So this isn't going to be a talk about how I'm not good enough for her?"

He grinned and nodded to the barman for a drink.

"She's our baby sister, man. In our eyes, no one is going to be good enough for her. But you're as close as anyone is going to get, brother, so I'm happy for you both. Just don't break her heart. I don't want to mess up that pretty face of yours."

He smiled when he said it, but I had no doubt he would happily mess up my face if I did the wrong thing by his sister. He had nothing to worry about. I had no intention of fucking up. I didn't need or want anything else. Just her. I glanced across the room at her as she walked in with Cassidy.

Christ, she's beautiful.

I was the luckiest fucking man in the world.

Caleb chuckled and shook his head. "Man, you've got it bad."

He was right.

I was about to head over to my queen when Ronnie appeared in front of me. Dressed in a sexy green dress with heels that went on forever, she was a knock out.

A deadly knock out.

I was wondering when she would pounce. Ronnie was fierce. A killer biker queen you didn't fuck with. If anyone was going to have something to say about my involvement with Chastity, it would be her.

"How about you take me for a push around the dance floor, Mr. La Montagne?"

I smiled. "Well, it would be my pleasure, Ms. Calley."

I led her out onto the dance floor just as the band started to play Buddy Guy's "*What Kind Of Woman Is This.*"

Ronnie didn't waste any time getting straight to the point.

"So, you and my daughter."

It was a trait I admired.

"Do you mind?"

She cocked an eyebrow at me.

"I don't hate the idea."

That surprised me.

"The age difference doesn't bother you?"

"I think it will impact your relationship eventually. I'm not sure how and I'm not sure how much. But what I do know is that my headstrong daughter has made up her mind to give you her heart, and no amount of resistance from me or the rest of the family is going to stop her."

"Your brother doesn't seem to think so."

"My brother loves her like a daughter so no one is ever going to be good enough for her. I think if you get to the crux of it, Michael is just as hurt as he is protective."

I pulled back to look at her. "Hurt?"

She rolled her eyes. "He'd never admit it because he's a stubborn fool. But you're like a brother to him. You're a part of Wendy, and he's always held you in high regard. You doing this behind his back, I think that is what hurts him. He knows you're good enough for Chastity. Hell, we all do. But my brother, he holds trust and honesty as the highest form of respect. It's an instinct that has kept him alive and president of the biggest MC in the South for a very long time. You broke that, and in doing that, you broke his heart."

I didn't know what to say.

But what Ronnie was saying was true.

Bull's resistance to Chastity and me being together was more about the trust I'd broken by not going to him about our involvement. I regretted him finding out the way he did, *hell*, the way he found out was a clusterfuck. But it happened. And now I had to repair what was broken that day.

I glanced over to where he was standing at the bar, a glass of scotch in his hand and his dark glasses fixed firmly in my direction. His jaw was set, and if his fingers gripped the glass any tighter it would shatter.

If I had been any other club member, he would've shot me.

"She's in love with you, Ruger. Don't fucking take it for granted," Ronnie said.

"I'm not planning to."

"Good." She leaned closer to whisper in my ear. "Because I've got a rusty pair of scissors at home with your name on them if you mistreat her."

"Rusty scissors?"

"They're meaner on the ball sac than a sharp blade." She raised an eyebrow. "There's also a chance you'll catch tetanus."

I ignored the dramatic threat, although, I had no doubt she meant it. Ronnie Calley didn't make idle threats.

"I'm not going to hurt her," I said sincerely.

Her bright blue eyes glittered over my face, scrutinizing me. Searching for a fault or a weakness in my story. But she wasn't going to find one.

"I believe you," she finally said, then she laughed. "Boy, you must have some balls on you, Ruger La Montagne. You could have any woman in town and you go and pick the niece of Bull Western and sister to the three Calley brothers." She shook her head and her dark curls bounced around her shoulders. "You've got to have some big stones to take on all of that."

"I love her," I said, meeting her bright blue eyes.

"Good. Because you're going to need that to ride out the fire and brimstone of Michael Western."

CHAPTER 45

CHASTITY

I was finally free of my bridesmaid's duties and ready to get my hands on my sexy ass boyfriend. But when I looked up, he was dancing with my mom.

"Oh, great!" I whispered, grabbing a tumbler of some kind of amber liquor from a passing waiter and downing it. Between my brothers' scrutiny, my mother's current inquisition, and my uncle's death stares from across the room, he probably felt like a man with a bounty on his head.

Not that he looked particularly fazed. He seemed to be taking it all in stride.

I walked over to where he was with my mom on the dance floor. "Mind if I cut in?"

"Of course not, baby girl." My mom smiled at me warmly. "He's all yours."

When she walked away, Ruger wrapped his arms around me.

"I've missed you," he said quietly, and the look of affection on his face filled my chest with warmth. "I'm dying to kiss you."

I wound my arms around his neck. "Then why don't you?"

His eyes searched mine. "If we do this, right here, right now, there's no turning back for me. Do you understand?"

I knew there would be resistance. But I was ready to weather the storm. Once people saw how happy we were—how good we were together—they would ease up and leave us be. Then we'd be free to explore this.

I whispered into his ear. "I'm all yours, baby. It's time we let them know."

Them being the entire MC who were already watching us curiously.

He grinned, and it was so delicious I couldn't wait for him to kiss me.

"Are you ready for this?" he asked.

"Are you kidding me? I was born ready." I smiled up at him. Nothing mattered as long as I was with him. Not the stares, not the inquisitive looks, not the raised eyebrows. I laced my hands behind his neck and looked up into his beautiful green eyes. "I love you."

Heat shimmered over his face and darkened in his eyes. "Then show me."

A small smile curled on my lips. Time to let our world know we were together. Time to show them that this was real, and that it was happening whether they liked it or not.

With my eyes riveted to his, I rose up and gently brushed my lips against his. He moaned and smiled, and took the kiss deeper by cupping my face in his hands and searing his lips to mine.

The kiss was sensual. Delicious. And deliberate.

Let them see what we had together.

I knew people were looking.

I knew there were whispers.

But damn it all to hell, I could care less and kissed my man like no one was watching.

CHAPTER 46

RUGER

"Let's go for a walk," Chastity said, pulling away from our kiss. She looked up at me through her lashes and I could see the lust in her eyes. Leaning up on her toes, she whispered in my ear. "I want you to fuck me in the apple grove."

She didn't need to ask twice. I hadn't seen my woman in twenty-four hours and I was fucking starving for a taste. Last night I had missed her in our bed. Missed the warmth of her body next to me. Now it was pressed up against me and doing things to all of my senses.

Taking her hand, I led her off the dance floor and down the stone steps in the direction of the rose garden. We followed the path through a floral archway, passed two security men dressed in black and into a field of lush green grass. The apple grove was on the other side of a small cobblestone fence, accessible through an old wooden gate.

As we made our way around the little stone barn, my woman stopped and pulled me to her, seeking my mouth with a searing kiss. I groaned in response and walked her backward until she was up against the brick wall, my hands roaming up and down the length of her like they were searching for Braille.

But she broke off our kiss and pushed me back until it was me up against the wall.

"I want your cock in my mouth," she whispered against my lips before dropping to her knees.

She had me unbuckled, unzipped and my hard cock springing free before I had a chance to say anything.

And who the fuck was I to argue.

Looking up at me through her lashes, she slid her kiss-swollen lips over the head of my erection and drew me into the velvety warmth of her mouth. I dropped my head back and groaned. My girl knew what I liked, and goddamn, she was giving it to me good. I tangled my fingers through her hair and bit down on my bottom lip, my hips starting to rock toward her succulent mouth as she continued to suckle and lick, and torture me with her tongue.

I looked down at her through lust-heavy eyes. Seeing her on her knees and giving me head was almost as much of a turn on as feeling the tease of her tongue and her beautiful mouth fucking me.

But I hadn't felt her pussy in more than a day, and that just wasn't right.

Before I hit the point of no return, I drew my angel to her feet and kissed her dirty, filthy, perfect fucking mouth.

I hastily hitched up her dress. When I felt how wet her panties were, I ripped them off and pushed her up against the wall with a growl.

She gasped but then laughed, and fixed me with dark eyes. "You want to fuck me?"

I hooked her leg over my arm.

"No, baby. I don't *want* to fuck you. I'm *going* to fuck you." With one thrust I was in her. She gasped once, and then again when I thrust into her a second time. She swallowed thickly, her eyes fluttering closed as my cock filled her again, and again, and again.

I buried my face into the warmth of her neck. Damn, she smelled so fine.

Felt so fine.

"I love what you do to me," she moaned. "How you make me feel..."

I was getting lost in her.

"Come in me, baby," she whispered in my ear. "Give me your baby."

Surprised by her words, I stopped thrusting into her tight pussy, and looked at her. "You want a baby?"

She shook her head. "No. I want *your* baby."

My cock pulsed inside her, and she bit down on her bottom lip.

As I ran the pad of my thumbs across her smooth cheeks, I searched her eyes. "Are you serious?"

She nodded and licked her lips. "I want everything with you. A life. A family. I'm ready, baby. I don't want to wait any longer. I love you. Let's just go for it."

The idea of making her pregnant almost made me come.

Pulling her face to mine, I kissed her hard. I felt so much goddamn love for her I wanted to give her the world and more.

Whatever she wanted, I would give it to her.

Sliding to the ground, I guided her down to my lap.

"I'll give you a baby," I said, securing her legs on either side of me. "If you'll be my wife."

Our eyes locked as she sank down on my cock again.

"I'd marry you in a heartbeat, Ruger La Montagne." She started to rock against me, and suddenly our apple grove tryst became so much more.

We had a future.
And I was going to make her my wife.

CHAPTER 47

RUGER

After the apple grove, we walked back to the reception where the party was in full swing. Wedding guests danced to Bob Seger on the dance floor, while others sat at the tables eating fried chicken and chugging beers. Bull was moodily leaning up against the bar, and when he saw us walk in, he stiffened.

I didn't want to bring it up here. Today was Chance and Cassidy's day. But feeling Bull's steely gaze on me from across the room wore down the last of my patience.

When Chastity went to the bathroom, I saw my chance with him and took it.

It was time to end this.

"You can't avoid me forever," I said, joining him at the bar. I signaled to the barman for a bourbon. "Whether you like it or not, I'm here and I'm not going away."

Bull's energy darkened next to me.

"There's more than one way to make someone disappear," he said ominously.

Accepting my drink, I turned to look at my president. "Nah, if you were going to do that you would've put a bullet in my head when we were at the cemetery."

His jaw tightened. "Don't be so sure. I've had plenty of time to reconsider."

I sighed and took a sip of my drink. "What's it going to take for you to accept that I'm with Chastity?"

"Hell freezing over."

I shook my head. "You can make this as hard or as easy you like. But either way, it's happening."

He took off his dark glasses and fixed his unholy eyes on me. "You didn't even have the balls to tell me."

The look on his face would terrify most men. But I wasn't afraid of Bull. And he knew it.

"At Chastity's request. She wanted to wait, and you know what, that was her right. It was her choice. And I wasn't going to take it away from her."

"You're really going to stand there and blame Chastity for this?"

"Blame? Blame has got nothing to do with this." I shook my head. "It may surprise you, Bull, but this isn't about you. The decisions Chasity and I made, we made for ourselves. Not you. Not the club. *Us*."

"There shouldn't even be a fucking *us*." He exposed his perfect white teeth as he gritted them.

"I love her. And you should know that I'm going to marry her."

He straightened. His body rigid. His face dark.

"Over my fucking dead body," he seethed.

"Don't fucking tempt me," I seethed back.

I was done with this. He needed to either fight me or fucking get over it.

I watched his throat work as he swallowed. Watched his jaw tighten as he gritted his teeth. "I'm warning you, Ruger. I'm seconds away from putting a bullet in you."

"This again? Fuck me, Bull, either do it or get over it."

If I hadn't been so distracted, I might've noticed them earlier. But I didn't, not until the four men in suits made their way up the cobblestones toward the reception area.

I didn't recognize them.

They were wearing black gloves and dark glasses.

They were out of place.

And their body language was way off.

Martel's men.

Somehow, they'd gotten through the security we had scattered all over the farm.

This wasn't good.

This wasn't going to end well.

I only had a moment to react.

To decide what to do.

Who to protect.

I had to get to her.

I'd never moved so fast in my life.

I called for everyone to take cover. I pulled out my gun and aimed as I ran. I called her name. I ran so damn fast and launched myself in front of her just as one of Martel's men raised his gun and started firing. My body took her down to the ground just as three bullets ripped through me and turned my world to black.

CHAPTER 48

CHASTITY

I couldn't breathe. Ruger was a dead weight on top of me. I could hear shooting and screaming all around me. I heard a shot fired and a body crash into a table and fall to the concrete nearby. Bullets rained down around us. I couldn't move, which probably saved my life because I had an overwhelming urge to run, even though I would more than likely die if I did. But Ruger had me shielded with his body.

But why wasn't he shooting back?

Seconds had passed since he'd thrown himself on me.

Maybe a minute?

I tried to shake Ruger, but he wouldn't budge.

Then, just like that, it was all over. I wriggled out from under Ruger to get my bearing and glanced around, dazed.

It was chaos. Tables were overturned and wedding decorations were destroyed. Flowers lay scattered all over the floor, decapitated and broken, laying amongst the glass and the debris, and the annihilated wedding cake.

Within minutes, the four intruders were dead. Well, three were dead. The fourth was busy having his face broken by my uncle's fists, his blood splattering in the air around him like a halo and covering the white tablecloth in red speckles. You didn't burst into the reception of a biker wedding and start firing without it ending badly for you.

I nudged Ruger.

"Baby, get up." But he didn't move. When I shook him, he rolled onto his back and I saw the blood stain spreading through the crisp white of his shirt. A new panic took up in me. A dread like I'd never known. "Ruger?"

And then the realization hit me in the face.

"No, no, no, no, no, no, no" I ripped open his shirt and let out a cry. Blood poured from three bullet wounds—three in his chest. I pressed my hands over the holes, but blood continued to rise up through my fingers and spill down his torso.

Everything happened in slow motion from that moment on. I started screaming. People around me were a blur. The fear in me more real than anything I'd ever felt.

Someone knelt next to me and I vaguely realized it was Indy. Caleb lifted me to my feet while Indy did what she could with Ruger.

"Are you okay, Chassy? Are you shot?" Caleb asked in a panic.

"Oh God, is he going to die?"

Caleb shook me. "Chassy! Are you hurt?"

I looked at my brother in a daze and slowly shook my head. The front of my dress was covered in blood, but it wasn't mine. It was Ruger's.

I looked from the blood on my hands to my brother. "Is he going to die?"

He didn't have to reply. I could see the answer written all over his face.

The sounds of sirens broke into the chaos. Police. Ambulance. It was complete bedlam.

I glanced over my shoulder at Indy performing chest compressions on Ruger. Everything became muted then, like I was floating underwater and watching the mayhem unfold above.

Before I realized it, we were being hustled into the back of an ambulance and the doors were closed with a loud bang.

Ruger died in the ambulance.

Twice.

And if it wasn't for Indy being in the back with us, I'm not sure he would've survived the travel to the hospital. She worked on him to keep him alive while I clung to his lifeless, bloody hand, my medical training instantly gone, and replaced with a fear that I was about to lose the love of my life.

Thankfully, by the time we got to the hospital he had a pulse.

But he wasn't out of the woods yet. He was in grave danger and as they rushed him into surgery there was a big chance he wasn't going to survive.

I paced back and forward across the ER waiting to hear something. *Anything.* I could barely stand it. I had no idea what was going on or how long I'd been there. I chewed down my thumb nail as I paced, my heart pounding, my skin rippling with goosebumps because I was still dressed in my bridesmaid dress, and it was colder than the Arctic Circle in there.

I looked down at my hands. They were covered in blood. *Ruger's blood.* But it wasn't just all over my hands, the front of my dress was soaked with it and there were smears of it up and down my arms.

As the hot sting of fresh tears burned their way down my cold cheeks, the doors to the ER burst open and Bull rushed in with my mom.

"Chastity, are you okay?" My mom rushed over to me while my uncle hung back.

As soon as my mom's arms went around me, I started to cry harder.

"I'm fine, but Ruger... they don't think he's going to make it."

I looked at my uncle and suddenly hated him. Grief and fear collided in me, and I let it erupt out of me in an explosion of anger aimed right at him.

"Why are you even here? You're probably happy he's going to die."

"That's my best friend in there."

"Your best friend?" I rounded on him, giving my anger full reign. I shoved him in the chest. "Your best friend? He's in here because of you!"

I wasn't sure that was exactly true. But I was blinded by pain and I needed someone to take some of it from me.

He turned his back on me and ran a hand through his hair.

"He saved my life. What more do you want?" I said angrily.

Bull swung back to look at me.

"What do I want? I want him to have kept his fucking hands off my niece. I want him to have not betrayed me by going behind my back with the one person I told him not to."

"Betrayed you! He never betrayed you. He would fucking die for you."

"He betrayed me the moment he touched you!"

We were yelling now.

"What do you want from him? To die because he fell in love with me? Because he makes me so damn happy? Because he treats me like a queen?" Tears spilled down my cheeks. "Because he loves me?"

"I want him to survive," he said, his eyes wild. "I want him to not have three bullets in him. I want my best friend back. But I want him to not have fucking touched you!"

"Why can't you be happy that I found someone who is good and decent and loves me like he does."

"Because he was never meant for you."

"How can you say that?"

"Because I told him to never go near you. They all know they're not to go near you. Every single King was warned."

"Why? Why did you make such a stupid rule?"

"Because you deserve better than this life!"

"It's not your choice!" I yelled.

Unable to stand another minute, I stormed away, my mind boiling with anger and fear and a terrible, terrible foreboding that Ruger was going to die. Leaving the waiting room, I found the smoker's area and bummed a cigarette from a plump orderly who looked as exhausted as I felt.

His eyes raked up and down my blood-soaked dress. "Rough night?"

My hands shook as I lit the cigarette.

"You could say that," I said, dragging in a lungful of smoke and barely holding back a cough. I wasn't a smoker. But if I didn't do something other than pace the ER and yell at my uncle, I was going to go insane.

"Want to talk about it?"

"Not really."

He shrugged. "Good. Because I'm no good at the whole comforting thing."

"And yet you work in a hospital."

"Yeah, well, my parole officer made me take this job."

I nodded. "I see."

His eyes rolled over my again, lingering on my chest area.

"Want to buy some weed?"

Again, I almost choked on the smoke. "No, I'm good. Thanks."

"You sure? I got this wicked stuff in my locker. A friend and I broke into the marijuana crop the Kings have growing out by the watermelon fields. Snuck in there under the cover of darkness and scored ourselves some wicked ganja."

He was lying.

"You've got some balls stealing off those bikers," I said, flicking the end of my cigarette with my thumb nail.

He puffed his chest out. "I can handle myself. I might not match them in size and brawn, but I can certainly outsmart them. Dumb fuckers."

Again, I nodded. "Right."

The glass door leading outside opened and Bull appeared in the doorway. My companion took one look at him and turned white. "Fuck."

"Oh yeah, *fuck* is about right," I murmured.

The orderly crushed his cigarette with his boot and whispered, "You know, I was only kidding about the whole marijuana thing, right? I didn't really break in."

"Oh, I know."

He wouldn't be standing in front of me if he did.

"So, no point mentioning it..."

"I wasn't going to."

His cheeks went red and he couldn't get out of the area fast enough.

"Thanks for the cigarette," I called after him. But he didn't reply and disappeared into the shadows.

My uncle walked up to me. "Since when do you smoke?"

I glared at him.

"Since my boyfriend took three bullets to the chest." I took another drag. "If you've come out here to yell at me—"

"I'm not going to yell at you."

"Good, because I'm not sure how many more of these I can stand," I said, holding up the half-smoked cigarette.

Bull took it from me and drew back on it. His anger stood between us like a wall and it made me want to cry, knowing how angry he was after everything that had happened. But it wasn't just his anger standing between us, I was angry, too.

I sat down at a barbecue table and he sat across from me. We were silent for a moment, both of us weighing the gravity of the situation before Bull finally said something.

"You know, in the whole time I knew him, I only ever saw your father cry once."

Taken by surprise at the random subject choice, I frowned and looked at him. "What?"

"It was the day you were born. After your mama gave birth to you, he came out and just stood there with this look on his face, like he'd just seen God. He shook his head as he looked at me with tears rolling down his face and he told me how perfect you were. 'The most perfect baby girl that ever there was', he said." He took a drag on the cigarette and looked nostalgic before blowing out a funnel of smoke. "Then he walked right on over to me and took me by the shoulders and he said, '*You promise me now that if anything ever happens to me, you'll be the father she needs. You tell me, she will always have someone strong watching over her*'. And I made him that promise, Chastity. I swore to your daddy that if he couldn't be there for you, I would be. And I've tried to be. For twenty-two years, I've watched over you like you were my own." He paused and his brows drew together. "Wendy and I used to love babysitting you when your daddy and mama went out. She'd always say how she couldn't wait to have a daughter just like you." Bull's voice wavered and he cleared his throat to hide it. "You know, she was pregnant when she died."

My eyes darted to his. "Aunt Wendy was pregnant?"

He looked infinitely sad. "Fifteen weeks."

I gasped and my hand shot to my mouth. "Did you know?"

He nodded. "She told me the day we got married. She didn't want to tell anyone until she was well and truly out of the first trimester."

I sat stunned. "I didn't know."

"The night she died… she was buying wine to celebrate finding out the sex of the baby. She was going to tell me over dinner, she said. Then I forgot to buy the damn wine and—" His emotion was raw on his face. "Following her death, I asked her doctor if it was a boy or a girl. I don't know if it was to torture myself, or if it was all part of the grieving process, but he did and he was able to confirm it was a girl."

Another piece of Bull's protective puzzle fell into place.

His daughter died with his wife.

"The only person I shared that with was Ruger." He sighed and I could see the pain etched in his face. "The amount of times I've thought about Wendy and how she'd still be alive if she never got involved with me."

"But she died in an accident."

"She died driving to get wine. Wine I was supposed to pick up for our dinner but I was too busy with club business to do it. If I had just put her before club business… but we don't always do that, you see, and it's our queens who pay, Chastity. It's our queens who have to bear the weight of their men being in the club. Can't you see, I don't want that for you."

It suddenly dawned on me why my uncle had never remarried.

He didn't want to make another woman a queen because he saw that title as a burden, not a blessing.

And it was exactly why he didn't want me getting involved with a club member.

I reached across the table.

"She didn't die because she was a queen, or because she was married to you, or because you were a King. She died because a college kid got drunk and decided to drive."

"Yes, but if I hadn't stayed back and put club business first, I would've gone home and picked up the wine along the way. Like I was supposed to. But I didn't and she died. Just like Mirabella died because she was married to Jacob. And Saskia before her."

Mirabella was shot dead by a psychopathic club member who was out for revenge on the club. He shot her to torture her husband who ended up committing suicide by putting his bike down in front of a truck.

Saskia was married to Liam, a club member from years ago. I remembered her fondly. When I was eleven she taught me how to apply makeup and gave me my first lipstick. A few months later, she and Liam were killed in the crossfire when a rival club shot up the clubhouse.

"Whether you like it or not, I'm already married to this club," I said. "I was born into it. It's in my blood. You can't protect me from it, and you don't need to."

He finished his cigarette and I watched him crush it beneath his big motorcycle boots. Despite wearing a suit and tie, he wasn't giving up his well-worn Harley Davidson boots for nothing.

He sighed and ran his hands through his inky black hair. When he looked up, his expression softened.

"So, you and Ruger, huh?"

"I love him," I said with conviction. "And I'm going to marry him whether you approve or not.

My uncle's jaw ticked, but then he nodded with appreciation. "Yeah, kid. I think I get that."

CHAPTER 49

RUGER

It hurt like a bitch. For two days, I lingered in and out of delirium. When I eventually woke up, they told me I had died a couple of times, but to be honest, I already knew that. I didn't know if it was the drugs, or my brain shutting down, or if it was something more esoteric and other-worldly, but at one stage I saw my sister, Wendy.

We were on the swing set in the backyard of our childhood home back in Louisiana and she was wearing the white dress and sunhat she used to love when she was a teenager. And goddamn, she looked just as beautiful and as carefree as I remembered. In the hazy sunlight her blonde hair glowed like a halo and her bright eyes were as big as emeralds. She was laughing and I realized how much I missed hearing her laughter.

"You're here," I said, feeling lightheaded.

She looked at me and laughed. "Of course, I am, where else would I be?"

I looked around us. The grass was very green and the clear blue sky was lit with sunlight.

"But you died," I said, wondering if I'd stepped out from a world where she was dead only to find it was nothing more than a dream.

She stopped swinging and turned to me, her beautiful face softening into a smile. "He needs to let me go, will you tell him that for me?"

I wrinkled my brow. "Who?"

"Tell him someone special is coming and he has to let me go. It's okay. It's time."

Fuck. I was high. I had to be.

"What are you talking about?"

She reached out and touched my jaw. "Go back to her, baby brother. You're going to make her so happy. The way that girl looks at you..." she sighed happily. "You're going to be so happy for a very long, long time."

I couldn't help but stare at her. It was unbelievable how good it felt seeing her again. To hear her. It had been almost twenty years since I had heard her voice and now she was here, smiling and talking to me.

"I miss you," I said.

She smiled at me softly. Almost regretfully. "I miss you, too."

An annoying beeping noise broke into the hazy peace of the afternoon, and somewhere in the distance I could hear voices, but looking around I couldn't see anything.

Wendy sucked in a deep breath and grinned, then leaned over and patted me on the knee. "Time to get back to it."

I didn't understand what was going on, but I knew I didn't want to leave.

"I don't want to go."

She looked surprised. "You don't?"

"If I go, I won't see you again."

She slid off the swing and stood in front of me. "You'll see me again. But not for a very long time."

The pulsating beep became a long, monotone beep, and Wendy pulled me to my feet. "Give me more blood, we need more blood."

I looked at her. What she said didn't make any sense. "What did you say?"

"Give me another milligram of epinephrine."

I started to feel woozy.

"Wendy..."

"He's crashing again, where's that epinephrine?"

I felt an overwhelming pull toward the ground, like I was going to pass out.

Wendy leaned in and whispered in my ear. "Don't forget to tell him."

When I woke up, my eyes opened onto a bright white ceiling light, before people slowly came into focus. Blinking, I let my eyes adjust before sucking in a deep breath.

Wendy was gone and I was in a world of fucking pain.

"Welcome back," a man in scrubs said as he leaned over me. "You gave us quite a scare."

I looked at him blankly as the world and everything that had happened came rushing back to me.

The door burst open and Chastity came flying in. She rushed toward me and wrapped her arms around my neck, crying into my throat.

"You scared me," she murmured, the heat of her breath over my skin making my heart squeeze with the familiarity.

I held her against me and ran my fingers down her spine. "I'm going to be okay."

She pulled back and straightened, raising an eyebrow at me. "You'd better be, Ruger La Montagne. You scared the hell out of me."

The doctor told me it took a while to stabilize me. That one of the bullets had come scarily close to my heart and caused a bleed they had struggled to control. Another was too difficult to remove because of where it was, so I would live the rest of my life with a bullet lodged in my chest cavity.

I reached up and touched Chastity's beautiful face. "Are you okay, baby?'

She sniffed back her tears. "You're the one lying in a hospital bed and you're asking me if I'm okay?"

"They didn't hurt you, did they?"

She shook her head. "I'm not hurt, thanks to you. You killed the one who was going to hurt me before he had the chance to. The others got caught in the crossfire. And I think my uncle took care of the fourth one."

"Did we lose anyone?"

"No." She shook her head. "Everyone else was okay. But, Ruger, if you hadn't noticed when you did... I wouldn't be standing here."

Tears fell down her cheeks and she trembled with emotion. I didn't blame her. Just the thought of her being hurt was more than I could take. Living without Chastity wasn't an option anymore. A world without her in it wasn't a world I wanted to be a part of.

But she was safe.

She glanced over her shoulder and my gaze followed. Bull lingered in the doorway looking confused and uncomfortable, and it occurred to me that for the first time ever, the *mighty* Bull Western didn't know what to do.

"You plan on standing in that doorway all day, or are you going to come in?" I said huskily. My throat was as rough as sandpaper and it was an effort to talk. Apparently, that happened when you had breathing tubes thrust down your esophagus.

But Bull continued to stall, and I saw his jaw tick as he shifted uncomfortably on his feet.

I sighed. "For fuck's sake, will you get your ass in here!"

Bull strode into the room and took off his glasses, and I could see he was concerned. Despite his bright, piercing eyes, the emotion was tight across his face.

"Are you going to die?" he asked.

"Not today."

He nodded. "Good."

"I thought you'd be pleased. Three bullet wounds to the chest..."

He looked at the monitors beeping around me. I was attached to so many different ones, I was surprised I didn't pick up Netflix.

"Well, it didn't feel nearly as satisfying as I had hoped."

Looking at him, I thought about Wendy.

He needs to let me go.

But I didn't say anything. It had been a dream. The visions of a dying brain as blood drained from my body.

Yet it had seemed so real.

Tell him someone special is coming and he has to let me go.

But I was going to keep it to myself.

Bull would probably put another bullet in me if I mentioned it.

"Has Martel been dealt with?" I asked, pushing the thought out of my mind.

He nodded. "Things have been put in place."

Meaning Bull was working up to something big. His retaliation would be lethal.

"I want in on it," I said.

"You need to get your strength back."

"I'll be out of here in a day."

There was no hope I would be out in a day. But it was worth a shot.

"Maybe, maybe not. Either way, I don't want to see your face until you're a hundred percent."

I frowned. I wanted revenge for this and I didn't like being shut out from the retaliation.

But then I looked at Chastity, and the strangest sense of peace and contentment washed over me, and my lust for revenge didn't matter anymore. She was what I needed. The goddess standing by my bed with bright blue eyes filled with affection and love.

"I'm going to go, give you and Chastity some alone time. Apparently, there's some talk about a fucking wedding you two are going to have."

Behind him, Chastity started to laugh through her tears.

My eyes met his, and when he gave me a nod, I realized it was his nod of approval.

"Try to stay out of trouble while you're in here," he said. Then leaning down, he whispered in my ear, "And remember, if you hurt her I *will* kill you."

But as he straightened, the fucker winked at me before he turned away and walked out the door.

If I wasn't in so much goddamn pain, I would smile.

Because Hell just froze over.

EPILOGUE

CHASTITY
Three months later

The crowd cheered as I leaned in and kissed my husband on the lips. Wolf whistles rippled through the late afternoon air, followed by clapping and loud cries of congratulations.

Pulling away, I looked up at Ruger and felt my heart twist with the intense love I felt every single time I looked at him. He was my husband now, and I was so batshit crazy for him I couldn't get the stupid grin off my face.

We were down by the river, near the clubhouse. The entire club and their loved ones had joined us in a beautiful grassy copse near the riverbank to watch us exchange our vows. It was a simple, no-fuss wedding. I had no bridesmaids and Ruger had no groomsmen. It was just the two of us standing before all of our friends and family as we became man and wife.

My uncle came up to us smiled. He patted Ruger on the back. "Welcome to the family, brother."

It made my heart squeeze with affection. Bull had come a long way in accepting our relationship. Only a few months ago, he wanted to murder Ruger for falling in love with me. But now even he couldn't deny what we had. One thing was for certain. We were meant for each other and no amount of craziness was ever going to come between us again.

After being released from a three-week stay in the hospital, Ruger had focused on getting his strength back and spent more time in rehabilitation and physical therapy than doing club business. But a month ago, he had resumed his position as the Kings of Mayhem sergeant-at-arms while I started work as an EMT at the same hospital where Indy worked as a doctor. I had nailed my final exams, especially biology, because I had the best damned study partner in the world.

And now I was married to him.

Gimmel Martel left town. I didn't know the full story but apparently the Kings of Mayhem had parked one of his trucks amongst his grapevines and set fire to it. The flames had spread to the entire vineyard and Eagle's Nest had burned to the ground. It was the reason Martel had sent four gunmen to Cassidy and Chance's wedding. It was payback.

I didn't know how Bull had retaliated. But I knew he would have. And I wasn't naïve to think that it was over. There was a war brewing, I had been around the club long enough to recognize when something big was about to happen.

It was the biker way of life.

But I refused to think about it. I had learned a long time ago not to worry about things before they happened. Even though my husband would be in the line of fire because of the position he held within the club, I was a queen. I would take our future as it came and face it like one.

As I ate wedding cake and stood with Honey and a now very pregnant Indy, Ruger came up and brushed a kiss across my shoulder.

"Let me steal you away for a moment," he whispered in my ear.

A secret thrill shot up my spine. The huskiness in his voice was a promise of some amazing sex to come.

And I couldn't wait to make love to him as my husband.

He took me by the hand and led me away from the celebrations and up a grassy knoll leading to the clubhouse.

"Where are we going?" I asked.

"It suddenly occurred to me that I never fucked you in my bedroom at the clubhouse."

I couldn't help but smile. I loved the way his mind worked. "That *is* true."

"And it seems somewhat rude of me not to."

"Again, that is true."

He paused to kiss me. "I think it's time we remedy that, what do you think?"

I looked at him through my lashes. "I think we're wasting time standing here talking about it."

He grinned and pulled me up the grassy slope and across the parking lot.

Inside the clubhouse, a few people lingered at the bar, but we ignored them as we raced for his bedroom. Next week, he would give it up. It was his choice. He never used it anymore and said he had no desire to sleep anywhere but in our bed, next to me.

Within seconds of stepping into the room, he had my dress off me and his face buried in my neck as he pinned me to the door.

Then, dropping to his knees, he kissed the tiny swell of my stomach.

We hadn't told anyone.

For now, it was our little secret.

A tiny little life growing inside of me.

Penny Dee

He guided me over to the bed, love and lust bright in his eyes. "You're so fucking beautiful."

I knelt on the bed and undid his belt buckle and black slacks, pushing them down his narrow hips. The sight of him, hard and thick, never failed to get me aroused quickly. I turned around. I wanted him to fuck me on his clubhouse bed and I wanted it to be hard, fast, and filthy.

"Lift your sexy ass up, baby." He guided my hips upward and pushed my legs further apart so I was completely exposed to him. He ran the head of his cock against my clit and I bit down on my lip.

"Oh, baby, you're so wet," he groaned.

I didn't have time to reply before he slid his cock into me with one smooth push, making me gasp at the sudden intrusion. Bliss flared in my clit. In this position I could feel every single inch of him. Every single *delicious* inch of him as he pushed in and out of me.

"Christ, you're so tight. So fucking tight." He put his hands on my hips and rocked into my wet pussy. I arched my back and moaned. "You make me so fucking hard, baby. There's no way I'm going to last."

"Make me come," I demanded. I didn't want this to be over. Every cell in my body was screaming for an orgasm. *My first orgasm as his wife.* "Make me come with your cock."

He pulled out and ran the broad head over my clit, detonating my orgasm immediately as a cry of pleasure roared out of us both. I felt him pump his cock with his hand, and the stickiness of his cum as he came all over my clit.

With a growl, he fell to the bed and pulled me into his arms. "I'm never going to get fucking tired of this."

"Good," I replied, kissing him gently on the lips. "Because it's too late to back out now. You've married me *and* knocked me up all in a matter of months. It's a bit late for any regrets."

He chuckled lightly and pressed a kiss to my forehead. "I could never regret anything about you."

While he pulled on his slacks, I went to the bathroom to clean up. Ruger's cum was sticky on my thighs and that wasn't going to work with my satin slip of a dress.

Sitting down, I glanced out the window. Outside, the sun had drifted further toward the horizon, painting the sky in shades of pink and gold. Music and voices drifted up from the river. Laughter floated on the fall air. Our wedding party was still very much in full swing.

I smiled happily to myself and played with the crown pendant Ruger had put around my neck only an hour ago.

I'm happy. So freaking happy.

It was amazing how much my life had changed in the last six months. All because of a burst water pipe in my apartment.

"We should probably get back to them before anyone notices us missing," I said, walking back into the room. But Ruger reached for my hand and sat me down on the edge of the bed.

"Before we go, I want to give you something."

Shirtless and looking so deliciously sexy in his black slacks and belt, he walked over to the dresser and pulled out a small box from one of the drawers. Walking back, he sat next to me on the bed and opened it.

I looked down at the ring sitting in the box and my mouth dropped open. When I looked up at him, a swirling fierce love whipped through me.

My skull ring.

The one I had given to him almost two decades earlier.

Emotion lodged in my throat. He had kept it all these years.

"I can't believe you actually kept it."

I had forgotten all about it.

"Of course, I did."

A sudden warmth poured into my chest. This beautiful, crazy man never failed to surprise me.

"Do you remember why you gave it to me?" he asked.

I tried to peel back the years, but the memory was murky.

"You gave it to me so I would be happy," he prompted.

Slowly, that day came back to me. It was the day we had buried his sister.

"I remember now." I paused as more of it replayed over in my mind. "I was drawing on the concrete and you came out for a cigarette."

"That's right."

"You were really sad. I could see it in your eyes. And I felt bad for you. I didn't want you to be sad... you were *broken-hearted*. So, I gave you my ring because it was a happy ring, and if you had it you wouldn't be sad anymore."

"And now I'm giving it back to you." He slid it onto my pinky. "Because I don't need it anymore. Because I have you and that kind of makes me the happiest guy on Earth."

My heart squeezed and I leaned in and kissed him. "So you're like the human version of Disneyland?"

He grinned against my lips. "Baby, Disneyland ain't got nothing on me."

His kiss was searing and delicious, and inside my heart pounded with love for him.

"I love you," he said.

"I love you, too."

And I did. He was my perfect forever after.

And I couldn't ask for anything more than that.

THE END

CONNECT WITH ME ONLINE

Check these links for more books from Penny Dee.

READER GROUP

For more mayhem join by FB readers group:
Penny's Queens of Mayhem
www.facebook.com/groups/604941899983066/

NEWSLETTER
https://bit.ly/364AFvo

WEBSITE
http://www.pennydeebooks.com/

INSTAGRAM
@pennydeeromance

EMAIL
penny@pennydeebooks.com

FACEBOOK

http://www.facebook.com/pennydeebooks/

ABOUT THE AUTHOR

Penny Dee writes contemporary romance about rock stars, bikers, hockey players and everyone in-between. Her stories bring the suspense, the feels and a whole lot of heat.

She found her happily ever after with an Australian hottie who she met on a blind date.

Printed in Great Britain
by Amazon

46238654R00165